Andrea Cesalpino and Renaissance Aristotelianism

Bloomsbury Studies in the Aristotelian Tradition

General Editor:

Marco Sgarbi, Università Ca' Foscari, Italy

Editorial Board:

Klaus Corcilius *(University of California, Berkeley, USA)*; Daniel Garber *(Princeton University, USA)*; Oliver Leaman *(University of Kentucky, USA)*; Anna Marmodoro *(University of Oxford, UK)*; Craig Martin *(Oakland University, USA)*; Carlo Natali *(Università Ca' Foscari, Italy)*; Riccardo Pozzo *(Consiglio Nazionale delle Ricerche, Rome, Italy)*; Renée Raphael *(University of California, Irvine, USA)*; Victor M. Salas *(Sacred Heart Major Seminary, USA)*; Leen Spruit *(Radboud University Nijmegen, The Netherlands)*.

Aristotle's influence throughout the history of philosophical thought has been immense and in recent years the study of Aristotelian philosophy has enjoyed a revival. However, Aristotelianism remains an incredibly polysemous concept, encapsulating many, often conflicting, definitions. *Bloomsbury Studies in the Aristotelian Tradition* responds to this need to define Aristotelianism and give rise to a clear characterization.

Investigating the influence and reception of Aristotle's thought from classical antiquity to contemporary philosophy from a wide range of perspectives, this series aims to reconstruct how philosophers have become acquainted with the tradition. The books in this series go beyond simply ascertaining that there are Aristotelian doctrines within the works of various thinkers in the history of philosophy, but seek to understand how they have received and elaborated Aristotle's thought, developing concepts into ideas that have become independent of him.

Bloomsbury Studies in the Aristotelian Tradition promotes new approaches to Aristotelian philosophy and its history. Giving special attention to the use of interdisciplinary methods and insights, books in this series will appeal to scholars working in the fields of philosophy, history and cultural studies.

Available titles:

A Political Philosophy of Conservatism, by Ferenc Hörcher
Elijah Del Medigo and Paduan Aristotelianism, by Michael Engel
Early Modern Aristotelianism and the Making of Philosophical Disciplines,
by Danilo Facca
Phantasia in Aristotle's Ethics, by Jacob Leth Fink
Pontano's Virtues, by Matthias Roick
The Aftermath of Syllogism, edited by Marco Sgarbi, Matteo Cosci
The Reception of Aristotle's Poetics in the Italian Renaissance and Beyond,
by Bryan Brazeau
The Scientific Counter-Revolution, by Michael John Gorman
Virtue Ethics and Contemporary Aristotelianism, edited by Andrius Bielskis,
Eleni Leontsini, Kelvin Knight
Aristotle's Syllogism and the Creation of Modern Logic, edited by
Lukas M. Verburgt and Matteo Cosci
The Legacy of Aristotelian Enthymeme, edited by Fosca Mariani Zini
Aristotelianism and Magic in Early Modern Europe, edited by Donato Verardi

Andrea Cesalpino and Renaissance Aristotelianism

Natural Philosophy in the Sixteenth Century

Edited by
Fabrizio Baldassarri and Craig Martin

BLOOMSBURY ACADEMIC
LONDON • NEW YORK • OXFORD • NEW DELHI • SYDNEY

BLOOMSBURY ACADEMIC
Bloomsbury Publishing Plc, 50 Bedford Square, London, WC1B 3DP, UK
Bloomsbury Publishing Inc, 1385 Broadway, New York, NY 10018, USA
Bloomsbury Publishing Ireland, 29 Earlsfort Terrace, Dublin 2, D02 AY28, Ireland

BLOOMSBURY, BLOOMSBURY ACADEMIC and the Diana logo
are trademarks of Bloomsbury Publishing Plc

First published in Great Britain 2023
This paperback edition published 2025

Copyright © Fabrizio Baldassarri, Craig Martin and Contributors, 2023

Fabrizio Baldassarri and Craig Martin have asserted their right under the Copyright, Designs and Patents Act, 1988, to be identified as Editors of this work.

For legal purposes the Acknowledgments on p. xiv constitute
an extension of this copyright page.

Cover image: 1600 ca, ITALY: The Italian ANDREA CESALPINO (1519–1603), physician, philosopher and botanist. Portrait engraving from XIX century by G. Guz. (© ARCHIVIO GBB/ Alamy Stock Photo)

All rights reserved. No part of this publication may be: i) reproduced or transmitted in any form, electronic or mechanical, including photocopying, recording or by means of any information storage or retrieval system without prior permission in writing from the publishers; or ii) used or reproduced in any way for the training, development or operation of artificial intelligence (AI) technologies, including generative AI technologies. The rights holders expressly reserve this publication from the text and data mining exception as per Article 4(3) of the Digital Single Market Directive (EU) 2019/790.

Bloomsbury Publishing Inc does not have any control over, or responsibility for, any third-party websites referred to or in this book. All internet addresses given in this book were correct at the time of going to press. The author and publisher regret any inconvenience caused if addresses have changed or sites have ceased to exist, but can accept no responsibility for any such changes.

A catalogue record for this book is available from the British Library.

A catalog record for this book is available from the Library of Congress.

ISBN: HB: 978-1-3503-2514-2
PB: 978-1-3503-2518-0
ePDF: 978-1-3503-2515-9
eBook: 978-1-3503-2516-6

Series: Bloomsbury Studies in the Aristotelian Tradition

Typeset by Integra Software Services Pvt. Ltd.

For product safety related questions contact productsafety@bloomsbury.com.

To find out more about our authors and books visit www.bloomsbury.com
and sign up for our newsletters.

Contents

List of Figures and Tables ix
List of Contributors xi
Acknowledgments xiv

1 Andrea Cesalpino. An Introduction *Fabrizio Baldassarri and Craig Martin* 1

Part 1 Philosophy

2 Andrea Cesalpino's Epistemology *Marco Sgarbi* 15
3 Philosophy, Medicine, and Humanism in Cesalpino's *Investigation into Demons* *Craig Martin* 33
4 Plato and Andrea Cesalpino's Aristotelianism: A Revealing Marginality *Eva Del Soldato* 53
5 Cesalpino on Sensitive Powers and the Question of Divine Immanence *Andreas Blank* 69
6 Andrea Cesalpino and the Rejection of the Celestial Spheres in Seventeenth-Century University of Edinburgh *David Malcolm McOmish* 87

Part 2 Botany and Mineralogy

7 Cesalpino's (Aristotelian) Philosophy of Plants: A Science of Botany in the Renaissance *Fabrizio Baldassarri* 107
8 Aristotelian Metaphysics of the Vegetative Soul and Early Modern Plant Physiology: A Comparison of Plant Functions in Aristotle, Pseudo-Aristotle, and Cesalpino *Quentin Hiernaux and Corentin Tresnie* 131
9 Paratextual Debates in *De plantis* (1583): On the Best Form of Botanical Prose, Garden and Things, and the Author-Figure of Cesalpino *Julia Heideklang* 153
10 Cesalpino's Mineralogy between Meteorology and Chymistry *Hiro Hirai* 171

Part 3 Medicine

11 Anatomy and Practice: Andrea Cesalpino's *Praxis universae artis medicae* *R. Allen Shotwell* 193

12 Simple and Compound Drugs in Late Renaissance Medicine: The
    Pharmacology of Andrea Cesalpino (1593) *Elisabeth Moreau*   209
13 Cesalpino's Theory of Disease: *De morbo gallico* in Context
    Carmen Schmechel   225

Index   243

List of Figures and Tables

Figures

7.1 [On the left] 157. Lupus salictarius. Pli: Lupulo (Humulus Lupulus L). [On the right] 158. Κάνναβις: Cannabis sativa: Canapa (Cannabis sativa L). Andrea Cesalpino, *Herbarium*, fol. 63. Courtesy of Sistema Museale di Ateneo, Museo di Storia Naturale (Botanica) of the Università di Firenze   110

7.2 [On the left] 214. Pharnaceon. Pli. tenuioris folii: Virga aurea Campestris (Solidago Virgaurea L). [On the right] 215. Eupatorium Avicennae (Eupatorium cannabinum L). Cesalpino, *Herbarium*, fol. 85. Courtesy of Sistema Museale di Ateneo, Museo di Storia Naturale (Botanica) of the Università di Firenze   111

7.3 [On the left] 395. Μανδραγόρας: Mandragoras mas (Mandragora veralis B). [On the bottom right] 396. Μανδραγόρας: Mandragoras foemina (Mandragorae microcarpae B). [On the top right] 397. Μόριον: Morion: Mandragoras 3° (Mandragora officinarum L). Cesalpino, *Herbarium*, fol. 148. Courtesy of Sistema Museale di Ateneo, Museo di Storia Naturale (Botanica) of the Università di Firenze   112

7.4 Cesalpino, section of the letter to Bishop Tornabuoni used as a preface to the herbarium. Courtesy of Sistema Museale di Ateneo, Museo di Storia Naturale (Botanica) of the Università di Firenze   115

9.1 Number of listed authorities within the paratexts of sixteenth-century printed herbals in relation to each first print edition (For Mattioli's *Discorsi* the first print edition by Vincenzo Valgrisi is considered). [©Julia Heideklang]   160

9.2 Comparison of the Authorities listed by Andrea Cesalpino and Mattioli: authorities constituting a core group of continuously invoked authors in sixteenth-century print herbals; Theophrastus as additionally shared ancient authority; southern European authorities who are quoted by both or Cesalpino only. [©Julia Heideklang]   161

11.1 Illustration of the internal structure of the kidney (III) from Felix Platter *De corporis humani structura et usu* (Basel: Froben 1583), 41. Platter copied Vesalius's illustration which contradicted the medieval view of the kidney containing a filtering membrane that was abandoned by Berengario earlier in the sixteenth century partly because of matters of practice. Public Domain   199

Table

9.1 Overview of paratexts in Cesalpino's *De plantis*, discussed in this chapter. © Julia Heideklang   156

List of Contributors

Fabrizio Baldassarri has a Marie Skłodowska-Curie Fellowship from Ca' Foscari University of Venice and Indiana University Bloomington, pursuing research on plants in pre-modern natural philosophy. He has co-edited the special issue "Manipulating Flora" in *Early Science and Medicine* (2018) and the volume *Vegetative Powers: The Roots of Life in Ancient, Medieval, and Early Modern Natural Philosophy* (2021), and he has edited the special issue "Plants in Early Modern Knowledge" in *Nuncius* (2022). He is author of *Il metodo al tavolo anatomico. Descartes e la medicina* (2021).

Andreas Blank holds a research position at Alpen-Adria Universität Klagenfurt, funded by the Austrian Science Fund (FWF). Previously, he has been Visiting Fellow at the Center for Philosophy of Science (University of Pittsburgh), the Cohn Institute for the History and Philosophy of Science and Ideas (Tel Aviv University), and the Istituto per il Lessico Intellettuale Europeo (ILIESI/CNR, Rome), as well as Visiting Associate Professor at the University of Hamburg and Bard College Berlin.

Eva Del Soldato is Associate Professor of Italian Studies at the University of Pennsylvania. Her research focuses on the early modern reception of ancient philosophical traditions, especially Aristotelianism and Platonism. She is the author of *Simone Porzio* (2010), *Early Modern Aristotle. On the Making and Unmaking of the Authority* (2020), and the editor of several volumes, including *Harmony and Contrast* (2022, with Anna Corrias).

Julia Heideklang is a postdoctoral researcher at Eberhard Karls Universität Tübingen in the Department of Philology. She obtained her master's degrees in Latin, Biology, and Classical Philology from the Humboldt University of Berlin. Her dissertation "Botanics in the Making (1500–1700): Communication and Construction of the Botanical Science in Early Modern Europe" focused on the paratexts of botanical writings in early modern Europe. She currently works in the DFG project "Versio latina" of Prof. Dr. Anja Wolkenhauer, examining the actors, functions, and aims of early modern translations into Latin.

Quentin Hiernaux is a research associate of the Fund for Scientific Research—FNRS. He is affiliated with the research center in philosophy (PHI) of the Université libre de Bruxelles and is a scientific collaborator at Meise Botanic Garden. His research focuses on the history and epistemology of plant science. He is more broadly concerned with the status of plants in the history of philosophy and in environmental ethics.

Hiro Hirai (PhD University of Lille 3, France) is a research associate at the Center for Science and Society, Columbia University. He has published widely on Renaissance and early modern natural philosophy, medicine, and alchemy, including *Le concept de semence dans les théories de la Renaissance* (2005) and *Medical Humanism and Natural Philosophy* (2011). He edited *Jacques Gaffarel between Magic and Science* (2014) and co-edited *Pseudo-Paracelsus: Forgery and Early Modern Alchemy, Medicine and Natural Philosophy* (2021). He is currently preparing his third monograph on Renaissance natural philosophy, medicine, and magic.

David Malcolm McOmish is research fellow at the Department of Philosophy and Cultural Heritage, Ca' Foscari, University of Venice, where he was Marie Curie Fellow, before which he was a research fellow at the Institute for Advanced Studies in the Humanities, University of Edinburgh. He works on the role of scholarly networks in institutional settings in shaping and transferring knowledge in natural philosophy and cosmology in the period 1560–1630, especially on transconfessional and transnational "cosmopolitan" academics and institutions.

Craig Martin is Associate Professor of the History of Science and Technology at Ca' Foscari University of Venice. He is the author of *Renaissance Meteorology: Pomponazzi to Descartes* (2011) and *Subverting Aristotle: Religion, History, and Philosophy in Early Modern Science* (2014). His translation of Girolamo Mercuriale's *On Pestilence* was published in 2022.

Elisabeth Moreau is an FNRS postdoctoral researcher at the Université libre de Bruxelles (Brussels, Belgium). Trained in history and philosophy of science, she has worked on medicine and matter theories in late Renaissance Europe. Her current postdoctoral project, "From the Alembic to the Stomach," is centered on the medical and alchemical conceptions of digestion and metabolism.

Carmen Schmechel currently holds a German Research Foundation—sponsored postdoctoral fellowship at the Institute for Philosophy of the Freie Universität Berlin, where she is exploring theories about ferments and fermentation in premodern European medicine and chemistry. Her broader interests extend to other theories of transformation of matter, such as distillation, sublimation, or metabolism, including the metaphorical usages of these terms and their philosophical backgrounds over the *longue-durée*.

Marco Sgarbi is Professor of History of Philosophy at Ca' Foscari University of Venice. Among his latest publications are *The Democratization of Knowledge in Renaissance Italy. The Philosopher and the People* (Amsterdam University Press, 2022) and *The Age of Epistemology. Aristotelian Logic in Early Modern Philosophy 1500–1700* (Bloomsbury, 2023).

R. Allen Shotwell is Professor of Humanities at Ivy Tech Community College. He holds a PhD in the History and Philosophy of Science from Indiana University, and his research focuses on anatomy and medicine in the renaissance. He is currently working on a book on early sixteenth-century anatomy and Berengario da Carpi.

Corentin Tresnie is Research Fellow of the Fund for Scientific Research—FNRS. He is affiliated with the research center in philosophy (PHI) of the Université libre de Bruxelles and the De Wulf-Mansion Centre of the KU Leuven. His main area of research is the history of early philosophical theories of education and cognitive improvement, with a focus on Platonisms in late antiquity. He also studies the legacy of ancient philosophy in early modern science.

Acknowledgments

The volume results from two organized panels at the RSA annual meeting of 2021 and an online event entirely devoted to Andrea Cesalpino, which took place on February 25–26, 2022, with the support of Ca' Foscari's Department of Philosophy and Cultural Heritage and the Center for Renaissance and Early Modern Thought and of the Department of History and Philosophy of Science and Medicine at Indiana University Bloomington. The panels and the conference have benefited from support from the European Union's Horizon 2020 research and innovation program under the Marie Skłodowska-Curie Grant Agreement n.890770, "VegSciLif." We thank Chiara Bariviera for her help with the bibliographies and index.

1

Andrea Cesalpino. An Introduction

Fabrizio Baldassarri and Craig Martin

In the *Dictionaire historique et critique* (1697), Pierre Bayle (1647–1706) included a short entry on Andrea Cesalpino that contains a few notes about his biography and intellectual significance. He wrote that Cesalpino "had been a highly skilled scholar in both philosophy and medicine. He was from Arezzo, and worked for a long period in Pisa, before becoming first physician of Pope Clement VIII. He died in Rome on February 23, 1603, aged 84 years."[1] Yet, he added something more. Influenced by Samuel Parker's reading of Cesalpino and by the criticisms made by Nicolaus Taurellus (1547–1606), he wrote that Cesalpino "abandoned the way of ordinary Peripatetic scholars in many aspects and to put it bluntly he was a bad Christian with respect to his opinions. His principles barely differed from those of Spinoza," while noting that "a modern author counts him among the greatest geniuses that has ever been seen."[2]

Bayle's account shows that Cesalpino enjoyed some renown in the seventeenth and eighteenth centuries, before his influence slowly faded. By the twentieth century, scholars often presented Cesalpino as anticipating later developments, just like Bayle had done. These studies, however, placed him not just as a precursor of Spinoza, but as a possible forerunner of William Harvey's discovery of the circulation of blood.[3] Moreover, scholars viewed his treatise on plants published in 1583, in which he provided a sound methodology to classify plants, as anticipating the ideas of John Ray (1627–1705) and Carolus Linnaeus (1707–78).[4] Although he is no longer considered central to the history of philosophy or to the discovery of the circulation of blood, Cesalpino has remained central to the history of botany. Nevertheless, Cesalpino's botany, however important and appreciated by Linnaeus, has been largely restricted to studies on Tuscany, removing him from the bigger picture of Renaissance Europe.[5]

The difficulties in understanding Cesalpino's ideas help explain his relative marginal place in contemporary scholarship in addition to giving motivation for reassessing his works. His unusual form of Aristotelianism had ramifications for theology. His attempt to harmonize metaphysics combined with an empirical understanding of nature. His philosophical framework was unattractive, if not distasteful, to some of his contemporaries. The Lutheran scholar Nicolaus Taurellus, who attempted to accommodate Aristotelian science with religious doctrine, accused Cesalpino of embracing impious positions. According to Taurellus, Cesalpino denied God's providence in human affairs, refused to accept a Christian understanding of the creation of the universe, and accepted Averroes' theory of the unicity of the passive intellect, a position that was condemned at the Fifth Lateran Council because of its ramifications for personal immortality. Taurellus blamed Cesalpino's impiety on an excessive faithfulness to Aristotle's philosophy and the negative influence of pagan and Arabic authors.[6] Taurellus's successors in Nüremberg continued the polemic against Cesalpino.[7]

While Taurellus's polemic perhaps reflects concerns among early modern Lutherans, his view of Cesalpino fails to correspond to his reception among Catholic authorities. Inquisitors of the Holy Office never accused him of heresy, and his works were never placed on the Index of Prohibited books. He even enjoyed the patronage of Clement VIII. Moreover, even though Taurellus considered him excessively committed to Aristotle, Guido Giglioni has highlighted Cesalpino's eclecticism, which reflected the presence of Platonism and Galenism, but at the same time makes interpreting his works difficult.[8] Above all, Cesalpino's writings are ponderous and at times ambiguous, making it difficult to understand the entirety of his thought.

Despite the relative neglect of recent scholars, Cesalpino enjoyed a prominent stature and held prestigious positions. He was director of the botanical garden in Pisa and was appointed professor of botany and medicine at the University of Pisa, a position that placed him close to the Medici court in Florence, a center for intellectual and cultural exchange. After he left Pisa, he became physician to Clement VIII (born Ippolito Aldrobrandini, 1536–1605) and taught medicine at La Sapienza, Rome's university. In these capacities, Cesalpino engaged in a wide range of intellectual interests, writing on logic, theology, demonology, natural philosophy, astronomy, geology, mineralogy, chymistry, botany, and medicine. In these writings, he proposed a new methodology for philosophical investigations into nature, as he aimed to perfect Aristotelian natural philosophy. Attentively observing plants and human bodies, Cesalpino described, ordered, and classified nature, which was at the core of developments in natural history and medicine.

While his Aristotelianism was in line with the philosophical achievements of sixteenth-century scholars, he also directly or indirectly influenced several important early modern scholars, including Galileo Galilei.[9] His doctrine of the celestial spheres was at the center of a vivid discussion at the University of Edinburgh, demonstrating that his thought remained relevant to seventeenth-century culture and education (see **David Malcom McOmish** in this volume). While recognizing his influence, in this volume, we interpret him not as a precursor of later philosophical and scientific doctrine, but we examine Cesalpino's ideas within the context of early modern thought and their influence in diverse fields of knowledge.

1. Biography

Cesalpino was likely born in 1524 or 1525, in the countryside near Arezzo, and not on June 6, 1519, as sometimes is claimed. While his date of birth still has not been determined with certainty, historical investigations in the late nineteenth and early twentieth century have provided important clues. In both *Vita ed opere di Andrea*

Cesalpino (1922) and *Tre medici aretini (A. Cesalpino, F. Redi e F. Folli)* (1936), Ugo Viviani demonstrated the unlikeliness that Cesalpino was born on June 6, 1519, as proposed by several historians and scholars—including Bayle. The origin of the mistake lies in a clue found in the register of baptism in Arezzo, which reports that on June 6, "Andrea et Giovanni of Bernardino of Andrea, *fazzerino (o fazzino)*" was baptized. Since the names correspond to Cesalpino's lineage—Giovanni was the name of his father, and Andrea the name of his grandfather—earlier historians understood this to refer to Cesalpino's birth. Yet, Viviani found another document that shows that on June 6 "Andrea et Giovanni was b[aptized], son of Bernardino d'Andrea d'Agnolino Painter (or *Sellario?*),"[10] making clear that on June 6, 1519, the child named Andrea Giovanni was the son of Bernardino, and therefore was not Cesalpino.

Unfortunately, neither Viviani nor anyone else has been able to discover the actual record of Cesalpino's baptism, which probably occurred in a parish in Arezzo's outskirts. Several other documents, however, confirm Viviani's interpretation. A note published by Giuseppe Lais, entitled "Documenti inediti di Andrea Cesalpino", reveals a report dated October 3, 1595, which concerns the inhumation of Filippo Neri, in which Cesalpino is said to have been "70 years" old, while another report dated April 17, 1599, Andrea Cesalpino is said to have been "74 years."[11] Viviani cited both documents and added a text of testimony Cesalpino gave in a case the Inquisition made against Jacopo Albergotti on November 24 1559, in which Cesalpino said he was thirty-five.[12] Finally, Viviani published documentation concerning Cesalpino's death in March 1603. In the Parish Archive of Sant'Eustachio in Rome it is written that "on the day of March 15, 1603, Andrea Cesalpini Florentine physician died and found burial in the Church of San Giovanni dei Fiorentini"; and in the Archival of this latter parish, Viviani found a document that attests that "on the day of March 15, 1603 G Cesare Cesalpino physician of the Parish of Sant' Eustachio, aged 78 … was buried in our Church."[13] This last document confirms that Cesalpino was likely born in 1524 or in 1525.[14]

Cesalpino enrolled at the University of Pisa in 1545 and followed courses taught by Simone Porzio (1496–1554) in philosophy, Guido Guidi (1508–69) in medicine, Realdo Colombo (1516–59) and Gabriele Falloppio (1523–62) in anatomy, and Luca Ghini (1490–1556) in simples.[15] He took his degree in medicine on March 20, 1551.[16] In the years surrounding the time when Cesalpino studied at the university, other important figures in medicine and botany were at Pisa. Andreas Vesalius performed public anatomical demonstrations in January 1544. Ulisse Aldrovandi likely attended some of Ghini's lectures in 1553 or 1554. Aldrovandi was close to Ghini and transcribed several of his lectures.[17] Although there is no direct correspondence between Aldrovandi and Cesalpino, in letters to other colleagues Aldrovandi expressed high esteem for Cesalpino's knowledge of botanical specimens.[18]

In 1555, Cesalpino succeeded Ghini as *prefectus* (Director) of the botanical garden of Pisa and as lecturer of simples. During these years, Cesalpino travelled within Italy, acquiring specimens for the botanical garden. He also received specimens from Europe and the West and East Indies. Around 1569, Cesalpino gave up the chair of *materia medica* for a professorship in practical medicine, succeeding Francesco Violi.[19] As ordinary professor of practical medicine his salary was 350 florins in 1585 and reached 400 florins in 1589 and 1590, respectable amounts but not the highest that the university paid.[20] In 1592, after Girolamo Mercuriale (1530–1606) was appointed to teach the same subject at a much higher salary and after quarrelling with Francesco de' Vieri (or Verino (II), 1524–91), Cesalpino moved to Rome, where he was appointed papal physician and taught medicine at La Sapienza. In Rome, Cesalpino enjoyed the company of Michele Mercati (1541–93), his former student in Pisa, who introduced him to the papal court. In addition to Mercati, Cesalpino taught the botanist and collector Johannes Faber (1574–1629) and Galileo, who would both become members of the Accademia dei Lincei. It has been reported that Cesalpino made a few microscopic observations of plants in the last period of his life with Galileo. Cesalpino died in Rome in 1603, where he was buried, in the church of San Giovanni dei Fiorentini.

Cesalpino's life was filled with controversy.[21] The University of Pisa was as famous for the excellence of its philosophical training as it was for scholastic battles.[22] Unlike many professors of philosophy, Cesalpino never wrote commentaries of Aristotelian texts. Rather, he published two collections of questions, which explored topics related to Aristotelian philosophy. Agonistic vehemence characterized the work of Cesalpino's teachers and friends such as Porzio and Girolamo Borro (1512–92). Porzio and Borro were staunch Aristotelians and most likely played a role in Cesalpino's intellectual development and in his adherence to Aristotle's philosophy. Cesalpino operated in a similar agonistic manner challenging his opponents. The most famous controversy took place in 1589–90, when Cesalpino opposed Verino's project for a Platonic School of philosophy. Doctrinal differences and philosophical interpretations shaped their hostility, which was likely long-lived, perhaps beginning after they offered their opinions about the alleged demonic possession of nuns in Sant'Anna Benedictine monastery in Pisa in 1574. In 1576, Verino published a *Discorso intorno a' dimoni, volgarmente chiamati spiriti*, in which he tried to combine a Platonic interpretation of demonology with Christian doctrine. Four years later, Cesalpino published the *Daemonum investigatio peripatetica*, with an Aristotelian perspective (see **Craig Martin**'s contribution in this volume).[23] Their hostilities grew throughout the 1580s, as Verino's Platonism was at odds with Cesalpino's Aristotelian philosophy—Verino contested Borro's work for similar reasons.[24] Verino's relationship with Borro was further complicated in 1582, when inquisitors accused Borro and Verino's son of possessing forbidden books and discussing suspect positions. Both Verino's son and Borro were eventually released from prison after intercessions from powerful ecclesiastical figures.[25] In 1589, Verino published the *Vere conclusioni di Platone conformi alla dottrina Christiana et a quella di Aristotele*, dedicated to Baccio Valori (1535–1606), in which he referred to the heretical teachers of philosophy, medicine, and logic that populated the University of Pisa. Although Verino did not include Cesalpino among the heretical teachers, Cesalpino found it necessary to inform Baccio Valori that there were no followers of Telesio in the medical school of Pisa and that Verino "under the shield of the Telesiani tried to hide his own philosophy."[26] The dispute faded away, as Verino died and Cesalpino left for Rome, but this quarrel shows that Cesalpino believed that his philosophy was consistent with Catholic theology (on the intersections between Plato and Cesalpino's Aristotelianism in his dispute with Verino, see **Eva Del Soldato**'s contribution in this volume).

Cesalpino was aware that his medical and natural philosophical views held implications for theology, and at times, he tried to accommodate his Aristotelianism with Catholic doctrine. Cesalpino's deep religiosity drove him into the brotherhood of San Filippo Neri (1515-95).[27] Not all, however, were convinced of the wholesomeness of his philosophical views. In 1597, Taurellus declared Cesalpino's interpretation of Aristotle to be impious for perniciously using Aristotelian ideas to discuss topics close to theology. Taurellus believed that Cesalpino endorsed pantheism, which made God the unifying principle of the universe and imbued all reality with a universal soul (for Taurellus's philosophical criticism, see **Andreas Blank**'s contribution in this volume).

Questions concerning the soul were central to Cesalpino's philosophical investigations. He rejected Porzio's materialist interpretation of Aristotle's psychology and followed a different line.[28] Cesalpino considered the soul's nature, location, immortality, and role as a source of life, ultimately exploring the idea of a universal presence of the soul that permeates nature. These ideas were crucial to his philosophy and had ramifications for his theories about plants, demons, the cosmos, and human physiology.

2. Soul and Life in Cesalpino's Thought

The investigation of soul threads throughout Cesalpino's work, connecting divine being with material nature. These discussions are apparent in both his philosophical works and his medical writings. Cesalpino began *Praxis universae artis medicae* with a meditation on the role of innate heat [*calidus innatus*], the most divine matter in living beings. Later in the text, he discussed the role of spirits in animating living bodies and provided a physiological investigation of the circulation of blood and the role of respiration. Blood and respiration form the subject matter of discussions in *Quaestiones peripateticae* (*QP*), book 5. Maintaining that the heart is the origin of all corporeal operations, he discussed the movement of blood as the vehicle of innate heat and spiritual powers, a subject noted by historians.[29] Cesalpino's interpretation of the movement of blood was influenced by Colombo's and Falloppio's anatomical writings. In line with medical instruction at Pisa, Cesalpino challenged some of Galen's tenets, without abandoning the larger Galenic synthesis.

Questions about soul and life surface in *De plantis* (*DP*) and *De metallicis*. In both cases, Cesalpino combined a philosophical systematization of nature with a natural historical classification and description of particulars. His attention to individual bodies is consistent with his matter theory, according to which the body is "*quantum* and *substantia* at the same time."[30] His direct observation of nature conducted at the Pisan botanical garden, the construction of two herbaria, and his observations of Vatican's mineral collection (and Michele Mercati's unfinished *Metallotheca*) played significant roles in Cesalpino's study of nature (on Cesalpino's mineralogy and history of metals, see **Hiro Hirai**'s contribution to this volume). In the study of plants, the vegetative soul is at the center of Cesalpino's explanation of vegetable life, as he devoted the first book of *DP* to plants' souls, discussing their location, nature, and functions, and establishing a classification of plants based on properties of the soul (see the contribution of **Corentin Tresnie** and **Quentin Hiernaux** in this volume). Cesalpino conceived minerals to be entirely deprived of life and soul, yet natural. He framed botany and mineralogy, fields that Aristotle's writings did not discuss in depth, within Aristotelian philosophy.

In conjunction with his privileging of observation, Cesalpino attempted to make use of logic to clarify the epistemic role of experience by providing a systematization and defining methodological principles to deal with observations of nature. Cesalpino's logical and epistemological assumptions provide a framework for his investigations into nature. In *QP*, Cesalpino developed methodological rules, which he applied to natural philosophy and especially on botany (on his epistemology and its application to botany, see **Marco Sgarbi** in this volume). Cesalpino's combination of a theoretical framework with the observation of natural particulars was innovative.

His medical works sought to frame medical theory in Aristotelian terms, at times combining Hippocratic ideas with an Aristotelian ones, such as in *Daemonum investigatio peripatetica* (*DIP*). In the dedicatory letter of *Quaestiones medicae* (*QM*), Cesalpino stressed that physicians should go back to the knowledge of the ancients, cleansed of the incorrect opinions of his contemporaries. In his view, later scholars had obscured ancient knowledge of both medicine and botany,[31] which he attempted to revise and perfect, for he proclaimed that modern discoveries can only be understood using ancient frameworks. For instance, the newly discovered remedies can only be theorized through the traditions of ancient medicine.[32] In *De medicamentorum facultatibus* (*DMF*), Cesalpino provided a list of remedies in forty-nine chapters, which form in essence a short treatise of *materia medica*. Cesalpino's botany was not only a philosophical systematization but also an empirical and pharmacological knowledge of specimens (on Cesalpino's study of plants, see **Fabrizio Baldassarri** in this volume).

In his works on practical medicine, which were posthumously collected in *Praxis universae artis medicae*, Cesalpino provided the reader with a broad investigation of diseases and ways of treating them, from fevers to *morbo gallicus* (see **Carmen Schmechel**'s contribution in this volume) to the diseases particular parts of the body. As a practitioner, Cesalpino was repeatedly called at Filippo Neri's bedside, as the latter suffered from heavy, painful beatings of the heart, which Cesalpino explained both in medical terms and in supernatural terms.[33]

Cesalpino's philosophy was a complex enterprise. Interrelations between metaphysics, epistemology, natural philosophy, and medicine shape the diverse layers of his thought. His natural philosophical texts bear metaphysical traces; a philosophical systematization frames his interpretation of plants and minerals, as he united the direct observation of specimens to a theoretical framework. Religion played a significant role in his life, and at times matters of faith influenced his analysis of Aristotle's philosophy, such as in *DIP*.

Cesalpino's medical and philosophical works exhibit many prominent themes of late Renaissance investigations of nature. His attitudes toward the ancients reflect Renaissance humanism. His embrace of Aristotle corresponds to the most vibrant philosophical traditions of sixteenth-century Italy. His development of ideas about method corresponds to attitudes about experience and observation embraced by Renaissance physicians. His classifications, collections, and observations of plants reflect the momentous changes that the field of natural history underwent in the decades before 1600.

3. Principal Works and Publications

- In 1563, he donated an herbarium to Alfonso Tornabuoni, now preserved in Florence. He prepared another one for Cosimo I de' Medici, which is lost. The surviving herbarium contains 768 specimens of 760 plant species, and it is one of the first herbaria ever produced in the modern era.

Cesalpino wrote the following printed works:

- In 1571, the *Peripateticarum quaestionum libri V* [QP], a series of philosophical questions in the line of Aristotelian doctrine, dedicated to the Grand Duke Francesco I de' Medici.
- In 1580, the *Daemonum investigatio peripatetica. In qua explicatur locus Hippocratis in Prognosticis si quid divinum in morbis habetur* [DIP].
- In 1583, *De plantis libri XVI* [DP], a classification and theoretical consideration of plants that applied the systematization found in the herbarium to a wide array of plants. It describes around 1,500 plants (on the paratextual parts of *DP*, see **Julia Heideklang**'s contribution in this volume).
- In 1593, a second edition of *QP* with the title *Quaestionum peripateticarum libri quinque* and *DIP*, together with the *Quaestionum medicarum libri II* [QM] and *De medicamentorum facultatibus libri II* [DMF], dedicated to the Grand Duke Ferdinand III (on Cesalpino's pharmacology, see **Elisabeth Moreau**'s contribution in this volume).
- In 1596, *De metallicis libri III*, dedicated to Pope Clement VIII, a work related to Michele Mercati's *Metallotheca*, the Vatican collection of minerals and metals in Rome.
- In 1602, *Artis medicae pars prima, de morbis universalibus*, that is, the first four books of *Praxis universae artis medicae*, in which he discussed practical medicine and the treatment of several diseases. In 1603, books 7 and 8 were printed in a second volume, entitled *Artis medicae, liber VII, de morbis ventris*. Both volumes were printed in Rome, by Zanetti. In 1605, the complete work, including books 5 and 6, was printed in Frankfurt with the title Κάτοπτρον, *sive Speculum artis medicae Hippocraticum*, and in 1606 it was printed in Treviso with the title *Praxis universae artis medicae* (on Cesalpino's anatomy and practical medicine, see **R. Allen Shotwell**'s contribution in this volume).
- In 1603, a short appendix to *DP* and *QP*, entitled *Appendix ad libros de plantis, et quaestiones peripateticas Andreae Cesalpini*. The *Appendix* is, however, incomplete.

A manuscript of Cesalpino's *Historiae ecclesiasticae compendium usque ad Annum Jubilei MDC* is at the Biblioteca Apostolica Vaticana (Vat. Lat. 35 600). An Italian translation by Luigi Condorelli was published in Rome in 1985.[34]

The spelling and punctuation of the Latin quoted in this volume have been modernized and systematized.

Notes

1. Pierre Bayle, *Dictionaire historique et critique* (Rotterdam: Reinier Leers, 1697), 1,2: 820: "a été un très-habile homme tant en Philosophie qu'en Medicine. Il étoit d'Arezzo, et il professa long tems à Pise; après quoi il devint premier Medecin du Pape Clement VIII. Il mourut à Rome le 23 de Fevrier 1603 à l'âge de 84 ans." There are several errors in this entry, see below. For a more recent summary of his intellectual biography, see Karl Mägdefrau, "Andrea Cesalpino (Andrea Caesalpinus) (1519–1603)," in *Dictionary of Scientific Biography*, ed. Charles C. Gillipsie (New York: Scribner, 1978), 80–1.
2. Bayle, *Dictionaire*, 1,2:820–1: "Il quitta la route ordinaire des Peripateticiens en plusiers choses, et pour bien dire, c'étoit un très-mauvais Chrétien eu égard aux opinions. Ses principes ne differoient guere de ceux de Spinosa…. Un auteur moderne le compte parmi les plus grans genies qu'on ait jamais vus." Bayle cited both Parker and Taurellus in the notes to his entry on Cesalpino.
3. For example, see: Carlo Colombero, "Andrea Cesalpino e la polemica anti-aristotelica e anti-spinoziana," *Rivista critica di storia della filosofia* 35, no. 4 (1980): 343–56; Silvano Chellini, *Antologia storica relativa alla scoperta della circolazione del sangue fatta da Andrea Cesalpino* (Pisa: Giardini, 1970).
4. Alan G. Morton, *History of Botanical Science: An Account of the Development of Botany from Ancient times to the Present Day* (London: Academic Press, 1981).
5. Cristina Bellorini, *The World of Plants in Renaissance Tuscany: Medicine and Botany* (Farnham: Ashgate, 2016).
6. Craig Martin, *Subverting Aristotle: Religion, History, and Philosophy in Early Modern Science* (Baltimore: Johns Hopkins University Press, 2014), 96–9.
7. Danilo Facca, *Early Modern Aristotelianism and the Making of Philosophical Disciplines* (London: Bloomsbury, 2020), 84–9.
8. On these interconnections, see Guido Giglioni, "Plantanimal Imagination: Life and Perception in Early Modern Discussions of Vegetative Power," in *Vegetative Powers: The Roots of Life in Ancient, Medieval, and Early Modern Natural Philosophy*, ed. Fabrizio Baldassarri and Andreas Blank (Cham: Springer, 2021), 325–45. Guido Giglioni, "Reading Galen's *De Naturalibus facultatibus* in the Early Modern Period," in *Galen and the Early Moderns*, ed. Matteo Favaretti Camposampiero and Emanuela Scribano (Cham: Springer, 2022), 9–35.
9. See, for instance, William R. J. Shea, "Galileo's Claim to Fame: The Proof that the Earth Moves from the Evidence of the Tides," *British Journal of the History of Science* 5 (1970): 111–27. For other possible influences on Galileo, see Michele Camerota and Mario O. Helbing, "Galileo and Pisan Aristotelianism: Galileo's *De motu antiquiora* and *Quaestiones de motu elementorum* of the Pisan Professors," *Early Science and Medicine* 5, no. 4 (2000): 319–65, at 327–8; Mario O. Helbing, "Mechanics and Natural Philosophy in Late 16th-Century Pisa: Cesalpino and Buonamici, Humanist

Masters of the Faculty of Arts," in *Mechanics and Natural Philosophy before the Scientific Revolution*, ed. W. Roy Laird and Sophie Roux (Dordrecht: Springer 2008), 185-93.

10 Ugo Viviani, *Tre medici aretini (A. Cesalpino, F. Redi e F. Folli)* (Arezzo: R. Accademia Petrarca Editrice, 1936), 12-13.

11 Giuseppe Lais, "Atti dell'Accademia Pontificia de' nuovi Lincei. Sessione Va del 16 aprile 1882 ... Documenti inediti di Andrea Cesalpino," *Atti dell'Accademia Pontificia de' nuovi Lincei*, 35 (1881-2): 95-102.

12 Viviani, *Tre medici aretini*, 14.

13 Ibid., 15. Viviani dismissed the two little mistakes in the documentation.

14 According to the documentation quoted, if exact, it is possible to speculate that Cesalpino was born between October 4 and November 24, 1524. See also John P. Arcieri, *The Circulation of Blood and Andrea Cesalpino of Arezzo* (New York: Vanni, 1945). R. Pazzaglia, "Andrea Cesalpino e la scoperta della circolazione del sangue nel terzo centenario della morte di Guglielmo Harvey," *Bollettino Memorie Società Tosco Umbra di Chirurgia* 19, no. 5 (1958): 454-64. R. Pazzaglia, "Il Cesalpino oggi," *Atti e Memorie dell'Accademia Petrarca Letteratura, Arti e Scienza di Arezzo* 40 (1970-1972, 1974): 206-12. Cf. Guido Moggi, "L'erbario di Andrea Cesalpino," *Gli erbari aretini da Andrea Cesalpino ai giorni nostri*, ed. Chiara Nepi and Enrico Gusmeroli (Firenze: Firenze University Press, 2008), 3-20.

15 On Porzio, see Eva Del Soldato, *Simone Porzio. Un aristotelico tra natura e grazia* (Rome: Edizioni di Storia e Letteratura, 2010). On Luca Ghini, see Dietrich von Engelhardt, "Luca Ghini (1490-1556) il padre fondatore della botanica moderna nel contesto dei rapporti scientifici europei del sedicesimo secolo," *Annali del Museo Civico di Rovereto, Sezione: Archeologia, Storia, Scienze naturali*, 27 (2011): 227-46. Paula Findlen, "The Death of a Naturalist: Knowledge and Community in Late Renaissance Italy," in *Professors, Physicians and Practices in the History of Medicine*, ed. Cynthia Klestinec and Gideon Manning (Cham: Springer, 2018), 155-95. On these teachings at the University of Pisa, see Manlio Iofrida, "La filosofia e la medicina (1543-1737)," in *Storia dell'Università di Pisa* (Pisa: Pacini, 1993), 1: 239-338.

16 Viviani, *Tre medici aretini*, 22.

17 See Sandra Tugnoli Pattaro, *La formazione scientifica e il "Discorso Naturale" di Ulisse Aldrovandi* (Trento: Unicoop, 1977), 40-2.

18 Regrettably, no direct reference to Aldrovandi surfaces in Cesalpino's text.

19 Angelo Fabroni, *Historiae academiae pisanae* (Pisa: Mugnaini, 1792), 2:55-7.

20 Galileo Galilei, *Le opere. Volume 19. Documenti e narrazioni biografiche di contemporanei* (Florence: Barbèra, 1907), 34-41.

21 Viviani reports of the alleged crime of Cesalpino, dismissing the case. See Viviani, *Tre medici aretini*, 41-52.

22 Paul F. Grendler, "The University of Florence and Pisa in the High Renaissance," *Renaissance and Reformation* 6, no. 3 (1982): 157-65; Charles B. Schmitt, "The Faculty of Arts at Pisa at the Time of Galileo," *Physis* 14 (1972): 243-72.

23 On the issues of Christian Platonism, see Martin Mulsow, "The Ambiguities of the *Prisca Sapientia* in Late Renaissance Humanism," *Journal of the History of Ideas* 65, no. 1 (2004): 1-13.

24 Charles B. Schmitt, "Girolamo Borro's *Multae sunt nostrarum ignorationum causae* (Ms. Vat. Ross. 1009)," in *Philosophy and Humanism: Renaissance Essays in Honor of Paul Oskar Kristeller*, ed. E. P. Mahoney (Leiden: Brill, 1976), 462-76; Craig Martin,

"Humanism and the Assessment of Averroes in the Renaissance," in *Renaissance Averroism and Its Aftermath: Arabic Philosophy in Early Modern Europe*, ed. Anna Akasoy and Guido Giglioni (Dordrecht: Springer, 2013), 65–79, at 76–7; Eva Del Soldato, *Early Modern Aristotle: On the Making and the Unmaking of Authority* (Philadelphia: University of Pennsylvania Press, 2020), 71–4.
25 Ugo Baldini and Leen Spruit, *Catholic Church and Modern Science: Documents from the Archives of the Roman Congregations of the Holy Office and the Index: Volume I: Sixteenth-century Documents* (Rome: Libreria Editrice Vaticana, 2009), 1,1:665, 815–17.
26 Viviani, *Tre medici aretini*, 32: "Ancorché il dott. Verino sotto lo scudo dei Telesiani cerchi di coprire il detto suo, nondimeno appresso molti non so come sia per essere accettata questa esposizione, attesto che de' Telesiani non vi è chi legga in Studio, né che abbia mandato fuori scritti, né che questi siano Medici come egli afferma." Viviani also included a letter Verino wrote to Baccio Valori on February 7, 1590 to counter Cesalpino's charge.
27 See Viviani, *Tre medici aretini*, 134–40.
28 See Carlo Colombero, "Il pensiero filosofico di Cesalpino," *Rivista critica di storia della filosofia* 32, no. 3 (1977): 269–84.
29 See, for example, Sigismund Peller, "Harvey's and Cesalpino's Role in the History of Medicine," *Bulletin of the History of Medicine* 23, no. 3 (1949): 213–35; Walter Pagel, "The 'Claim' of Cesalpino and the First and Second Editions of his *Peripatetic Questions*," *History of Science* 13 (1975): 130–8.
30 Colombero, "Il pensiero filosofico di Cesalpino," 282.
31 See Luciana Repici, "Cesalpino e la botanica antica," *Rinascimento* 45 (2005): 47–87.
32 Andrea Cesalpino, *Quaestiones medicarum*, "Serenissimo Ferdinando Magno Hetruriae Duci III," fol. A1v: "Nova quidem remedia atque optima nostris temporibus reperta sunt antiquis incognita, at utendi occasio non a quolibet tenetur, sed ab iis tantum, qui veterum medicinam didicerunt."
33 See Catrien G. Santing, "'Deus rotator and the Microrotator': Blood as the Source of Life in the Life and Works of Andrea Cesalpino," in *Blood—Symbol—Liquid*, ed. Catrien G. Santing and Jetze J. Touber (Leuven: Peeters, 2012), 137–56, at 152–4.
34 Andrea Cesalpino, *Historiae ecclesiasticae*, tr. Luigi Condorelli (Rome: De Luca, 1985).

Bibliography

Primary Sources

Bayle, Pierre. *Dictionaire historique et critique*. 2 vols. Rotterdam: Reinier Leers, 1697.
Cesalpino, Andrea. *Historiae ecclesiasticae*, translated by Luigi Condorelli. Roma: De Luca, 1985.
Cesalpino, Andrea. *Quaestionum medicarum libri II*. Venice: Giunta, 1593.
Galilei, Galileo. *Le opere. Volume 19. Documenti e narrazioni biografiche di contemporanei*. Florence: Barbèra, 1907.

Secondary Sources

Arcieri, John P. *The Circulation of Blood and Andrea Cesalpino of Arezzo*. New York: Vanni, 1945.

Baldini, Ugo, and Leen Spruit. *Catholic Church and Modern Science: Documents from the Archives of the Roman Congregations of the Holy Office and the Index: Volume I: Sixteenth-century Documents*. Rome: Libreria Editrice Vaticana, 2009.
Bellorini, Cristina. *The World of Plants in Renaissance Tuscany: Medicine and Botany*. Farnham: Ashgate, 2016.
Camerota, Michele, and Mario Helbing. "Galileo and Pisan Aristotelianism: Galileo's *De motu antiquiora* and *Quaestiones de motu elementorum* of the Pisan Professors." *Early Science and Medicine* 5, no. 4 (2000): 319–65.
Chellini, Silvano. *Antologia storica relativa alla scoperta della circolazione del sangue fatta da Andrea Cesalpino*, Pisa: Giardini, 1970.
Colombero, Carlo. "Andrea Cesalpino e la polemica anti-aristotelica e anti-spinoziana." *Rivista critica di storia della filosofia* 35, no. 4 (1980): 343–56.
Colombero, Carlo. "Il pensiero filosofico di Cesalpino." *Rivista critica di storia della filosofia* 32, no. 3 (1977): 269–84.
Del Soldato, Eva. *Early Modern Aristotle: On the Making and Unmaking of Authority*. Philadelphia: University of Pennsylvania Press, 2020.
Del Soldato, Eva. *Simone Porzio. Un aristotelico tra natura e grazia*. Rome: Edizioni di Storia e Letteratura, 2010.
Fabroni, Angelo. *Historiae academiae pisanae*. 3 vols. Pisa: Mugnaini, 1791–5.
Facca, Danilo. *Early Modern Aristotelianism and the Making of Philosophical Disciplines*. London: Bloomsbury, 2020.
Findlen, Paula. "The Death of a Naturalist: Knowledge and Community in Late Renaissance Italy." In *Professors, Physicians and Practices in the History of Medicine*, edited by Cynthia Klestinec and Gideon Manning, 155–95. Cham: Springer, 2018.
Giglioni, Guido. "Plantanimal Imagination: Life and Perception in Early Modern Discussions of Vegetative Power." In *Vegetative Powers: The Roots of Life in Ancient, Medieval, and Early Modern Natural Philosophy*, edited by Fabrizio Baldassarri and Andreas Blank, 325–45. Cham: Springer, 2021.
Giglioni, Guido. "Reading Galen's *De Naturalibus facultatibus* in the Early Modern Period." In *Galen and the Early Moderns*, edited by Matteo Favaretti Camposampiero and Emanuela Scribano, 9–35. Cham: Springer, 2022.
Grendler, Paul F. "The University of Florence and Pisa in the High Renaissance." *Renaissance and Reformation* 6, no. 3 (1982): 157–65.
Helbing, Mario O. "Mechanics and Natural Philosophy in Late 16th-Century Pisa: Cesalpino and Buonamici, Humanist Masters of the Faculty of Arts." In *Mechanics and Natural Philosophy before the Scientific Revolution*, edited by W. Roy Laird and Sophie Roux, 185–93. Dordrecht: Springer 2008.
Iofrida, Manlio. "La filosofia e la medicina (1543–1737)." In *Storia dell'Università di Pisa*, vol. 1, 239–338. Pisa: Pacini, 1993.
Lais, P. Giuseppe. "Atti dell'Accademia Pontificia de' nuovi Lincei. Sessione Va del 16 aprile 1882 … Documenti inediti di Andrea Cesalpino." *Atti dell'Accademia Pontificia de' nuovi Lincei* 30 (1881–2): 95–102.
Mägdefrau, Karl. "Andrea Cesalpino (Andrea Caesalpinus) (1519–1603)." In *Dictionary of Scientific Biography*, edited by Charles C. Gillispie, 80–1. New York: Scribner, 1978.
Martin, Craig. "Humanism and the Assessment of Averroes in the Renaissance." In *Renaissance Averroism and Its Aftermath: Arabic Philosophy in Early Modern Europe*, edited by Anna Akasoy and Guido Giglioni, 65–79. Dordrecht: Springer, 2013.
Martin, Craig. *Subverting Aristotle: Religion, History, and Philosophy in Early Modern Science*. Baltimore: Johns Hopkins University Press, 2014.

Moggi, Guido. "L'erbario di Andrea Cesalpino." *Gli erbari aretini da Andrea Cesalpino ai giorni nostri*, edited by Chiara Nepi and Enrico Gusmeroli, 3–20. Florence: Firenze University Press, 2008.

Morton, Alan G. *History of Botanical Science: An Account of the Development of Botany from Ancient Times to the Present Day*. London: Academic Press, 1981.

Mulsow, Martin. "The Ambiguities of the *Prisca Sapientia* in Late Renaissance Humanism." *Journal of the History of Ideas* 65, no. 1 (2004): 1–13.

Pagel, Walter. "The 'Claim' of Cesalpino and the First and Second Editions of his *Peripatetic Questions*." *History of Science* 13 (1975): 130–8.

Pazzaglia, R. "Andrea Cesalpino e la scoperta della circolazione del sangue nel terzo centenario della morte di Guglielmo Harvey." *Bollettino Memorie Società Tosco Umbra di Chirurgia* 19, no. 5 (1958): 454–64.

Pazzaglia, R. "Il Cesalpino oggi." *Atti e Memorie dell'Accademia Petrarca Letteratura, Arti e Scienza di Arezzo* 40 (1970–2, 1974): 206–12.

Peller, Sigismund. "Harvey's and Cesalpino's Role in the History of Medicine." *Bulletin of the History of Medicine* 23, no. 3 (1949): 213–35.

Repici, Luciana. "Cesalpino e la botanica antica." *Rinascimento* 45 (2005): 47–87.

Santing, Catrien G. "'Deus rotator and the microrotator': Blood as the Source of Life in the Life and Works of Andrea Cesalpino." In *Blood—Symbol—Liquid*, edited by Catrien G. Santing, and Jetze J. Touber, 137–56. Leuven: Peeters, 2012.

Schmitt, Charles B. "Girolamo Borro's *Multae sunt nostrarum ignorationum causae* (Ms. Vat. Ross. 1009)." In *Philosophy and Humanism: Renaissance Essays in Honor of Paul Oskar Kristeller*, edited by Edward P. Mahoney, 462–76. Leiden: Brill, 1976.

Schmitt, Charles B. "The Faculty of Arts at Pisa at the Time of Galileo." *Physis* 14 (1972): 243–72.

Shea, William R. J. "Galileo's Claim to Fame: The Proof that the Earth Moves from the Evidence of the Tides." *British Journal of the History of Science* 5 (1970): 111–27.

Tugnoli Pattaro, Sandra. *La formazione scientifica e il "Discorso Naturale" di Ulisse Aldrovandi*. Trento: Unicoop, 1977.

Viviani, Ugo. *Tre medici aretini (A. Cesalpino, F. Redi e F. Folli)*. Arezzo: R. Accademia Petrarca, 1936.

Viviani, Ugo. *Vita e opere di Andrea Cesalpino*. Arezzo: Bennati, 1922.

von Engelhardt, Dietrich. "Luca Ghini (1490–1556) il padre fondatore della botanica moderna nel contesto dei rapporti scientifici europei del sedicesimo secolo." *Annali del Museo Civico di Rovereto, Sezione: Archeologia, Storia, Scienze naturali* 27 (2011): 227–46.

Part One

Philosophy

2

Andrea Cesalpino's Epistemology

Marco Sgarbi

1. Historiographical Introduction

In a classic study on the treatises of logic in sixteenth-century Italy, Cesare Vasoli wrote that the first pages of the 1571 *Peripateticae Quaestiones (QP)* "are evidence—more than eloquent—of the problems of logic and of the rational systematization of knowledge that an Aristotelian master should face with some urgency at that time, opened, however, to the new experimental and creative epistemology."[1] In another article, Vasoli emphasized that:

> [Cesalpino's] appeal to experience and to the use of logical tools essentially aimed to make sensible data clear and to provide rational rules for the construction of science [and] had a more advanced and innovative meaning than the flawless examinations of Paduan logicians, who were great interpreters of the Peripatetic tradition, but still unable to transform the commentary to the texts of the *Organon* into a search for new methodological principles of science.[2]

This provocative suggestion has never been picked up by scholars, who have focused their attention on other aspects of Cesalpino's intellectual activity as anatomist, botanist, and mineralogist. This activity, which characterizes Cesalpino as an all-around naturalist, has been explored in recent years with detailed investigations that show his originality and his capacity to open up new threads of research.[3]

In contrast, scholars have paid scarce attention to Cesalpino's philosophy. A number of studies emphasize the objections raised by Nicolaus Taurellus and Samuel Parker, while others foreground his animistic and vitalistic conception of nature, which would make of him a forerunner of Spinoza.[4] Cesalpino's logical and epistemological assumptions and ideas that support, inform, and stimulate his natural investigations have been consistently neglected. Kristian Jensen alone has provided an insightful investigation into Cesalpino's method for the foundation of botany as an independent discipline, though omitting to offer any characterization of the epistemological background or theoretical innovations.[5]

In this paper, I aim to explore Cesalpino's logic and epistemology by (1) examining his theoretical reflections and (2) assessing whether these came to affect his practice and activity as a naturalist. Indeed, it was not unusual for Aristotelian philosophers to teach, preach, and practice three very different approaches to natural investigations all at the same time. As interpreters of Aristotle, they explain the Aristotelian texts in the most faithful way, most of the times referring to other commentators, but without doubting or criticizing the validity of his thought or of his philosophical system. As theorizers they had an idealized method or epistemology, which it was their confirmed intention to follow. Equally, as practitioners they often adopted a mixed methodology in studying nature. These three models were usually perceptible in the different literary genres in which a natural philosopher elaborated his ideas. In commentaries the reference was always Aristotle's text and his commentators, while original conceptions were usually developed in treatises. However, in observations and reports, assorted approaches were generally pursued in referring both to first-hand experience and to the opinions of past authorities. Cesalpino never wrote a commentary to Aristotle's texts. His works mainly tackle academic questions or disputations on Aristotelian topics or treatises. They articulate not a slavish or pedantic devotion to Aristotle's works, but rather fresh and original ideas capable of transforming the Aristotelian tradition.

2. Reading Aristotle

The preface to the first book of the *Peripateticae quaestiones* is a dense and detailed methodological reflection on how to proceed in doing philosophy, especially in relation to authorities, and especially in relation to Aristotle, the one regarded as the best. It was quite common to introduce at the very beginning of a treatise or even a lecture an explanation of an author's philosophical approach. This was the case with Jacopo Zabarella's famous *Praelectio* to the academic year 1568 on how to read Aristotle correctly.[6]

Following Aristotle, Cesalpino emphasized that human beings have an innate desire to seek the truth and know things, but only very few have achieved or discovered new knowledge. The advancement of learning is very slow, and this is the reason why across the ages many philosophers have focused their attention on relatively similar questions in order to establish perfect answers.[7] This search for the truth over time—*veritas filia temporis*—constitutes the final goal of philosophy, in particular of natural philosophy, as Pietro Pomponazzi also emphasized in his *De incantationibus*.[8] However, according to Cesalpino this goal is never achievable—at least not in any comprehensive form—because the boundaries of knowledge are continually and perpetually being extended by the human mind. Definitive answers and ultimate truth are thus intrinsically impossible for human beings. This impossibility of grasping the truth does not lead to a kind of skepticism, but rather for Cesalpino stimulates contributions to the development and progress of knowledge.

Mastering authorities is for Cesalpino essential for advancing the field of knowledge, but he advocated avoiding simply repeating what has already been said and overcoming possible errors. Past philosophers are genuine treasures that enable a step forward in knowledge to take place. However, the study of past ideas and doctrines should not prevent new discoveries. Philosophy cannot be reduced to a form of commentary, which, as already mentioned, Cesalpino himself never practiced. This is particularly true in the case of Aristotle for whom many "barbarian commentators" have spent more than a thousand years merely explicating and interpreting his thought, producing nothing but errors and thus concealing and burying the truth under a curtain of dust.[9] This attitude has led philosophy away from its rightful path of finding the truth, generating not real thinkers, but admirers of a pagan authority, namely Aristotle, who in order to preserve these words are apt to contrast them with the sacred and revealed truth of religion.[10] This attachment to the Aristotelian texts and Aristotle's words contributes neither to the advancement of knowledge nor to the discovery of the truth.

Cesalpino was clearly referring to the most recent Aristotelian interpretations of his day, like that of Pietro Pomponazzi, which argued for the incompatibility of Aristotelianism with Christianity. Doing Aristotelian philosophy does not mean doing philosophy or seeking new knowledge in itself, says Cesalpino, departing from what many of his associates and other philosophers of the time believed. This particular variety of "bad philosophy" fills Aristotelian doctrines with errors, which must be purified before any progress in the search for the truth can be made. For this reason, Cesalpino aimed in this work to purge Aristotelian texts of impurities, and then provide a correct reading of Aristotle's ideas from which point it might then be possible to establish the truth.

This purging is a hard task and a difficult enterprise for Cesalpino because the minds of his fellow thinkers have been so entirely shaped by these impious interpretations of Aristotle that they cannot see the truth. Any attempt, therefore, to revise their reading of Aristotle seems to threaten to overturn the authority of Aristotle and equally the status quo: the idea of saying something different or new in comparison with what has been written in Aristotelian texts is an act of arrogance.[11] Against this charge of overturning authority, Cesalpino reacted by stating that "it is superfluous to write what has been already written," and that whoever seeks the truth then should bring something new to what has previously been acquired.[12] This truth must be achieved without the use of a verbose style, which most of the time tends to obscure and impede knowledge. Language is important only for the sake of clarity, but not for conveying doctrines.[13]

In his *Peripateticae quaestiones*, Cesalpino's idea is to discuss the truth "according to the words of the prince of the Peripateticians—Aristotle—and according to his principles of investigation."[14] Cesalpino advanced the idea of a methodological investigation of nature *Aristotelis iuxta propria principia*, as also his mentor Simone Porzio had done.[15] Cesalpino tackled six different questions, which were highly debated within the Aristotelian tradition in the sixteenth century. Yet he never explicitly mentioned his polemical target or references, discussing Aristotle— according to the bidding of his methodology—only through the primary texts, not those of commentators or interpreters. The six problems are as follows: (1) how to know universals from particulars—that is, how to transform experience into science; (2) why all definitions are reducible to demonstration; (3) why first philosophy, that is, metaphysics, uses neither demonstration nor definition; (4) how the various sciences differ according to the kind of the substances; (5) how the differences of substances are connected to the kinds of the predicaments; (6) why the last difference is not sufficient for explaining or determining things. Cesalpino dealt with each of these questions by stating theses, raising objections, and formulating possible solutions. And of the six, it is the first that shapes his epistemology and has a major impact on what was considered Cesalpino's main achievement, his system of classifying plants.

3. Classification System

Before dealing with the first question, it is important to provide at least a brief description of Cesalpino's classification system, because only in this way it is possible to appreciate the magnitude and import of his epistemological perspective in making botany a true science, as opposed to merely specimen-collecting as was typical in the Renaissance times.

The idea that botany was not a true and autonomous discipline—but rather a kind of appendix to medicine, based on *historiae* of plants—comes from Pseudo-Aristotle and Theophrastus, and surfaced anew in the sixteenth century with the rediscovery of classical texts. What is remarkable is not that botany was not conceived as an independent discipline separable from medicine, but that it was not understood as a science at all from the strict Aristotelian perspective, according to which science was certain and universal knowledge of causes through demonstration.

In the pseudo-Aristotelian *De plantis*, the author states concerning the classification of plants that it was only possible to indicate the various classes "by general inferences, and by giving examples and descriptions," that is, without employing any instrument of science such as demonstration.[16] No science, that is scientific knowledge, of plants was possible for this Pseudo-Aristotle. The accidental and contingent nature of knowledge regarding plants is evident also in Theophrastus's *Historia plantarum*. Aristotle's pupil maintains that the "plant is something various and manifold, and so it is difficult to describe in universal terms."[17] He adds that scientific demonstration or proof is absent from botanical investigation, and that it is impossible "to seize on any universal character which is common to all."[18] In botany "some characteristics are the same in all, merely in the sense that all have analogous characteristics," but there are no universal features.[19] There was no instrument or method for attributing feature or distinguishing mark to the essence of the plant.

This lack was probably one of the main reasons why Aristotelian works on plants were neglected in the Renaissance period. They do not provide tools for scientific investigation but relegate the field of botany to the realm of opinion, where no certainty, necessity, or universality was possible. This absence of method, in perhaps what was one of the most "method-focused" centuries in the history of philosophy, discouraged scholars from making these works the basis of their own. Indeed, these works were essentially histories and collections rather than theoretical reflections. Obsessed by method as they were, Renaissance natural philosophers felt an urgency to acquire an epistemology that would establish botany as a science. And this was what Cesalpino did. This epistemology represents the solid background for his botanical classification, which was elaborated following the Aristotelian tradition.

Cesalpino had a clear idea of the epistemological situation of botany, even before he wrote the *Peripateticae quaestiones*. Indeed, in his letter to Alfonso Tornabuoni, that dates to September 14, 1563, he recognized that the number of plants is almost infinite and that infinitude cannot be understood by the human intellect. Nonetheless, this infinitude does not diminish the possibility of providing a scientific knowledge of plants. His purpose is to find a method for collecting under specific labels different kinds of plants with common characteristics in such a way as to reduce the overall multiplicity and thus make scientific knowledge possible. He openly contested Dioscorides' attempt at this, considering it a failure because the Greek naturalist did not follow a method and an order, without which only confused histories can be written. Using Dioscorides' a-methodical approach means for Cesalpino appealing only to experience, which is not a trustworthy method when it comes to dealing with an infinite number of plants. Theophrastus's attempt to organize and classify plants seems more successful in Cesalpino's eyes, because he at least tried to bring the infinity of plants under a small number of labels. However, his classification still remains unscientific in that he did not follow a proper method for establishing accurate similarities and their true differences.

The general weakness of these classificatory systems is a lack of theorization of the sensible data gathered by experience. Indeed, Cesalpino criticized those who wrote on simples who failed to develop their knowledge with the proper study of natural philosophy. The mere collection of herbs and plants does not provide real science. This experience must be methodical. But Cesalpino also opposed those "philosophers" who comment on the causes of things without ever having had experience of what they are dealing with.[20]

Cesalpino's objection was a common criticism not only raised against botanists, but also found in classic descriptions of the sects of ancient physicians who adopted either (1) an empirical approach, dismissing any universal claims or statements about the causes of diseases; or (2) a rationalist standpoint, neglecting any empirical research. For Cesalpino, the perfect methodology was a mix of these two approaches. Neither spiders, nor ants—to borrow the words of Francis Bacon—but bees. And it is an epistemology of bees that Cesalpino attempted to develop with his own classification system. Indeed, employing a compelling metaphor, he suggested that his enterprise is like that of a pianist, who, before playing a sonata, tests all the piano keys to check whether there is something missing or wrong. Experience and reason should work together in order to provide scientific or universal knowledge. The process of classification helps to achieve this knowledge in a quick and easy manner. Furthermore, classification provides a good instrument for committing knowledge to memory and also helping recall, in being based on a rational system perfectly deducible through logical arguments.

As has often been observed, Cesalpino's classification is Aristotelian because it is based on the substance-essential characteristics distinction. A full account of Cesalpino's theory of classification is provided in Chapter 13 of the first book *De plantis*.[21] Here he was looking for "similarities and dissimilarities of the forms that constitute the substance of plants."[22] He discarded the investigation of accidental characteristics or attributes since they do not lead to the immediate knowledge of substance but provide a further specification for the type of plant. These accidental attributes are comparable to aspects such as their use, or medical properties, or provenance. But through these attributes the cause or "reason for the substance is entirely unknown, as just as their ultimate differences remain unknown."[23] It is necessary, therefore, to circumscribe and narrow down all characteristics into an essential one. Here Cesalpino makes a clear reference to his first of the *Peripateticae quaestiones*, which I will turn to shortly.

In Chapter 13, Cesalpino explained that plants differ from all other living beings, because their essential feature—that is, their form—is vegetative soul. However, this difference is not sufficient to characterize the many specimens of plants, and hence further categorizations must be added. Since—scholastically speaking—*operari sequitur esse*, and vice versa, plants must be qualified according to their operations. The first of these for a plant is nutrition, while the second is procreation. And so the classification must be based on these two operations, which together characterize the substance of plants. This classification is grounded in Aristotle's metaphysical principles. However, the recognition of the various differences among these operations is made through experimental observation. The way in which these operations are attributed essentially or not to the substance of plants follows another dynamic.

Cesalpino's classification is Aristotelian not because it is based on the substance/accident paradigm, but principally because his epistemology is distinctively Aristotelian. The decision to classify according to substance and accidents does not depend on adherence to, or agreement with, Aristotle, who never employed this kind of classification in either the *History of Animals* or *Parts of Animals*. Rather, his attachment to the Aristotelian tradition is evident because its logic of discovery of these essential attributes is eminently Peripatetic. In particular, it belongs to that form of Aristotelianism which during the Renaissance debated the best method of investigation for natural philosophy and questioned the validity of the regressus theory—in particular, the intermediate stage—as an instrument capable of providing new scientific discovery. This form of Aristotelianism is evident in the first of the *Peripateticae quaestiones*, and Cesalpino is himself conscious of this debt by referring to this method in Chapter 13. Without a proper understanding of the first question, it is impossible to appreciate why, according to Cesalpino, his classification did not lead to false categorizations or distinctions, but rather to true scientific knowledge.

4. Renaissance *Regressus*

The novelty of Cesalpino's thinking is perceptible if we contextualize it within the more general framework of the sixteenth-century discussion on regressus, and, more specifically, its intermediate stage. In the Renaissance, regressus theory comprises three main stages. The first stage is a kind of resolution or analysis, and usually employs the tools of induction and of an argument from effects to cause or *prius nobis*. The intermediate process is variously named mental consideration, intermediate consideration of the intellect, negotiation of the intellect, intermediate negotiation of the intellect, intermediate discourse of the intellect, examination, mental examination, meditation, application and intention of the mind, and work of the mind. The third stage is a form of composition or synthesis, and usually argues from cause to effects or *prius naturae*. The main objective of the intermediate stage was to provide solid foundations and principles from the material given by sensation and experience to the third stage in order that the final moment of regressus could stage a scientific demonstration. The means of achieving this goal varies among authors. One of the first theorizers of the intermediate stage of regressus, Agostino Nifo (1469/1470—1538),[24] believed that this result can be achieved by conceiving of the intermediate stage as a form of composition and division, which leads to definition:

> And for negotiation of the intellect we meant composition and division, by means of which the understanding discovered the cause, that is, the definition. We called the first process the discovery of the cause, of its existence (*quod est*), but negotiation discovered the definition of the effect. Subsequently in the second process, the effect was known according to its essence (*propter quid*) by means of a causal definition.[25]

In particular:

> This negotiation is composition (*compositio*) and division (*divisio*). For when the cause itself has been discovered, the intellect composes and divides until it knows the cause in the form of a middle term. For though cause and middle term be the same thing, they differ in their aspect. For it is called the cause in as much as the effect proceeds from it, whether it be better known than the effect or not. But it is a middle term in as much as it is a definition. From effect to cause is thus the procedure of discovering the cause; negotiation is directed toward the cause as a middle term and a definition. But since a definition is discovered only through composition and division, it is through them that the cause is discovered in the form of a middle term, from which we can then proceed to the effect.[26]

In opposition to Nifo, Girolamo Balduino denied the validity of the process of composition and division for finding definitions.[27] He introduced another logical process of discovery which is totally independent of regressus. This process reduces the discovered cause to a formal cause, extracting the essence of the cause. However, in response to the question "what is the tool employed to know the essence?" which constitutes the definition, Balduino answers that

> one cannot give a specific [that is, general] rule to this. The reason is that, according to the first book of the *Ethics* and the second book of the *Metaphysics*, the way of knowing the subject-matter and the essence is specific to the [various] arts.[28]

Balduino shifted the problem of negotiation outside of the regressus, awarding to the specific methods of each discipline the role of finding definitions. In this way he clearly undermined the possibility of a general method or logic for scientific discovery; he made clear that it is not a universalizable process, even if leading to the definition of the cause.

A lack of faith in the intermediate stage of regressus had been expressed by Alessandro Piccolomini in his *Commentarium de certitudine mathematicarum* (1547),[29] when against the supporters of regressus theory he had posited not only that he had never understood what they meant by negotiation of the intellect, but also that they were introducing an opaque element into a logical process. In *L'instrumento della filosofia* (1551) Piccolomini agreed with Balduino: definition is the only tool that allows for reciprocity between the two kinds of demonstration by providing not only the existence of the cause but also its essence, and thus identifying the convertible middle term for the demonstration *propter quid*. After stating that it is hard and laborious to "make the definitions of things," and after excluding Platonic division as a method for finding a definition because it does not lead to necessary conclusions, Piccolomini proposes the combined use of "three ways, that is, division, composition and then syllogism."[30] In other words, even if Piccolomini denied the validity of the negotiation, he reintroduced it by stealth in positing the combined process of these three methods.

Piccolomini placed great emphasis on the activity of composition—in particular, of the genus with the differences—and he establishes two methodical rules. First, it is necessary to combine the differences gradually, without jumping to the conclusion, and this should be done with reference to extent of their proximity, starting with those closest to what needs to be defined. Second, the genus should be divided systematically into differences, which are necessary for reconstructing what is being defined. For the work of the mind that takes place according to these two rules he employs a term from the Italian vernacular, *negotio*, which seems to be an implicit allusion to the negotiation of the intellect.[31] However, Piccolomini pointed out that these two rules are not always sufficient. Indeed, it may happen that there is no easy choice between two contradictory differences when attributing to a genus, and in this specific case one should appeal to sensation and experience, which can be helpful in affirming or negating which of the two differences is the true one. Nonetheless, Piccolomini was aware of the weakness of sensation, which can only know the accidents of things. Since sensation and experience cannot always be diriment, the intellect exchanges and substitutes common characteristics for essential and proper characteristics, thus falling into error and not determining the real definition and nature of a thing.[32] The role of sensation remains pivotal, and this is the reason why

> philosophers have sweated in discovering with long observation and care, with anatomies and dissections of animals, plants, stones and of any other thing, in order to understand well which nature, part and condition were attributed and led to these or those accidents, in such a way as to know gradually the proper accidents of things.[33]

Piccolomini closed his investigation by saying that these observations, anatomies, and dissections, intent on finding the true differences, are essential to the foundation of scientific knowledge, opening up empirical and experimental approaches typical of early modern philosophy.[34]

Girolamo Capivacci, similarly, in his *On the Differences of Doctrines* (1562), focused on the role of definition instead of negotiation, giving special emphasis to the experimental dimension.[35] According to Capivacci, true definition is possible through resolution. This resolution is not a form of division through which one enumerates the individuals of a species, or the species of a kind; rather, it is a process that proceeds from individuals to species and kinds in order to identify the essential elements of an individual, dismissing the accidents and establishing thus the true definition.[36] This process determines the presence and absence of distinctive characteristics in individuals, which makes possible the formation of groups of individuals with a specific definition. This working of the intellect generates the basis for scientific knowledge: indeed, through this logical process it is possible to discover the formal definition of an individual, a definition that will be sufficiently general to act as the principle for the following demonstration *propter quid*.

Cesalpino developed his own original epistemology from the ashes of these logical reflections, applying his ideas directly to the study of plants. This development becomes eminently clear in examining the first of the *Peripateticae quaestiones*.

5. Cesalpino's Version of Regressus

The first question is the most relevant from an epistemological standpoint, and it was the beginning of all discussions and debates on method in the sixteenth century. Although his thinking is not properly speaking dependent on Aristotle's logical works, Cesalpino tackled the problem by examining the *Proem* to *Physics*. Furthermore, he took an original stance on a specific elaboration of the regressus theory.

Cesalpino immediately recognized a difficulty in Aristotle's position which warrants explanation in order to lend coherence to his thought. According to Aristotle, individual and singular things are best known because they are acquired through sensation, while universals are quintessentially more remote. Nonetheless, Aristotle aims to investigate the principles of natural bodies by proceeding from universals, which are first known by nature, but far removed from our immediate understanding. How is it possible to solve this apparent contradiction in the Aristotelian text, especially considering that the whole is better known to us than the parts, and the whole is known in a confused not distinct way?[37]

Cesalpino points out that all our knowledge, or—better—every kind of apprehension, is achieved either through sensation or through intellect. By sensation we come to know things, but indistinctly, starting from a generic knowledge and arriving later at an understanding of detail. This limitation becomes very clear, for Cesalpino, if we consider a plant: it is easier to say simply that it is a plant rather than to determine immediately its species as fig or oak—that is, its specific difference. The plant is the confused whole, while the species is the part. It is much easier to characterize something vaguely as "plant," than as "*a* plant" in a determinate way. The determination of the specific difference is an addition of the intellect.[38] In general, sensible knowledge is always confused and indistinct, for when something is known through sensation, what is acquired is a generic knowledge that has many characteristics that are not immediately distinguishable. Only the intellect can know and distinguish the various characteristic marks that determine the concept of a thing.[39] In Cesalpino, there is, therefore, an epistemological priority of intellectual knowledge over sensible knowledge, following Aristotle, according to whom no science of the singular is possible.

Cesalpino pointed out that the operation of the intellect as a way of grasping this generic and confused knowledge from the particular is called induction.[40] In order to elucidate this confused and indistinct knowledge arising out of sensation and generated by induction, Cesalpino pinpointed the necessity of division. By division it is possible to identify the individual species. In this process, the generic concept is identified first, being the first thing that the mind conceives of. As such, this generic concept is something which all things share or have in common (*quae omne conveniunt*). Cesalpino believed that the capacity of the intellect to perceive distinctions within a generic concept, and so to specify better the object of knowledge, is a kind of "habit" acquired over time. Once every characteristic mark has been identified, it is possible to compose them into a definition, the only instrument capable of providing scientific knowledge. Therefore, the discovery of knowledge is conceived as being based on three operations: (1) induction, (2) division, (3) definition.[41]

More specifically, by induction "we intuit similarity and agreement," by division "dissimilarity and difference," and by definition "the univocal substance." More specifically, "induction makes universals from singulars and offers all intelligible material to the mind," "division finds the differences between universals, which are the individual species," and "definition triggers the resolution of the species into their principles up to the elements."[42] These three operations encompass what Renaissance Aristotelians characterized as the intermediate stage of the regressus, that is, that set of logical processes capable of transforming what was accidental and derived from sensation into universal principles of science. Once the essential characteristics that pertain to substance are extracted, scientific knowledge of the object becomes possible. This methodology illuminates why Cesalpino believed scientific knowledge of plants to be possible, and thus for botany to be transformed into a genuine and independent science.

If the epistemology starts with induction—that is, working from experience and sensation—Cesalpino ponders once more why Aristotle suggests proceeding in the discovery of nature's first principles from universal to singular, instead of vice versa. Is Aristotle considering the principles as hypothesis?[43] This is Cesalpino's dilemma. The problem is that the principles are discovered by induction and sensation, "but the number and nature of principles cannot be obtained either by induction or by definition."[44] Indeed, the definition supposes that its object is known, but it has no clear cognition of it, while induction infers only the unity of the manifold but does not show the number or specific differences. What should be done—Cesalpino explained—is "the division of universal concepts into singular concepts," and this is what Aristotle meant when at the beginning of the *Physics* he affirmed the necessity of proceeding from universals to singulars.[45] Cesalpino was clearly stretching his own interpretation of Aristotle. Indeed, Aristotle himself criticized division as a logic of discovery, for it would have been only able to clarify existing knowledge, but not to invent new ideas.

Cesalpino believed, furthermore, that at the beginning of the *Physics* Aristotle mentioned only one of the three processes that lead to knowledge of the principles. Cesalpino's explanation is that induction and division are performed unconsciously by the mind through an insensible act of the understanding (*increscente intellectu*).[46] Most of the time, the mind does not need to collect a large number of singulars to establish the essence but can jump directly to the definition. However, when the essence is not immediately graspable, then a long experiential process of discovery must be undertaken in order to obtain a reliable definition. This insensible act performed by the understanding directly recalls the negotiation of the intellect.

This overall epistemological framework allowed Cesalpino to develop a methodology which makes it possible to transform botany into a true science because the conclusions it reaches are couched as universal and necessary.

6. Conclusion

In his *Κάτοπτρον, sive speculum artis medicae Hippocraticum* (1605)—as Eugenio Garin has already pointed out[47]—Cesalpino elaborated a mixed methodology in which combined experience and reason are capable of discovering new knowledge:

> Common people bring to the sick medications of which they have learned the powers and they do that often very advantageously, perhaps with a profit greater than that obtained with a science that is profound but without experience. The knowledge of remedies derives first of all from experience. ... The knowledge of a remedy in the hands of a misinformed person, however, is like a sword in the hands of one taken by madness. ... The true physician is one who knows how to join experience with reason. Experience brings knowledge of remedies; reason selects the opportunity for their application.[48]

This statement reflects his epistemological considerations on plants, in which sensible experience and reason represent two essential components for acquiring scientific knowledge. Sensible experience is not a mere collection of observations—that is, a compilation of different histories—but the result of a series of experiments and interventions in nature in order to assess whether a particular difference pertains essentially to the substance of the plant. In arguing so, Cesalpino applied Aristotelian methodology and epistemology to the realm of plants—something that Aristotle himself had not dared to do.

This closely bonded relation between experience and reason reappears in Cesalpino's most famous student, Galileo Galilei, who championed "sensate experience" and "certain demonstration." We know little or nothing about Galileo's apprenticeship with Cesalpino. He studied with him in Pisa between 1582 and 1584, but perhaps close contact and scientific collaboration continued even thereafter. Indeed, a curious account exists that connects the two philosophers. A late eighteenth-century report compiled by Giovanni Calvi stated that natural history gained immense advancement through the introduction of the microscope, and the two protagonists of this new path in the history of science were Cesalpino and Galileo. With microscopes it is possible to achieve a detailed observation of minuscule things, things which, even if they held close to the eye, remain almost invisible. Galileo observed, in their particular parts and structure, minuscule animals which are called insects. But before Galileo, according to Calvi, it was Cesalpino that had used the microscope to study the seeds (*seminibus*) of plants, the smallest roots and seeds (*germen*), and all the other smallest parts of herbs, their structure and manner of nutrition.[49]

This account connects Galileo and his teacher, but it finds no supporting evidence in any other document or source of the time. Research has demonstrated that in sixteenth-century Tuscany it was common to investigate plants and animals with spectacles and lenses. The instrument consisted of a concave metal mirror, and there is a famous example relating to the anatomy of a bee provided by Giovanni Rucellai in his poem *The Bees* (1539).[50] Rucellai, in whose garden's anatomies were frequently performed, explains that in order to have a more detailed knowledge of bodies one should take a clear and concave mirror, and from the metal it will be possible to see the magnified image. In such a way, there will be made visible all the parts and organs of a bees, which are invisible to the naked eye. This kind of microscopical investigation should be performed not only on the bodies of the animals, but on plants too.

Furthermore, there is little doubt that these kinds of microscopical investigations were carried out even within the walls of the universities. The emphasis on structures and modes of nutrition that these microscopical observations made possible was instrumental to Cesalpino in creating his own classification system. But experimental observations were not in themselves enough to generate scientific knowledge. Microscopical observations of attributes had further to be rationalized and systematized in order to test whether they were essential or not. This kind of testing became possible as a result of the specific epistemology that Cesalpino developed in his reinterpretation of the Aristotelian regressus.

Notes

1   Cesare Vasoli, *Profezia e ragione* (Napoli: Morano, 1974), 445.
2   Cesare Vasoli, *Studi sulla cultura del Rinascimento* (Manduria: Lacaita, 1968), 344.
3   Ugo Viviani, *Vita e opere di Andrea Cesalpino* (Arezzo: Bennati, 1922); Carlo Colombero, "Il pensiero filosofico di Andrea Cesalpino," *Rivista Critica di Storia della Filosofia* 32 (1977): 269–84; Guido Moggi, "Andrea Cesalpino, botanico," *Atti e Memorie dell'Accademia Petrarca di Lettere, Arti e Scienze* 42 (1976–78): 235–49; Hiro Hirai, *Le concept de semence dans les théories de la matière à la Renaissance, de Marsile Ficin à Pierre Gassendi* (Turnhout: Brepols, 2005), 157–75; Luciana Repici, "Andrea Cesalpino e la botanica antica," *Rinascimento* 45 (2005): 47–87.
4   Carlo Colombero, "Andrea Cesalpino e la polemica anti-aristotelica e anti-spinoziana," *Rivista Critica di Storia della Filosofia* 35 (1980): 343–56; Cecilia Muratori, "Seelentheorien nördlich und südlich der Aplen: Taurellus's Auseinandersetzung mit Cesalpinos *Quaestiones peripateticae*," in *Nürnbergs Hochschule in Altdorf*, ed. Hanspeter Martin (Köln-Wiemar-Wien: Böhlau, 2014), 41–66.
5   Kristian Jensen, "Description, Division, Definition: Caesalpinus and the Study of Plants as an Independent Discipline," in *Renaissance Readings of the Corpus Aristotelicum*, ed. Marianne Pade (Copenhagen: Museum Tusculanum Press, 2001), 185–206.

6   Mario Dal Pra, "Una oratio programmatica di G. Zabarella, nov. 1585," *Rivista Critica di Storia della Filosofia* 21 (1966): 286–90.
7   Andrea Cesalpino, *QP* (1571), preface, sig. a8r: "Nemini profecto mirum videi debet, si veritatem, cuius cognoscendae omnibus hominibus natura inditum est desiderium, vix tamen attingere datum est paucis. Quamquam enim eius initium maxime simplex est, et natura clarissimum, apertissimumque; multiplici tamen rerum, ab eo prodeuntium compage involuitur, ut nobis, qui sponte nostra psectamus externa potius quam interna, difficilime pateat. Hac de causa illud effectum est, ut cum tot seculis philosophi innumeri summis laboribus, et studiis diuturnis in perquirenda veritate laboraverint, optatam tamen metam interdum non attingerit."
8   Pietro Pomponazzi, *De incantationibus*, ed. Vittoria Perrone Compagni (Florence: Olschki, 2011), 171.
9   Cesalpino, *QP* (1571), preface, sig. a8r: "Si enim non fuisset Democritus, Empedocles Anaxagoras, alique multi, & tandem Plato; non fuisset Aristoteles, quod duce philosophia ad dignitatis summum fastigum pervenisse videtur, quando annis iam fere bis mille, in unius Aristotelis doctrina intelligenda studium omne impenditur. Quanquam illud etiam factum est, ut ob quorundam barbarorum Commentarios, qui ob acre ingenium autoritatem et primarium locum in Peripatetica disciplina sibi vendicarant; tanta caligo oborta sit, ut conscriptis aliis innumeris in Commentatores Commentarijs, Philosophia in errores impegerit inextricabiles."
10 Ibid., preface, sig. a8v: "Hanc profecto divinitus revelatam sacrae literae nobis tradiderunt: eandem sponta naturae multi philosophi, saltem balbutientes, indicarunt, non enim dissentire, ullum eorum quae sunt, veritati opertet. Multos tamen, minime pudet, quo minus sua fateantur inscitiam, iis quae certissima sunt, contradicere, et argumentorum deceptiunculas demonstrationes putare, atque huiusmodi suasionibus sacram veritatem evertere."
11 Ibid.: "Huiusmodi igitur initio confisus, enixus sum Peripateticam disciplinam multorum altercationibus involutam, pro viribus mihi concessis evolvere, ut summi philosophi sententiae cum non parva humani generis iactura delitescentes, in apertum exeant, et reliquis ad veritatis complementum facientibus via sternant. Difficilem profecto aggressus sum provinciam, sed libentissime susceptam. Nam et si opiniones consuetae, quae diu iam in qui in iis multum insuadarunt, extirpari nequeant in eorum tamen gratiam, qui sunt veritatis studiosi, nec veneno impiorum adhuc confecti, pleniorem laborem non recusavi. Damnabunt forte multi hoc institutum, quod temerarium videatur, putare me videre, quae oculatissimi illi, & tam celebres autores non viderunt."
12 Ibid.: "Quibus illud respondeo: Superfluum esse scribere quae scripta sunt; nolle autem sua communicare, qualiacumque fuerint, aut ignaviae, aut invidiae tribui oportere."
13 Ibid., preface, sig. a9r: "Veritatis enim nuditas, quo suam prae se ferat pulchritudinem, non verborum amplitudine, aut alii oratinis fucis indigere videtur: neque tamen sermonis impuritate eandem sordescere fas est. Interim vero utilissima in scientiis vocabula minime abhorreo."
14 Ibid.: "secundum Aristotelis Peripateticorum Principis sententiam, aut secundum tradita ab eodem principia investigantur."
15 Eva Del Soldato, *Simone Porzio. Un aristotelico tra natura e grazia* (Roma: Edizioni di storia e letteratura, 2010).
16 Pseudo-Aristotle, *De plantis*, 819b14–15.
17 Theophrastus, *Hist. pl.* I, 1, 10.

18 Ibid.
19 Ibid.
20 Viviani, *Vita e opere di Andrea Cesalpino*, 82–3: "Se bene il numero delle piante, Monsignore Reverendissimo, cresce quasi in infinito, et questo dall'intelletto humano non si può comprendere, nondimeno con il raccorne molte in una simiglianza, et ridurle in questo modo a breve numero, facilmente se ne può haver quella cognitione, che a noi s'aspetta. … Altri hanno raccolto ciò che hanno trovato scritto de' Semplici, ma senza ordine, da' quali non si può cavare altro che una historia assai confusa et molto difficile, anzi impossibile mandarla a memoria … per avere una generale cognitione di tutte, non è suffitiente, perciocchè è impossibile haver avuto esperientia di tutte quelle che ci si rappresentano dinanzi. … e fra Semplicisti pochissimi sono quelli che habbino congiunto questa professione con li studii di Philosophia, senza la quale non è possibile farvi frutto alcuno. E fra i filosofi di qualche conditione, pochissimi sono che habbino messo e loro studii nelle cose particolari, come sono i semplici, ancorchè tutto il nervo della philosophia consista in quello. … Et per dare principio a quest'impresa, ho fatto come quel sonatore, il quale innanzi che cominci la sonata, fa prima una ricercata, per vedere se nessun tasto vi è che scordi."
21 Fabrizio Baldassarri, "Early Modern Philosophy of Plants and the Unwelcome Guest: Pseudo-Aristotle's *De Plantis*", in *Peri phyton. Trattati greci di botanica in Occidente e in Oriente*, ed. Maria Fernanda Ferrini and Guido Giglioni (Macerata: EUM, 2020), 237–64.
22 Andrea Cesalpino, *De plantis libri XVI* (Florence: Marescotti, 1583), 26: "Cum autem formarum similitudines, & dissimilitudines quaeramus, ex quibus constat Plantarum substantia, non autem eorum, quae accidunt ipsis."
23 Ibid., 26–7: "Haec enim omnia accidentia sunt, sed substantiae ratio forte incognita est, incognitis differentiis ultimis, ut multi putant, id circo oportere per accidentia circumscribere."
24 See Ennio De Bellis, "Nifo, Agostino," in *Encyclopedia of Renaissance Philosophy*, ed. Marco Sgarbi (Dordrecht: Springer, 2022), 3: 2341–54.
25 Agostino Nifo, *Collectanea ac commentaria in libros* De anima (Venezia: Scoto, 1522), fol. 20vb.
26 Agostino Nifo, *Aristotelis Physicarum acroasum hoc est naturalium asuscultationum liber interprete* (Venice: Scoto, 1508), fols. 7vb–8ra.
27 See Giovanni Papuli, *Girolamo Balduino. Ricerche sulla logica della Scuola di Padova nel Rinascimento* (Manduria: Lacaita, 1967).
28 Girolamo Balduino, *De regressu demonstrativo* (Naples: Cancer 1557), fol. 11rb.
29 See Alessio Cotugno, "Piccolomini," in *Encyclopedia of Renaissance Philosophy*, ed. Marco Sgarbi (Dordrecht: Springer, 2022), 3: 2551–4.
30 Alessandro Piccolomini, *L'instrumento della filosofia* (Roma: Valgrisi, 1551), 203: "la via di far tal'acquisto depende iniemmente da queste tre vie, cioè da la divisione, da la compositione, ed dal sillogismo."
31 Ibid., 204.
32 Ibid., 203–8.
33 Ibid., 209: "grandatamente sudarono i Filosofi, in cercar con osservationi, con avvertenze di lunghi tempi, con anatomie, ed secamenti di animali, di piante, di pietre, et d'ogni alra cosa: accio che ben contemplando qual natura, qual parte, & qual conditione si attribuisse, ed conseguisse a questo, o quello accidente, potesser così venir'à conoscere a poco a poco gli accidenti proprii de le cose."

34 Ibid., 210.
35 See Giuliano Gliozzi, "Capodivacca, Girolamo," in *Dizionario biografico degli Italiani* (Rome: Treccani, 1975), vol. 18, 649–51.
36 Girolamo Capivacci, *De differentiis doctrinarum, logicis, philosophis, atque medicis* (Padova: Pasquati, 1562), fol. 120v.
37 Cesalpino, *QP* (1571), fol. 1r: "propter quid iubet Aristoteles ad investiganda corporum naturalium principia procedendum esse ex universalibus in singularia tanquam ex notioribus nobis in ea, quae natura sunt notiora?"
38 Ibid.: "Et in intellectu plantam, aut arborem, aut animal, prius concipimus, quam oleam, aut ficum, aut canem: facilius enim est de quodam animali, animal enunciare indistincte, quam huiusmodi animal determinate."
39 Ibid.: "Confusa enim est singularium cognitio, universalium autem distincta."
40 Ibid.: "An ubique notius nobis est ipsum totum quam pars, et ipsum confusum quam distinctum? Patet autem inductione."
41 Ibid., fol. 1v: "Triplici ergo progressu, ut in aliis plerisque natura solet, perfectionem attingimus: inductione scilicet, divisione, definitione."
42 Ibid., ibid.: "Inductione quidem similitudinem et convenientiam intuemur; Divisione, dissimilitudinem et differentiam; Definitione, propriam uniuscuiusque substantiam. Inductione ex singularibus universalia facit, et materiam omnem intelligibilem menti offert; Divisio differentiam universalium invenit tendens in ea, quae specie sunt individua; Definitio autem species in sua principia resolvit usque ad elementa, incipiens a singularibus."
43 Ibid., fol. 2r: "Sed propter quid ad principiorum naturalium inventionem praecipit Aristoteles ab universalibus in singularia procedendum esse, non autem e converso, cum tamen etiam universalia partes sint singularium? An principia esse supponitur?"
44 Ibid.: "inductione enim et sensu iam prius id invenisse oportet: quot autem et quae sint, neque inductione, neque definitione haberi potest."
45 Ibid.: "Definitio enim supponit notum id esse quod definitur; sed quae sint principia, adhuc incertum est; Inductio autem nec numerum nec distinctionem ostendit, sed unitatem solum in multis colligit. Relinquitur igitur, ut divisione conceptuum universalium in singulares, haberi possit id quod quaerimus."
46 Ibid.: "Duo autem illi processus, qui definitionem antecedunt, inductio scilicet, et divisio, aliquando nobis minime animadvertentibus fiunt, paulatim increscente intellectu."
47 Eugenio Garin, *Storia della filosofia italiana* (Torino: Einaudi, 1966), 634.
48 Andrea Cesalpino, Κάτοπτρον, *sive Speculum artis medicae Hippocraticum* (Frankfurt: Becker, 1605), 39–40: "Sic enim videmus multos ex plebe remedia aegrotantibus proponere, cum vires quorundam medicamentorum didicerint, et saepe utiliter, imo magis, quam qui profundiorem scientiam tenent, sed absque experientia. ... Videmus expertos magis id, quod intendunt, consequi, quam illos qui rationem absque experientia tenent. Cognitio enim remediorum ab experientia praecipue habita est. Nihil autem refert, sive is, qui utitur, saepe expertus fuerit, sive acceperit ab iis, qui experti sunt. Caeterum remediorum notitia apud imperitos est veluti ensis in manu stulti, nam temerarius eorum usus multos interimit, casu autem sanat. Sed ille optimus medicus est, qui experientiam cum ratione coniunxit. Experientia in remediorum notitia consistit; ratio in usu eorundem oportuno."
49 Giovanni Calvi, *Commentarium inserviturum historiae Pisani vireti botanici academici* (Pisa: De Pizzorni, 1777), 55–6: "Immensa etiam historiae ipsius naturae accessio facta fuit a microscopio, quod Galileius, paullo ante Caesalpini

mortem, adinvenit, et pluries confecit, quo minimas observare penitus datur res, quae, licet oculis proximae, tamen prorsus sunt invisibiles. Minimorum praecipue animalium, quae insecta dicuntur, partes, earumque structuram observavit Galileius, microscopio quo inde seminibus plantarum minima radicem, et germen, aliasque perexiguas herbarum partes, et structurae ac nutritionis modum, detexisse ante omnes Caesalpinus dicitur, qui, utpote Peripateticus, corruptionem plantarum matrem autumabat."

50   See Vincent Ilardi, *Renaissance Vision from Spectacles to Telescopes* (Philadelphia: American Philosophical Society, 2007), 45.

Bibliography

Primary Sources

Pseudo-Aristotle, *De plantis*. In Aristotle. *Minor Works*, translated by Walter Stanley Hett. Cambridge, MA: Harvard University Press, 1936.
Balduino, Girolamo. *De regressu demonstrativo*. Naples: Cancer 1557.
Calvi, Giovanni. *Commentarium inserviturum historiae Pisani vireti botanici academici*. Pisa: De Pizzorni, 1777.
Capivacci, Girolamo. *De differentiis doctrinarum, logicis, philosophis, atque medicis*. Padova: Pasquati, 1562.
Cesalpino, Andrea. *De plantis libri XVI*. Florence: Marescotti, 1583.
Cesalpino, Andrea. Κάτοπτρον, *sive Speculum artis medicae Hippocraticum*. Frankfurt: Becker, 1605.
Cesalpino, Andrea. *Peripateticarum quaestionum libri quinque*. Venice: Giunta, 1571.
Nifo, Agostino. *Aristotelis Physicarum acroasum hoc est naturalium auscultationum liber interprete*. Venice: Scoto, 1508.
Nifo, Agostino. *Collectanea ac commentaria in libros De anima*. Venezia: Scoto, 1522.
Piccolomini, Alessandro. *L'instrumento della filosofia*. Rome: Valgrisi, 1551.
Pomponazzi, Pietro. *De incantationibus*, edited by Vittoria Perrone Compagni. Florence: Olschki, 2011.
Theophrastus. *De historia plantarum*. In Theophrastus, *Enquiry into Plants and Minor Works on Odour and Weather Signs*, translated by Arthur Hort. 2 vols. Cambridge, MA: Harvard University Press, 1961.

Secondary Sources

Baldassarri, Fabrizio. "Early Modern Philosophy of Plants and the Unwelcome Guest: Pseudo-Aristotle's *De Plantis*." In *Peri phyton. Trattati greci di botanica in Occidente e in Oriente*, edited by Maria Fernanda Ferrini and Guido Giglioni, 237–64. Macerata: EUM, 2020.
Colombero, Carlo. "Andrea Cesalpino e la polemica anti-aristotelica e anti-spinoziana." *Rivista critica di storia della filosofia* 35, no. 4 (1980): 343–56.
Colombero, Carlo. "Il pensiero filosofico di Cesalpino." *Rivista critica di storia della filosofia* 32, no. 3 (1977): 269–84.
Cotugno, Alessio. "Piccolomini." In *Encyclopedia of Renaissance Philosophy*, edited by Marco Sgarbi, 3: 2551–4. Dordrecht: Springer, 2022.

Dal Pra, Mario. "Una *oratio* programmatica di G. Zabarella, nov. 1585." *Rivista Critica di Storia della Filosofia* 21 (1966): 286–90.
De Bellis, Ennio. "Nifo, Agostino." In *Encyclopedia of Renaissance Philosophy*, edited by Marco Sgarbi, 3: 2341–54. Dordrecht: Springer, 2022.
Del Soldato, Eva. *Simone Porzio. Un aristotelico tra natura e grazia*. Rome: Edizioni di storia e letteratura, 2010.
Garin, Eugenio. *Storia della filosofia italiana*. Torino: Einaudi, 1966.
Gliozzi, Giuliano. "Capodivacca, Girolamo." In *Dizionario biografico degli Italiani*, 18:649–51. Rome: Treccani, 1975.
Hirai, Hiro. *Le concept de semence dans les théories de la matière à la Renaissance, de Marsile Ficin à Pierre Gassendi*. Turnhout: Brepols, 2005.
Ilardi, Vincent. *Renaissance Vision from Spectacles to Telescopes*. Philadelphia: American Philosophical Society, 2007.
Jensen, Kristian. "Description, Division, Definition: Caesalpinus and the Study of Plants as an Independent Discipline." In *Renaissance Reading of the Corpus aristotelicum*, edited by Marianne Pade, 185–206. Copenhagen: Museum Tusculanum Press, 2000.
Moggi, Guido. "Andrea Cesalpino, botanico." *Atti e Memorie dell'Accademia Petrarca di Lettere, Arti e Scienze* 42 (1976–8): 235–49.
Muratori, Cecilia. "Seelentheorien nördlich und südlich der Aplen: Taurellus's Auseinandersetzung mit Cesalpinos *Quaestiones peripateticae*." In *Nürnbergs Hochschule in Altdorf*, edited by Hanspeter Marti and Karin Marti-Weissenbach, 41–66. Cologne: Böhlau, 2014.
Papuli, Giovanni. *Girolamo Balduino. Ricerche sulla logica della Scuola di Padova nel Rinascimento*. Manduria: Lacaita, 1967.
Repici, Luciana. "Cesalpino e la botanica antica." *Rinascimento* 45 (2005): 47–87.
Vasoli, Cesare. *Profezia e ragione*. Napoli: Morano, 1974.
Vasoli, Cesare. *Studi sulla cultura del Rinascimento*. Manduria: Lacaita, 1968.
Viviani, Ugo. *Vita e opere di Andrea Cesalpino*. Arezzo: Bennati, 1922.

3

Philosophy, Medicine, and Humanism in Cesalpino's *Investigation into Demons*

Craig Martin

Andrea Cesalpino signaled his allegiances in the titles or subtitles of *Quaestiones Peripateticae* (QP) and *Daemonum investigatio peripatetica* (DIP). Besides the obvious Aristotelian outlook, the latter work's subtitle, in its first edition, points to a further inspiration, namely Hippocrates, as it promises the treatise will explain a passage in the Hippocratic *Prognostic*, that asks "if there is something divine in diseases." Cesalpino's Hippocratic orientation was again advertised in the Frankfurt edition of the *Ars medica*, as the editors retitled it Κάτοπτρον, sive Speculum artis medicae Hippocraticum. These titles reflect Cesalpino's conception of his medical and philosophical projects. Despite often veering in unchartered directions, Cesalpino proclaimed to favor Hippocrates and Aristotle, considering them to agree with and at times oppose Galen.

Cesalpino's allegiances to these ancient authorities reflected the views of leading medical theorists and practitioners in the second half of the sixteenth century. Contrasting Aristotle to Galen characterized the approach of several professors at Padua, in particular anatomists, in the latter years of Cesalpino's life, and several physicians linked Hippocrates and Aristotle because of similarities between the *Problemata* and *Airs Waters Places*.[1] Cesalpino, however, showed less concern with these issues, and instead focused on the divine in *DIP*. In doing so, he engaged in debates about the interpretation of Hippocratic texts that went back to Galen, which were revived in the sixteenth century. He used historical analysis, textual hermeneutics, and philosophical argument to assimilate Aristotle's and Hippocrates' views about the divine and to explain what he believed was their shared position. In addition to promoting Hippocrates as more pious than Galen, he strove to present the Hippocratic conception of the divine as agreeing with Aristotelian views about the soul and nature, as developed in the *QP*.

Cesalpino accepted the tenets of Christian theology yet distinguished them from philosophical knowledge. For him, philosophy simultaneously offered a path for explaining demons and the divine yet was inadequate for clarifying the mysteries of the faith. In his account of demons, he wrote that through Christianity we can know (*nosse*) what philosophers have struggled to explain, as if they were stuttering, but human ingenuity can never attain theology's revealed truth as laid out by the doctors of the Church, who teach that demons are fallen angels, whose essences are "sub-divine." Cesalpino contended that he did not want to dispute what "is explained by the most lucid and learned doctors of the Roman Church," but that it will be sufficient to show that demons can be explained in agreement with the principles of the natural world.[2] The causes of nature, however, are linked to the divine, according to Cesalpino's understanding of Aristotelian philosophy. Accordingly, Cesalpino's considerations of demons invoke discussions of the boundaries of nature and its relation to the divine, the supernatural, and the artificial.

Jonathan Seitz in his analysis of physicians' roles in witchcraft trials in early modern Venice argues that among the available medical authorities there was no one accepted view about the relation between naturalistic and demonic explanations of apparent possessions. In his account, on the extreme of the naturalistic side sat Girolamo Cardano; in the middle, Antonio Benivieni and Jean Fernel offered the possibility of the supernatural; and Giovanni Battista Codronchi recounted his own experiences with the divine.[3] To the contrary, Stuart Clark, in his magisterial *Thinking with Demons*, found consensus. He argued that all early modern philosophical and medical accounts of demons treated them as natural.[4] Seitz does not mention Cesalpino's *DIP*, and Clark passed over him quickly, grouping him with physicians who discussed demons and maintaining that there was a link between Pietro Pomponazzi's and Cesalpino's views, despite Cesalpino's repeated rejection of naturalistic positions that Pomponazzi had advanced.[5] Regardless of his relation to Pomponazzi, the question of whether to define Cesalpino's demonology as naturalistic is not straightforward. His conceptions of the natural and the divine are not neatly separated. Indeed, it is the intermixing of the natural, the divine, and the artificial that he explored as he analyzed the line "if there is something divine in diseases" taken from Hippocrates' *Prognostic*, a passage, which he linked to Aristotle's *On Divination during Sleep*, which maintained that "nature is daimonia."[6]

1. Cesalpino's History of Medicine

Cesalpino's practical medical writings provide a historical justification for connecting Aristotle and Hippocrates. Following a lengthy humanist tradition of tracing out medical genealogies, in the dedication of the second part of the *Ars medica*, Cesalpino summed up medicine's past.[7] He contended that the first inventors of medicine discovered the art of healing through chance and dreams, and only later thinkers added philosophical arguments to the field.[8] Since at that time, the Presocratics disagreed about philosophical principles, and since every philosopher also taught medicine, it was difficult to find consensus and come to certain conclusions. The lack of philosophical consensus led to the rise of the sects of Empiricists, who rejected all philosophical arguments as fallacious and relied only on experience. Others, however, found the empirical path faulty and sought out better established philosophical principles, forming the sect of Rationalists or Dogmatists. Soon after, the Methodist sect arose, which reduced medicine to a few universal and evident principles. The medicine of the Methodists was unsatisfactory, according to Cesalpino, because their universal principles gave no account for particular cures and procedures. They failed to discern the minute individual differences essential to medical practice. At this point in Cesalpino's historical narrative, Hippocrates arrives. He joined philosophical dogma to medical understandings developed from experience.[9] Then, Aristotle adopted Hippocrates' philosophical dogma, according to Cesalpino's account.[10] His depiction of Hippocrates' combining experience and logic closely fit the method he proposed for the *QP*.[11]

According to Cesalpino, in the next centuries, Galen declared Hippocrates' medicine the best but deemed it undeveloped. He elaborated Hippocratic ideas, which in turn were transformed by Arabic and Latin physicians, who frequently provoked controversies. Cesalpino presented himself as adhering to recent learned Italian physicians who sought to construct a medicine free of Arabic sources, while adhering to Greek learning. He pointed to two Tuscans, Leonardo Giacchini and Guido Guidi, as models for this return to Greek medicine.[12]

Both Giacchini and Guidi likely influenced Cesalpino's historical approach. In the 1540s, while Cesalpino was a student, Giacchini taught theoretical medicine at Pisa, where he promoted Galen's teaching. He displayed hostility toward the Arabic medical tradition in polemics against Mesue and Avicenna, despite writing a commentary on the ninth book of Al-Razi's *Ad Almansorem*.[13] Guido Guidi, whom Cesalpino referred to as his teacher, took a chair in medicine at Pisa in 1548. He pioneered surgical techniques based on humanistic research.[14] Despite offering slightly different understandings of Hippocrates' history and allegiances, both Giacchini and Guidi emphasized Hippocrates' blending of theory and experience. Guidi, in his commentary on the Hippocratic *On Joints*, wrote that Hippocrates was no Empiricist despite being an assiduous an "observer of experiments," since he demonstrated the import of his observations with rational arguments. In his view, Hippocrates' surgical teachings required theoretical knowledge about the human body.[15] Giacchini credited Hippocrates with the establishment of the Rationalist sect while still employing experience to discover diseases of the whole substance and the properties of poisons.[16] Giacchini's works possibly influenced Cesalpino in other ways. Several doctrines key to Cesalpino's exposition on the celestial character of innate heat and about demons resonate with the preface that Girolamo Donzellini wrote for Giacchini's commentary on Al-Razi's *Ad Almansorem*.

Despite presenting himself as part of this sixteenth-century tradition of returning to the Greeks, Cesalpino maintained that he did not aim to contradict but only wanted to clarify what others had left untouched. He wrote that "Hippocratic medicine derives from philosophical principles and agrees more with Aristotle than Plato," emphasizing that Galen's preference of Plato over Aristotle led to many difficulties for his medical theories.[17] Throughout Cesalpino's writings, especially in those that focus on medicine, he presented the concordance of Hippocrates and Aristotle in relation to principles of natural philosophy, which in turn he found to agree with, or at least not contradict, Christian theology. His attempts to reconcile Hippocrates and Aristotle are pronounced in his demonology, which depended on philosophical conclusions developed in *QP* and on a selective hermeneutic approach to Hippocratic and Aristotelian writings.

2. Peripatetic Investigations into Demons

Medical questions framed some of the most famous philosophical considerations of demons of the sixteenth century. The premise of Pietro Pomponazzi's *De incantationibus*, which was completed in the 1520 but first printed in 1556, was a request to explain three astounding examples of seemingly inexplicable recoveries from disease and injury. Hypothesizing about these recoveries led to broader considerations of the plausibility of demonic causation and miracles.[18] Similarly, Cesalpino identified his initial motivations for writing *DIP* as being an outbreak of preternatural possession among nuns in Pisa. Cesalpino's Hippocratic turn in this work marked new ground. Pomponazzi did not cite Hippocrates in *De incantationibus*, and, at the time he published the work, Cesalpino had scarcely referred to Hippocrates in his printed writings. In *QP*, there is little consideration of Hippocratic writings, besides a reference to *On the Nature of the Child*, which suggested that Aristotle erred when he wrote that semen evaporates.[19] There are, however, signs of animosity toward Galen, who earned Cesalpino's scorn, for supposed errors in anatomy and for understanding respiration and the heart's functioning differently than Aristotle did.[20]

Situating *DIP* only in a medical context, however, overlooks central parts of the argumentation and its relation to ideas espoused in *QP*. Cesalpino's main concerns went beyond determining whether Aristotle or Hippocrates held demons to exist, as Pomponazzi rejected or as was discussed by more recent scholars, such as Giano Matteo Durastante and Francesco Verino (II), a rival and colleague of Cesalpino at Pisa.[21] Although Cesalpino, at times addressed the issue of Aristotle's true view, much of the argumentation is an attempt to explain demonic phenomena, using Aristotelian principles. In this sense, Aristotle's philosophy, with its connections to Hippocratic principles, is the starting point, not the goal of the inquiry. As such Cesalpino followed the approach and methodology of *QP*, which were also not an attempt at establishing Aristotle's true views but rather an application of Aristotelian concepts that arrived at new conclusions.[22]

DIP was first printed in 1580 as a standalone treatise and again in 1593 together with *QP* and *Quaestiones medicae*. The two versions are largely but not entirely the same. In the later version, material has been added, shifted, and deleted, and many chapter breaks were moved. In both versions, Cesalpino accepted demonic activity as a theological, legal, historical, and medical fact. In the earlier edition's dedicatory letter to Giovanni de' Tonsis, a nobleman from Milan, he explained that he aimed to put forward a view that corresponds to theology, although he understood his approach as not being part of theology but only philosophy.[23] The opening chapter in both editions presents the motivation for the treatise as an investigation into whether the nuns recently vexed by demons in Pisa was natural or supernatural.[24] If it were deemed supernatural, then medicine could provide no help, according to the Pisans. Cesalpino's solution navigates these two possibilities, finding a compromise that allows for the existence of the supernatural but also retains the possibility of medical intervention. In later chapters of *DIP*, he returned to the case of the Pisan convent, after discussing philosophical explanations and laying out examples of demonic activity confirmed by history or by legal testimony. Cesalpino's discussion of demons includes both medical and philosophical concerns and authorities, as he depended on ideas about intelligences, the soul, and causation, many of which were discussed in QP.

3. Demonic and Divine Nature in Aristotle and Hippocrates

The initial chapters, in which Cesalpino discussed demons according to the opinions of Hippocrates, Galen, Aristotle, and Plato, set the stage for Cesalpino's philosophical exposition. Like in his other works, Cesalpino failed to identify recent opponents or allies, largely hiding the intellectual context of the work. Nevertheless, these discussions place him in the middle of heated natural philosophical and medical debates. The treatise's subtitle in the 1580 printing declares that it explains the passage in the Hippocratic *Prognostic* that advises physicians to be able to recognize the nature of diseases, their powers, and "if there is something divine in diseases."[25] The *Prognostic* was one of the most widely read Hippocratic treatises through the Middle Ages and early modern period; it formed part of the *Articella* and was a mainstay in universities' curricula.[26] The passage that interested Cesalpino attracted considerable discussion beginning with Galen's commentary on it. Cesalpino disagreed with Galen, whom he accused of being impious, not just in his interpretation of this passage, but also in his theory of the soul, which Cesalpino read as materialist, interpreting Galen as identifying the soul with temperament. Cesalpino's understanding of this passage from the *Prognostic* stands out from many of his contemporaries in two ways. He used it to differentiate Hippocrates and Galen, and he believed that the "divine" referred to the soul and innate heat or vital spirit within the human body rather than to meteorological or celestial forces.

Galenism greatly conditioned Renaissance readings of Hippocratic texts.[27] Galen's systemization of Hippocratic doctrines codified bodily temperaments, humors, spirits, and faculties, and his judgments about the authenticity of Hippocratic writings affected sixteenth-century perceptions of the composition of the Hippocratic corpus.[28] As Galen's commentaries on the *Aphorisms*, *Prognostic*, and *Epidemics* became more widely read after the printing of the Aldine editions, Galen as textual interpreter and historian gained greater weight. For example, Girolamo Mercuriale, in his *Censura Hippocratis*, used Galen's views in his determination of the authenticity of Hippocratic treatises.[29] Yet, Mercuriale recognized limits to Galen's authority as a reader of Hippocrates, and at times disagreed with Galen's interpretation of Hippocratic texts.[30] Others, such as Girolamo Cardano, attempted to shed allegiance to Galen, replacing him with other authorities—in the case of Cardano by linking Hippocrates to Ptolemy.[31] Both Mercuriale and Cardano disputed Galen's interpretation of the passage in the *Prognostic* that refers to the divine in diseases.

In his commentary on Hippocrates' *Prognostic*, Galen argued that this passage could not refer to God's providence or divine anger as a cause of disease. He contended that Hippocrates never considered God to be a cause but only paid attention to natural affections. Furthermore, it could not refer to some unknowable cause of critical days, because elsewhere Hippocrates explained their material origins. Therefore, for Galen, the use of the word divine in Hippocrates refers not to Godly matters. Rather, the word referred to the "constitution of the ambient air," that was responsible, in his eyes, for epidemics.[32] Galen's view gained detractors in late antiquity, the Middle Ages, and among Cesalpino's contemporaries.[33] In the decades before Cesalpino, a rich debate about Galen's position emerged.

None of the most prominent participants in the debate before Cesalpino had linked the passage from the *Prognostic* to demons, although Mercuriale, like Cesalpino, connected the passage to Aristotle's views about innate heat.[34] Cristóbal de Vega, a professor of medicine at Alcalá, in his 1551 commentary on the *Prognostic* and Galen's commentary on it, adhered closely to Galen's view that the divine referred to the constitution of air, which potentially was an underlying cause of plagues. Vega wrote that the passage means "if a disease has some derivation from the air."[35] He pointed out that divine causes are not mentioned anywhere else in this book, surmising that Hippocrates passed over them because the constitution of air was discussed in the *Epidemics* and the *Aphorisms*. Cesalpino's teacher, Guido Guidi expanded on the Galenic interpretation in his discussions of the causes of syphilis, in his posthumous volume on practical medicine. He wrote that the primary cause of syphilis was "the divine that Hippocrates noted in disease," namely the air affected by stellar forces that had brought the disease to humans.[36]

Galen's opinion, however, failed to convince others. Girolamo Cardano, in his commentary on the *Prognostic*, first printed in 1568, explicitly disagreed with Vega, while attacking Galen's interpretation. Cardano criticized Galen for using *On the Sacred Disease* as support for his position, despite having judged the work to be inauthentic. Rather, Cardano pointed to the stars and planets. Unlike Guidi, however, Cardano dismissed the idea that Hippocrates had ever called the air divine. In his view it must refer to the heavens, tying the passage from the *Prognostic* to *On Fleshes*, which refers to the immortal heat of heavenly ether, and to a line in *Airs, Waters, Places* that maintains that a physician must know astrology (*astrologia*).[37] Accordingly, Cardano linked the passage to his own interests in prediction through the stars.

Cesalpino forged a new interpretative path for this passage from the *Prognostic*. He rejected that it referred to the air or the heavens as divine. "If it is necessary to call divine what depends on the heavens divine," he wrote, "then the entire production of nature is divine," since Aristotle wrote in the *Meteorology* that the sublunary world is governed by the heavens.[38] Rather, according to Cesalpino's interpretation, the divine, for Hippocrates, does not refer to something that derives from natural causes, like the heavens or a quality of the ambient air, but to "afflictions that abound in the part of the body in us that is divine."[39] He argued that there is no need to naturalize this passage given that there are other places where Hippocrates considered the divine in this way, citing a passage at the start of *On the Nature of Woman*, which reads "the divine is most especially the cause in humans," and a line from *Decorum*, where the philosophical physician is likened to a god, a passage that Girolamo Donzellini quoted in his preface to Giacchini's commentary on Al-Razi.[40] Cesalpino noted that many other passages support Hippocrates' endorsement of the divine, even if the authenticity of those works might be debatable. Nevertheless, the question of authenticity is ambiguous, in his view. For example, Cesalpino noted, like Cardano, that Galen cited *On the Sacred Disease*, even though Galen did not think it was by Hippocrates.[41] Cesalpino put forward unorthodox ideas about the authenticity of Hippocratic works. In addition to using *On the Sacred Disease*, against Mercuriale's judgment, he accepted that Hippocrates wrote *On Ancient Medicine*, believing that the treatise gave support to the ideas that secondary qualities are more important for understanding the powers of medications than the four primary qualities are.[42]

Recent scholars have been accepting of Galen's interpretation of the passage from the *Prognostic*.[43] To the contrary, according to Cesalpino, Galen, "who was addicted to no religion," erred because he thought that Hippocrates did not recognize anything divine in the sublunary world or in humans.[44] "What is divine in disease," Cesalpino argued, must be connected to what is divine in humans, namely the soul. He contended that the soul is divine according to Hippocrates, who agrees with Aristotle. Pointing to Galen's supposed impious views about soul as a major difference from Hippocrates' and Aristotle's, Cesalpino implicitly disagreed with several prominent medical theorists who had assimilated Hippocrates' and Galen's views. For example, Giambattista Da Monte, while lecturing on Avicenna's *Canon* at Padua in the 1540s, contended that Hippocrates, Galen, "and perhaps Aristotle" identified substantial form of humans, and thus soul, with the temperament that is "educed from matter." In Da Monte's view, Hippocrates' and Galen's position conflicts with the tenets of Christian theology, which cannot be proven and must be grasped only through faith. Nevertheless, he defended the Hippocratic and Galenic opinion based on "philosophical principles," judging it inopportune to mix philosophy and theology.[45] Donato Antonio Altomare, professor of medicine at Naples, argued in a similar vein that Hippocrates and Galen agreed about the human soul's bodily dependence, noting that their view ran counter to the truth of Christianity.[46] Girolamo Donzellini, however, in the preface to Giacchini's commentary on Al-Razi, affirmed a materialist understanding of Galen's theory of soul, that identified soul with temperament, without contending that Hippocrates shared the theory.[47]

Cesalpino's identification of the soul with the divine positioned him within an evolving debate about the divine, the soul, and the human body. In *DIP*, he argued that the human mind (*mens*) is an immortal substance separated from matter. Its proper function (*operatio*) is not joined to the body, although there are other functions of the soul that can be affected by changes in the temperament of the body. Speaking according to medicine, as he believed Hippocrates did, Cesalpino shifted toward a material understanding of soul, writing that the soul should be thought of as innate heat, which is the principle of life and death. Moving to Aristotle's view, Cesalpino argued that the innate heat appears to have something divine in it, citing *Generation of Animals* 2.3, where Aristotle wrote that semen contains breath (*pneuma*) "that is analogous to the stars" and that semen possesses a principle that is separable from matter in semen, a principle that belongs to "animals which have something divine (to wit, what is called the reason)."[48] In *QP*, Cesalpino cited these passages, making nearly identical arguments, as he argued that this innate heat or spirit, crucial to the functioning of the heart and blood, provided connections between living beings and the divine.[49]

This passage from *Generation of Animals* had been at the middle of a controversy, that has its roots in the Middle Ages, but became central to Renaissance discussions of the nature of human seed and soul. At the turn of the sixteenth century, Niccolò Leoniceno, taking on Pietro d'Abano, argued that the vital heat that Aristotle referred to in *Generation of Animals* is not celestial but merely proportional to the heavenly body.[50] Jean Fernel, implicitly arguing against Leoniceno, contended that this vital heat was identical to the heavenly matter.[51] Donzellini adopted a position similar to Leoniceno's in his preface to Giacchini's work, attributing to Aristotle's philosophy, a subtle, warm, bodily spirit (*spiritus*) that is "proportional to the element of the stars," which he tied to the human mind.[52] Cesalpino took a slightly different tack. Adopting a view that Leoniceno and Donzellini had put forward, he interpreted Aristotle as saying that humans possess an innate heat proportional to the celestial heavens. The innate heat or spirit, which is found in semen, however, is not the same as heavenly body but rather produces the same things that the heavens generate through motion and light. Thus, unlike Fernel and many of those who supported the astrological tradition, he thought innate heat is not heavenly *per se* but produces the same effects as the heaven.[53]

Continuing with the idea of the proportionality between the heavens and the sublunary world, Cesalpino argued that it would be wrong to assign all corruptible bodies an eternal divine intelligence. Nevertheless, since all corruptible things consist in prime matter, which is not generated and incorruptible, it is reasonable to suppose the existence of an immortal intelligence that assists prime matter, in the same way that the moving intelligences assist celestial bodies. Cesalpino wrote, somewhat inaccurately, that this immortal intelligence is what Aristotle was thinking about in *On the Parts of Animals* 1.5, when Heraclitus is quoted as saying that "also the gods are here," while inviting guests into what might be a kitchen.[54] Here the two versions differ, as the 1593 one offers an extended argument and the quotation attributed to Heraclitus changes. The 1580 version reads "everything is full of the gods," a statement that Aristotle attributed to Thales not Heraclitus.[55] The 1593 version has Heraclitus saying that the "immortal gods are not missing anywhere," which is closer to the text of *On the Parts of Animals*.[56] But the conclusion remains the same even if the phrasing is altered; namely, prime matter receives the divine, which has a heavenly principle, meaning that "not only in humankind but also in all of nature, something immortal is contained, namely a divine intelligence."[57] This principle that acts on the three dimensions of prime matter is insufficient, however, for understanding the corruptions of the world. Therefore, Cesalpino introduced a third principle, namely privation. Unlike for his teacher Simone Porzio, for Cesalpino, privation is active; it is the flip side of the intelligence that generates.[58] The divine intelligence generates the forms of natural beings, while privation corrupts them. These natural forms participate in the beautiful, while their privation is participation in the ugly.[59]

This argument gives a foundation for the presence of the divine in nature and thereby provides a solution to the meaning of the passage of the *Prognostic*. Yet more is needed to explain demons. To establish the existence of demons, using the concepts of form and privation, Cesalpino made an analogy between the divine intelligence and humans, interpreted Aristotle's statement that "nature is *daimonia*," and appealed to authority. He wrote that humans are the only mortal substances that have a "supernatural" aspect because only humans use the intellect, and in fact doing so is in accordance with their essence. At times, the operations of the divine part, which is good and beautiful, shine forth in the world, and at times from the opposite part, evil and ugly. The ancients seemingly correlated these kinds of intelligence and privation to *eudaemones* and *cacodaemones*, or angels and demons, which were intermediaries between God and mortals for Plato and Aristotle, according to Cesalpino.[60]

4. Demonic Works and the Factive Intellect

In Cesalpino's view, Aristotle showed he accepted demons, in *On Divination during Sleep*, a short treatise in the *Parva naturalia*, in which he stated that "all nature is *daimonia*."[61] In this treatise, Aristotle rejected the idea that some dreams foretell the future because God sends them. Instead, he wanted a natural cause, namely the power of the imagination.[62] The images in the soul, however, are moved by an intelligence, which Aristotle, and his contemporaries, referred to as a demon, according to Cesalpino. Cesalpino maintained that Aristotle, despite his acceptance of the reality of demons, failed to discuss their powers and properties, because he considered them to be abstracted substances and therefore not part of discussions of natural philosophy.[63] While Aristotle left out discussions of demons, numerous ancients spoke about magic with reference to demons, so there was no need for Aristotle to do so, in Cesalpino's opinion.

Cesalpino provided two responses to those who thought that Aristotle definitively dismissed the existence of demons. The first is that there is abundant testimony of the existence of demons and their actions in ancient poetical and mythological writings, in legal proceedings, and in medical inquiries. Cesalpino categorized demonic practices, mustering examples taken from recent events and the past. The second response is that those who maintain that Aristotle denied the existence of demons misinterpret what demons are by positing that they are physical spirits composed of an aerial matter, following Plato.[64] Instead, according to Cesalpino, demonic intellects, unlike the celestial ones that are assigned a body, are immaterial and they alter sublunary matter by applying spirits and aerial matter. The demonic intellect, which applies these natural substances, however, is not the speculative intellect, because the speculative intellect is directed only toward knowing the truth and discarding falsehood. The speculative intellect cannot be directed to a work (*opus*). Rather demons use the active or factive intellect.[65]

Cesalpino used the distinction between the factive and speculative intellect to differentiate the powers of demons from those of celestial orbs and to define the supernatural. While the movements that derive from celestial intellects are natural, those that come from demons are artificial and thus beyond the works of nature, that is, they are supernatural. Despite using only natural means, demonic works can be considered supernatural in the same way that human craft goes beyond nature.[66] Accordingly, the actions of physicians and demons parallel each other. Physicians do not directly alter bodies, but prescribed medications do. Similarly, demons, although being able to move bodies, do not alter them, since they lack tangible qualities. Rather using natural substances, demons introduce spirits into bodies that move the organs contrary to the will. Given that the soul resides in the heart, according to Cesalpino, if this polluted spirit harms the heart, sudden death ensues. The dirty nature of the spirit is evident in the sulfuric stench and putrefaction that is emitted during exorcisms.[67] Yet these spirits should not be taken as divine, as Plato allegedly believed. Rather, demonic possessions and hallucinations are the result of natural substances that have been set in motion by demons. According to Cesalpino, witches find the substances demons use and apply them in black magic. Despite deriving from natural substances, the demonic effects are not natural, since what comes from nature must have an internal principle of movement, following Aristotle's teachings in the *Physics*.[68]

Citing QP, Cesalpino elaborated the role of the factive intellect used by demons. He stated that the speculative intellect possessed by the celestial intelligences and humans is concerned with the knowledge of universals. The motions of nature arise out of a natural appetite linked to the celestial speculative intellect. This intellect, however, is distinct from the ones that demons use for their nefarious acts.[69] These acts are beyond nature (*supra naturam*) in the same way the works of artisans are. Cesalpino theorized that demons prepare subtle and powerful spiritous substances, which are like form purged of crass matter. Demons act like physicians, when they prepare medicines by distillation and extract the spirituous properties from plants and minerals. The spirit supposedly used by demons moves and acts quickly like poisons in the air during plagues, in vipers' venom, and in contagious diseases, an explanation for why accused witches are often alleged to be found with concoctions made from snakes and frogs. In Cesalpino's view, demons prepare subtle and invisible substances, which in turn witches collect and apply.[70] While Pomponazzi thought it was implausible that demons keep their tools in pillboxes that have never been observed, Cesalpino believed that inquisitors had found them in witches' lairs.[71]

These substances that demons use can affect the mind without being sensed, a possibility that Cesalpino maintained Aristotle supported. The imagination, according to Aristotle's *On Divination during Sleep*, can be affected without sensation, in Cesalpino's reading. In this work, Aristotle explained that dreams can be altered by bodily parts, by what Cesalpino called the animal spirit, a subtle matter that connects the brain to sense organs and the rest of the body. Vapors arising from food digesting in the stomach, for example, can interfere with the imagination and produce nightmares.[72] Cesalpino likened his explanation of demonic affects to those found in the famed discussion of melancholy in the Aristotelian *Problemata* 30.1, which associated the powers of Sibyls and soothsayers with a naturally melancholic temperament.[73] Cesalpino interpreted Aristotle as reducing the ability to divine future events to natural causes. Yet, in Cesalpino's interpretation the black bile is not the cause of the divination and oracular abilities but merely prepares the body to receive an external movement, as he believed was explained in the *On Divination during Sleep*.[74]

In that treatise, Aristotle theorized that dreams could signal the future, especially the onset of diseases. Aristotle maintained that people often fail to notice faint sense stimuli because they are overwhelmed by a flood of sensations. While asleep, however, some people can feel these slight sensations, and at times the faculties of perception exaggerate them, so a small noise becomes loud thunder in a dream. Similarly, the first stages of diseases caused by humoral imbalance might be felt in sleep despite being imperceptible while conscious. In this manner, a dream can signal future disease.[75]

Besides these harbingers of physical distress, Aristotle thought it might be possible that other kinds of movements and perceptions might enter dormant souls prompting the receiver to use these vivid reveries for divination. Certain kinds of people are more susceptible to these telling dreams, according to Aristotle. Categorizing humans by their temperaments and by their mental capacities, he thought that the melancholic, those with unstable minds, the garrulous, and the simple-minded are prone to possessing this extraordinary divinatory ability because their own thoughts are not strong enough to obscure these faint stimuli.[76] That melancholics are given to such experiences might suggest a physiological explanation tied to a profound naturalism—and indeed, some have interpreted this work as such. Pomponzzi emphasized that nearly everyone who experiences such dreams are melancholic.[77] Yet, Aristotle tempered the possibility of such a naturalistic reading by writing that while God does not send dreams, they are still of a divine origin (*daimonia*), just as all of nature comes from the divine (*daimonia*) yet is not in itself divine (*theia*).[78] Aristotle's use of the word *daimonia* fit nicely with Cesalpino's reading of the concept of the divine in Hippocratic works, which he believed referred to lower gods.

Cesalpino's interest in this work went beyond Aristotle's identification of nature with the demonic. He addressed Aristotle's *On Divination during Sleep* in the final question of *QP*. There, he concluded that, although infrequent, it is possible that the imagination is moved without sensing. Not only are we able to imagine many things that are impossible or do not exist, but also faint images that are not normally perceptible can be perceived through dreams. For Cesalpino, this passage shows the need of a "more divine cause" and that those who have veridic dreams possess a "more divine nature."[79] *On Divination during Sleep*, therefore helped Celsalpino define a "more divine cause" in addition to explain how demons can create hallucinations. Just as sometimes it is possible to dream true things because of the motions of blood in the body, demons can cause illusions by altering the body, in particular the heart and the brain.

Aristotle's *On Divination during Sleep* paved the way for Cesalpino's philosophical explanation of demonic acts, and Hippocratic medicine provided him a foundation for potential cures and their limits. Given that the effects of demons on the body are supernatural and thus at times do not correspond to the natural course of diseases, physicians can easily diagnose demonic disease when the supernatural effects are obvious. Cesalpino cited hallucinations concerning "obscene body parts" as an unmistakably supernatural effect.[80] He believed, however, that it was more difficult to diagnose demonic possession when all bodily afflictions are identical to those that can appear in illnesses that have strictly natural causes. For example, the symptoms of a "third species of epilepsy" correspond to those of demonic possession. The difficulty in diagnosing demonic actions is compounded by the expertise of demons. Often the impure substance sent by the demons is hidden in a very small particle that harms the natural functions.[81] Yet, unless the demons' tools are found, it is most difficult or even impossible to judge whether diseases arise naturally or demonically.

Given physicians' limited ability to diagnose all cases of demonic possession and since "as long as the *maleficium* persists the affliction is not eliminated through natural remedies," Cesalpino pointed to two methods of removing demonic influence: magic and religion, two areas of knowledge that he believed to be "maximally distant from each other."[82] In his view magic employed "superstitious means," while religion used "divine and sacred names." Hippocrates and other ancients, however, did not discern between upper and lower divinities. Here he cited again the passage from the *Prognostic*, stating that the word *divinum* "instead must be said *daemonium*," and thus would correspond to Aristotle's usage in *On Divination during Sleep*.[83]

Cesalpino believed that, because of the ancients' lack of distinction between the demonic and the divine, great care must be taken in navigating ancient authors. He reserved special scorn for unnamed recent writers on the Cabala, who, in his eyes, falsely promised to move divine powers. These writers must be avoided, in his view.[84] Many of the natural cures found in Pliny and Dioscorides are ineffective and, even worse, are combined with superstitions, since there is no way to rein in demons' actions.[85] Some hope, however, may be found in the possibility of limiting the actions of the natural substances that the demon used. Since demons use substances that are like poisons, antidotes such as the Alexipharmaca, theriac, and the Mithraditic antidotes, which have been tested through long experience, offer the best prospect. They, however, can only work in conjunction with religion. He wrote, "it must be combatted partly by religion, partly by the aforementioned antidotes."[86] Yet in agreement with his earlier statements, he refrained from discussing religion since it was beyond the scope of the treatise.

5. Conclusion

In Cesalpino's account of demons, Hippocrates and Aristotle promote the explanatory power of spirits for understanding the divine within humans and the powers that demons use to affect the imagination and body. The divine plays two interconnected roles and explains the innate heat within humans and the immaterial powers midway between the celestial intelligences and the sublunary. Hippocratic texts referred to the divine in disease, which Cesalpino tied to the soul. Aristotle called nature "demonic," which Cesalpino interpreted as referring to lower divinities. For Cesalpino, humans and demons are linked by being the only beings that use the factive intellect to produce artificial effects that are beyond nature. Both humans and demons initiate motion with their minds but are only capable of altering subjects using natural substances. Demons, however, differ from artisans by being incorporeal and by making substances that surpass human knowledge and evade human perception. Cesalpino agreed with Pomponazzi that it was absurd to imagine demons to be aerial creatures, yet he disagreed in significant ways. Pomponazzi considered it impossible that demons applied natural products, which would be visible, but Cesalpino considered it not just reasonable, but speculated on the types of materials they used.

Whereas Pomponazzi cast doubt on the demonology of the Catholic Church, Cesalpino's account supported its major tenets. Foremost, he accepted its threatening reality. Moreover, he emphasized that Aristotle recognized divine aspects of nature and the soul. The 1593 version of the treatise, perhaps, attempts to highlight the orthodoxy of his position even more than the 1580 version. In the later version, after conceding that his purpose was not to discuss theological matters or to use religion and prayers against black magic, he added two sentences in favor of giving the sacraments to a patient before medical assistance, because they can help the soul and combat magic. Forcing a seemingly contradictory reading of Hippocrates' *On the Sacred Disease*, he contended that the practices of the Catholic Church parallel those of Hippocrates' time, when they used chants and religious rites to invoke divine powers. Moreover, he mustered the Hippocratic texts *On the Nature of Woman* and *On the Diseases of Young Girls* to support religious cures.[87]

Physicians at inquisitorial processes in Venice exhibited attitudes like Cesalpino's. They were hesitant to proclaim demonic possession in trials, despite expressing belief in demons in private.[88] In *DIP*, Cesalpino highlighted the difficulties and limitations of medicine when faced with suspected cases of demonic possession. Even though in a few cases the demonic signs are unmistakable, Cesalpino emphasized the uncertainties involved with diagnosing demonic possession and differentiating it from natural maladies, since the natural instruments demons use can produce the same effects as diseases that arise solely from natural causes. The curative powers of medicine are also limited, in his view, and in many cases only religion can help the possessed. In practice, however, Cesalpino took a stand on the presence of divine signs in the human body. In 1595, Cesalpino was part of a commission of physicians that testified that an autopsy showed that Filippo Neri's heart suffered from a supernatural and miraculous inflammation.[89]

The differences between the two versions of *DIP* point more to corrections of religious ideas than of revisions regarding the connections between Hippocrates and Aristotle. In his *Ars medica*, published another decade after the second version, Cesalpino again opined about the nature of the divine in Hippocratic and Aristotelian philosophies. Marshalling even more Hippocratic texts, such as *On Fleshes*, which he attributed to Democritus and called *On Principles,* once again Cesalpino compared the innate heat to the heavenly ether. Citing *Generation of Animals* 2.3, he wrote that this spirit "responds analogously to the element of the stars" and is responsible for the powers of the soul that distinguish humans from animals, being present in semen and in the human mind that is separable from the body. Its power (*vis*) derives not from the four elements but is celestial.[90] The opening chapters, while reiterating the philosophical foundations of *On Demons*, differ in one major way, namely, the polemic against Galen drops out, as Cesalpino identified Galen's wisest and most powerful craftsman with God. Thus, up to end of his career, Cesalpino championed the reconciliation of Aristotle and Hippocrates to help explain the presence of the divine in humanity and the connections between God and nature.

Notes

1   Andrew Cunningham, "Fabricius and the 'Aristotle Project' in Anatomical Teaching and Research at Padua," in *The Medical Renaissance of the Sixteenth Century*, ed. Andrew Wear, Roger K. French, and Iain M. Lonie (Cambridge: Cambridge

University Press, 1985), 195–222; Tawrin Baker, "Why All This Jelly? Jacopo Zabarella and Hieronymus Fabricius ab Acquapendente on the Usefulness of the Vitreous Humor," in *Early Modern Medicine and Natural Philosophy*, ed. Peter Distelzweig, Benjamin Goldberg, and Evan Ragland (Dordrecht: Springer, 2016), 59–88; Simone de Angelis, "From Text to the Body: Commentaries on *De Anima*, Anatomical Practice and Authority around 1600," in *Scholarly Knowledge: Textbooks in Early Modern Europe*, ed. Emidio Campi et al. (Geneva: Droz, 2008), 205–27; Craig Martin, "Lodovico Settala's Aristotelian *Problemata* Commentary and Late-Renaissance Hippocratic Medicine," in *Early Modern Medicine and Natural Philosophy*, ed. Distelzweig, Goldberg, and Ragland (Dordrecht: Springer, 2016), 19–42.

2   Andrea Cesalpino, *Daemonum investigatio peripatetica. In qua explicatur locus Hippocratis in Prognosticis si quid divinum in morbis habetur* (Florence: Giunta, 1580), fol. 8r: "explicatae sunt a doctissimis ac lucidissimis romanae ecclesiae doctoribus." Andrea Cesalpino, *Daemonum investigatio peripatetica* (Florence: Venice: Giunta, 1593), fol. 152v.

3   Jonathan Seitz, *Witchcraft and Inquisition in Early Modern Venice* (Cambridge: Cambridge University Press, 2011), 181–91.

4   Stuart Clark, *Thinking with Demons: The Idea of Witchcraft in Early Modern Europe* (Oxford: Oxford University Press, 1997), 151–60.

5   Ibid., 189–90, 243.

6   Aristotle, *Div. somn.* 1.463b12–15; For an analysis of the *fortuna* of the Aristotelian passage in the Middle Ages and early modern period, see Christoph Sander, "Der Dämon im Text lateinische Lesarten von *De somno* 453b22 und *De divinatione per somnum* 463b12 zwischen 1150 und 1650," *Recherches de Théologie et Philosophie médiévales* 83, no. 2 (2016): 245–311.

7   For the origins of this humanist tradition in the fifteenth century, see Giovanni Tortelli and Gian Giacomo Bartolotti, *Two Histories of Medicine of the XVth Century*, ed. and trans. Dorothy M. Schullian and Luigi Belloni (Milan: Stucchi, 1954).

8   Bartolotti described the role of chance and dreams in the early development of medicine, see *Two Histories*, 29–31.

9   Andrea Cesalpino, *Artis medicae pars II. De morbis particularibus internarum partium* (Rome: Zannetti, 1603), sig. †2v–†4v.

10 Ibid., sig. †4r–†4v.

11 See Marco Sgarbi's contribution to this volume.

12 Cesalpino, *Artis medicae pars II.*, sig. †4v–†5v.

13 Leonardo Giacchini, "Adversus Mesuem et vulgares medicos omnes tractatus," in *Novae academicae florentiane opuscula adversus Avicennam et medicos neotericos* (Venice: Giunta, 1533), fols. 34r–47v; Leonardo Giacchini, *In nonum librum Rasis ad Almansorem regem commentaria* (Basel: Perna, 1564), 2.

14 Cesalpino, *Artis medicae pars II*, sig. †5v; Guido Guidi, *Chirugia e graeco in latinum conversa cum nonnullis commentariis* (Paris: Galterius, 1544); Vivian Nutton, "Humanist Surgery," in *The Medical Renaissance of the Sixteenth Century*, ed. Andrew Wear, Roger K. French, and Iain M. Lonie (Cambridge: Cambridge University Press, 1985), 75–99, at 87–9.

15 Guidi, *Chirurgia*, 280: "maxime experimentorum spectator, iisque omnia comprobavit, quae multis fretus rationalibus argumentis invenit."

16 Giacchini, *In nonum librum Rasis*, 2.

17 Cesalpino, *Artis medicae pars II*, sig. †5v–†6r: "Hippocraticam medicinam ex philosophiae principiis emanantem, cum Aristotele magis consentire quam cum Platone."

18 Pietro Pomponazzi, *De incantationibus*, ed. Vittoria Perrone Compagni (Florence: Olschki, 2011), 3–5.
19 Andrea Cesalpino, *Peripateticarum quaestionum libri quinque* (Venice: Giunta, 1571), fol. 98r; Aristotle, *Gen. an.* 2.3.737a10; Hippocrates, *Nat. puer.* 13 (7.491L).
20 Cesalpino, *QP* (1571), fols. 107v–109r.
21 Mark Edward Clark and Kirk M. Summers, "Hippocratic Medicine and Aristotelian Science in the 'Daemonum investigatio peripatetica' of Andrea Cesalpino," *Bulletin of the History of Medicine* 69, no. 4 (1995): 527–41; Giano Matteo Durastante, *Problemata* (Venice: Ziletti, 1567), 23–41; Francesco de' Vieri, *Discorso intorno a' dimoni, volgarmente chiamati spiriti* (Florence: Sermartelli, 1576), 13–27; Francesco de' Vieri, *Liber in quo a calumniis detractorum philosophia defenditur et eius praestantia demonstratur* (Rome: Ruffinelli, 1586), 69.
22 See Sgarbi in this volume.
23 Cesalpino, *DIP* (1580), sig. B1r.
24 Cesalpino, *DIP* (1580), fol. 4r; Cesalpino, *DIP* (1593), fol. 145r.
25 "Si quid divinum in morbis habetur." Cf. Hippocrates, *Prognostic* 1 (2.112L). As Eva Del Soldato points out in her chapter in this volume, the subtitle is not found in the 1593 printing.
26 Pearl Kibre, "Hippocrates Latinus Repertorium of Hippocratic Writings in the Latin Middle Ages (VII)," *Traditio* 37 (1981): 267–89.
27 Vivian Nutton, "Hippocrates in the Renaissance," in *Die hippokratischen Epidemien: Theorie-Praxis-Tradition*, ed. Gerhard Baader and Rolf Winau. *Sudhoffs Archiv* 27 (Stuttgart: Franz Steiner, 1989), 420–39; Nancy G. Siraisi, *The Clock and the Mirror: Girolamo Cardano and Renaissance Medicine* (Princeton: Princeton University Press, 1997), 119–21.
28 Vivian Nutton, "Hippocrates in the Renaissance," 423–4, Nancy G. Siraisi, "History, Antiquarianism, and Medicine: The Case of Girolamo Mercuriale," *Journal of the History of Ideas* 64, no. 2 (2003): 231–51, at 247. For the slow dissolution of the Galenic version of Hippocratism, see Wesley D. Smith, *The Hippocratic Tradition* (Ithaca, NY: Cornell University Press, 1979), 13–31.
29 Girolamo Mercuriale, *Censura operum Hippocratis* (Venice: Giunta, 1585), sig. B2v–E1v.
30 Girolamo Mercuriale, *De pestilentia* (Padua: Mietti, 1577), 23.
31 Siraisi, *Clock and Mirror*, 119–21.
32 Galen, *In Hippocratis Prognosticum commentaria* 1.4.18b.21K (CMG 5.9.2, p. 208).
33 Stephanus of Athens, *In Hippocratis Prognosticum commentaria III*, ed. and trans. John M. Duffy in *CMG* XI (Berlin: Akademie-Verlag, 1983), 1.17, 1,2: 62–4; Taddeo Alderotti, *Expositiones in divinum Pronosticorum Ipocratis librum* (Venice: Giunta, 1527), fol. 197v.
34 Mercuriale, *De pestilentia*, 23–4.
35 Cristóbal de Vega, *Liber Prognosticorum Hippocratis* (Lyon: Beringos, 1551), 26: "id est, si quam habeat morbus ex aere dependentiam."
36 Guido Guidi, *De curatione generatim partis secundae sectio secunda* (Venice: De Franceschi, 1586), fol. 47r: "Prima causa unde ortus est et adhuc durat gallicus morbus, est divinum illud quod Hippocrates in morbis notavit, aer videlicet qui syderum vi quondam afffetionem contrahit, ob quam in corpora nostra hanc pestem infert." The printed marginal note indicates the *Prognostic*.
37 Girolamo Cardano, *In Hippocratis Coi Prognostica commentarii* (Basel: Petri, 1568), 15; Hippocrates, *De carnibus* 2 (8.584L); Hippocrates, *Aer.* 2 (2.14L).
38 Cesalpino, *DIP* (1580), fol. 5r; Cesalpino, *DIP* (1593), fol. 146r: "Praeterea si propter coelum divina dicenda essent, quae ab eo pendent, omne opus naturae divinum esset." Aristotle, *Mete.* 1.2.339a21–23.

39 Cesalpino, *DIP* (1593), fol. 150r: "intellexerit huiusmodi affectus, qui redundant in corpus ex parte, quae divina est in nobis."
40 Cesalpino, *DIP* (1593), fol. 150r; Hippocrates, *Nat. mul.* 1 (7.312L); Hippocrates, *Decorum* 5 (9.232L); Giacchini, *In nonum librum Rasis*, sig. *1r.
41 Cesalpino, *DIP* (1593), fol. 150r.
42 Andreas Cesalpino, *Quaestionum medicarum libri II* (Venice: Giunta, 1593), 174–6; Mercuriale, *Censura*, sig. D3r–D3v; Cesalpino, *DIP* (1593), fol. 167v.
43 Fridolf Kudlien, "Das Göttliche und die Natur im Hippokratischen Prognostikon," *Hermes* 105, no. 3 (1977): 268–74; Oswei Temkin, *Hippocrates in a World of Pagans and Christians* (Baltimore: Johns Hopkins University Press, 1991), 191–2.
44 Cesalpino, *DIP* (1580), fol. 8v; Cesalpino, *DIP* (1593). 145v: "Galenus utpote qui nulli religioni esset addictus."
45 Giambattista Da Monte, *In prima fen libri primi Canonis Avicennae explanatio* (Venice: Constantini, 1554), fols. 58r–60r; Nancy G. Siraisi, *Avicenna in Renaissance Italy: The Canon and Medical Teaching in Italian Universities after 1500* (Princeton: Princeton University Press, 1987), 290–1.
46 Donato Antonio Altomare, *Omnia opera* (Lyon: Rouillé, 1565), 21.
47 Giacchini, *In nonum librum Rasis*, sig. *1v.
48 Aristotle, *Gen. an.* 2.3.736b29–737a10. Translation, slightly altered, from *The Complete Works of Aristotle*, ed. Jonathan Barnes (Princeton, NJ: Princeton University Press, 1984), 1: 1143–4.
49 See Andreas Blank's contribution to this volume.
50 Hiro Hirai, "Formative Power, Soul, and Intellect in Nicolò Leoniceno Between the Arabo-Latin Tradition and the Renaissance of the Greek Commentators," in *Psychology and the Other Disciplines: A Case of Cross-Disciplinary Interaction (1250–1750)*, ed. Paul J. J. M. Bakker, Sander W. de Boer, and Cees Leijenhorst (Leiden: Brill, 2012), 297–324, at 303–12.
51 Jean Fernel, *On the Hidden Causes of Things*, ed. and trans. John M. Forrester and John Henry (Leiden: Brill, 2005), 1.7–8, 492–512.
52 Giacchini, *In nonum librum Rasis*, sig. *2v–*3r: "Spiritus porro, quibus et substantiae summa tenuitas, splendor et calor almus, clemens, suavis, et blandus inest, elemento stellarum proportione respondere, Aristoteles affirmavit." The printed marginal note cites Aristotle, *Gen. an.* 2.3.
53 Cesalpino, *DIP* (1580), fols. 5v–6r; Cesalpino, *DIP* (1593), fols. 146v–147r.
54 Aristotle, *Part. an.* 1.5.645a15–23.
55 Aristotle, *De an.* 1.5.411a7–10.
56 Cesalpino, *DIP* (1580), fol. 6r; Cesalpino, *DIP* (1593), fol. 147r.
57 Cesalpino, *DIP* (1580), fol. 6r; Cesalpino, *DIP* (1593), fol. 149r: "non solum in homine sed et in tota natura immortale quid contineri intelligentiam."
58 Cesalpino, *DIP* (1580), fol. 6r; Cesalpino, *DIP* (1593), fol. 149r; Simone Porzio, *De rerum naturalium principiis* (Naples: Scoto, 1561), fol. 4r.
59 Cesalpino, *DIP* (1580), fol. 6v; Cesalpino, *DIP* (1593), fol. 149v.
60 Cesalpino, *DIP* (1580), fols. 6v–7v; Cesalpino, *DIP* (1593), fols. 151v–152r.
61 Aristotle, *Div. somn.* 2.463b12–15.
62 Aristotle, *Div. somn.* 1.462b21–24; 1.463a22–32.
63 Cesalpino, *DIP* (1580), fol. 7v; Cesalpino, *DIP* (1593), fol. 152v.
64 Cesalpino, *DIP* (1580), fol. 8v, 15v; Cesalpino, *DIP* (1593), fols. 153v, 159r–159v.
65 Cesalpino, *DIP* (1580), fol. 15v; Cesalpino, *DIP* (1593), fols. 159v–160r.
66 Cesalpino, *DIP* (1580), fol. 21v; Cesalpino, *DIP* (1593), fol. 165v.

67 Cesalpino, *DIP* (1580), fol. 21r; Cesalpino, *DIP* (1593), fol. 165r.
68 Cesalpino, *DIP* (1580), fol. 21v; Cesalpino, *DIP* (1593), fol.165v; Aristotle, *Ph.* 2.1.192b8-16.
69 Cesalpino, *DIP* (1580), fol. 16r; Cesalpino, *DIP* (1593), fol. 160r.
70 Cesalpino, *DIP* (1580), fols. 16v-17r; Cesalpino, *DIP* (1593), fol. 162r-162v.
71 Pomponazzi, *De incantantionibus*, 13.
72 Cesalpino, *DIP* (1580), fol. 19v; Cesalpino, *DIP* (1593), fol. 163r.
73 [Ps.] Aristotle, [*Pr.*] 30.1.954a34-37.
74 Cesalpino, *DIP* (1580), fol. 21v; Cesalpino, *DIP* (1593), fol. 165v.
75 Aristotle, *Div. somn.* 1.463a8-22.
76 Aristotle, *Div. somn.* 2.463b15-19.
77 Pomponazzi, *De incantationibus*, 125; Angus Gowland, "Melancholy, Imagination, and Dreaming in Renaissance Learning," in *Diseases of the Imagination and Imaginary Disease in the Early Modern Period*, ed. Yasmin Haskell (Turnhout: Brepols, 2011), 53-102, at 73-97.
78 Aristotle, *Div. somn.* 2.463b13-15.
79 Cesalpino, *QP* (1571), fols. 126v-127r.
80 Cesalpino, *DIP* (1580), fol. 22r: "qui patiuntur praestigia aut circa partes obscaenes." This sentence was cut from the 1593 edition. Cf. Cesalpino, *DIP* (1593), fol. 166r.
81 Cesalpino, *DIP* (1580), fol. 22v; Cesalpino, *DIP* (1593), fol. 166r.
82 Cesalpino, *DIP* (1580), fol. 23r-23v; Cesalpino, *DIP* (1593), fols. 166v-167r: "Quamdiu enim maleficium persistit, affectio non caedit remediis naturalibus;" "Reperio autem duas rationes inter se maxime distantes."
83 Cesalpino, *DIP* (1580), fol. 23v; Cesalpino, *DIP* (1593), fol. 167r: "Unde Hippocrates divinum vocavit quod in morbis habetur, cum potius daemonium dicendum esset."
84 Cesalpino, *DIP* (1580), fol. 23v; Cesalpino, *DIP* (1593), fol. 167r-167v.
85 Cesalpino, *DIP* (1580), fols. 23v-24r; Cesalpino, *DIP* (1593), fols. 167v-168r.
86 Cesalpino, *DIP* (1580), fol. 24v; Cesalpino, *DIP* (1593), fol. 168v: "partim religione partim antidotis praedictis pugnandum est."
87 Cesalpino, *DIP* (1593), fol. 167v. Cf. Cesalpino, *DIP* (1580), fol. 23v. Hippocrates, *Morb. sacr.* 1 (6.358); Hippocrates, *Nat. mul.* 1 (7.312L); Hippocrates, *Virg.* 1 (8.468L).
88 Seitz, *Witchcraft*, 187-94.
89 Bradford A. Bouley, *Pious Postmortems: Anatomy, Sanctity, and the Catholic Church in Early Modern Europe* (Philadelphia: University of Pennsylvania Press, 2017), 61-3.
90 Andrea Cesalpino, *Artis medicae pars prima, de morbis universalibus* (Rome: Zannetti, 1602), 5-12, at 8: "Calor vocatur, non ignis, sed spiritus proportione respondens elemento stellarum."

Bibliography

Primary Sources

Alderotti, Taddeo. *Expositiones in divinum Pronosticorum Ipocratis librum*. Venice: Giunta, 1527.
Altomare, Donato Antonio. *Omnia opera*. Lyon: Rouillé, 1565.
Aristotle. *Generation of Animals*, translated by A. L. Peck. Cambridge, MA: Harvard University Press, 1943.

Aristotle. *The Complete Works of Aristotle*, edited by Jonathan Barnes. 2 vols. Princeton: Princeton University Press, 1984.
Cardano, Girolamo. *In Hippocratis Coi Prognostica commentarii*. Basel: Petri, 1568.
Cardano, Girolamo. *Opera omnia*, edited by Charles Spon. 10 vols. Lyon: Huguetan and Ravaud, 1663.
Cesalpino, Andrea. *Artis medicae pars prima, de morbis universalibus*. Rome: Zannetti, 1602.
Cesalpino, Andrea. *Artis medicae pars II. De morbis particularibus internarum partium*. Rome: Zannetti, 1603.
Cesalpino, Andrea. *Daemonum investigatio peripatetica. In qua explicatur locus Hippocratis in Prognosticis si quid divinum in morbis habetur*. Florence: Giunta, 1580.
Cesalpino, Andrea. *Daemonum investigatio peripatetica*. Florence: Venice: Giunta, 1593.
Cesalpino, Andrea. *Peripateticarum quaestionum libri quinque*. Venice: Giunta, 1571.
Cesalpino, Andrea. *Quaestionum medicarum libri II*. Venice: Giunta, 1593.
Da Monte, Giambattista. *In prima fen libri primi Canonis Avicennae explanatio*. Venice: Constantini, 1554.
Durastante, Giano Matteo. *Problemata*. Venice: Ziletti, 1567.
Fernel, Jean. *On the Hidden Causes of Things*, edited and translated by John M. Forrester and John Henry. Leiden: Brill, 2005.
Galen. *Opera omnia*, edited by Karl Gottlieb Kühn. 20 vols. Leipzig: Karl Knobloch, 1821–33.
Giacchini, Leonardo. "Adversus Mesuem & vulgares medicos omnes, tractatus." In *Novae academicae florentiane opuscula adversus Avicennam & medicos neotericos*. Venice: Giunta, 1533: fols. 34r–47v.
Giacchini, Leonardo. *In nonum librum Rasis ad Almansorem regem commentaria*. Basel: Perna, 1564.
Guidi, Guido. *Chirugia e graeco in latinum conversa cum nonnullis commentariis*. Paris: Galterius, 1544.
Guidi, Guido. *De curatione generatim partis secundae sectio secunda*. Venice: De Franceschi, 1586.
Hippocrates. *Prognostic. Regimen in Acute Diseases. The Sacred Disease. The Art. Breaths. Law. Decorum. Physician (Ch. 1). Dentition*, translated by W. H. S. Jones. Cambridge, MA: Harvard University Press, 1923.
Mercuriale, Girolamo. *Censura operum Hippocratis*. Venice: Giunta, 1585.
Mercuriale, Girolamo. *De pestilentia*. Padua: Mietti, 1577.
Pomponazzi, Pietro. *De incantationibus*, edited by Vittoria Perrone Compagni. Florence: Olschki, 2011.
Porzio, Simone. *De rerum naturalium principiis*. Naples: Scoto, 1561.
Stephanus of Athens. *In Hippocratis Prognosticum commentaria III*, edited and translated by John M. Duffy. Volume 11 of *Corpus Medicorum Graecorum*. Berlin: Akademie-Verlag, 1983.
Tortelli, Giovanni and Gian Giacomo Bartolotti. *Two Histories of Medicine of the XVth Century*, edited and translated by Dorothy M. Schullian and Luigi Belloni. Milan: Stucchi, 1954.
Vega, Cristóbal de. *Liber Prognosticorum Hippocratis*. Lyon: Beringos, 1551.
Vieri, Francesco de'. [Verino] *Discorso intorno a' dimonii, volgarmente chiamati spiriti*. Florence: Sermartelli, 1576.
Vieri, Francesco de'. [Verino] *Liber in quo a calumniis detractorum philosophia defenditur & eius praestantia demonstratur*. Rome: Ruffinelli, 1586.

Secondary Sources

Baker, Tawrin. "Why All This Jelly? Jacopo Zabarella and Hieronymus Fabricius ab Acquapendente on the Usefulness of the Vitreous Humor." In *Early Modern Medicine and Natural Philosophy*, edited by Peter Distelzweig, Benjamin Goldberg, and Evan Ragland, 59–88. Dordrecht: Springer, 2016.

Bouley, Bradford A. *Pious Postmortems: Anatomy, Sanctity, and the Catholic Church in Early Modern Europe*. Philadelphia: University of Pennsylvania Press, 2017.

Clark, Mark Edward, and Kirk M. Summers. "Hippocratic Medicine and Aristotelian Science in the *Daemonum investigatio peripatetica* of Andrea Cesalpino." *Bulletin of the History of Medicine* 69, no. 4 (1995): 527–41.

Clark, Stuart. *Thinking with Demons: The Idea of Witchcraft in Early Modern Europe*. Oxford: Oxford University Press, 1997.

Cunningham, Andrew. "Fabricius and the 'Aristotle Project' in Anatomical Teaching and Research at Padua." In *The Medical Renaissance of the Sixteenth Century*, edited by Andrew Wear, Roger K. French, and Iain M. Lonie, 195–222. Cambridge: Cambridge University Press, 1985.

de Angelis, Simone. "From Text to the Body: Commentaries on *De Anima*, Anatomical Practice and Authority around 1600." In *Scholarly Knowledge: Textbooks in Early Modern Europe*, edited by Emidio Campi, Simone de Angelis, Anja-Silvia Goeing, and Anthony Grafton, 205–27. Geneva: Droz, 2008.

Gowland, Angus. "Melancholy, Imagination, and Dreaming in Renaissance Learning." In *Diseases of the Imagination and Imaginary Disease in the Early Modern Period*, edited by Yasmin Haskell, 53–102. Turnhout: Brepols, 2011.

Hirai, Hiro. "Formative Power, Soul, and Intellect in Nicolò Leoniceno between the Arabo-Latin Tradition and the Renaissance of the Greek Commentators." In *Psychology and the Other Disciplines: A Case of Cross-Disciplinary Interaction (1250–1750)*, edited by Paul J. J. M. Bakker, Sander W. de Boer, and Cees Leijenhorst, 297–324. Leiden: Brill, 2012.

Kibre, Pearl. "Hippocrates Latinus Repertorium of Hippocratic Writings in the Latin Middle Ages (VII)." *Traditio* 37 (1981): 267–89.

Kudlien, Fridolf. "Das Göttliche und die Natur im Hippokratischen Prognostikon." *Hermes* 105 (1977): 268–74.

Martin, Craig. "Lodovico Settala's Aristotelian *Problemata* Commentary and Late-Renaissance Hippocratic Medicine." In *Early Modern Medicine and Natural Philosophy*, edited by Peter Distelzweig, Benjamin Goldberg, and Evan Ragland, 19–42. Dordrecht: Springer, 2016.

Nutton, Vivian. "Hippocrates in the Renaissance." In *Die hippokratischen Epidemien: Theorie-Praxis-Tradition*, edited by Gerhard Baader and Rolf Winau, 420–39. *Sudhoffs Archiv* 27. Stuttgart: Franz Steiner, 1989.

Nutton, Vivian. "Humanist Surgery." In *The Medical Renaissance of the Sixteenth Century*, edited by Andrew Wear, Roger K. French, and Iain M. Lonie, 75–99. Cambridge: Cambridge University Press, 1985.

Sander, Christoph. "Der Dämon im Text lateinische Lesarten von *De somno* 453b22 und *De divinatione per somnum* 463b12 zwischen 1150 und 1650." *Recherches de Théologie et Philosophie médiévales* 83, no. 2 (2016): 245–311.

Seitz, Jonathan. *Witchcraft and Inquisition in Early Modern Venice*. Cambridge: Cambridge University Press, 2011.

Siraisi, Nancy G. *Avicenna in Renaissance Italy: The Canon and Medical Teaching in Italian Universities after 1500*. Princeton: Princeton University Press, 1987.

Siraisi, Nancy G. "History, Antiquarianism, and Medicine: The Case of Girolamo Mercuriale." *Journal of the History of Ideas* 64 (2003): 231–51.

Siraisi, Nancy G. *The Clock and the Mirror: Girolamo Cardano and Renaissance Medicine*. Princeton: Princeton University Press, 1997.

Smith, Wesley D. *The Hippocratic Tradition*. Ithaca, NY: Cornell University Press, 1979.

Temkin, Oswei. *Hippocrates in a World of Pagans and Christians*. Baltimore: Johns Hopkins University Press, 1991.

4

Plato and Andrea Cesalpino's Aristotelianism: A Revealing Marginality

Eva Del Soldato

In 1576, when Andrea Cesalpino was a professor of practical medicine, a chair of Platonism *in die festivo* was established at the University of Pisa.[1] To hold it was Francesco de' Vieri (or Verino (II), 1524–91), a professor of philosophy and main advocate for the chair.[2] Verino was fittingly described as "very Aristotelian, but old-style, that is at the same time a Platonist."[3] Indeed, Verino kept the substantial agreement between Plato and Aristotle as a constant motif in his writings and evidently in his teaching. After only three years, however, the Platonic chair *in die festivo* was suspended, probably because of tensions with other university *magistri*. Girolamo Borro (1512–92), for example, another *ordinario* in philosophy and better-paid competitor of Verino, had made clear his anti-Platonic feelings and his diffidence toward attempts at reconciling Plato with Aristotle.[4] Verino was then forced to teach only the "regular" Aristotelian curriculum, but he did not abandon his veneration for Plato, and accordingly did not give up the hopes to revive one day the Platonic chair. Over the years, he composed several works lobbying for the restauration of the chair, and in 1589 he likely thought to be closer to reach his goal. That year Verino published his *Vere conclusioni*, a work in which he tried to prove the agreement of Plato and Aristotle on crucial doctrines, and proposed a revised teaching curriculum including both philosophers.[5] Written in the vernacular, the *Vere conclusioni* was a sort of *manifesto*, intended at displaying the virtues of Plato and his philosophy not as much to university insiders as to influential patrons in the Medicean court. This largely explains why Cesalpino was not pleased with the *Vere conclusioni*.

Cesalpino had received the book from Verino himself, at the behest of the patron he shared with Verino, Baccio Valori (1535–1606), and one passage in the work infuriated him.[6] In that passage of the *Vere conclusioni* Verino referred to "heretical teachers of philosophy, medicine, and logic" from whom one would learn wicked principles and

---

I am grateful to Fabrizio Baldassarri, Craig Martin, and all the participants of the Cesalpino workshop for their precious feedback. All translations of Aristotle's works are from *Complete Works of Aristotle, The Revised Oxford Translation*, ed. Jonathan Barnes, 2 vols. (Princeton: Princeton University Press, 1985). Other translations are mine, if not stated otherwise.

deduce wicked conclusions, adding in counterbalance a list of individuals who were instead to be considered good teachers.[7] This list included some of Verino's colleagues in philosophy and medicine at Pisa, many of whom had been dead for a long time, but not Cesalpino. Cesalpino read the omission of his name as an implicit suggestion, on Verino's part, that he was one of those heretical teachers of wicked principles. Confronted by an enraged Cesalpino, Verino appealed to Valori and claimed that he was instead attacking no better identified "Telesiani," as he did in a courtly dispute at the presence of two late Medici dames years before.[8] This response did not satisfy Cesalpino, who replied back that in Pisa there was no trace of *Telesiani*.[9] Baccio Valori had nonetheless reassured Cesalpino that his reputation was unscathed, advising him not to be bothered further by the issue.[10] Verino himself was happy to close the incident, and thanked Valori for his mediation.[11]

On the basis of the extant documents, it seems that the episode had no consequences on the career of both men and, aside from Cesalpino's obvious disliking of Verino, there is no evidence that he was behind the failure of Verino's attempts at reintroducing the Platonic chair.[12] For sure, toward Verino's hero—Plato—Cesalpino seemed rather to nurture a substantial disinterest. And such an attitude, in those times, was in many ways notable.

Even if the chairs of Platonism were precarious and very few in number, in the second half of the sixteenth century it was indeed almost a given that a close dialogue with Plato characterized the teaching of the traditional Aristotelian texts.[13] In the promotion of this Platonic wave significant credit belonged to teachers of medicine, who were interested in questions of *methodus*, but the trend was no less common in the teaching of philosophy.[14] Not only *magistri* who sympathized for Plato, like Francesco Piccolomini (1523–1607), but also those of solid Aristotelian allegiance, such as Francesco Vimercato (d. 1569) and Federico Pendasio (d. 1603), equally introduced Plato and his doctrines in their lectures, in their commentaries, and in their works.[15] These men shared the same exegetical concern: it would be impossible to understand Aristotle without an adequate knowledge of Plato's philosophy. There was also the awareness that Aristotle did not always report faithfully Plato's doctrines, another consideration that favored this "informal" introduction of Plato within university halls.[16]

Cesalpino's philosophical writings, in which Plato is mentioned only rarely and superficially, suggest that he was alien to this approach. One probable explanation is that Cesalpino, unlike these other *magistri*, was engaged in something different from a mere interpretative work of the Aristotelian text. He himself admitted it introducing the *Quaestiones peripateticae* (1571 and 1593), a work that openly rejected the commentary tradition. As Cesalpino wrote, in the QP the different subjects were discussed not via a textual exegesis of Aristotle, but "according to … Aristotle's opinions, or according to the principles he passed on."[17] Cesalpino wanted to keep the discourse exclusively within the boundaries of the Aristotelian realm, identifying the principles that allow the entire universe to work and on which he could build his own description of the world, even when touching questions that have not been thematically discussed in the *corpus Aristotelicum*. In this sense, Cesalpino's philosophical mission seems directed at perfecting Aristotelianism as a philosophy that can explain the entire reality, either by correcting it from within, for example by emphasizing its immanentistic character,[18] or by supporting its compatibility with religion and so rejecting any sort of double truth. Cesalpino read Aristotle with Aristotle, and his goal was to make Aristotelianism coherent with itself and, as much as possible, with the religious exigencies of his own times.

To this, one has to add that—as highlighted by many contributions in this volume—Cesalpino was extremely hesitant to give traces of his readings and sources, and Plato was certainly no exception. This attitude was largely connected to the self-imposed Aristotelian boundaries of his philosophical investigations. Yet, to make things worse, the few explicit references of Plato that we find in Cesalpino are—as noticed above—disappointing and superficial, to the extent that one can question if he was directly familiar with the Platonic dialogues or was actually relying on Aristotle even when referring to Plato's doctrines.

As already mentioned, Cesalpino's patron at that time of his Pisan teaching was Baccio Valori. Valori has been credited with the construction of a Ficinian "Platonic hub," grounded in the tradition of his family.[19] Even after leaving Pisa for Rome, Cesalpino kept an intense correspondence with Valori. In January 1594 he sent Valori a letter in which he eagerly affirmed his loyalty to the Medici family, through the description of the facade he had designed for his house in Pisa, a facade that paid homage to the Florentine rulers. Together with the inscription "UNITAS SUPERIUS, DUALITAS INFERIUS," the facade was decorated by an elaborated composition of triangles and spheres that alluded to the *palle medicee*. This interplay of geometrical shapes was coherent with the meaning of the motto, displaying the imperfection of multiplicity and the perfection of unity, which was evidently granted by the Medici's rule. Such a design had a philosophical foundation that Cesalpino explained to Valori:

> Plato had as principles of all things unity and duality, unity as the form, and duality as the matter under the name of great and small, as reported many times by Aristotle. And that for a good reason, because what is one brings perfection in all things, and he calls this unity form. He calls imperfection every multiplicity, and says that is born out of matter; since it is divisible, and since the first multiplicity is the duality, under this name [Plato] means the matter.[20]

The nod to Plato was likely intended to please Valori. Yet the reference was more Aristotelian than Platonic, being based—and Cesalpino did not hide it—on what Aristotle reported about Plato, in *Metaphysics* 1.6.987b18–22 and *Physics* 1.4.187b17–19. Crucially, this was not an isolated instance because the same passage is quoted twice in QP. The first occurrence is in a section on multitude in separate substances. Cesalpino argued that in separate substances multitude is in part present, and in part not. Substances, in fact, are nonetheless the result of a composition and therefore are a multitude, because only the first simple act is unique. In support of this claim, Cesalpino quoted and discussed a passage from *Metaphysics* 12.8.1074a33–34, in which Aristotle affirmed that all the things which are many in number, have matter. It is here that Cesalpino inserted the Platonic reference, as presented by Aristotle in *Metaphysics* 1 and *Physics* 1. The passage in QP, because of its phrasing, likely represented the Latin original of what Cesalpino wrote to Valori in 1594 and works as a mere—one could even say ornamental—confirmation of what he had already stated on solidly Aristotelian bases.[21]

The second occurrence of the Platonic "great" and "small," in the chapter on the dependance of dry and humid on hot and cold, is even more *en passant*. Here Cesalpino mentioned the Platonic doctrine briefly, in a sort of doxographic section, listing the position of those who claimed that dry and humid, but also cold and hot, depended on quantity, and more precisely on rarefaction and condensation: "and Plato wanted great and small to be the principles."[22] The position to which Plato, among others, is associated is nonetheless dismissed by Cesalpino.

In these cases, therefore, Cesalpino spoke of Plato on the basis of the information he found in the Aristotelian *corpus*. If one considers the other passages in the *Quaestiones peripateticae* in which Cesalpino mentioned Plato, one will hardly find a more serious engagement with the actual text of Platonic dialogues and letters.

The first reference to Plato in the text is mostly rhetorical and occurs in the preface. Here, Cesalpino inserted Plato in a genealogical list of great thinkers like Democritus, Empedocles and Anaxagoras, who made possible Aristotle's sublime achievements. Plato, in a few words, would have been a teleologically oriented step, useful to achieve Aristotle's unparalleled greatness:

> This is the effect of that cause, that even if for so many centuries, innumerable philosophers worked hard ... searching the truth, nonetheless they sometimes did not reach their desired goal. However, we owe them our gratitude, since by transmitting to their successors the things they found, made easier the way to investigate subsequent things. Indeed, had been not Democritus, Empedocles, Anaxagoras, and many others, and finally Plato, there would have been no Aristotle, thanks to whom philosophy seems to have reached the highest peak of authority ...[23]

Whoever looks closely would immediately realize that the passage is nothing more than a re-elaboration of a famous section in *Metaphysics* 2.1.993b12-18, in which Aristotle said that we need to be grateful to those who came before us in spite of their shortcomings, because they paved the way toward the truth: "if there had been no Phrynis, there would have been no Timotheus." The name of Plato, therefore, is simply implicated in an intertextual Aristotelian game.

Other occurrences in the *QP*, even if posited in theoretically oriented sections, confirm the impression that Cesalpino's mentions of Plato and his doctrines were prompted by Aristotelian needs and grounded on Aristotelian texts. The mention of Plato coupled with the Pythagoreans in one of the opening *quaestiones*, "Sciences are distinguished according to the genus of the substances," is an aside entirely based on *Metaphysics* 1.4.985b23ff. Their shared position that mathematics and first philosophy would partially overlap was in any case promptly rejected by Cesalpino, quoting texts from *Metaphysics* 7 and 11. An important chapter in the first book of *QP* is entitled "A single difference, even if it is the ultimate difference, is not sufficient to express what has to be explained."[24] The discussion on the nature of definition was crucial for Cesalpino's botany and his classificatory efforts. Cesalpino believed that a single ultimate difference cannot be considered equal to the species and that is not enough to constitute the essence of a thing and therefore to offer its definition.[25] In fact, according to Cesalpino, a definition must be obtained from several ultimate differences deriving from multiple divisions of the genus.[26] However, to prove this point, Cesalpino had to cope with the difficulties caused by a passage in *Metaphysics* 7.12.1037b18ff. that tore many of his Aristotelian contemporaries as well.[27] In the passage Aristotle seemed to accept the use of dichotomy in definition, something that he nonetheless vehemently rejected in *Parts of Animals* 1.2.642b5ff., criticizing those authors who "propose to reach the ultimate forms of animal life by dividing the genus into two differences." Aristotle did not name his target, but Cesalpino easily identified him: Plato.[28] Cesalpino made sense of the apparent conflict between *Metaphysics* 7 and *Parts of Animals* 1 by claiming that in the former text Aristotle was not expressing his opinion "verum ex veris," but actually displaying the shortcomings of Plato's erroneous division.[29] If Aristotle did not say it explicitly, this was because he had already written against Plato's *methodus* in other works, and in *Metaphysics* 7 wanted instead to show the unity that characterizes definitions.[30] Again in this *quaestio*, Cesalpino's references to Plato are all mediated through Aristotle and not founded in Platonic works.

This treatment is not spared to Plato even when discussing psychological issues, one of the most distinctive aspects of his thought. There is one incidental reference to the Platonic self-moving soul, in a *quaestio* focused on the circular movement of the heavens ("The circulatory movement of the heavens is an imitation of the intelligences").[31] Plato's definition of the soul as a self-moving substance, even if useful to understand the operation of the intelligences, was immediately corrected by Cesalpino, observing that one could properly speak of movement only for bodies, but not in reference to indivisible substances, and that for this reason Aristotle said that every movement happens in time (e.g. *Physics* 8.1.251b17ff.). Aristotle offered an extensive discussion of the Platonic self-moving soul in *On the Soul* 1.3.405b34ff., suggesting again that Cesalpino used the Aristotelian text when referring to a Platonic doctrine, rather than—in this case—to the *Timaeus* itself. And indeed, the doctrine was invoked by Cesalpino in an exquisitely Aristotelian perspective. The same can be said for the mention of Plato in the section entitled "Among mortal souls, only human souls are immortal" ("Mortalium solas hominum animas immortales esse").[32] This chapter was crucial to Cesalpino's affirmation of the exceptional nature of human souls, grounding his position on Aristotle's words. But how to conciliate this position with the individuality of the souls and their numerability? Does this mean that the only immortality one can achieve would be *secundum speciem*? One of the problems that Cesalpino had to solve in this context, while supporting a multiplicity of immortal souls, is embedded in a difficulty raised against Plato's *Timaeus* (37d). How could there be, in fact, something which is generated but not corrupted? There could not have been a soul of Socrates, before Socrates came to existence, since it would not have been possible for the soul to be participated by something which did not exist yet. Nonetheless, this very generated soul would not be corrupted after the death of Socrates. The main issue with this position is that there would be an infinity *in actu*.

Cesalpino's solution to the *dubitatio* saved the privilege of the human soul precisely relying on Aristotelian principles, that is by evoking the doctrine of the continuum which is potentially infinitely divisible, but not all at once, instead *successive* (cf. *Physics* 3.7.207b1ff.). In the same way the immaterial substance would contain the multitude of the souls. This solution allowed Cesalpino to preserve—against Averroes—the individuality of the human immortal soul, though allowing a unique immaterial substance. But Plato's doctrine from the *Timaeus*—supporting that something generated could be incorruptible—was also immediately neutralized by the Aristotelian framework and according to the rules of the cosmology of *On the Heavens*. It was in that work (1.10.280a29-31) that Aristotle explicitly mentioned and dismissed the Platonic position. Evidently, that passage was behind Cesalpino's mention of the criticisms against Plato. This occurrence further confirms that Cesalpino's Plato was a second-hand version of the ancient philosopher, constantly filtered through the *corpus Aristotelicum*.

Something slightly different seems to happen in the medical sections of the *Quaestiones*. In the *quaestio* "The heart is not only the principle of the arteries, but also of the veins" (*Cor non solum arteriarum sed et venarum ac nervorum esse principium*), Cesalpino argued plants can live without sensation, while in animals sensation cannot be without the inferior vegetative soul.[33] This genuine Aristotelian doctrine (*On the Soul* 3.12.434a23-24) highlights the mistake made by Plato with his "anatomy of the soul." Plato localized the vegetative soul in the liver, but since an animal deprived of its liver does not necessarily die, this would erroneously suggest something impossible: that an animal could live without the vegetative soul.[34] Cesalpino's endgame in this *quaestio* was to bring support to the Aristotelian cardiocentrism and to the unity of the soul. Yet, in *On the Soul*, Aristotle did not openly attack Plato for locating a part of his tripartite soul in the liver. He simply mentioned (1.5.411b5-6), with no reference to the name of his teacher, that "some hold that the soul is divisible, and that we think with one part and desire with another." Also, in the *Timaeus*, Plato spoke of the soul located in the liver as the desiderative soul (70d ff.), not as the vegetative. However, several authors had declared the equivalence between Plato's desiderative soul and Aristotle's vegetative soul, most notably—in the case of Cesalpino—Galen.[35] In fact, only a few pages later in the same *quaestio*, Cesalpino criticized Galen for having followed Plato in identifying three souls that are distinct not only with respect to their faculties, but also with respect to their locations.[36] These considerations, along with the incidental mention of Plato's opinion, suggest once again that Cesalpino almost certainly did not resort to Plato's original text for his quotation, even when not using Aristotle as his direct source.

From what has just been expounded, a few possible conclusions already emerge: Plato appeared rarely throughout QP. When mentioned, Plato's doctrines were not discussed on the basis of his own works, but usually according to what Aristotle wrote of them. Consequently, Plato was typically criticized by Cesalpino. To that, it must be added that in QP there are no explicit quotations from other Platonic authors and interpreters.[37]

After considering QP, therefore, one could conclude that Cesalpino did not have a "Platonic" library of his own, and that in any case had little interest in Plato's philosophy, which in his perspective had been overcome by what Aristotle built. And yet, another work by Cesalpino, the *Daemonum investigatio peripatetica*, would suggest—at least at first glance—a different attitude. In this text Cesalpino was certainly more generous in quoting Platonic dialogues, and in various occasions appeared even sympathetic to Plato. But was *DIP* actually presenting a more Platonic side of Cesalpino?

Looking at the context in which the *DIP* was conceived, and its purpose, can help to correctly make sense of the use Cesalpino made of the *authoritates Platonis* in this work. Cesalpino's *DIP* is a work devised and written for a precise reason: in 1574, in the Sant'Anna Benedictine monastery in Pisa, three nuns were tormented by demons. The demons were apparently quickly and easily defeated. Yet, the episode provoked debates in the city, and at least two printed works: a 1576 vernacularization of a Latin treatise by our Francesco Verino (II), and Cesalpino's *DIP*, which first appeared in 1580.[38] Both works had been requested at the time of the incident by the Archbishop Pietro Giacomo Bourbon Del Monte, who had prematurely died in 1575. Verino's work posited more emphasis on theological issues, while Cesalpino framed his treatise as an explanation of an ambiguous sentence in Hippocrates' *Prognostic* (I).[39] Yet, they both concluded that demons had to be admitted not just from a religious perspective, but also from the point of view of the natural philosopher. And, crucially, both Verino and Cesalpino agreed that Plato as much as Aristotle did not deny the existence of demons.

If this position is unsurprising for Verino, it could appear unexpected in a committed Aristotelian like Cesalpino. However, *DIP* seems a work composed in radical opposition to Pomponazzi's *De incantationibus*, in which—famously—the existence of demons was denied *in via Aristotelis*. This denial was philosophically coherent with Pomponazzi's Aristotelianism which, unlike Cesalpino's, supported a mortalistic reading of *On the Soul*. In *DIP*, Cesalpino began his discussion precisely starting with the soul. As mentioned above, *DIP* is presented as an *explanatio* of a contested sentence from Hippocrates' *Prognostic*, in which the Greek physician wondered if diseases could have divine causes as well. Interpreting the text, Galen had rejected the idea that his predecessor would have admitted divine causes. According to Galen, what Hippocrates meant as divine was simply the effects of circulating air ("aeris ambientis conditionem").[40] This is where Cesalpino intervened, pointing out that if Galen supported such an erroneous position, this was only because he denied that anything immortal or divine could be contained by the inferior world. Galen clearly stated this in *The Faculties of the Soul Follow the Mixtures of the Body* (*Quod animi mores sequantur corporis temperamentum*), where he rejected the immortality of the rational part of the soul, as described by Plato, associating the soul to a heat (*calidum*) subject to generation and corruption.[41] By denying something divine in men, Galen *a fortiori* denied the divine in all other substances inferior to them. Following the opposite path, what Cesalpino needed to prove was therefore that something divine is present in men, and then consequently in all the other substances. This first foundational point is easily gained by highlighting the divine nature of the *mens*, an immortal substance coming from outside and separated from matter, whose operation does not communicate with the operation of the body. Aristotle demonstrated this, which was approved—among others—by Plato.[42] The following pages draw the consequences of this pivotal statement, to explain the error of Galen. But what is notable here is that

Cesalpino aligned Aristotle and Plato, opposing this latter to Galen. The agreement of Aristotle and Plato on the immortality of the rational soul was in fact the necessary premise to their agreement on the existence of the demons, and—crucially—to prove that a demonology *in via Aristotelis* was possible.

One could wonder if Cesalpino was repeating in *DIP*, under an opposite sign, the strategy adopted by Pomponazzi in his *De incantationibus*. In that work, Pomponazzi had equally suggested a substantial agreement between Plato and Aristotle on the subject of the demons, but in his case both philosophers rejected their existence.[43] Even if Pomponazzi was not persuaded by the possibility of a complete harmony between Plato and Aristotle, though elsewhere he did not exclude that Plato believed the human soul to be mortal, this qualified agreement brought him—in the context of *De incantationibus*—important argumentative support.[44] This move was indeed convenient to combine the positions of the philosophers against Christian religion, and to somehow defuse the meaning of the Aristotelian denial of the existence of demons as the stance of natural reason in a general sense. Cesalpino, unlike Pomponazzi, did not want to establish a stark opposition between philosophy and faith, though highlighting their distinct realms. In his case claiming that both Plato and Aristotle equally supported the existence of demons meant showing that human philosophy and Christian theology did not collide (even though theology had the last word).[45]

In order to admit the reality of demons, Cesalpino's Aristotelian treatment had to embrace Plato, converting in a sort of alliance the disagreement between the two philosophers occasionally implied in *QP*. Cesalpino needed this also because, unlike Aristotle, Plato wrote quite extensively about demons. The best Cesalpino could say, when comparing the positions of the two philosophers, is that while Plato openly admitted the existence of demons, Aristotle never excluded them from the realm of natural things.[46] Therefore, to face this topic, Plato's authority and definitory terms were necessarily useful. Indeed, in *DIP* there are numerous direct references to Platonic dialogues, not filtered this time through Aristotle, and Plato is recognized as authoritative in the discussion of the issues at stake.

Yet these references to Plato throughout *DIP* are quite anodyne, and several of Plato's quotations are condensed in a single section. In it, Cesalpino first mentioned the intermediary nature of demons as described in the *Symposium* (202e–203a). He continued saying that among the different demons, one is Eros (*Symposium*, 203a), and that Plato said they were also divine shepherds of men (*Statesman*, 272e), and even wise and blessed men who have conversations with the divine (*Symposium*, 203a). Through a collage of quotes from the *Teages* (128d ff.), the *Apology of Socrates* (27c–d), and the *Cratylus* (397e ff.), Cesalpino then introduced the Socratic demon and the idea that demons are guardians of men. In the passage from the *Apology* to which Cesalpino referred, Socrates asked his accusants how it was possible that a man who proclaims the existence of demons could deny the existence of gods. Cesalpino appropriated this argument, a few lines below, *pro domo sua* and in a quite sophistical way: after listing all the mentions of demons he could find in the Aristotelian corpus, Cesalpino proclaimed that since Aristotle spoke of demons, he evidently believed in their existence, "as Socrates concluded."[47]

Plato's definition of demons as a "natura media," in any case, was easily reconcilable with the few scattered indications about demons left by Aristotle, for example in *On Divination in Sleep* (2.463b16), when he claimed that dreams are demonic, for nature is demonic and not divine.

Plato is quoted as a source also to compare his words with contemporary anecdotes about demonic interventions: at one point, discussing divine possessions, Cesalpino reports the case of a man "apud nos" who drew milk from the water of a river, referring to a passage in the *Ion* (534a), about "Bacchic maidens who draw milk and honey from the rivers when under the influence of Dionysus."[48] What Plato wrote in the same passage of the divine possession of the poets was indeed useful, according to Cesalpino, to understand not only that men could possess abilities not because of their mind and their art, but also how they could produce things that go beyond human strengths.

Even if it is worth mentioning that this very passage from the *Ion* was extensively quoted also by Pomponazzi in his *De incantationibus*,[49] precise references like this one may be helpful both to reconstruct Cesalpino's Platonic library and to understand how he read Plato. In terms of works, Cesalpino included in *DIP*—as seen—the *Ion*, the *Cratylus*, the *Symposium*, the *Teages*, the *Apology of Socrates*, the *Phaedrus*, and the *Statesman*. The wording of these quotations, which were for the most part paraphrased, suggests moreover that Cesalpino read these texts relying on Ficino's Latin translations. On the other hand, precisely because Cesalpino is quoting the traditional Platonic passages which were invoked in discussions of demonology, one could doubt if, again, he was using a "second-hand" Plato.

Cesalpino's *DIP* was published again with the *Quaestiones* in 1593, with some differences in its organization and order.[50] In this second edition, the sections in which Plato is mentioned were not internally modified (an exception being the removal from the second edition of the only reference to Hermes Trismegistus).[51] This seems to confirm the fact that Plato's quotations played after all in the economy of *DIP* a formal role, mostly useful to validate the Aristotelian perspective that Cesalpino discussed.

***

Unlike many *magistri* of his time, Cesalpino was not interested in establishing a dialogue between Plato and Aristotle, mostly because his non-exegetical but "productive" approach to Aristotelianism did not require that. Eager to remain within the boundaries of Aristotelianism, and to improve it on the basis of its own principles, Cesalpino simply accepted what Aristotle wrote of his teacher, avoiding a constant and direct engagement with Platonic texts. This explains why Cesalpino did not have to virulently attack Plato, even when criticizing him: he did not need to protect the authority of Aristotle and his philosophy, which in his perspective occupied by default the domineering position. Equally, the self-sufficiency of Aristotelianism explains why attempts at reconciling Plato and Aristotle, like those of Verino, were alien from Cesalpino's theoretical outlook. Yet, in Cesalpino's view, Plato could also work as a useful crutch for Aristotle, in subjects for which the *corpus Aristotelicum* needed further support. For this reason, when discussing demonology in *DIP*, Cesalpino strategically accepted a sort of essential agreement between the two philosophers, in order to enlarge the field of application of Aristotelianism while endorsing a position acceptable to religious orthodoxy. But even in this case Plato was for Cesalpino little more than a background actor, as it was appropriate for an investigation named "peripatetica."

Notes

1. On the Platonic chair see at least Simone Fellina, *Platone allo Studium Fiorentino-Pisano (1576–1635): l'insegnamento di Francesco de' Vieri, Jacopo Mazzoni, Carlo Tomasi, Cosimo Boscagli, Girolamo Bardi* (Verona: Scripta, 2019).
2. Aside from Fellina, *Platone allo Studium Fiorentino-Pisano (1576–1635)*, 24–7, on de' Vieri at the University of Pisa see Armando F. Verde, "Il 'Parere' del 1587 di Francesco Verino sullo Studio pisano," in *Firenze e la Toscana dei Medici nell'Europa del '500. Atti del Colloquio internazionale di Firenze, 9–14 giugno 1980* (Florence: Olschki, 1983), 1:71–94.
3. This is what was annotated on the frontispiece of an exemplar of Francesco De' Vieri, *Trattato della lode, dell'honore, della fama, et della gloria* (Florence: Marescotti, 1580), today at the Biblioteca Riccardiana, Florence (signature PPP 3985): "L'Autore è Peripatetico molto ma alla antica cioè insieme Platonico." See Paolo Pissavino, "L'altro sole di Francesco de' Vieri," in *Atti del Convegno internazionale di studi su Bernardino Telesio* (Cosenza: Accademia Cosentina, 1990), 207–20.
4. Charles B. Schmitt, "Girolamo Borro's *Multae sunt nostrarum ignorationum causae* (Ms. Vat. Ross. 1009)," in *Philosophy and Humanism: Renaissance Essays in Honor of Paul Oskar Kristeller*, ed. Edward P. Mahoney (Leiden: Brill, 1976), 462–76. On Borro's and Verino's salaries between 1576 and 1580 see Jonathan Davies, *Culture and Power: Tuscany and Its Universities 1537–1609* (Leiden: Brill, 2009), 252–7.
5. Francesco De' Vieri, *Vere conclusioni di Platone conformi alla dottrina Christiana et a quella di Aristotele* (Florence: Marescotti, 1589).
6. Several letters by Cesalpino to Baccio Valori, including this one, are contained in the MS Magliabechiano XIV 29 (II.V.169) at BNCF, and published in Ugo Viviani, *Il trattato sui Sapori inedito, dedicato a Baccio Valori ed il carteggio, in gran parte inedito, di Andrea Cesalpino con Baccio Valori, col Granduca di Toscana, con Bianca Cappello, con Belisario Vinta e con l'Albergotti, con l'aggiunta delle sue lettere dedicatorie, delle tre sue testimonianze sulla malattia e sull'esumazione di S. Filippo Neri e di una lettera di Giovambattista Cesalpino* (Arezzo: Bennati, 1916).
7. The passage is in de' Vieri, *Vere conclusioni*, 40–1.
8. Verino had indeed polemicized several times with Telesio and his followers in his writings, implicitly in the manuscript entitled *Conclusione del libro della natura dell'universo* (1576 ca.), BNCF, Magliabechiano XII. At fol. 41v, Verino made a reference to the same anti-Telesian dispute in presence of "*Signora Donna* Isabella Medici nelli Orsini and ... *Signora Donna* Leonora di Toledo ne' Medici," that he will mention in his letter to Valori, in 1590, and explicitly in the expanded version of de' Vieri, *Trattato delle metheore* (Florence: Marescotti, 1582), 227. On Verino and Telesio see Eugenio Garin, "Telesiani minori," *Rivista critica di storia della filosofia* 26 (1971): 199–204, at 202; Pissavino, "L'altro sole di Francesco de' Vieri." Laura Carotti, *Astri, fortuna, libero arbitrio: discussioni filosofiche tra '400 e '600* (Florence: Olschki, 2021),

22, suggests instead that Verino equated Cesalpino with the *Telesiani*. There actually exists an edition of the *Quaestiones peripateticae* published together with Telesio's *De rerum natura iuxta propria principia* (*Tractationum philosophicarum tomus unus: in quo continentur. I II III. Philippi Mocenici, Veneti, Universalium institutionum contemplationes ad hominum perfectionem, quatenus industria parari potest, contemplationes V Andreae Caesalpini, Aretini, Quaestionum peripateticarum libri V Bernardini Telesii, Consentini, De rerum natura iuxta propria principia libri IX: Opus multiplici eruditione refertum, ac literarum humanarum sacrarumque studiosis omnibus apprime necessarium: index, librorum omnium, summas et praecipua capita complectens, post praefationem adiectus est* ([Geneva]: Vignon, 1588)), yet the volume was aimed to present two radically opposed attitudes toward Aristotelianism, as expressly mentioned by the editor of the volume in his preface. Verino's letter to Valori is published in Verde, "Il 'Parere,'" 84–6.

9 Viviani, *Il trattato sui Sapori inedito*, 34.
10 Ibid., 35.
11 Verde, "Il 'Parere,'" 84–6.
12 Of a different opinion is Paola Zambelli, "Scienza, filosofia, religione nella Toscana di Cosimo I," in *Florence and Venice: Comparisons and Relations, Acts of Two Conferences at Villa I Tatti in 1976–1977*. 2 vols. (Florence: La Nuova Italia, 1979–80), 2:3–52. The chair was eventually reintroduced in 1591, the year Verino died. It has to be noted that, unlike Cesalpino, de' Vieri had some problems with the Inquisition because of prohibited books in his possessions. See Vincenzo Lavenia, "La medicina dei diavoli: il caso italiano, secoli XVI–XVII," in *Médecine et religion: compétitions, collaborations, conflits (XIIe–XXe siècles)*, ed. Maria Pia Donato, Luc Berlivet, Sara Cabibbo, Raimondo Michetti, and Marilyn Nicoud (Rome: École Française de Rome, 2013), 164–94, at 175.
13 See Eva Del Soldato, *Early Modern Aristotle: On the Making and Unmaking of Authority* (Philadelphia: University of Pennsylvania Press, 2020), 62; Eva Del Soldato, "Between Past and Present: Paganino Gaudenzi (1595–1649) and the *Comparatio* Tradition," in *Harmony and Contrast: Plato and Aristotle in the Early Modern Period*, ed. Anna Corrias and Eva Del Soldato (Oxford: Oxford University Press, 2022), 172–88; Maude Vanhaelen, "Teaching Plato in Sixteenth-Century Italy," in *Plato in the Italian Universities*, ed. Eva Del Soldato and Maude Vanhaelen (Turnhout: Brepols, forthcoming).
14 Maude Vanhaelen, "What Is the Best Method to Study Philosophy? Sebastiano Erizzo and the 'Revival' of Plato in Sixteenth-Century Venice," *Italian Studies* 71, no. 3 (2016): 311–34.
15 Del Soldato, *Early Modern Aristotle*, 54–68.
16 Craig Martin, "Interpreting Plato's Geometrical Elements in Renaissance Aristotle Commentaries," in *Harmony and Contrast*, 149–71.
17 Cesalpino, *QP* (1593), sig. A2r–v. On Cesalpino's approach to Aristotle, especially in the botanical context but also in the *Quaestiones*, see also the observations by Luciana Repici, "Andrea Cesalpino e la botanica antica," *Rinascimento* 45 (2005): 47–87, at 50. Repici also notes Cesalpino's hostility towards commentaries. More on this topic in Luciana Repici, "Aristotele e la generazione spontanea," *Antiquorum philosophia* 12 (2018): 77–89, at 85, where Cesalpino is defined as a "systematizer" and "reviser" of the Aristotelian thought.
18 A similar attitude characterized Cesalpino's teacher, Simone Porzio. See Eva Del Soldato, *Simone Porzio. Un aristotelico tra natura e grazia* (Rome: Edizioni di Storia e Letteratura, 2010).

19 Mark Jurdjevic, *Guardians of Republicanism: The Valori Family in the Florentine Renaissance* (Oxford: Oxford University Press, 2008), 61–2.
20 See Viviani, *Il trattato sui Sapori inedito*, 38–9: "Platone metteva per principio di tutte le cose l'unità e la dualità, intendendo per unità la forma, et per dualità la materia, sotto nome di grande et piccolo, come in più luoghi cita Aristotile. E questo meritatamente, perchè quello, che dà la perfezione in tutte le cose, è uno, et la forma dice questa unità. Ogni moltitudine dice imperfettione, et nasce dalla materia; per esser ella divisibile, et per esser la prima moltitudine dualità, sotto questo nome intende la materia."
21 Cesalpino, *QP* (1593), fol. 28r: "Idcirco Plato sub nomine dualitatis materiam intelligebat, cum ex uno et dualitate fieri dicebat omnia quae fiunt. Idque recta ratione, a forma enim unitas ubique provenit, a materia autem multitudo et divisio."
22 Ibid., fol. 79v: "Et Plato magnum et parvum principia esse voluit."
23 Cesalpino, *QP* (1593), sig. A1r-v: "Hac de causa illud effectum est, ut cum tot seculis philosophi innumeri … in perquirenda veritate laboraverint, optatam tamen metam interdum non attigerint. Quibus tamen ob id maxime habendae a nobis sunt gratiae, quod a se inventa cum posteris tradiderint ad ulteriora perscrutanda iter facilius reddiderunt. Si enim non fuisset Democritus, Empedocles, Anaxagoras, aliique multi, et tandem Plato, non fuisset Aristoteles, quo duce philosophia ad dignitatis summum fastigium pervenisse videtur …"
24 Ibid., fol. 16v: "Unicam differentiam etiam si ultima fuerit, non sufficere ad ipsum quid est explicandum."
25 Ibid., fol. 20v.
26 The *quaestio* is recalled in Cesalpino, *DP*, 27.
27 On these debates and the originality of Cesalpino's solution see Kristian Jansen, "Description, Division, Definition. Caesalpinus and the Study of Plants as an Independent Discipline," in *Renaissance Readings of the Corpus Aristotelicum. Papers from the Conference Held in Copenhagen 23–25 April 1998*, ed. Marianne Pade (Copenhagen: Museum Tusculanum, 2001), 185–206; Ian Maclean, "White Crows, Graying Hair, and Eyelashes: Problems for Natural Historians in the Reception of Aristotelian Logic and Biology from Pomponazzi to Bacon," in *Historia: Empiricism and Erudition in Early Modern Europe*, ed. Gianna Pomata and Nancy G. Siraisi (Cambridge, MA: The MIT Press, 2005), 147–79.
28 Cesalpino, *QP* (1593), fol. 16v, but also fols. 18v, 19v.
29 Ibid., fol. 16v: "Putaverunt enim illud Aristotelem concludere tanquam verum ex veris, non tanquam absurdum ex pravo definiendi modo secundum divisionem, ut Plato faciebat."
30 Ibid., fol. 17v.
31 Ibid., fol. 33r: "*Caeli circulationem imitationem esse intelligentiae.*"
32 Ibid., fol. 45v.
33 Ibid., fol. 115r.
34 Possible tensions appear in the *Questionum medicarum libri duo*, fol. 226r-v, in which Cesalpino suggested a relationship between vegetative functions and the sense of touch. This position situated in an Aristotelian framework a doctrine Cesalpino found in Galen, and that Galen recovered from Plato's *Timaeus*, 77b. This confirms, again, that Cesalpino's references to Platonic doctrines were not founded on Plato's works themselves. On the relationship between digestion and touch in Cesalpino see Guido Giglioni, "Plantanimal Imagination: Life and Perception in Early Modern Discussions of Vegetative Power," in *Vegetative Powers: The Roots of Life in Ancient,*

Medieval and Early Modern Natural Philosophy, ed. Fabrizio Baldassarri and Andreas Blank (Cham: Springer, 2021), 325–45, at 331–3.

35 See, for example, Galen, *Opera omnia*, ed. Karl Gottlob Kühn. 20 vols. (Leipzig: Karl Knobloch, 1821–33), 4: 782. On the topic see Dag Nikolaus Hasse, "Plato arabico-latinus. Philosophy, Wisdom Literature, Occult Sciences," in *The Platonic Tradition in the Middle Ages: A Doxographic Approach*, ed. Stephen Gersh and Maarten J. F. M. Hoenen (Berlin and New York: De Gruyter, 2002), 31–66, at 40–2.

36 Cesalpino, *QP* (1593), fol. 116v: "Putavit [Galenus] enim Platonem insequutus triplicem esse animae principatum non solum facultatibus, sed et locis distinctum." See also note 34 above on Galen as a source of Platonic doctrines for Cesalpino.

37 I found only one explicit mention of Marsilio Ficino in Cesalpino's *opera*, in *De metallicis libri tres* (Rome: Zannetti, 1596), 172, with reference to Ficino's *argumentum* to the *Critias*.

38 Francesco De' Vieri, *Discorso intorno a' dimonii, volgarmente chiamati spiriti* (Florence: Sermartelli, 1576). The original Latin version is the MS Riccardiano 1223, Biblioteca Riccardiana, Florence. Some analogies between de' Vieri's work and Cesalpino's are noted by Carotti, *Astri, fortuna, libero arbitrio*, 24. On the two works see again Zambelli, "Scienza, filosofia, religione"; Lavenia, "La medicina dei diavoli."

39 "Et si quid Divinum in morbis habetur, illiusque quoque ediscere providentiam" ("if there is anything divine about the disease, the doctor should know how to prognosticate it too,") translation in Jacques Jouanna, "Hippocrates and the Sacred," in *Greek Medicine from Hippocrates to Galen: Selected Papers* (Leiden: Brill, 2012), 97–118, at 109. The sentence is present in almost all the Greek manuscripts but is today widely considered an interpolation (see Hippocrates, *Prognostic. Regimen in Acute Diseases. The Sacred Disease. The Art. Breaths. Law. Decorum. Physician (Ch. 1). Dentition*, trans. W. H. S. Jones (Cambridge, MA: Harvard University Press, 1923), 8). The emphasis on the Hippocrates' *Prognostic* disappeared from the frontispiece of the second edition of *DIP* printed in 1593. See *DIP* 1593, fol. 145r.

40 Ibid., fol. 145v.

41 Galen, *Opera omnia*, 4: 767–822. On the debates around the Hippocratic passage see Jouanna, "Hippocrates and the Sacred."

42 Cesalpino, *DIP* (1593), fol. 146v: "In homine igitur contineri partem divinam, quae mens appellatur immortalem substantiam extrinsecus innascentem a materia separatam, cui propria est operatio non communicans cum operatione corporis, demonstratum est ab Aristotele, eandem concessit Plato, et omnes ferme philosophi praestantiores."

43 More precisely, Pomponazzi (I quote from the first printed edition, Pietro Pomponazzi, *De naturalium effectuum causis, sive de incantationibus* (Basel: Petri, 1556), 217–18, 327) suggested that Plato would have said to approve of the existence of demons only to teach ignorant men. See also note 44 below.

44 For Pomponazzi's perplexity about the harmony of Plato and Aristotle, see Pomponazzi, *De incantationibus*, 218. Pomponazzi suggested that maybe Plato did not believe in the immortality of the soul in Pietro Pomponazzi, *Apologia* (Bologna: Rubiera, 1518), fol. 22r.

45 See, for example, Cesalpino, *DIP* (1593), fol. 152v: "Testatur et Plato haec et caetera huiusmodi, quo pacto natura se habeant, nec facile sciri posse, nec si quis sciat aliis persuderi. Quod igitur mirum si Aristoteles ob praedictas causas disputationem huiusmodi praetermiserit? Nobis autem ac caeteris omnibus Christianam fidem sequentibus gratiae prae caeteris Deo optimo maximo habendae sunt, quod divina

quadam sorte datum est ea nosse, in quibus tot Philosophi propriis viribus nixi veluti balbutientes haesitarunt. Quae enim humanum ingenium attingere nunquam potuisset revelata nobis sunt in sacra Theologia, et quae in ea minus aperta erant, explicata sunt a doctissimis ac lucidissimis romanae ecclesiae doctoribus."

46 The quotation is from the dedication letter to Giovanni de' Tonsi, Knight of Saint Stephen, which appears only in the first edition (Cesalpino, *DIP* (1580), fol. [3v]: "Daemones qui apertissime a Platone conceduntur, et ab Aristotele nequaquam excluduntur e rerum natura.")

47 Cesalpino, *DIP* (1593), fol. 151r–v and Cesalpino, *DIP* (1580), fol. 7r–v. Also de' Vieri, *Discorso intorno a' dimonii*, 14v, claimed that Aristotle did not deny the existence of demons because he mentioned them in some of his writings.

48 Cesalpino, *DIP* (1593), fol. 159r and Cesalpino, *DIP* (1580), fol. 15r.

49 Pomponazzi, *De incantationibus*, 136–7.

50 The differences are indeed mostly formal, even if Mark E. Clark and Kirk M. Summers, "Hippocratic Medicine and Aristotelian Science in the *Daemonum investigatio peripatetica* of Andrea Cesalpino," *Bulletin of the History of Medicine* 69, no. 4 (1995): 527–41, suggest otherwise.

51 See Cesalpino, *DIP* (1580), fol. 7v. One could speculate if the removal of the reference to Hermes Trismegistus was connected to the hostility against *prisca sapientia* that was shared by many members of the Roman curia in the wake of the Patrizi affair. Yet, in the same 1593 edition, Trismegistus's name was not removed from the dedication letter to *QP*, addressed to Francesco de' Medici. See Cesalpino, *QP* (1593), sig. †iiir.

Bibliography

Manuscripts

MS Magliabechiano XII 11, Biblioteca Nazionale Centrale Firenze, Florence.
MS Magliabechiano XIV 29 (II.V.169), Biblioteca Nazionale Centrale Firenze, Florence.
MS Riccardiano 1223, Biblioteca Riccardiana, Florence.

Primary Sources

Aristotle. *The Complete Works of Aristotle*, edited by Jonathan Barnes. 2 vols. Princeton: Princeton University Press, 1984.
Cesalpino, Andrea. *Daemonum investigatio peripatetica. In qua explicatur locus Hippocratis in Prognosticis si quid divinum in morbis habetur*. Florence: Giunta, 1580.
Cesalpino, Andrea. *Daemonum investigatio peripatetica*. Venice: Giunta, 1593.
Cesalpino, Andrea. *De metallicis libri tres*. Rome: Zannetti, 1596.
Cesalpino, Andrea. *Quaestionum peripateticarum libri quinque*. Venice: Giunta, 1593.
Galen. *Opera omnia*, edited by Karl Gottlob Kühn. 20 vols. Leipzig: Karl Knobloch, 1821–33.
Hippocrates. *Prognostic. Regimen in Acute Diseases. The Sacred Disease. The Art. Breaths. Law. Decorum. Physician (Ch. 1). Dentition*, translated by W. H. S. Jones. Cambridge, MA: Harvard University Press, 1923.
Pomponazzi, Pietro. *Apologia*. Bologna: Rubiera, 1518.
Pomponazzi, Pietro. *De naturalium effectuum causis, sive de incantationibus*. Basel: Petri, 1556.

Vieri, Francesco de'. *Discorso intorno a' dimonii, volgarmente chiamati spiriti*. Florence: Sermartelli, 1576.
Vieri, Francesco de'. *Trattato della lode, dell'honore, della fama, et della gloria*. Florence: Marescotti, 1580.
Vieri, Francesco de'. *Trattato delle metheore*. Florence: Marescotti, 1582.
Vieri, Francesco de'. *Vere conclusioni di Platone conformi alla dottrina Christiana et a quella di Aristotele*. Florence: Marescotti, 1589.

Secondary Sources

Carotti, Laura. *Astri, fortuna, libero arbitrio: discussioni filosofiche tra '400 e '600*. Florence: Olschki, 2021.
Clark, Mark E., and Kirk M. Summers. "Hippocratic Medicine and Aristotelian Science in the *Daemonum investigatio peripatetica* of Andrea Cesalpino." *Bulletin of the History of Medicine* 69, no. 4 (1995): 527–41.
Davies, Jonathan. *Culture and Power: Tuscany and Its Universities 1537–1609*. Leiden: Brill, 2009.
Del Soldato, Eva. "Between Past and Present: Paganino Gaudenzi (1595–1649) and the comparatio Tradition." In *Harmony and Contrast: Plato and Aristotle in the Early Modern Period*, edited by Anna Corrias and Eva Del Soldato, 172–88. Oxford: Oxford University Press, 2022.
Del Soldato, Eva. *Early Modern Aristotle: On the Making and Unmaking of Authority*. Philadelphia: University of Pennsylvania Press, 2020.
Del Soldato, Eva. *Simone Porzio. Un aristotelico tra natura e grazia*. Rome: Edizioni di storia e letteratura, 2010.
Fellina, Simone. *Platone allo Studium Fiorentino-Pisano (1576–1635): l'insegnamento di Francesco de' Vieri, Jacopo Mazzoni, Carlo Tomasi, Cosimo Boscagli, Girolamo Bardi*. Verona: Scripta, 2019.
Garin, Eugenio. "Telesiani minori." *Rivista critica di storia della filosofia* 26 (1971): 199–204.
Giglioni, Guido. "Plantanimal Imagination: Life and Perception in Early Modern Discussions of Vegetative Power." In *Vegetative Powers: The Roots of Life in Ancient, Medieval and Early Modern Natural Philosophy*, edited by Fabrizio Baldassarri and Andreas Blank, 325–45. Cham: Springer, 2021.
Hasse, Dag Nikolaus. "Plato arabico-latinus. Philosophy, Wisdom Literature, Occult Sciences." In *The Platonic Tradition in the Middle Ages: A Doxographic Approach*, edited by Stephen Gersh and Maarten J. F. M. Hoenen, 31–66. Berlin: De Gruyter, 2002.
Jensen, Kristian. "Description, Division, Definition—Caesalpinus and the Study of Plants as an Independent Discipline." In *Renaissance Reading of the Corpus aristotelicum*, edited by Marianne Pade, 185–206. Copenhagen: Museum Tusculanum Press, 2000.
Jouanna, Jacques. "Hippocrates and the Sacred." In *Greek Medicine from Hippocrates to Galen: Selected Papers*, 97–118. Leiden: Brill, 2012.
Jurdjevic, Mark. *Guardians of Republicanism: The Valori Family in the Florentine Renaissance*. Oxford: Oxford University Press, 2008.
Lavenia, Vincenzo. "La medicina dei diavoli: il caso italiano, secoli XVI-XVII." In *Médecine et religion: compétitions, collaborations, conflits (XIIe-XXe siècles)*, edited by Maria Pia Donato, Luc Berlivet, Sara Cabibbo, Raimondo Michetti, and Marilyn Nicoud, 164–94. Rome: École Française de Rome, 2013.

Maclean, Ian. "White Crows, Graying Hair, and Eyelashes: Problems for Natural Historians in the Reception of Aristotelian Logic and Biology from Pomponazzi to Bacon." In *Historia: Empiricism and Erudition in Early Modern Europe*, edited by Gianna Pomata and Nancy G. Siraisi, 147–79. Cambridge, MA, and London: The MIT Press, 2005.

Martin, Craig. "Interpreting Plato's Geometrical Elements in Renaissance Aristotle Commentaries." In *Harmony and Contrast*, edited by Anna Corrias and Eva Del Soldato, 149–71. Oxford: Oxford University Press, 2022.

Pissavino, Paolo. "L'altro sole di Francesco de' Vieri." In *Atti del Convegno internazionale di studi su Bernardino Telesio*, 207–20. Cosenza: Accademia Cosentina, 1990.

Repici, Luciana. "Aristotele e la generazione spontanea." *Antiquorum philosophia* 12 (2018): 77–89.

Repici, Luciana. "Cesalpino e la botanica antica." *Rinascimento* 45 (2005): 47–87.

Schmitt, Charles B. "Girolamo Borro's *Multae sunt nostrarum ignorationum causae* (Ms. Vat. Ross. 1009)." In *Philosophy and Humanism: Renaissance Essays in Honor of Paul Oskar Kristeller*, edited by Edward P. Mahoney, 462–76. Leiden: Brill, 1976.

Vanhaelen, Maude. "Teaching Plato in Sixteenth-Century Italy." In *Plato in the Italian Universities*, edited by Eva Del Soldato and Maude Vanhaelen. Turnhout: Brepols, forthcoming.

Vanhaelen, Maude. "What Is the Best Method to Study Philosophy? Sebastiano Erizzo and the 'Revival' of Plato in Sixteenth-Century Venice." *Italian Studies* 71, no. 3 (2016): 311–34.

Verde, Armando F. "Il 'Parere' del 1587 di Francesco Verino sullo Studio pisano." In *Firenze e la Toscana dei Medici nell'Europa del '500. Atti del Colloquio internazionale di Firenze, 9–14 giugno 1980*, 2 vols., 1: 71–94. Florence: Olschki, 1983.

Viviani, Ugo. *Il trattato sui Sapori inedito, dedicato a Baccio Valori ed il carteggio, in gran parte inedito, di Andrea Cesalpino con Baccio Valori, col Granduca di Toscana, con Bianca Cappello, con Belisario Vinta e con l'Albergotti, con l'aggiunta delle sue lettere dedicatorie, delle tre sue testimonianze sulla malattia e sull'esumazione di S. Filippo Neri e di una lettera di Giovambattista Cesalpino*. Arezzo: Bennati, 1916.

Zambelli, Paola. "Scienza, filosofia, religione nella Toscana di Cosimo I." In *Florence and Venice: Comparisons and Relations, Acts of Two Conferences at Villa I Tatti in 1976–1977*, 2 vols., 2: 3–52. Florence: La Nuova Italia, 1979–80.

5

Cesalpino on Sensitive Powers and the Question of Divine Immanence

Andreas Blank

The origin of sensitive powers was one of the many issues in Cesalpino's natural philosophy that the Altdorf-based physician and natural philosopher Nicolaus Taurellus (1547–1606) criticized in his *Alpes caesae* (1597).[1] Apart from many concerns concerning physiological details, Taurellus argued that Cesalpino's account of the role of vital heat in the framework of a cardiocentric physiology of sensation has theological implications that could be incompatible with the Christian doctrine of creation. In particular, Taurellus objected to what he understood to be Cesalpino's conception of the divine intellect inherent in animate beings, both individuals living beings and the universe as a whole. On first sight, one may conjecture that Taurellus's theological concerns rested on a misinterpretation of Cesalpino's natural philosophy. In Cesalpino's *Quaestiones peripateticae* (1571 and 1593) and *Daemonum investigatio peripatetica* (1580 and 1593), the relation between the causal role of vital heat in producing sensation and the causal role of the divine intellect in functioning as the first origin of motion is characterized as an analogy. Did Taurellus simply mistake a claim about an analogy relation for a claim about an inherence relation?

The question, of course, is what grounds the analogy relation to which Cesalpino was undoubtedly committed. Is it a mere (rather loose) similarity between causal functions of different entities? Or is it the conjecture that the same entity that is responsible for the first origin of motion is also responsible for the origin of sensation in animate beings? Taurellus's interpretation may draw attention to aspects of Cesalpino's natural philosophy that have not found much attention from commentators. One aspect is Cesalpino's account of divine self-reflection as a principle of final causation inherent in animals. This account does not reduce to the stipulation of a causal relation between the divine intellect and the striving found in animals; rather, Cesalpino's view that the divine intellect at the same time is the object desired and the entity that desires itself points toward a sense in which some divine activity can be said to be operative in animals. The other aspect is Cesalpino's account of divine self-reflection as a principle of final causation inhering in the heavens.

I will proceed as follows. First, I will show that Taurellus's theological objection is directed at one of Cesalpino's arguments for cardiocentric physiology. Then I will argue that the use of analogical reasoning in *Daemonum investigatio peripatetica* leaves room for asking whether Taurellus has seen something significant. Subsequently, I will argue that the role that Cesalpino assigns in *Quaestiones peripateticae* to final causation in the origin of the vegetative and sensitive powers of living beings goes beyond the limits of analogical reasoning. Finally, I will argue that the same holds for Cesalpino's account of how a single divine intellect animates the universe by animating the heavens.

1. Sensitive Powers and Cardiocentric Physiology

Cardiocentric physiology is built around the claim that the heart is the principal organ in sanguineous animals, in the sense that the proper functioning of other organs depends on some causal influence deriving from the heart, while the heart can continue to function well without an influence of the same kind deriving from other organs. One might conjecture that Cesalpino's version of cardiocentric physiology is connected with his views concerning the circulation of the blood.[2] However, as Andrew Cunningham has pointed out, Realdo Colombo (c. 1516–59), whose discovery of the pulmonary circulation Cesalpino took up, maintained that the brain, not the heart, is the principal organ.[3] Thus, the question of the principal organ was quite independent from specific views concerning the circulation of the blood. Rather, it involved questions concerning the causal role of theoretical entities such as vital heat in nutrition, growth, and sensation.

To argue for cardiocentric physiology, Cesalpino took up several strands of thought from Aristotle. One of them is the argument that, because nutrition is due to the element of fire, and the heart is the origin of heat, the heart is the first organ to be nourished.[4] Another strand is the argument that, because blood is the ultimate aliment, and in the development of the fetus appears for the first time in the heart, the heart is the organ from which the nutrition and augmentation of other body parts originate.[5] Cesalpino also adopted Aristotle's view that, in sanguineous animals, there is no sensation in any part that lacks blood.[6] Like Aristotle, he explained this through the view that the sensitive soul is one actually and belongs to one part primarily[7] because otherwise the sensitive soul could not judge the difference between several senses.[8]

Going beyond Aristotle, Cesalpino developed a series of arguments of his own to support cardiocentric physiology. For present purposes, it will suffice to focus on the argument that triggered Taurellus's objection that Cesalpino's version of cardiocentric physiology leads to unacceptable theological consequences—the argument from the possibility of dividing lower animals into parts that all have vegetative and sensitive powers. Cesalpino argued that "animals that are less distinct, have a closer union of these vessels: this is why it happens that they can stay alive for some while, for they do not have distinct principles but rather principles that are diffused throughout the vessels."[9] Cesalpino maintained that some lower animals can be divided such that the separated parts have the same vegetative and sensitive powers as the whole animal. For example, if a worm is cut into pieces, all the vegetative and sensitive powers of the soul can be observed in each part that were observable in the whole, "as if they were inseparable from each other."[10] Cesalpino remarked that the persistence of the vegetative and sensitive powers of the entire animal in the separated parts also indicates an answer to the question of "how the eternal and the mortal are numerically one."[11] As he argued, from the experiences such as the division of a worm "it follows that in all bodies, together with a material form, there inheres an immaterial form."[12] And finally, he conjectured that this could be the sense of Thales' saying (reported by Aristotle) that everything is full of Gods.[13]

Cesalpino's reasoning is certainly puzzling because it leaves out any of the intermediary steps that could have led him from observations about the persistence of sensitive powers in separate worm parts to the divine nature of an immaterial form inherent in bodies. Some, but not all these steps could be filled in by considering how he takes up and modifies the late scholastic theory of sensible species. The question that the theory was meant to answer is how sensible qualities can be represented (in different material media and in the states of the sensitive soul) without carrying the material substrate with them.[14] There was a strong tendency to understand sensible species as immaterial entities that are capable of travelling through matter, thereby making their mode of transmission enigmatic; but there were also attempts at understanding them as modifications of material substrates (such as changes in shape and motion).[15] Cesalpino distinguished material species inherent in the sensory organs from immaterial sensible species that allow the common sense to compare the impressions of the different senses. As he puts it, "in an organ and a body, a species is received with quantity and divisibly, which is why it turns out that at the same time the same part of the body cannot sense contraries, such as light and darkness, heat and coldness."[16] Since we can observe in ourselves the ability to judge contrary sensible qualities, it is necessary to presuppose the existence of an entity that itself is indivisible.[17] The role of immaterial sensible species for the workings of the common sense would explain why Cesalpino held that the persistence of sensitive powers in separated worm parts indicates the presence of an immaterial form in each part.

Still, it remains enigmatic why Cesalpino connected the idea of an immaterial form in sensitive beings with Thales' saying that "everything is full of Gods." The lack of argumentative connection at this place could indicate that what Cesalpino had in mind is merely analogical or metaphorical. This, however, is not how Taurellus understood the passage. Taurellus commented: "I wonder about Cesalpino's imprudence: ... What others have with the best judgement distinguished—God and nature—he dared to confuse."[18] For Taurellus, this is by no means a side issue because, in his preface to *Alpes caesae*, he makes clear that the main motivation of his critique of Cesalpino derives from theological concerns. In Taurellus's view, what is problematic about Cesalpino's physiology of sensation is that it implies that God is not separated from matter and, hence, is not understood as an efficient cause of things; rather, God is understood as their constitutive cause (*rerum causa constituens*).[19] As Taurellus maintains later in the text, Cesalpino's view amounts to nothing other than "to confuse the substance of God and of all other things in such a way that each thing in some respect is said to be God himself."[20] Did Taurellus simply misunderstand Cesalpino?

2. Vital Heat and Analogical Reasoning in *Daemonum investigatio peripatetica*

On first sight, some aspects of the treatment of vital heat in Cesalpino's *Daemonum investigatio peripatetica* could point in that direction.[21] Cesalpino there discussed vital heat in the context of his discussion of the sense in which fever could be regarded to be something divine. In this context, he referred to Aristotle's view that the heat of the fertile seed is not fiery but stands in an analogy to the heavenly bodies.[22] Understanding talk about what is divine in fever from the perspective of this analogy may suggest that what Cesalpino has in mind is nothing other than an analogy between the causal role of vital heat in the production of fever and the role of the divine being in celestial causation. But consider how Cesalpino explained the analogy:

> Vital heat is a body that is more divine than elements, although it is constituted by them; and rightly it corresponds to the element of the stars not only with respect to the fecundity, which it possesses from the intelligence that is contained in it, but also with respect to the immortality and purity of the subject.[23]

My conjecture is that the "subject" mentioned Cesalpino is prime matter. This is suggested when he claims that sublunar bodies have an "eternal corporeal nature"—which cannot refer to the concrete material objects (that is, "secondary matter") that undergo change, generation, and corruption.[24] If so, then one of the analogies that Cesalpino had in mind is the analogy between the Aristotelian conception of the eternity of prime matter and the Aristotelian conception of the eternity of heavenly matter. But there is an aspect that goes beyond the limits of analogical reasoning. Cesalpino connected his conception of prime matter with Aristotle's view that, in all natural things, there inheres beauty.[25] As he explained:

> "Beautiful" is said with respect to the goal for whose sake nature acts, and whose origin is said to derive from the heavens. For this divine being that is eternal is by its nature always the cause of the best condition in contingent things. But that the first body that receives this divinity is prime matter, is evident from this: It is something that by its own nature strives for what is divine, good and desirable.[26]

Hence, in Cesalpino's view both the source of the striving characteristic for prime matter and its object are described as being divine. And the same holds of the nature of prime matter itself: "What flows without motion and change from the divine essence is also something divine and immortal."[27]

There is a further aspect of analogical thought in Cesalpino's discussion of vital heat. The comparative use of "being more divine" suggests that vital heat should not be regarded to be something divine without qualification. One important qualification results from the consideration that vital heat is described as being constituted by elements, which implies that there is a corporeal aspect to vital heat. In this respect, vital heat differs from the divine intelligence, which is described as being indivisible and devoid of extension.[28] But, again, there is an aspect that seems to go beyond the limits of analogical reasoning. The causal powers of vital heat are described in a way that suggests that it cannot be reduced to the causal powers of elements and their composition. As Cesalpino put it, "because in the spirit or innate heat the animal power inheres actually, not in fire nor in other elements, this body is called 'more divine': for it actually receives the power of the divine intelligence."[29] What is more, the reception of a power from the divine intelligence does not seem to reduce to a causal influence. Otherwise, it could not be explained why Cesalpino speaks of the fecundity that vital heat "possesses from the intelligence *that is contained in it.*" Evidently, the containment relation goes beyond a causal relation, even though the nature of containment of the divine intelligence in vital heat is not further spelled out here. If so, then the analogy between the powers of vital heat and the powers of divine intelligence may be grounded in the presence of divine intelligence in vital heat.

3. Sensitive Powers and the Origin of Substantiality in *Quaestiones peripateticae*

Of course, the passages from *Daemonum investigatio peripatetica* are puzzling. But they leave room for asking whether Taurellus may have been right when he ascribed a conception of divine immanence to Cesalpino. And Cesalpino seems to have been aware that more needed to be said. Immediately after the cited passages, he referred the reader to his account of the origin of multiplicity from the unity of the divine being developed in *Quaestiones peripateticae*.[30] Apparently, he did not think that there is a tension between these two works but rather wanted them to be read in conjunction. In fact, the latter work offered a much more detailed discussion of the sense in which the divine intellect could be understood to be contained in vital heat.

It will be useful to start with the interpretation that Taurellus gave of Cesalpino's views concerning the origin of multiplicity. Taurellus presented the following summary:

> Because Aristotle taught that all the multitude of things arise from matter, Cesalpino has put down this great doctrine, namely, that there is a unique incorporeal substance. Because he neither wanted to make souls corporeal nor to admit their multitude, he maintained that they are parts of a unique incorporeal substance and stand in relation to multitude only with respect to their underlying matter.[31]

Such a reading could be supported by Cesalpino's view that the different ways in which things are distinguished from each other depend on the different ways in which things "participate in being," that is, on the different ways in which things "descend from a unique substance."[32] However, Cesalpino was faced with the problem of specifying how the divine intellect could animate less perfect beings without thereby making the life of less perfect beings its final cause—the perfection of the divine intellect implies that it is the goal of everything but does not exist for the sake of anything.[33] To provide a solution, Cesalpino invoked Aristotle's conception of divine self-reflection. As Cesalpino noted, for Aristotle the divine intellect's understanding "is a substance, for it is identical with what is understood, and it is the understanding of the understanding."[34] As Cesalpino argued, self-reflection leads the divine intellect to think everything that can be thought—hence, also to think of the multiplicity of possible substances that the divine intellect could animate.[35] At the same time, because self-reflective thought originates from the divine intellect and has only the contents of the divine intellect as its object, it does not detract anything from the perfection of the divine being "in so far as it is the most perfect being, it distributes being to all others and confers perfection upon them; but in so far as it is understanding, it confers upon things the desire for perfection."[36]

How could the relation between the divine being and the desire for perfection found in natural objects be characterized? Cesalpino wrote about divine, "speculative" intellect:

> The speculative intellect ... is a substance that persists by itself, and is desirable not for the sake of any further being; it imparts perfection to those beings that by their nature are capable of desiring, and it does so not by acting in some way, or by introducing something into matter ..., but rather by educing through its presence that form for which matter has an aptitude by its nature.[37]

In this passage, Cesalpino distinguishes two ways of thinking about the relation between the divine intellect and the natural world. One way of thinking invokes the idea that God acts upon things that are external to the divine being. A special case of such action would involve introducing one natural object into another natural object (which are both external to God). Another way of thinking starts from the hypothesis of divine presence in natural objects and asks about the consequences that this presence has. Clearly, Cesalpino adopted the second way of thinking. As he put it: "Separate elements ... do not contain actually this divine being, but only potentially, but mixtures contain it actually, and, for this reason, they are actually substances."[38] The relation of a divine being to mixtures here is characterized as a relation of being-contained-in, which confirms that what Cesalpino has in mind is not only a causal relation between a divine being and powers of the mixture but also a relation of inherence.

Interestingly, the causal role of a divine being that is actually present in the mixture that constitutes the body of a living being is described in terms of a concept widely used in early modern natural philosophy: the concept of *eductio*. This concept is built around the idea that complex material composites possess causal power that cannot be reduced to the causal powers of their constituents and the composition of these constituents.[39] In contrast to other non-reductionist natural philosophers, Cesalpino does not believe that the occurrence of new causal powers is a basic feature of complex material composites that cannot be explained further; rather, he explains the occurrence of such new powers through the presence of the divine intelligence in living beings. Living beings thereby possess properties that are not the properties of the divine intelligence. In this sense, it is informative to speak of an analogy between the substance of living beings and the substance of the divine intelligence. At the same time, the striving for perfection found in living is identical with the striving characteristic of the divine intelligence. This is why living beings are substances only because they depend upon the substance of the divine intelligence.

Taken together, these passages suggest the view that a single divine intellect can be the origin of a multiplicity of natural powers not only because the divine intellect, through self-reflection, comprises an infinite complexity of thoughts, but also because, by animating material composites, the divine intellect brings forth new causal powers that cannot be reduced to the powers of elements. For this reason, Cesalpino held that there is more than one sense in which unity is the origin of multiplicity:

> From what has been said it is clear how a single intelligence contains all the acts of understanding things, for it is like the measure of all things. However, it is evident that things relate to each other as acts of understanding do; hence, it is not impossible that a multiplicity arises from the one. This also becomes clear from the reduction of entities to the one and from the way in which the kinds of substances are described according to addition and subtraction ... Hence, insofar as it is simply and as it is described with respect to the subtraction of all matter, there is a unique and simple substance.[40]

Thus, one sense in which multiplicity arises from the one has to with the dependence of things on the divine understanding. A plurality of things comes about because there is a plurality of divine acts of understanding, to which the things correspond. Another sense in which multiplicity arises from the one has to do with the role of matter in bringing about plurality. This is the sense in which Cesalpino spoke of "addition" and "subtraction": "adding" matter to the single incorporeal substance leads to a plurality of natural beings, "subtracting" matter from the plurality of natural beings leads to the single incorporeal substance. But if living beings are nothing but the divine intellect to which matter is added, then the active principle that brings about vegetative and sensitive powers cannot be anything other than the divine intellect. If so, then divine self-reflection itself is understood as a principle of goal-directed activity inherent in living beings.

4. Sensitive Powers and the Animation of the Universe in *Quaestiones peripateticae*

The same conception of divine immanence can be found in Cesalpino's account of the animation of the universe. As Cesalpino believed, "it is reasonable to assume that the universe is animate, if the heaven is animate ... for in animals, the soul is not necessarily in the whole body, but it suffices that it is in a principal part such as the heart."[41] Accordingly, "the universe is something organic, for it consists of similar parts that are in a certain way prepared to carry out some action, but the nature of organs arises only from the soul, for this is the being of the soul."[42] Taurellus was very much aware of this analogy and ascribed to Cesalpino the claim that the first mover is "a constitutive part of the heavens" (*coeli pars constituens*).[43] This reading is closely connected to Taurellus's already mentioned reading that, for Cesalpino, God is a "constitutive cause of things."[44]

The analogy between the animation of the universe through the animation of the heavens and the animation of the body through the animation of the heart plays a central role. Cesalpino's analogy between how the divine intellect animates the universe by animating the heavens and how vital heat animates animals by animating their heart was meant to specify the sense in which a single divine intellect can be the origin of animation for a multiplicity of heavenly bodies (and thus to offer an alternative to the Aristotelian theory of a plurality of movers of heavenly bodies). This is how he explained why it is not necessary to multiply intelligences:

> It is ... as if we hold that the soul had many parts because it confers the power of sensation to many parts while, by itself, it is one and resides indivisibly in the heart, as Aristotle maintained. But that intelligences are many in this sense is not repugnant to the unity and simplicity of intelligence that we advocate. For as the same soul is called vision in the eye but hearing in the ear, so can the same intelligence, in so far as it moves the moon, be ascribed to the moon, in so far as it moves Saturn, be ascribed to Saturn, and so on.[45]

According to this analogy, to animate the universe, the divine intelligence need not be present to all parts of the universe. It suffices that the divine intelligence be present to the heavens, which corresponds to the principal organ in sanguineous animals, as long as it is capable of bringing forth causal powers also in regions of the universe where it is not present. Cesalpino develops the analogy further by ascribing to final causation a role in the animation of the universe that is closely similar to the role that he ascribed to final causation in the animation of living beings. As he maintained, in order to be moved by final causation, the heavenly bodies must have the power of striving for the highest good since "what is loved, moves the heavenly bodies, but they could not desire and love it unless they understand the good itself."[46] Cesalpino's suggestion seems to be that the divine intellect does not bring forth any separate act of understanding in an animate substance. Presumably, such an act of understanding would be diminished in perfection due to the matter constitutive of the individual. This, however, is not what Cesalpino assumed to take place. Rather, he held that "the highest and optimal good, which in the highest degree exists only as a single being, fills out everything with the desire for it, and what is simply good is good for each being taken individually without any contamination through matter or diminution of any essence."[47] If no diminution of essence takes place, it seems most plausible to assume that the understanding that underlies the striving of heavenly bodies is nothing other than the understanding of the divine intelligence. This reading is supported by how Cesalpino developed the analogy between the animation of living beings and the animation of the universe:

> To think that what is moved and what desires and what understands is the same and in the same respect would be foolish, for even in animals, these do not happen with respect to the same part. Motion is perfected through the nerves and the

joints; the appetite is located in the heart or its analogue; the power of sensation is located in the sensory organs, while the power of the mind is separate. Something similar must be said with respect to the heavens. For there are three things: the body that is moved; the moving intelligence; and a third being through which it is moved, the appetite. What is moved, what desires, and what understands is the same being, but not with respect to the same parts or powers. Hence, motion inheres according to the nature of body, for this is moved primarily; it understands according to the intelligence, for this is the proper operation of the intellect that does not communicate with the body; but it desires according to the composite, for loving, hating and desiring belong to the composite consisting of soul and body.[48]

This way of developing the analogy between the animation of living beings and the animation of the universe is interesting for two reasons: First, it supports the reading that the understanding that causes the striving of heavenly bodies is identical with the understanding of the divine intelligence. Second, it takes up Cesalpino's view that the actual presence of the divine intellect in material composites "educes" new causal powers—the powers that are characteristic of an animate being. In one sense, thus, the powers of animate beings are not the same as the powers of the divine intellect. This is why it is informative to speak about an analogy between the causal role of the vital heat in an organic body, the causal role of the first mover in the heavens, and the activity of the divine intellect considered in itself. But at the same time, the analogy is grounded on a claim about inherence. Vegetative and sensitive powers could not come into being without the inherence of the divine intellect in the vital heat. And the striving of heavenly bodies could not come into being without the inherence of the divine intellect in the different regions of the heavens.

Taurellus noted that Cesalpino's characterization of the relation between God and the material world allows for two diverging interpretations, both of which, however, are in conflict with the doctrine of creation. One interpretation suggested by Taurellus has it that "things depend on the first being only insofar as these bodies are animate or substances. For [Cesalpino] maintained that each substance is a substance only through participation in the first being."[49] Taurellus observed that, according to this line of thought, "neither prime matter, nor secondary matter—that is, a body that is not animate—depends on the first being. If this is the case, it is necessary *that, in order for there to be dependence on the first being, something must preexist that has actuality but is not animate by itself.*"[50]

This is the first sense in which Cesalpino's account of divine immanence could be incompatible with the view that the world is created. If prime matter (and hence a constituent of all concrete natural beings that can be described as secondary matter) precedes dependence on God and is a condition for it, then prime matter (and hence all concrete natural beings) cannot be the outcome of creation. A further aspect that is incompatible with the doctrine of creation is Cesalpino's view that the new causal powers brought about in animate beings by the presence of the divine intelligence arise by necessity. Cesalpino understood this to be a consequence of the nature of divine self-reflection:

It suffices that there is some separate speculative intellect, which does not understand for the sake [of an animate being]; rather, it understands for its own sake and persists in its own perfection; consequently, the other substances that depend on it are *by necessity* imbued with the appetite; this perfection is called the nature of each single being, and by means of it every natural motion becomes more perfect.[51]

Cesalpino's reasoning seems to be that, if the divine essence consists in self-reflection, it is impossible for the divine intelligence not to reflect upon itself. But if self-reflection comes about by necessity, then also the new causal powers that result in material composites from the presence of the divine intellect must arise in a non-contingent manner. Moreover, describing the perfection of divine self-reflection as the nature of each single animated being strongly confirms the reading that divine self-reflection is understood inhere in animate beings.

How problematic Taurellus found these aspects of Cesalpino's thought becomes clear in his response to a second, diverging interpretation of Cesalpino's theory of animation that he took into consideration: "But if you maintain *that everything that exists has not only animation but also existence from the first being*, there would be a flowing of essences from the first being."[52] While in *Daemonum investigatio peripatetica*, Cesalpino explicitly stated such a view, in *Quaestiones peripateticae* one finds the vaguer idea that "prime matter depends on this first actuality, which means that what is divisible depends on what is indivisible and multiplicity on the one; for the division of matter is the cause of multiplicity."[53] What is missing from the description given in *Quaestiones peripateticae* is the specific reference to notions such as appetition, goodness, and divine essence. But what is found is an element absent from the description given in *Daemonum investigatio peripatetica*: the view that prime matter depends on the first being in a way that does not presuppose any kind of potentiality on the side of the first being. As Cesalpino argued, "otherwise, there would be an infinite regress. For prior to this potentiality, another actuality would be required, in which this potentiality is founded."[54] Cesalpino's argument seems to move from the plausible assumption that every potentiality must be founded upon actuality to the assumptions that every potentiality in one entity has to be founded upon the actuality of another entity. Speaking of an infinite regress also seems to imply the assumption that the actuality of the entity upon which potentiality is grounded in turn presupposes potentiality in a third entity, and so on. Taurellus contested the latter two assumptions. He denied that supposing that divine agency presupposes potentiality leads to an infinite regress, writing "for actuality and potentiality do not stand in the same relation. In order for potentiality to occur, another actuality necessarily must exist before: but not vice versa."[55] He maintained that both potentiality and actuality can be regarded as characteristic of God:

Because the potentiality, due to which we say that things depend on GOD, does not depend on GOD but rather belongs to GOD himself and is in GOD himself, namely a necessary power of the divine essence: which nevertheless does not act out of necessity but rather according to the will of God himself.[56]

Here, the central disagreement Taurellus has with Cesalpino's account of the relation between God and world comes to the fore. Taurellus was clear that Cesalpino's conception would lead to necessitarianism not only with respect to the soul's powers but also with respect to the existence of natural particulars:

> If things do not depend on GOD through an intermediary potentiality, they exist necessarily ... What exists necessarily always existed and always will exists necessarily. For what once did not exist, has been made at some time; and it has been made through some preexisting potentiality. Our Christian faith sufficiently teaches how impious it is to assume that all things depend on GOD in such a way that they have not been made by him or that they cannot be changed by him.[57]

Taurellus agreed with Cesalpino that certain features follow with necessity from the divine essence. But unlike Cesalpino, he included among the qualities that necessarily follow from the divine essence the ability to use will. And the use of will presupposes the ability to choose between acting and not acting. As Taurellus put it: "we ... ascribe truly and piously potentiality to our God, such that he can act when he wants to and that he can also not act."[58] Because potentiality involves a space of alternative possibilities, it is incompatible with necessity. And if creation presupposes the power of the will to choose between acting and not acting, then the necessitarian consequences of Cesalpino's account of the relation between God and the world seem to be incompatible with the doctrine of creation.

5. Concluding Remarks

In this article, I have used some of Taurellus's observations as a framework for interpreting Cesalpino's account of the origin of sensitive powers. It may be worth the while to indicate that the approach taken here leads to results that diverge significantly from an influential recent interpretation of Cesalpino's understanding of blood and vital heat. According to Catrien G. Santing, Cesalpino's project should be understood in the context of the early modern reception of spiritual interpretations of natural particulars such as blood prominent in late medieval theology. In this tradition, blood acquired a variety of spiritual meanings—ranging from the incarnation and suffering of Christ to the workings of the Holy Spirit.[59] And it is well documented that allusions to this tradition can be found in early modern works on anatomy and physiology.[60] In Santing's view, when Cesalpino talks about vital heat as a divine principle inherent in blood his aim was to offer support for such spiritual interpretations of blood.[61] However, while there cannot be any question about Cesalpino's loyalty to Catholicism, it is not evident that his theoretical reflections were concerned with Counterreformation theology. To my knowledge, Cesalpino did not discuss Christ, the Holy Spirit, the doctrine of creation, or any of the specific theological doctrines that divided Catholicism from other denominations.

The absence of specifically Christian issues, let alone of topics central to the dynamics of confessionalization, may allow for an alternative interpretation of

Cesalpino's analogical use of blood and vital heat. Cesalpino's cardiocentric physiology may turn out to have not been motivated by the desire to instantiate a pattern of thought well entrenched in the Catholic tradition and but rather by the desire to think through the Aristotelian conception of a self-reflexive divine intellect that functions as the final cause for natural particulars and the universe as a whole—a conception that can function as explanation for a wide range of natural phenomena, ranging from the origin of vegetative, sensitive and rational powers to the motion of heavenly bodies. The analogies that Cesalpino drew between animate substances, the animate universe and the divine intellect is grounded on the claim that the divine intellect is a constituent of animate substances and the animate universe. For this reason, Cesalpino held that the vegetative and sensitive powers characteristic of animate beings could not come about without the striving of the divine intellect, and that the same holds for the striving characteristic of heavenly bodies. If so, then Taurellus may to have been on the right track when he ascribed to Cesalpino a conception of God as a constitutive cause of living beings and the universe.

Notes

1 For an overview of this work, see Cecilia Muratori, "Seelentheorien nördlich und südlich der Alpen," in *Nürnbergs Hochschule in Altdorf. Beiträge zur frühneuzeitlichen Wissenschafts- und Bildungsgeschichte*, ed. Hanspeter Marti and Karin Marti-Weissenbach (Cologne: Böhlau, 2014), 41–66. On Taurellus's life and works, see Andreas Blank, "Nicolaus Taurellus," *Stanford Encyclopedia of Philosophy*, ed. Edward N. Zalta, 2016 edition, revised 2021. For overviews of Taurellus's metaphysics, see Peter Petersen, *Geschichte der aristotelischen Philosophie im protestantischen Deutschland* (Leipzig: Felix Meiner, 1921), 219–58; H. C. Mayer, *Nikolaus Taurellus, der erste Philosoph im Luthertum, Nikolaus Taurellus, der erste Philosoph im Luthertum. Ein Beitrag zum Problem von Vernunft und Offenbarung* (PhD Diss., University of Göttingen, 1959); Ulrich Gottfried Leinsle, *Das Ding und die Methode. Methodische Konstitution und Gegenstand der frühen protestantischen Metaphysik.* 2 vols. (Augsburg: Maro Verlag, 1985), 147–65; Siegfried Wollgast, *Philosophie in Deutschland zwischen Reformation und Aufklärung, 1550–1650* (Berlin: Akademie Verlag, 1988), 148–53. On the reception of Cesalpino in Altdorf, see Martin Mulsow, "Ambiguities of the Prisca Sapientia in Late Renaissance Humanism," *Journal of the History of Ideas* 65, no. 1 (2004): 1–13, at 7–9.

2 From the 1880s onward, these views have led to scholarly controversies that came to a close with Walter Pagel, *William Harvey's Biological Ideas. Selected Aspects and Historical Background* (New York: Karger, 1967), 169–209; Walter Pagel, "The Claim of Cesalpino and the First and Second Editions of his 'Peripatetic Questions,'" *History of Science* 13, no. 2 (1975): 130–8; Jerome J. Bylebyl, "Cesalpino and Harvey on Portal Circulation," in *Medicine and Society in the Renaissance. Essays to Honor Walter Pagel*, ed. Allen G. Debus (New York: Science History Publications, 1972), 1:39–52; Jerome J. Bylebyl, "Nutrition, Quantification and Circulation," *Bulletin of the History of Medicine* 51 (1977): 369–85.

3 Andrew Cunningham, "The Principality of Blood. William Harvey, the Blood, and the Early Transfusion Experiments," in *Blood—Symbol—Liquid*, ed. Catrien

G. Santing and Jetze J. Touber (Leuven: Peeters, 2012), 193–205, at 204, n. 8; see Realdo Colombo, *De re anatomica libri XV* (Venice: Bevilacqua, 1559), 15.
4   Cesalpino, *QP* (1593), fol. 115v; see Aristotle, *Resp.* 4.482b29–36.
5   Cesalpino, *QP* (1593), fol. 115v; see Aristotle, *Gen. an.* 2.4.740a16–22. For Cesalpino's adoption of these doctrines, see Catrien G. Santing, "'For the Life of a Creature is in the Blood' (Leviticus 17:11). Some Considerations on Blood as the Source of Life in Sixteenth-Century Religion and Medicine and their Interconnections," in *Blood, Sweat and Tears. The Changing Concepts of Physiology from Antiquity into Early Modern Europe*, ed. Manfred Horstmanshoff, Helen King, and Claus Zittel (Leiden: Brill, 2012), 415–41, at 433–4.
6   Cesalpino, *QP* (1593), fol. 127v; see Aristotle, *Part. an.* 2.10, 565b19–21.
7   Cesalpino, *QP* (1593), fol. 127v; see Aristotle, *Part. an.* 3.5.687b22–24.
8   Cesalpino, *QP* (1593), fol. 127v; see Aristotle, *De an.* 3.2.426b20-22; Aristotle, *Sens.* 7.449a10-17.
9   Cesalpino, *QP* (1593), fol. 131r: "animalia quae minus distincta sunt, communionem hanc vasorum arctiorem habent, unde fit ut divisa vivere aliquamdiu possint, principia enim non habent distincta, sed velut disseminata in ductibus."
10 Ibid., fol. 43r.
11 Ibid.: "quomodo aeternum et mortale unum numero sunt."
12 Ibid.: "sequetur in omnibus corporibus cum forma materiali et immaterialem quoque inesse."
13 Ibid.; see Aristotle, *De an.* 1.5.411a8.
14 For detailed discussion, see Anneliese Maier, "Das Problem der 'species sensibiles in medio,' und die neue Naturphilosophie des 14. Jahrhunderts," *Freiburger Zeitschrift für Philosophie und Theologie* 10 (1963): 3–32.
15 For an example of the latter approach in the natural philosophy of Girolamo Fracastoro, see Andreas Blank, "Julius Caesar Scaliger on Corpuscles and the Vacuum," *Perspectives on Science* 16 (2008): 137–59, at 142–4.
16 Cesalpion, *QP* (1593), fols. 135v–136r: "in organo et corpore recipitur species cum quantitate et divisibilis, idcirco non contingit eodem tempore contraria sentire ut lumen et tenebras, calidum et frigidum secundum eandem partem corporis."
17 Ibid., fol. 135v: "At cum sensus iudicat diversa vel contraria, actu patitur et multitudinem recipit. Quomodo igitur unus erit tunc actu sensus? Quod si non fuerit unus, quomodo iudicare diversitatem poterit? Necesse igitur est indivisibile esse id quod iudicat."
18 Nicolaus Taurellus, *Alpes caesae. Hoc est, Andreae Caesalpini Itali, monstrosa & superba dogmata, discussa & excussa* (Frankfurt: Palthenius, 1597), 936: "Ideo Caesalpini miror imprudentiam. ... quod ea quae optimo consilio Deus, et natura distinxerunt, ipse ausit confundere."
19 Ibid., 25–6.
20 Ibid., 309: "Quid hoc quaeso est aliud quam Dei rerumque ceterarum omnium substantias ita confundere ut unaquaeque Deus ipse dicitur esse aliqua ex parte?"
21 On the natural philosophy in this work, see Mark E. Clark and Kirk M. Summers, "Hippocratic Medicine and Aristotelian Science in the *Daemonum investigatio peripatetica* of Andrea Cesalpino," *Bulletin of the History of Medicine* 69, no. 4 (1995): 527–41.
22 Aristotle, *Gen. an.* 2.3.736b29-727a7. On this passage, see Friedrich Solmsen, "The Vital Heat, the Inborn Pneuma, and the Aether," *Journal of Hellenic Studies* 77 (1957): 119–23. For critical discussion, see Anthony Preus, "Science and Philosophy in

Aristotle's Generation of Animals," *Journal of the History of Biology* 3 (1970): 1–52, at 35–8; Gad Freudenthal, *Aristotle's Theory of Material Substance: Heat and Pneuma, Form and Soul* (Oxford: Clarendon Press, 1999), 19–29, 40–6, 114–29; James G. Lennox, *Aristotle's Philosophy of Biology* (Cambridge: Cambridge University Press, 2001), 229–49.

23 Cesalpino, *DIP* (1593), fol. 148r: "Ostensum est ... calidum innatum corpus esse divinius quam elementa, quamvis ex illis constituatur. Et merito respondere elemento stellarum non solum ratione foecunditatis, quae ab intelligentia habetur in eo comprehensa, sed etiam ratione immortalitatis subiecti et puritatis."

24 Ibid., fol. 147r.

25 Aristotle, *Part. an.*, 1.5.645a23-27.

26 Cesalpino, *DIP* (1593), fol. 147r: "Significavit autem id ... pulchrum ... rationem finis, cuius gratia natura agit, et cuius principium caelitus dicitur. ... Nam Divinum illud, quod sempiternum est, causa semper est sua natura melioris conditionis in rebus contingentibus. Corpus autem primum recipiens hanc divinitatem esse materiam primam, hinc patet. Haec enim est, quae secundum suam ipsius naturam appetit id, quod divinum est, bonum et appetibile."

27 Ibid.: "quod sine motu et mutatione fluit a divina essentia, divinum quoque et immortale sit."

28 Cesalpino, *QP* (1593), fol. 30v.

29 Cesalpino, *DIP* (1593), fol. 148v: "Quia ... in spiritu seu calore innato inest actu facultas animalis, non in igne nec caeteris elementis, ideo divinius hoc corpus dicitur: recipit enim actu virtutem divinae intelligentiae."

30 Ibid.

31 Taurellus, *Alpes caesae*, 26: "Cum enim docuisset Aristoteles omnem rerum multitudinem a materia proficisci; magnum hinc dogma Caesalpinus instituit: unicam videlicet esse substantiam incorpoream. Ne vero vel corporeas faceret animas vel earum cogeretur admittere multitudine, has unius illius incoporeae substantiae partes aliquas esse professus est: quae pro subiecta materia multitudinis subeant rationem."

32 Cesalpino, *QP* (1593), fol. 9v: "alio modo quatenus ipsum esse diverso modo participant, ab uno quodam quae substantia est descendentia."

33 Ibid., fol. 32v.

34 Ibid., fol. 35r: "Quoniam vero huiusmodi intellectio substantia est, idem enim cum intelligibili, et est intellectionis intellectio" See Aristotle, *Metaph.* 12.9.4.1074b32–34.

35 Cesalpino, *QP* (1593), fol. 35r.

36 Ibid., fol. 35v: "Quatenus enim perfectissimum ens est, caeteris esse distribuit et perficit omnia; quatenus autem intellectio est, perfectionis desiderium rebus indit."

37 Ibid., fol. 32v: "Speculativus ... intellectus substantia existens per se, non alterius gratia appetibilis, ea quae apta nata sunt appetere, perficit, non agendo quippiam, aut introducendo in materia aliquid ...; sed per sui praesentiam educendo ex potentia materiae formam ad quam apta nata est."

38 Ibid., fol. 22r-v: "Elementa separata ... actu non continent divinum hoc, sed potentia solum, in mixtione autem etiam actu, idcirco et actu sunt substantiae."

39 On early modern theories of *eductio*, see Andreas Blank, "The Question of Emergence in Protestant Natural Philosophy, 1540–1610," *Hungarian Philosophical Review* 61 (2017): 7–22; Andreas Blank, "Sixteenth-Century Pharmacology and the Controversy between Reductionism and Emergentism," *Perspectives on Science* 26 (2018): 157–84; Andreas Blank, "Instrumental Causes and the Natural Origin

40 Cesalpino, *QP* (1593), fols. 35v–36r: "Patet igitur ex dictis quo pacto unica intelligentia omnium rerum intelligentias contineat, est enim tanquam mensura omnium. Quemadmodum autem se habet intellectiones, sic etiam et res ipsas esse manifestum est; ab uno igitur multitudinem descendere non est impossibile. Patet etiam ex reductione entium ad unum, et ex modo quo substantiarum genera dicuntur secundum additionem et ablationem. … Quatenus igitur simpliciter est, et per ablationem omnis materiae dicitur, unica et simplex est substantia."

41 Ibid., fol. 21v: "Esse autem animatum ipsum universum, si coelum animatum est, rationi est consentaneum. … Nam et in animalibus non est necesse animam in toto corpore esse, sed sufficit esse in principali parte ut corde."

42 Ibid.: "universum organicum quiddam est, constat enim ex similaribus certo modo dispositas ad aliquod opus, organorum autem natura non nisi ab anima est, haec enim est animae esse."

43 Taurellus, *Alpes caesae*, 133.

44 See above, note 19.

45 Cesalpino, *QP* (1593), fol. 36r: "Ob multitudinem … formarum materialium non est necesse intelligentias multiplicari. Ratione autem moventium orbes coelestes, quemadmodum Aristoteles multitudinem substantiarum immobilium constituit, sic intelligentiarum multitudo ponenda videtur. … Simile igitur esset ac si animam sentientem multas habere partes censeremus, quia multis instrumentis vim sentiendi tribuit, cum tamen per se una sit et indivisibilis in corde sedens, ut voluit Aristoteles. Hoc autem modo intelligentias multas esse non repugnat unitati et simplicitati intelligentiae, quam posuimus. Ut enim eadem anima sentiendi in oculo visus appellatur, in aure autem auditus; sic eadem intelligentia quatenus quidem Lunam movet, Lunae ascribitur: quatenus autem Saturnum Saturno, et de caeteris eodem modo."

46 Ibid., fol. 32v: "amatum movet corpora celestia, appetere autem et amare haec non possunt, nisi intelligant ipsum bonum."

47 Ibid., fol. 29r: "Idcirco summum bonum et optimum unum maxime existens omnia implet sui desiderio, et quod simpliciter est bonum, unicuique sigillatim sit bonum absque infectione materiali aut diminutione aliqua essentiae."

48 Ibid., fol. 32v: "Credere autem idem esse et secundum idem id quod movetur, et quod appetit, et quod intelligit, non nisi fatuum, est, non enim secundum eandem partem haec fiunt etiam in animalibus. Motus enim secundum nervos et articulos perficitur; appetitus autem in corde aut proportionali consistit, virtus autem sentiendi in propriis organis, mentis autem virtus separata est. Similiter dicendum de coelo. Cum enim in eo tria sint, id quod movetur, corpus; movens, intelligentia; et tertium quo movetur, appetitus. Unum quidem aliquod est, quod movetur, quod appetit, et quod intelligit, non tamen secundum easdem partes aut potentias. Secundum igitur corporis naturam motus inest, hoc enim primo movetur: secundum intelligentiam intelligit, haec enim propria est intellectus operatio non communicans cum corpore; secundum autem coniunctum appetit, amare enim et odisse et desiderare affectiones sunt coniuncti ex anima et corpore (*De an.* 1.1.403b16–19)."

49 Taurellus, *Alpes caesae*, 755: "Atque ita ut id solum quo haec corpora sunt animata vel quo sunt substantiae a primo ente dependeant."

50 Ibid., 755–6: "Unde liquet neque materiam primam neque secundam, hoc est, corpus, quod non sit animatum a primo ente dependere. Quae cum ita sint necesse est *ut sit dependentia a primo ente, praeexistere aliquid, quod sit actu: sed quod ex se non sit animatum.*"

51 Cesalpino, *QP* (1593), fol. 32r: "sufficit speculativum esse quendam intellectum separatum, qui non huius quidem gratia intelligat (non enim esset ultimus finis, cum ad opus aliud dirigeretur) sed sui quidem gratia intelligente, et in sua perfectione persistente, reliquis substantiis ab ipso pendentibus, *ex necessitate* appetitus ille innascatur, quae natura dicitur uniuscuiusque, a quo omnis motus naturalis perficitur" (my emphasis).

52 Taurellus, *Alpes caesae*, 756: "Si vero *non animari, sed esse velis a primo ente quicquid est*, hic essentiarum ex primo ente erit defluxus."

53 Cesalpino, *QP* (1593), fol. 99r: "Primam … materiam ab illo actu pendere concedimus qui primus est, ab indivisibili scilicet divisibile, et ab uno multitudo; materiae nanque divisio multitudinis est causa."

54 Ibid.: "dicimus dependentiam entium a primo ente non supponere ex necessitate praeexistentem potentiam, sic enim processus esset in infinitum. Nam ante illam potentiam alter actus requireretur, in quo fundaretur potentia."

55 Taurellus, *Alpes caesae*, 755: "Non enim eadem actus et potentiae est ratio. Ut potentia sit, actum praeexistere necesse est, at non viceversa."

56 Ibid., 756-7: "Nam potentia, per quam res a DEO dependere dicimus, non dependet a DEO: sed ipsius est DEI. Et in ipso est DEO divinae scilicet essentiae virtus necessaria, quae non agit tamen necessario, sed pro ipsius DEI voluntate."

57 Ibid., 756: "Si res a DEO non dependent per intermediam potentiam, necessario sunt. … Quod necessario est id semper fuit, et semper erit necessario. Nam quod aliquando non fuit, aliquando factum est, et quidem per praeexistentem potentiam. Res autem omnes a DEO ita dependere ut ab eo factae non sint nec ab eo mutari possint, nostra fides Christiana satis docet, quam sit impium."

58 Ibid., 748: "nos … et vere, et pie nostro Deo potentiam ascribimus ut facere possit ea, quae vult, et possit etiam non facere."

59 See Miri Rubin, *Corpus Christi. The Eucharist in Late Medieval Culture* (Cambridge: Cambridge University Press, 1991); Caroline Walker Bynum, *Wonderful Blood: Theology and Practice in Late Medieval Northern Germany and Beyond* (Philadelphia: University of Pennsylvania Press, 2007).

60 See Luigi Lazzerini, "Anatomy and Blood Sacrifices in the Renaissance Period: The Frontispiece of *De Humani Corporis Fabrica* by Andreas Vesalius and the Sacrificial Scene," in Santing and Touber, *Blood—Symbol—Liquid*, 83–101; Rina Knoeff, "Unspeakable Blood. Menno Simons versus Martin Micron on Menstrual Blood, Sin and the Doctrine of Incarnation," in Santing and Touber, *Blood—Symbol—Liquid*, 103–15.

61 Catrien G. Santing, "'For the Life of a Creature Is in the Blood'"; Catrien G. Santing, "*Deus rotator* and the Microrotator: Blood as the Source of Life in the Life and Works of Andrea Cesalpino," in Santing and Touber, *Blood—Symbol—Liquid*, 137–56.

Bibliography

Primary Sources

Aristotle. *Generation of Animals*, translated by A. L. Peck. Cambridge, MA: Harvard University Press, 1943.

Aristotle. *The Complete Works of Aristotle*, edited by Jonathan Barnes. 2 vols. Princeton: Princeton University Press, 1984.

Cesalpino, Andrea. *Peripateticarum quaestionum libri quinque*. Venice: Giunta, 1571.

Cesalpino, Andrea. *Quaestionum peripateticarum libri quinque*. Venice: Giunta, 1593.
Colombo, Realdo. *De re anatomica libri XV*. Venice: Bevilacqua, 1559.
Taurellus, Nicolaus. *Alpes caesae, Hoc est, Andreae Caesalpini Itali, monstrosa & superba dogmata, discussa & excussa*. Frankfurt: Palthenius, 1597.

Secondary Sources

Blank, Andreas. "Instrumental Causes and the Natural Origin of Souls in Antonio Ponce de Santacruz's Theory of Animal Generation." *Annals of Science* 76 (2019): 184–209.

Blank, Andreas. "Julius Caesar Scaliger on Corpuscles and the Vacuum." *Perspectives on Science* 16 (2008): 137–59.

Blank, Andreas. "Julius Caesar Scaliger on Plants, Species, and the Ordained Power of God." *Science in Context* 25, no. 4 (2012): 503–23.

Blank, Andreas. "Nicolaus Taurellus." In *Stanford Encyclopedia of Philosophy*, edited by Edward N. Zalta. 2016 edition, revised 2021.

Blank, Andreas. "Sixteenth-Century Pharmacology and the Controversy between Reductionism and Emergentism." *Perspectives on Science* 26 (2018): 157–84.

Blank, Andreas. "The Question of Emergence in Protestant Natural Philosophy, 1540–1610." *Hungarian Philosophical Review* 61 (2017): 7–22.

Bylebyl, Jerome J. "Cesalpino and Harvey on Portal Circulation." In *Medicine and Society in the Renaissance. Essays to Honor Walter Pagel*, edited by Allen G. Debus, 2 vols, 1: 39–52. New York: Science History Publications, 1972.

Bylebyl, Jerome J. "Nutrition, Quantification and Circulation." *Bulletin of the History of Medicine* 51 (1977): 369–85.

Bynum, Caroline Walker. *Wonderful Blood: Theology and Practice in Late Medieval Northern Germany and Beyond*. Philadelphia: University of Pennsylvania Press, 2007.

Clark, Mark E., and Kirk M. Summers. "Hippocratic Medicine and Aristotelian Science in the *Daemonum investigatio peripatetica* of Andrea Cesalpino." *Bulletin of the History of Medicine* 69, no. 4 (1995): 527–41.

Cunningham, Andrew. "The Principality of Blood. William Harvey, the Blood, and the Early Transfusion Experiments." In *Blood—Symbol—Liquid*, edited by Catrien G. Santing, and Jetze J. Touber, 193–205. Leuven: Peeters, 2012.

Freudenthal, Gad. *Aristotle's Theory of Material Substance: Heat and Pneuma, Form and Soul*. Oxford: Clarendon Press, 1999.

Knoeff, Rina. "Unspeakable Blood. Menno Simons versus Martin Micron on Menstrual Blood, Sin and the Doctrine of Incarnation." In *Blood—Symbol—Liquid*, edited by Catrien G. Santing, and Jetze J. Touber, 103–15. Leuven: Peeters, 2012.

Lazzerini, Luigi. "Anatomy and Blood Sacrifices in the Renaissance Period: The Frontispiece of *De Humani Corporis Fabrica* by Andreas Vesalius and the Sacrificial Scene." In *Blood—Symbol—Liquid*, edited by Catrien G. Santing, and Jetze J. Touber, 83–101. Leuven: Peeters, 2012.

Leinsle, Ulrich Gottfried. *Das Ding und die Methode Methodische Konstitution und Gegenstand der frühen protestantischen Metaphysik*. 2 vols. Augsburg: Maro Verlag, 1985.

Lennox, James G. *Aristotle's Philosophy of Biology*. Cambridge: Cambridge University Press, 2001.

Maier, Anneliese. "Das Problem der 'species sensibiles in medio,' und die neue Naturphilosophie des 14. Jahrhunderts." *Freiburger Zeitschrift für Philosophie und Theologie* 10 (1963): 3–32.

Mayer, H. C. *Nikolaus Taurellus, der erste Philosoph im Luthertum, Nikolaus Taurellus, der erste Philosoph im Luthertum. Ein Beitrag zum Problem von Vernunft und Offenbarung.* PhD diss., University of Göttingen, 1959.

Mulsow, Martin. "The Ambiguities of the *Prisca Sapientia* in Late Renaissance Humanism." *Journal of the History of Ideas* 65, no. 1 (2004): 1–13.

Muratori, Cecilia. "Seelentheorien nördlich und südlich der Aplen: Taurellus's Auseinandersetzung mit Cesalpinos *Quaestiones peripateticae*." In *Nürnbergs Hochschule in Altdorf*, edited by Hanspeter Marti and Karin Marti-Weissenbach, 41–66. Cologne: Böhlau, 2014.

Pagel, Walter. "The 'Claim' of Cesalpino and the First and Second Editions of His *Peripatetic Questions*." *History of Science* 13, no. 2 (1975): 130–8.

Pagel, Walter. *William Harvey's Biological Ideas. Selected Aspects and Historical Background*. New York: Karger, 1967.

Petersen, Peter. *Geschichte der aristotelischen Philosophie im protestantischen Deutschland*. Leipzig: Felix Meiner, 1921.

Preus, Anthony. "Science and Philosophy in Aristotle's Generation of Animals." *Journal of the History of Biology* 3 (1970): 1–52.

Rubin, Miri. *Corpus Christi. The Eucharist in Late Medieval Culture*. Cambridge: Cambridge University Press, 1991.

Santing, Catrien G. "'Deus rotator and the microrotator': Blood as the Source of Life in the Life and Works of Andrea Cesalpino." In *Blood—Symbol—Liquid*, edited by Catrien G. Santing, and Jetze J. Touber, 137–56. Leuven: Peeters, 2012.

Santing, Catrien G. "'For the Life of a Creature Is in the Blood' (*Leviticus* 17:11). Some Considerations on Blood as the Source of Life in Sixteenth-Century Religion and Medicine and their Interconnections." In *Blood, Sweat and Tears. The Changing Concepts of Physiology from Antiquity into Early Modern Europe*, edited by Manfred Horstmanshoff, Helen King, and Claus Zittel, 415–41. Leiden: Brill, 2012.

Solmsen, Friedrich. "The Vital Heat, the Inborn Pneuma, and the Aether." *Journal of Hellenic Studies* 77 (1957): 119–23.

Wollgast, Siegfried. *Philosophie in Deutschland zwischen Reformation und Aufklärung, 1550–1650*. Berlin: Akademie Verlag, 1988.

6

Andrea Cesalpino and the Rejection of the Celestial Spheres in Seventeenth-Century University of Edinburgh

David Malcolm McOmish

The following essay represents a case study on the reception of the work of Italian natural philosopher Andrea Cesalpino in early modern tertiary education. It has developed out of a larger study of the ways in which significant intellectual developments in the early modern period were exchanged across transnational networks and then presented and conceptualized within regional universities and formal education more broadly.[1] This study will examine evidence from formal education in the early seventeenth century of the reception of Andrea Cesalpino's writings on the doctrine of the celestial spheres from his five-book study the *Quaestiones peripateticae* (hereafter *QP*).[2] Primarily, it will examine how his views on this topic were framed within an evolving debate on the nature of the superlunary universe, from the time of the publication of *QP* in the late sixteenth century onwards. The textual evidence for this study pertains to the University of Edinburgh, one of early modernity's rising university centers, whose reformers, lecturers, and senior administrators were part of a broader European network of educationalists. It provides evidence for the ways in which Cesalpino's views on celestial spheres were discussed within academia across Europe in the late sixteenth century and early seventeenth century at a time when the issue was particularly contested. As other contributors to this volume highlight, Cesalpino did not cite contemporaries. This makes the task of determining the relationship between his work and its contemporary context less straightforward. However, as will be seen in the following discussion, it is possible to see the place that his contemporaries thought his work occupied within a particular branch of intellectual activity.

The point of academic reference for this essay is, as mentioned, the University of Edinburgh, which was becoming a center of trans-European scholarly activity at this time. Its educational program was developed by experienced and respected academics from across Europe and reflected intellectual trends from across regional hubs. Within this well-connected scholarly community, Edinburgh provided an environment for its students and lecturers to examine new intellectual developments with a noteworthy degree of awareness of their broader contemporary significance. Within this context, it is possible to form an understanding of Cesalpino's place within contemporary scholarship. It suggests that Cesalpino's late sixteenth-century view on celestial spheres was understood as a noteworthy example within the Aristotelian philosophical tradition. It was also presented as ill-suited to meet the challenges and opportunities presented by developments in mathematics, optics, and instrumental observation at the start of the seventeenth century. The academic sources that provide the main evidence base for the following discussion come from Edinburgh's published university disputations, lectures notes, and manuscript sources. These sources reveal the geographical spread of the nodes of the pan-European networks operating in Edinburgh and bring into focus how Cesalpino's ideas were understood within the broader European debates on the nature of the universe.

1. Wandering Scholars and the University of Edinburgh

Recognition of the political entanglements of the University of Edinburgh in this period makes it easier to understand how it could make ideas imported from across Europe and its confessional and cultural divides accessible to its students. From its foundation in the later sixteenth century, the university became a focus for power struggles between the state and the increasingly militant church.[3] In the first half of the seventeenth century, it was administered and developed by individuals who were particularly close to the King of Scotland, King James VI. After becoming King of England in 1603, James attempted to foster cultural initiatives that derived benefit from and benefitted the new polity. It was during this period that a series of reforms, both administrative and intellectual, led to a transformation of the University, the most visible sign of which was that James himself became its protector and had it renamed "King James' College" in his honor. This move was, in King James's own words, motivated by the need to protect the university from the "evil eye" of those who harbored ill-will toward it. Although James did not explicitly state who this was, the Church authorities in Scotland were undoubtedly the target.[4] Thereafter, Edinburgh emerged as a distinct educational space within the new cultural landscape of post-union Britain. The institution became a place where scholars who had participated in the scholarly "vast wanderings" of the period, regardless of confessional background, were able to return and participate in its development under the King's protection.

Many of those involved in King James's political activities at this time were also involved in the reform of education at Edinburgh. Four representative figures in Edinburgh from the period provide insight into the ways in which knowledge could pass through and across regional centers in this political environment. They were the jurist and writer Thomas Craig, educated in Paris; the academics Adam King and Patrick Sands, educated in Paris and Venice, respectively; and the doctor John Jolie, educated in Basel. Craig was involved in writing a series of legal tracts justifying the creation of a United Kingdom of Great Britain through the political and legal union between England and Scotland (Thomas Craig, *De Unione* (1604), and *Jus Feudale* (1603)). Craig was also appointed to the commission in Edinburgh to find a new Latin grammar book for use in the schools. Craig was the elder brother of John Craig, professor of mathematics at Frankfurt an der Oder, student of Paul Wittich, tutor of Duncan Liddel, and one-time friend and later adversary of Tycho Brahe.[5] Also part of the same commission was the academic Adam King, whose work was the main conduit through which the ideas of Andrea Cesalpino were passed to generations of students at Edinburgh. King had been a much-respected professor of mathematics and philosophy and a senior administrator at the University of Paris for many years.[6] Active during the important period from the late sixteenth to early seventeenth century, he was especially interested in philosophical and mathematical work on infinity, on motion, the work on refraction of his predecessor in the royal chair at Paris, Jean Pena, the various writings on the supernova and comets of the period, and the writings of Johannes Kepler and Galileo. King wrote a cosmological manual containing 160,000 words, which was recommended by King James's Lord Chancellor, Lord Seton, for use in education at Edinburgh.[7] As we shall see, this work became a crucially important mechanism through which the well-connected King funneled knowledge (in the present case that of Cesalpino) from the central circuits in which he moved to the subgroups of the periphery of Edinburgh. Another member of King James's educational commission was Venice-educated Patrick Sands. Sands became principal of the University of Edinburgh in 1620, where he presided over the establishment of the Chair of Mathematics at the University, and the introduction of Adam King's cosmology manual into the formal educational experience.[8] Finally, the fourth representative figure is academic administrator, doctor, political advisor, and poet John Jollie. He and Patrick Sands were part of the administrative body of the University of Edinburgh responsible for choosing new lecturers.[9] He was the son-in-law of Lord Seton, the Lord Chancellor, Adam King's patron. Jollie was commissioned by King James to found a Royal College of Physicians at Edinburgh, along with his close friends Venice-educated George Sibbald and Adam King's son-in-law Alexander Kincaid.[10] In addition to these educational activities, all four were active in furthering the political agenda of King James at home and abroad.[11]

The four identified above were, as indicated, representative of the wandering scholars who return to Edinburgh at this period. A key aspect of the entire group, including the wider friends and family circuits of which they were part, was that, although they shared bonds of family, friendship, and intellectual culture, they were from markedly different confessional backgrounds. Both their upbringing and respective academic experiences when younger reflected this multi-confessional aspect.[12] Across the early seventeenth century, the make-up of the lecturers, student body, and the corporate body's patronage network highlights that Edinburgh continued to be a place where religious background was not a barrier to participation in the life of the university. Unsurprisingly, a significant characteristic of the university in this period was its receptivity to ideas and texts from across Europe and across its national and confessional divides. While it was Britain's first post-reformation university, Edinburgh was also arguably the first college on the island whose fundamental development can be understood in a cultural context that transcended traditional national and confessional confines. This makes it a fascinating case study for gaining a broad overview of how the period's contested topics were understood across regional educational hubs and above and beyond confessional or national restrictions.

2. The Doctrine of the Celestial Spheres

Debate on the nature of the superlunary universe presents a particularly fertile topic in this regard. Edinburgh's wandering scholars were heavily invested in this contested topic from the middle of the sixteenth century through to the early to middle seventeenth century. The question of the nature, composition, and validity of the doctrine of the celestial spheres exercised both astronomers and philosophers from its inception in Aristotle's *On the Heavens* and *Metaphysics* onwards.[13] The basic outline of the doctrine in Aristotelian thought as it existed in early modernity held that the planets were embedded in nested spheres. The movement of the planets were the result of the movement of the spheres onto which they were fixed. These spheres were material in nature in the Aristotelian tradition, although of a type that was different to and separate from sublunary matter.[14] The materiality of the spheres is evidenced by their counteracting nature, which, Aristotle suggests, may account for motion.[15] The number of these spheres and the nature of the motion(s) that moved them was more difficult to define. Aristotle himself was unsure and felt that the matter of the number of spheres was one for astronomy (the intermediate discipline between mathematics and philosophy) to solve.[16] Ptolemy, the exceptionally influential ancient astronomer, whose work was epitomized and became canonical in the medieval period in the *Sphaera Mundi* of Johannes de Sacrobosco, rejected Aristotle's mechanical link between the planets and their spheres. His view on impetus to motion for the planets was rooted in the alternative Platonic tradition that imagined an internal motive force moved the planets, which then accounted for the other movements within and along the sphere to which they were attached.[17] From antiquity through to the early modern period, variations on these basic themes played out within the Aristotelian and Platonic traditions.

In 1557 Pena, a Royal Professor at the University of Paris, published an edition of Euclid to which he added an introduction outlining conclusions he had drawn from contemporary work on optics.[18] In it, Pena concluded that the lack of detectable refraction in light travelling through the heavens beyond the moon meant that there can be no physical boundaries (i.e., material celestial spheres) in the superlunary universe below the fixed stars, as Aristotle and the doctrine of the spheres dictated. There then followed a series of developments that cast further doubt upon the existence of the spheres as physically real and that subsequently filtered into formal education across Europe. Several astronomers, mathematicians, and philosophers observed the supernova of 1572 and the comet of 1577, including Italian philosopher Girolamo Cardano, Danish astronomer Tycho Brahe, and the Jesuit mathematician Christoph Clavius.[19] They agreed that these phenomena existed in three-dimensional space above the moon and that the movement of the comet especially could not be reconciled with the doctrine of the spheres. Even before the appearances of the supernova and comet, the Parisian educationalist Petrus Ramus explicitly rejected the doctrine and, furthermore, called for a rejection of all planetary hypotheses.[20] Not conforming to Ramus's extreme rejection of all hypotheses, Kepler attempted the marry the fruitful approach of detailed observation of the skies with sound philosophical principles to find an plausible alternative.[21]

The Edinburgh reformers were intimately familiar with both the ideas of those rejecting the spheres and the individuals themselves. Adam King, who held a Royal Chair after Pena at Paris, and who was the Peter Ramus Professor (*Petrorameus Professor*) of Philosophy and Mathematics at Paris, drew deeply from Pena's Euclid edition in his own work. As will be seen below, he characterized Cesalpino's work within the broader context of the ideas of Pena. Thomas and John Craig, Adam King, and John Napier were in direct contact with Tycho Brahe in relation to his work on the comets.[22] They were also part of a broader circle around Brahe that included both Duncan Liddel and Kepler.[23] Adam King's younger brother Clement and their mutual acquaintance Patrick Sands maintained links with Thomas Seget, who was part of Kepler's circle of friends.[24] Through vocational entanglements and bonds of family and friendship, the educationalists at Edinburgh were enmeshed within the web of scholars, philosophers, mathematicians, and astronomers across Europe who were actively involved in dismantling of the doctrine of the celestial spheres from Pena's Euclid in 1557 through to Kepler's *Harmonices mundi* of 1619.

3. Cesalpino's *Quaestiones Peripateticae* 3.4

A brief introduction to Cesalpino's actual words in relation to the Aristotelian doctrine of the celestial spheres outlined above will set the scene for discussion of how his views on the subject were framed and presented within formal education at Edinburgh. The main section of the *QP* that contains those views, and which is cited in the Edinburgh lecture notes, is framed by two direct references to those Cesalpino sees as the object of his discussion. At the beginning of *QP* 3.4, Cesalpino states that it is the opinion of all astrologers that heaven is composed of many globes mutually interlinked with each other.[25] These globes are thought, he wrote, to be moved circularly around specific poles and cardinal points, and heaven is spherical in shape. Cesalpino then begins to dismantle what he sees as the absurdities of the system created by the astronomers. He starts with the physical impossibility of the existence of nested, interlocking spheres. Aristotle's *Physics*, according to Cesalpino, demonstrates that motion is not possible in a vacuum.[26] Indeed, there can be no physical resistance in a vacuum, of the type that initiates motion, that is, there can be no friction or resistance necessary for motion for bordering celestial spheres if a vacuum exists between them: "it is impossible that motion happens in a vacuum; for there is no contact."[27] Consequently, physical touch between the spheres for motion is needed to initiate motion. According to Cesalpino, the celestial spheres would require abrasive properties on their surfaces that would interlock with and move the bordering spheres, which they cannot possess: "There is no succession of parts touching each other by turns, upon which motion depends."[28] Additionally, in the same passage he wrote that, even if this were not the case, the physical stresses on individual spheres in such a system, brought about from above, below, and internally would result in irreconcilable contrary motions, especially for the middle spheres, and they would be torn apart. These two factors of location (vacuum) and resistance (interlocking spheres) dictated that the heavens could not be divided into spheres and that they must therefore be rejected: "If indeed these things said about the nature of the location and resistance are true, it is impossible that heaven is constructed out of mutually interlocking spheres."[29] Cesalpino's rejection of the doctrine of spheres is constructed out of Aristotelian physical principles and presented as a rejection of the absurd hypotheses of the astronomers.

The final framing reference to the astronomers completes the main section of his discussion of the spheres. Cesalpino here highlights the absurd lengths to which mathematical astronomers must go to save the phenomena of interlocking spheres, using homocentric models and eccentric solutions, double movements in epicycles for planets resulting from this, and, moreover, correcting deferent points to preserve all.[30] Consequently, Cesalpino concludes, the heavens must be thought of as a single continuum, a single sphere, within which a series of circles move, all of which are moved in a single movement by the same force.[31] According to Cesalpino, this model was in agreement with Aristotle's words: "we say, therefore, that Aristotle's opinion was that all heaven is one continuous body."[32] In his introduction and in this specific passage, Cesalpino is explicitly addressing problems that he determines have been created by astronomers with a philosophical solution. As will become clear, it is the philosophical nature of Cesalpino's rejection of the celestial spheres that informed how he was presented to students at Edinburgh.

4. Cesalpino and Edinburgh

The multiple pathways of knowledge exchange from across Europe outlined above, which conditioned the intellectual environment of Edinburgh, are not immediately perceptible in the official records of the university. There survive an abundance of printed disputations that record the public disputations undertaken by the lecturers and students at the graduation ceremony for each undergraduate class. Edinburgh was the first Scottish university to publish these records, and, despite being a relatively new institution, produced more of them across the first half of the seventeenth century than the older, more established Scottish universities.[33] The *Theses* have been recognized as important evidence that highlights the curious position Edinburgh held as the only place in Scotland where we find any evidence of an emergent scientific culture.[34] The evidence contained in the *Theses* has puzzled scholars because, formally at least, the curriculum from Edinburgh seemed to conform to the largely scholastic and dogmatically Aristotelian curriculum of other reformed universities in Britain.[35] However, two additional layers of textual evidence exist for Edinburgh that demonstrate that the "anomalous" content within the *Theses* is actually evidence of a *de facto* alternative educational experience, which was shaped by the academics and itinerant scholars mentioned above. They are student notebooks (i.e., lecture dictates) and Adam King's cosmological commentary.[36] They allow us to reconstruct a relatively comprehensive picture of the educational experience at the University. They reveal a relationship with the nascent sciences of early modernity at Edinburgh that is inextricably enmeshed within the broader international context of knowledge exchange and operative networks.

They allow us to see evidence of the reception of Cesalpino in Edinburgh, especially how Edinburgh's wandering scholars understood his place within contemporary thought across Europe. Cesalpino is not cited or mentioned by name in any of the published *Theses Philosophicae* for Edinburgh. The absence of his name, however, is the result of a double editorial process of preparing the cosmological commentary for lectures in the classroom and, in turn, preparing those lectures for public performance at graduation. The student dictates that survive from across the seventeenth century are comprehensive and reflect the lecturers' spoken word. However, their quotations of secondary or primary sources do not always contain citational information, and this is true of the dictates where Cesalpino's text is being quoted or paraphrased. Adam King's cosmological commentary, Dk.7.29, written between 1595 and 1616 after his return to Edinburgh from Paris, fills in the citational gaps.[37] Dk.7.29 provided the content for a remarkable portion of Edinburgh's lectures on natural philosophy and the sciences; and the *Theses* and dictates represent a partial reproduction of its content. The pervasive influence upon the dictates and *Theses* of this manuscript makes it clear that it was the main point of reference for cosmological study in the classroom across the first half of the seventeenth century.[38] Dk.7.29 is the most detailed evidence of the efforts of the above educators and disciplinary specialists, as they attempted to reform university and vocational teaching in Edinburgh.

A close reading of Dk.7.29 reveals both the presence in formal education at Edinburgh of Andrea Cesalpino's work and more importantly its nature. *QP* is the source of several unattributed quotations spread across twenty years and found in the published student disputations known as the *Theses philosophicae*. The "Theses physicae," that is, the natural philosophical theses contained in the *Theses philosophicae* for the graduating year 1624–8 at Edinburgh, present a robust articulation of Aristotelian cosmology. "Thesis Physica" XIV opens with the proposition that: "All understand that the neighboring surfaces of the celestial spheres have been rubbed down to an evenness as completely as nature is able to bring about."[39] This passage recapitulates Aristotle, *On the Heavens* 2.4.287b15–27, which is quoted and cited in Cesalpino *QP* 3.4. However, the first corollary, or as they are called in the Edinburgh disputations, "appendix," adds that, as a consequence, there can be no extremities of protrusions that would facilitate the touch between one sphere and another necessary for celestial motion.[40] Both of these assertions, the initial thesis, and its primary corollary, also form the main argumentative structure and content of Cesalpino's position as outlined above. However, the final appendix of "Thesis Physica" XIV from 1628 rejects the notion that such a model is the only one that can be followed: "they are quite wrong who opine that the turning of the celestial spheres comes about from only the abrasion of surface, which exchange of contact brings about."[41] "Thesis Physica" XIV and its corollaries are, in essence, the articulation of an abstract celestial system reliant upon tangible external impetus to motion, articulated from within the Aristotelian tradition, and then rejected on those specific terms.[42] Appendices 2 and 3 of thesis XIV offer an alternative philosophical position, incorporating some of those Aristotelian positions (i.e., on living force within celestial bodies as discussed at *On the Heavens* 2.13.294a22) developed by Julius Caesar Scaliger in his theories on motive intelligences.[43]

The two types of celestial systems presented in the *Theses* and appendices (and dictates) are derived in their entirety from Dk. 7.29. They are verbatim sections taken from it and edited for the classroom and edited again for the public disputations. Here is the passage on the two types of motive forces from Dk. 7.29:

> But whoever says that the turning of the celestial spheres happens through only the friction of surfaces, which tactile interchange brings about, is quite mistaken. Indeed, a sphere does not turn around another sphere through contact unless, where contact happens, the surfaces should be rough and unequal, like we see on the wheels of clocks; all understand that the neighboring surfaces of the celestial spheres have been rubbed down to an evenness as completely as nature is able to bring about. So that, where one should push on or push back another, there would be utterly no inequality of bordering protrusions to bring about exchanged friction and abrasion. Therefore, they are not moved through contact. Rather each one is moved by an attendant intelligence. The first moves its own sphere only by means of intellection of itself, and the other spheres by the way in which it moves its own. However, the intellects closer to us move by means of a twin intellection: one from itself through which they turn their own spheres; the other when they comprehend the first. Hence they become one with the latter [i.e., first], through the presence of the intellection, as if through an irradiation exchange; so that it copies the rotation of that one and follows it.[44]

The arrangement of the text is the only clearly noticeable difference between the *Theses* and the lecture notes. The first clause of the passage is appropriated largely unchanged to create Appendix 4 in the student theses; clause three ("orbium autem caelestium …") is reproduced verbatim as the main thesis; clause four is Appendix 1; and the rest of the passage from Dk.7.29 is used to produce Appendices 2 and 3, respectively, in the published disputations.[45] The rearrangement of the text is part of a process of making the general argument from the source text more disputational for the public context, in which participants strove to demonstrate argumentative agility when rejecting both nested interlocking spheres (main thesis and Appendix 1) and one single sphere with planes and circles (Appendices 2–4). However, the differing verbal form at the beginning of the passage (singular "fallitur" in Dk.7.29 and plural "falluntur" in the published theses) highlights that Adam King had someone in mind regarding the propagation of the Aristotelian notion of interlocking-spheres. King explicitly states in the preceding passage that it is Cesalpino who propagated the view:

> Andrea Cesalpino, (book 3 of the *Peripatetic Disputations*, Disputation 4) since he stated that the spheres bordering upon each other could not be moved unless through the exchange of reciprocal contact, and frictional exchange across their surfaces; and that each of the spheres are drawn around by the turning of the bordering one in motion; he thinks that it therefore necessarily follows that the highest sphere would have to be moved not only by its own motion, but by the motion of the lower sphere immediately bordering it; that the middle spheres be moved threefold, by their own motion, and by the twin movement on each side of the lower and upper spheres; and so it is dragged in different

directions by contrary motions, finally at the lowest sphere, only by their own motion and the motion of those nearby. Which is absurd and impossible [Cesalpino thinks]. [So] he determines that heaven ought not to be divided into neighboring spheres.[46]

It is Cesalpino's rejection of the celestial spheres that is abstracted and presented to the students. We find it in "Thesis Physica" XIV from 1628 in bit-sized chunks, shorn of its full context, the result of the lecturer's attempts to highlight the students' facility in proposing, opposing, and debating closely prescribed philosophical positions. These positions are extracted and crafted from the more prolonged discussion of the concepts found in the student dictates by the lecturers.[47] Therefore, taken together, they represent what were considered important philosophical positions, quoted in the classroom, and rendered in abridged form in the disputations.

In "Thesis Physica" XIV Appendices 2 and 3, we find Cesalpino's explanation presented in opposition to intellective force or intellection, accompanied with a direct quote from Scaliger's work. In the quoted passage, Scaliger develops Aristotle's idea on the prime mover, which Aristotle identified as God, but Scaliger slightly recasts as an intelligence that is under orders from God to move itself and inspire the neighboring spheres to move (freely) according to God's plan. King's juxtaposition of one interpretation of motive force (Cesalpino) with another (Scaliger) from within the broader Aristotelian tradition presents Cesalpino's rejection of the spheres as unnecessarily restrictive within its own Aristotelian parameters. This understanding of late sixteenth century Aristotelian philosophy and motive force was central enough to the students' education at Edinburgh that, for the showcase public disputations for their graduation ceremony, they recited an edited form of it to open debates on the causes of motion across the early to mid-seventeenth century. King's interpretation of Cesalpino's ideas on motive force and Scaliger's motive intellection reappear throughout the Edinburgh theses, dictates, and lecture notes as the exemplars of late Aristotelian cosmology at Edinburgh.[48]

The broader discussion of the celestial spheres in Dk.7.29, of which this passage is part, also reveals how students at Edinburgh were encouraged to think that these recent philosophical attempts to reform the old paradigms were increasingly unsustainable in the late sixteenth to early seventeenth century. Cesalpino's work was introduced to students in the context of recent Aristotelian views on the celestial spheres and cosmic motion. Cesalpino is presented as arguing against the idea of a multiplicity of spheres in the heavens as an Aristotelian, reflecting Cesalpino's own rhetoric. Dk.7.29 precedes its introduction to this Aristotelian context with a censure of those who rely exclusively either upon their senses or their reason for judgment:

Those from the ancients who have confused the senses with thought (as Aristotle says), and have taken up no other judgment about the universe than that which is established through the senses; as long as they would observe no division of the celestial spheres with their eyes, they determined that there is no body of heaven, in which the stars are moved, unless a continuous whole ... Now certain moderns wish to be seen correct not through the testimony of their senses, but with the firm influence of their reason, in their destruction of the celestial spheres.[49]

In the next sentence, King singles out Cesalpino as the representative of the latter group who do not observe what they discuss. The following discussion of Cesalpino and Scaliger's views is part of a broader examination in Dk.7.29 of the role of *a priori* and *a posteriori* knowledge, geometrical modelling (and the application of mathematics generally), and philosophical discourse. In his introduction to this discussion, King warns that such an unbalanced approach to examining the natural world results in ignorance of the significance of phenomena like parallax, refraction, and other areas that can reveal the vast distances that exist between planets and other astronomical phenomena. The entire passage in question is also found in the published *Theses* from Edinburgh, and replicated verbatim in the graduation "Theses Astronomicae" from the 1612–16 class:

> Our vision, subject to and processed through a bodily instrument, has acquired a function that has been defined within certain established quasi boundaries of qualities and limited by nature ... So, unless they [observed phenomena] are subjected to the measurements of geometric proofs with a particularly agile attentiveness of the mind, then scare anything certain can be stated about the stars.[50]

According to King, this approach allowed the wise in previous and current generations to agree that the heavens contain orbs moving through space at greatly divergent distances, and that those who think the universe made up of one sphere are not considering the evidence properly.[51] This, then, provides the argument against any system (explicitly Cesalpino's) that promotes the idea of circles and planes locked onto a single sphere.

As indicated above, the educational importance of this extended discussion from Dk.7.29 at Edinburgh is attested by the repeated citation of sections of it in the *Theses*. The passage containing the extended Cesalpino discussion in Dk.7.29 is also replicated in the graduation theses across a generation.[52] This section of Dk. 7.29 is significant for our understanding of the collapse of Aristotelian philosophy and what followed it in the academy in Europe in this period and is dealt with in greater detail elsewhere.[53] However, it must be addressed in part here because it provides an insight into the characterization of Cesalpino's work within contemporary discussions on how to integrate both philosophical and astronomical approaches in examining the universe. A series of writers are cited by Adam King in Dk.7.29 as having produced insoluble problems for natural philosophers: "Jean Pena, Tycho Brahe, Christoph Rothmann, Johannes Kepler and other recent writers have created much greater trouble for antiquity through their work on the comets and refraction."[54]

The passage above highlights the presence in formal education at Edinburgh of a fundamental intellectual shift that was taking place throughout Europe. It begins by stating that the philosophical tradition itself ("antiquity") is now in particular difficulty. Refraction and comets are the instruments that spell trouble. Quoting all the authors mentioned above, King explains to students that the absence of multiple refractions in the lights of the stars through elemental spheres or any mediating optical filters that celestial spheres would surely produce, suggests that arguing for their existence is difficult. King states, if we look at the very accurate observations of Brahe and Kepler, the most likely scenario is that a single filter, the earth's atmosphere, marks the boundary between the sublunary and superlunary world. The refraction argument is no major obstacle to Cesalpino's ideas, of course, as his cosmological model presented an Aristotelian system capable of withstanding any objections based upon a lack of discernable physical spheres. Cesalpino's cosmology was unable to withstand a system where planets and orbs were determined to be moving freely above the moon at varied distances and speeds, though. It is the work on comets that present Cesalpino's system with insurmountable problems. "Thesis Astronomica" Vll for the graduating class 1612–16 states:

> Through clear and compelling proof, many astronomers of great reputation have concluded that the comet, which was visible for almost three months in the year 1577, remained consistently above the Moon in the region of ether, as evidenced by its motion being slower than lunar motion, by the line from the celestial equator which it traced with its own motion, and its lesser angular divergence from the Moon's, which was often scarcely perceptible.[55]

This section is taken unchanged from Dk.7.29, fol. 39v, where it rounds off discussion on the proofs from atmospheric refraction. Although, King writes, transparent spheres may exist that are solid within the model Kepler and Brahe suggest (if they are so far away from the observer that no discernible refraction takes place), it is now impossible to accept this. Comets move through the area thought by previous generations and by more recent philosophers to be the domain of the solid spheres and they also travel at varying distance above the moon and below the fixed stars. King's conclusion is clear and unequivocal: "I do not see how we can free heaven, in which the new stars and comets were generated and disappeared, from mutation or maintain the doctrine of the spheres, whose settled and determined paths the comets do not follow."[56] Within this context, King explicitly states that both geometrical modeling and an agile mind are required to be able to say anything coherent about the stars. Cesalpino's single sphere with planes and circles and Ptolemy's celestial spheres have no validity when subjected to this approach.

5. Conclusion

As the evidence for Edinburgh shows, Cesalpino was presented as an interesting voice within the later Aristotelian tradition. He provided a philosophical starting point for lecturers and students to process and examine the changes that were taking place in academic conjecture on universe from the middle of the sixteenth century into the early seventeenth century. Here Cesalpino's reception provides an excellent opportunity to witness how avowedly Aristotelian and philosophical conclusions were viewed in relation to the specialist approaches. Moreover, the very specific nature of the evidence from Edinburgh, with its multi-national scholarly perspective, operating within a particularly eventful timescale from Pena to Kepler, provides a fascinating insight into how the philosophy of Cesalpino was characterized, as debates on the nature of the universe evolved across Europe in a period of significant change in methods and methodologies. Cesalpino may not have articulated his own position explicitly in relation to his contemporaries, but in the evidence for Edinburgh we can see with a degree of clarity what place his contemporaries thought that he held in this important debate.

Notes

1. Larger study: ENNSE, funded by EU's Horizon 2020 scheme under the Marie Curie Project GA n. 892528. David Malcolm McOmish, "Not Just a Lawyer: Thomas Craig and Humanist Edinburgh," *The Innes Review* 67, no. 2 (2016): 93–106; David Malcolm McOmish, "The Scientific Revolution in Scotland Revisited," *History of Universities* 21, no. 2 (2018): 153–72; David Malcolm McOmish, "European Networks and the Reformation of the University of Edinburgh: The University of Edinburgh's Astronomical Disputations from the Graduating Class of 1612–1616," in *The Bloomsbury Anthology of British University Literature*, ed. Lucy R. Nicholas and Gesine Manuwald (London: Bloomsbury, 2022), 177–201.
2. Andrea Cesalpino, *Peripateticarum quaestionum libri V* (Florence: Giunta, 1571).
3. Michael Lynch, "The Origins of Edinburgh's 'Toun College,'" *The Innes Review* 33 (1982): 3–14.
4. Thomas Craufurd, *History of the University of Edinburgh from 1580 to 1646* (Edinburgh: A. Neill, 1808), 85.
5. Owen Gingerich and Robert Westman, "The Wittich Connection: Conflict and Priority in Late Sixteenth-century Cosmology," *Transactions of the American Philosophical Society* 78, no. 7 (1988): 1–148; Adam Mosley, "Tycho Brahe and John Craig: The Dynamic of a Dispute," in *Tycho Brahe and Prague: Crossroads of European Science*, ed. John Robert Christianson et al. (Frankfurt: Harri Deutsch, 2002), 71–83; Pietro Daniel Omodeo, "Traces of a University Career in Renaissance Brandenburg: The Scottish Mathematician and Physician John Craig at Frankfurt on Oder," *History of Universities* 21, no. 2 (2018), 130–52.
6. John Durkan, "Adam King: Church Papist," *The Innes Review* 52, no. 2 (2001): 195–9.
7. MS Dk.7.29, University of Edinburgh Library.
8. MS Dk.7.29, University of Edinburgh Library, fol. 5r.
9. Craufurd, *History of the University*, 101.
10. See introduction to Anonymous, *Consilia medicinalia* (Edinburgh: Finlason, 1620).
11. Jamie Reid-Baxter, "Adam King's Soteria," http://www.philological.bham.ac.uk/king/; John Milward, *Iacobs Great Day of Trouble, and Deliuerance. A Sermon Preached at Pauls Crosse, the Fifth of August 1607. vpon His Maiesties Deliuerance from the Earle Gowries Treason and Conspiracie by Iohn Milvvarde Doctor of Diuinitie* (London: Stansby, 1610). John Jollie, *Epithalamium et gratulatio* (Heidelberg: Lancelot, 1613); John Jollie, Συζητησις *medica de internis oculorum affectibus* (Basel: Genathius, 1613).
12. Lord Seton and Adam King were both Catholics educated in Rome and Paris: Durkan, "Adam King," 195–9; Alexander Bower, *The History of the University of Edinburgh: Chiefly Compiled from Original Papers and Records*, vol. 1 (Edinburgh: Alexander Smellie, 1817), 144; David Calderwood, *History of the Kirk of Scotland* 6 (Edinburgh: Wodrow, 1845), 518; McOmish, "Not Just a Lawyer," 101–2.

13 Edward Grant, *Planets, Stars, and Orbs: The Medieval Cosmos, 1200–1687* (Cambridge: Cambridge University Press, 1994), 324–70; Eric John Aiton, "Celestial Spheres and Circles," *History of Science* 19, no. 2 (1981): 75–114, at 76–7.
14 Ibid., 77.
15 Ibid., 78.
16 Ibid., 77.
17 Ibid., 84.
18 Miguel A. Granada, "Did Tycho Eliminate the Celestial Spheres before 1586?," *Journal for the History of Astronomy* 37, no. 2 (2006): 125–45, at 128–9. For Pena's dependence upon the work of Gemma Frisius, see Aiton, "Celestial Spheres," 101–2.
19 James M. Lattis, *Between Copernicus and Galileo: Christoph Clavius and the Collapse of Ptolemaic Cosmology* (Chicago: University of Chicago Press, 1994), 147–50.
20 Aiton, "Celestial Spheres," 102–3.
21 Eric John Aiton, "Johannes Kepler and the Astronomy without Hypotheses," *Japanese Studies in the History of Science* 14 (1976): 77–100; Aiton, "Celestial Spheres."
22 McOmish, "Not Just a Lawyer," 95–9.
23 McOmish, "Scientific Revolution," 161–2; Edward Rosen, "Thomas Seget of Seton," *Scottish Historical Review* 28, no. 105,1 (April 1949): 91–5; Stefano Gattei, "The Wandering Scot Thomas Seget's Album amicorum," *Nuncius* 28, no. 2 (2013): 345–463.
24 Thomas Seget, *Album Amicorum*, MS Vat. Lat. 9385, Biblioteca Apostolica Vaticana, Vatican City, fol. 83r.
25 Cesalpino, *QP* (1571), fol. 53r; Aristotle, *Cael.* 2.4.287a6–12.
26 Cesalpino, *QP* (1571), fol. 53r-v: "ex demonstratione Aristotelis, 4. Phy. text. 71 ubi probatur, in vacuo non posse fieri motum." Aristotle, *Ph.* 4.9.215a1–30.
27 Cesalpino, *QP* (1571), fol. 53v: "in vacuo impossibile motum fieri; nihil enim tangitur."
28 Ibid., "successio partium se invicem tangentium, in qua motus consistit."
29 Ibid., fol. 54v: "Si igitur vera sunt, quae de loci natura et resistentia dicta sunt, impossibile est ex sphaeris se invicem complectentibus coagmentari caelum."
30 Ibid., fol. 55r: "Haec atque alia huiusmodi incommoda sequuntur, si caelum ex sphaeris componatur."
31 Ibid., fol. 55v: "Ex circulis igitur coagmentata est caeli sphaera secundum quos motus sempiternus peragitur." [Therefore the sphere of heaven has been composed out of circles, around which perpetual motion is realized].
32 Ibid., fol. 55r: "Dicimus igitur Aristotelis sententiam fuisse totum caelum continuum quoddam corpus esse." See Aristotle, *Cael.* 2.8.290a6–7.
33 Giovanni Gellera, "Natural Philosophy in the Graduation Theses of the Scottish Universities in the First Half of the Seventeenth Century" (PhD diss., University of Glasgow, 2012), 15–16; Christine M. Shepherd, "Philosophy and Science in the Arts Curriculum of the Scottish Universities in the 17th Century" (PhD diss., University of Edinburgh, 1974), 357–65.
34 Gellera, *Natural Philosophy*, 17; Paul Wood, "The Scientific Revolution in Scotland," in *The Scientific Revolution in National Context*, ed. Roy Porter and Mikulas Teich (Cambridge: Cambridge University Press, 1992), 263–87, at 263–5.
35 McOmish, "Scientific Revolution," 155–8; John L. Russell, "Cosmological Teaching in the Seventeenth-Century Scottish Universities: Part 1," *Journal for the History of Astronomy* 5 (1974): 122–32.
36 For a list of the extant notebooks for Edinburgh, see Shepherd, *Philosophy and Science*, 344–55.

37 Dk. 7.29 does not contain specific reference to its completion date. However, the letter from the Lord Chancellor, which recommends it for educational use, is dated August 5, 1616. Adam King wrote that he returned to Scotland in late 1595, see Dk. 7.29, fol. 6v. English spies also noted his return in December 1595, see Durkan, "Adam King," 197.
38 McOmish, "European Networks."
39 William King, *Theses philosophicae* (Edinburgh: Johannes Wreittoun, 1628), "Theses Physicae," 14: "Orbium caelesium continguas superficies, laevore, quantum natura efficere potuit, perfectissimo expolitas, omnes intelligunt."
40 King, *Theses Philosophicae*, "Theses Physicae," 14.1: "Qua alter alterum secum promoveat aut retardet, nulla omnino est extremitatum contiguarum inaequalitas, quae mutuam attritionem pariat."
41 King, *Theses Philosophicae*, "Theses Physicae" 14.4: "Longe falluntur, qui orbium caelestium conversionem ex sola superficierum attritione, quam mutatio contactus efficiat, fieri autumant."
42 This abstract system is recapitulated in other *Theses* across a generation, e.g., "Theses Physicae" and "Theses Astronomicae" (especially II) from 1612 to 1616.
43 Julius Caesar Scaliger, *Exotericarum exercitationum liber quintus decimus de Subtilitate, ad H. Cardanum* (Paris: Vascosan, 1557), 68.2. For discussion of Scaliger's development of motive intelligences, see Kuni Sakamoto, *Julius Caesar Scaliger, Renaissance Reformer of Aristotelianism: A Study of His Exotericae Exercitationes* (Leiden: Brill, 2016), 94–8.
44 King, Dk. 7.29, fol. 39r: "At longe fallitur, qui orbium caelestium conversionem, ex sola superficierum attritione, quam mutatio contactus efficiat fieri autumat; neque enim orbis orbem circumagit contactu, nisi qua contactus fit, superficies asperae sint et inaequales ut in horologiorum rotis videmus: orbium autem caelestium contiguas superficies, laevore quantum natura efficere potuit perfectissimo expolitas, omnes intelligunt ut qua alter alterum secum promoveat, aut retardet, nulla omnino sit extremitatum contiguarum inaequalitas; quae mutuam attritionem aut affricationem pariat. Non moventur ergo per contactum sed a sua quisque intelligentia assistente. Sola enim sui intellectione, suum movet orbem prima aliosque simili quo suum modo. Citeriores vero mentes gemina movent intellectione: una sui, quo suos rotant orbes, altera cum intelligunt primam qua cum hac unum fiunt, per praesentiam intellectionis, quasi irradicationem mutuam ut illius imitentur et sequantur conversionem."
45 McOmish, "European Networks," 194–5, 211.
46 King, Dk. 7.29, fol. 39r: "Andreas Caesalpinus, (lib.3. Quaest. Peripateticarum. Quaest.4.) dum statuit contiguos orbes nisi mutui contactus mutatione et superficierum attritu non posse moveri et unumquemque orbium contigui mobilis conversione circumduci. Hinc consequi oportere putat supremum orbem non suo tantum sed contigui etiam inferioris motu cieri, medios orbes triplici, suo proprio, et gemino utrinque contingentium superioris ac inferioris ideoque in adversas partes, contrariis motionibus distrahi infimum demum, solo suo et ambientis contigui. Quae siquidem absurda sunt et impossibilia; caelum in contiguos orbes non esse dividendum censet."
47 In the daily lectures for the 1616–20 class on Aristotle, *Physics* book 4, on the vacuum and location, the above section is replicated, but without citing Cesalpino, see *Dictates of George Livingston*, MS Dc.10.29, Edinburgh University Library, Edinburgh, fol. 58v. See Dc. 10.29, fols. 57r–58v for full discussion on the subject.

48 See McOmish, "European Networks," passim but note 8 especially.
49 Dk. 7.29, fols. 38v–39r: "Qui e veteribus sensum cum mente (ut author est Aristoteles) confuderunt; nec aliud de rebus iudicium tulerunt: quam quod sensui comprobaretur: dum nullam orbium caelestium divisionem oculis usurparent: non nisi unum continuum caeli corpus, in quo moveantur sidera, statuerunt … Qua recentiorum nonnulli illam orbium caelestium naturam, tot retro saeculis creditam, non sensuum iudicio, sed firmis rationum momentis, e medio tollere iure videri volunt."
50 Dk. 7.29. fol. 38v: "Visio nostra corporeo addicta et exercita organo, actionem certis quibusdam circumstantiarum quasi terminis definitam et circumscriptam a natura obtinuit: quos ultra citrave sese expedire, aut officio suo apte defungi nequeat … ut nisi vivaciore mentis opera, ad geometricarum demonstrationum trutinam expendantur; certi quicquam de iis vix statui queat." See McOmish, "European Networks"; "Thesis Astronomica" III and accompanying note.
51 Dk. 7.29, fol. 39r: "Si multiplicem motuum in sideribus anomaliam, et variata subinde intervalla, vel leviuscule observassent: nunquam uni caelo astra omnia affixent. [If they had even slightly marked the many irregularities of movements among the stars, and their repeatedly changed distances, they would never have attached all the stars to a single heaven.]" See Grant, *Planets, Stars, and Orbs*, 271–5 for other ancients who thought this.
52 For the 1612–16 class and the 1628 class attested above, see McOmish, "European Networks." Dk. 7.29 continued to be quoted extensively and verbatim at Edinburgh up to the middle of the seventeenth century, see *Dictates of Alexander Hepburn*, MS Dk. 5.5, Edinburgh University Library, Edinburgh, 1643–4.
53 McOmish, "European Networks;" "Thesis Astronomica" VII and accompanying notes.
54 Dk. 7.29, fol. 39v: "Maius antiquitati negotium facessunt, Ioannes Pena, Tychon Brahaeus, Christophorus Rothmannus, Ioannes Keplerus aliique recentiorum; refractionum et cometarum argumento."
55 Dk.7.29, fols. 39v–40r: "Cometam a.d. 1577 tribus fere mensibus conspicuam, ex uniformi eius motu tardiore Lunari, ex ductu maximi circuli quem motu proprio designavit, ex Parallaxj minore Lunari, et interdum vix sensili: plerique magni nominis astronomi in aetheris regione Luna superiori constitisse evidenti et firma demonstratione collegerunt."
56 Dk.7.29, fol. 40r: "non video, qui caelum in quo nova sidera et cometae generentur ac evanescunt, a mutatione vindicare, aut orbium doctrinam sustinere possimus: quorum certam ac definitam revolutionem cometae non sequantur."

Bibliography

Manuscripts

MS Dc. 10.29, Edinburgh University Library, Edinburgh.
MS Dk. 5.5, Edinburgh University Library, Edinburgh.
MS Dk. 7.29, University of Edinburgh Library, Edinburgh.
MS Vat. Lat. 9385, Biblioteca Apostolica Vaticana, Vatican City.

Primary Sources

Aristotle. *The Complete Works of Aristotle*, edited by Jonathan Barnes. 2 vols. Princeton: Princeton University Press, 1984.
Cesalpino, Andrea. *Peripateticarum quaestionum libri quinque*. Venice: Giunta, 1571.
Cesalpino, Andrea. *Quaestionum peripatetricarum libri quinque*. Venice: Giunta, 1593.
Consilia medicinalia. Edinburgh: Finlason, 1620.
King, William. *Theses philosophicae*. Edinburgh: Wreittoun, 1628.
Scaliger, Julius Caesar. *Exotericarum exercitationum liber quintus decimus de Subtilitate, ad H. Cardanum*. Paris: Vascosan, 1557.

Secondary Sources

Aiton, Eric John. "Celestial Spheres and Circles." *History of Science* 19 (1981): 75–114.
Aiton, Eric John. "Johannes Kepler and the Astronomy without Hypotheses." *Japanese Studies in the History of Science* 14 (1976): 77–100.
Bower, Alexander. *The History of the University of Edinburgh: Chiefly Compiled from Original Papers and Records*, 3 vols. Edinburgh: Alexander Smellie, 1817.
Calderwood, David. *History of the Kirk of Scotland* 6. Edinburgh: Wodrow, 1845.
Craufurd, Thomas. *History of the University of Edinburgh from 1580 to 1646*. Edinburgh: A. Neill, 1808.
Durkan, John. "Adam King: Church Papist." *The Innes Review* 52, no. 2 (2001): 195–9.
Gattei, Stefano. "The Wandering Scot Thomas Seget's Album Amicorum." *Nuncius* 28, no. 2 (2013): 345–463.
Gellera, Giovanni. "Natural Philosophy in the Graduation Theses of the Scottish Universities in the First Half of the Seventeenth Century." PhD diss., University of Glasgow, 2012.
Gingerich, Owen, and Robert Westman. "The Wittich Connection: Conflict and Priority in Late Sixteenth-century Cosmology." *Transactions of the American Philosophical Society* 78, no. 7 (1988): 1–148.
Granada, Miguel A. "Did Tycho Eliminate the Celestial Spheres before 1586?" *Journal for the History of Astronomy* 37 (2006): 125–45.
Grant, Edward. *Planets, Stars, and Orbs: The Medieval Cosmos, 1200–1687*. Cambridge: Cambridge University Press, 1994.
Jollie, John. *Epithalamium et gratulatio*. Heidelberg: Lancelot, 1613.
Jollie, John. Συζήτησις *medica de internis oculorum affectibus*. Basel: Genathius, 1613.
Lattis, James M. *Between Copernicus and Galileo: Christoph Clavius and the Collapse of Ptolemaic Cosmology*. Chicago: University of Chicago Press, 1994.
Lynch, Michael. "The Origins of Edinburgh's 'Toun College.'" *The Innes Review* 33 (1982): 3–14.
McOmish, David Malcolm. "European Networks and the Reformation of the University of Edinburgh: The University of Edinburgh's Astronomical Disputations from the Graduating Class of 1612–1616." In *The Bloomsbury Anthology of British University Literature*, edited by Lucy R. Nicholas and Gesine Manuwald, 177–201. London: Bloomsbury, 2022.
McOmish, David Malcolm. "Not Just a Lawyer: Thomas Craig and Humanist Edinburgh." *The Innes Review* 67, no. 2 (2016): 93–106.
McOmish, David Malcolm. "The Scientific Revolution in Scotland Revisited." *History of Universities* 21, no. 2 (2018): 153–72.

Milward, John. *Iacobs Great Day of Trouble, and Deliuerance. A Sermon Preached at Pauls Crosse, the Fifth of August 1607. vpon His Maiesties Deliuerance from the Earle Gowries Treason and Conspiracie by Iohn Milvvarde Doctor of Diuinitie.* London: Stansby, 1610.

Mosley, Adam. "Tycho Brahe and John Craig: The Dynamic of a Dispute." In *Tycho Brahe and Prague: Crossroads of European Science*, edited by John Robert Christianson et al. 71–83. Frankfurt: Harri Deutsch, 2002.

Omodeo, Pietro Daniel. "Traces of a University Career in Renaissance Brandenburg: The Scottish Mathematician and Physician John Craig at Frankfurt on Oder." *History of Universities* 21, no. 2 (2018), 130–52.

Reid-Baxter, Jamie. "Adam King's Soteria." http://www.philological.bham.ac.uk/king/.

Rosen, Edward. "Thomas Seget of Seton," *Scottish Historical Review* 28, no. 105,1 (April 1949): 91–5.

Russell, John L. "Cosmological Teaching in the Seventeenth-Century Scottish Universities: Part 1." *Journal for the History of Astronomy* 5 (1974): 122–32.

Sakamoto, Kuni. *Julius Caesar Scaliger, Renaissance Reformer of Aristotelianism: A Study of His Exotericae Exercitationes*. Leiden: Brill, 2016.

Shepherd, Christine M. "Philosophy and Science in the Arts Curriculum of the Scottish Universities in the 17th Century." PhD diss., University of Edinburgh, 1974.

Wood, Paul. "The Scientific Revolution in Scotland." In *The Scientific Revolution in National Context*, edited by Roy Porter and Mikulas Teich, 263–87. Cambridge: Cambridge University Press, 1992.

Part Two

Botany and Mineralogy

7

Cesalpino's (Aristotelian) Philosophy of Plants: A Science of Botany in the Renaissance

Fabrizio Baldassarri

Despite the general claim that a theoretical approach to botany only developed in the late seventeenth century, and that Renaissance botany was a mere collection and identification of specimens, the recent studies of plants in the early modern time have shed light on a more complex situation.[1] In his well-known monograph, *The Science of Describing*, Brian Ogilvie has highlighted four moments in Renaissance science, which perfectly apply to sixteenth-century botanical studies.[2] Accordingly, the first phase is the philological attempts to identify specimens for medical aims; the second reveals a naturalistic attention to plants; the third enhances an exchange of specimens and the fabrication of herbaria as well as the construction of botanical gardens, while the fourth phase emphasizes the production of a theoretical framework to classify plants. However, the interconnection of these features surfaced throughout the sixteenth century. A specific case is found in the work of Andrea Cesalpino, whose botanical text, *De plantis libri XVI* [*DP*] (1583), represents a climax in Renaissance botany and reveals a combination of such diverse phases, as Cesalpino incorporated a theoretical approach to botany with the practical attempt to identify and classify plants, uniting the study of plant life and functioning with the systematization of plants in an original way.[3]

A theoretical attention to plants was not new. Around thirty years before the publication of Cesalpino's *DP*, Girolamo Cardano (1501–76) and Julius Caesar Scaliger (1484–1558) had attempted to place plants within a natural philosophical framework, investigating the properties of plants within a theoretical aim. Yet, a philosophical

---

Financial support for the research for this paper was provided from the European Union's Horizon 2020 research and innovation programme under the Marie Skłodowska-Curie Grant Agreement n.890770, "VegSciLif." I would like to thank my supervisors, Marco Sgarbi and Domenico Bertoloni Meli for their insights and suggestions. I benefitted from comments and discussions at the panel "Andrea Cesalpino: A Physician, Philosopher, and Botanist in Renaissance Italy," I organized at RSA 2021 online, and also at the workshop Craig and I co-organized in 2022. I am thankful to the participants and discussants of all workshops, and especially to Craig Martin for his comments, and to Brenton M. Wells for both his comments and the discussions on this topic.

interpretation of plants had already surfaced even earlier in Raffaello Maffei's (1451–1522) *Commentariorum urbanarum libri XXXVIII* (Rome 1506; Paris 1516), as botany acquired "a more 'philosophical' character [which] made [its] connection to (or dependence on) medicine and pharmacy a little less evident."[4] In Cardano and Scaliger, such a philosophical attention to plants gained momentum. In both *De subtilitate rerum* (1550) and *De rerum varietate libri XVII* (1558), Cardano reduced the properties, characteristics, and life of plants to a few rules, as he understood the study of plants to be the study of the internal structure and activities working in them. Accordingly, this investigation would produce a systematization to their variety, as a theoretical frame would help understand the diversity of plants and classify them. While Scaliger eagerly opposed Cardano in the *Exercitationes exotericae de subtilitate* (1557), as they debated the functions of plants and their principle, namely the vegetative soul, he also published a series of commentaries on ancient texts on plants. These texts are *In libros duos qui inscribuntur De plantis, Aristotele autore, libri duo* (1556), on the Pseudo-Aristotelian *De plantis*; and *Commentarii et animadversions in sex libros De causis plantarum Theophrasti* (1566) and *Animadversiones in historia Theophrasti* (1584), on Theophrastus make possessive by adding's botanical oeuvres. As a result, Scaliger proposed a philosophical investigation of the properties of plants within an Aristotelian line, but moving outside of this frame, as he inquired whether plants may have more powers than those deriving from the vegetative soul and ultimately proposed an alternative definition of plant life.[5]

Thus, a theoretical approach to plants, concentrating on the cause and nature of plant activities, and how they were reflected in their differentiation, formed a significant part of Renaissance knowledge. Cardano's and Scaliger's investigations reveal the degree to which plants were intertwined in natural philosophy in the middle of the Cinquecento, as scholars not only accumulated or identified vegetal bodies, but also investigated their nature, faculties, and principles, and provided a theory to the study of plants.

However far from this conflict, Cesalpino uncovered another attempt to place plants within a philosophical framework. His perspective was innovative. On the one hand, Cesalpino was an Aristotelian philosopher, and grounded botany on a philosophical program, connecting Theophrastus's classification of plants with an attempt to rewrite Pseudo-Aristotle's *De plantis* in a more orthodox way.[6] On the other hand, Cesalpino was also a botanist and the director of the Botanical garden in Pisa, and produced two herbaria, ultimately equipping a science of plants with botanical observation and experimentation. A fascinating combination of diverse features ultimately emerged.

In this chapter, I first present Cesalpino's interest in botany, his work at the Botanical garden as a professor and the production of a herbarium in 1563. Second, I discuss the epistolary preface to the herbarium, in which he nuanced several epistemological and methodological issues, consistent with a philosophical approach to plants. Third, I investigate the more theoretical and philosophical section of Cesalpino's *De plantis*, namely Book 1, in which he applied an Aristotelian philosophy to botany. In the conclusion, I lay out Cesalpino's original philosophy of plants and its reception.

1. Cesalpino's Botanical Aims: Exchanges of Specimens, the *Herbarium*, and Exotics

In 1544, Cesalpino moved to Pisa from Arezzo to study medicine and botany and graduated on March 20, 1551. He had studied under Luca Ghini (1490–1556), who promoted the observation and cultivation of plants as well as the foundation of the botanical garden in Pisa. Ghini was at the center of a huge net of scholars exchanging specimens and botanical knowledge. And Cesalpino likely benefitted from several of these connections. For instance, Ulisse Aldrovandi was in good relationship with Ghini, whom he met in Bologna in 1551 and later visited in Pisa in 1553, when he likely attended Ghini's classes.[7] It is therefore possible that Cesalpino and Aldrovandi were acquainted by the early 1550s, for it is likely that Cesalpino remained in Pisa after his graduation, although there is no evidence of any direct contact and no direct letters between the two have survived.[8] Four years later, in 1555, when Ghini moved to Bologna, Cesalpino succeeded him as a Prefect of the botanical garden and lecturer of simples.[9] In Pisa, Cesalpino's career grew in a context of botanical observation, and both Ghini and Cesalpino were renowned among naturalists at the time.[10] Pierre Belon (1517–64) and Matthias de L'Obel (or Lobel, 1538–1616), among others, praised Cesalpino's botanical knowledge and the richness of the Pisan botanical garden, as they exchanged specimens with him, revealing that Cesalpino's interest in plants did not merely consist of a theoretical approach.[11]

This is testified to by his fabrication of two *horti sicci*. In 1563, he donated a herbarium to Bishop Tornabuoni, which resulted from several years of work in the botanical garden, while he had prepared another one dedicated to Cosimo I de' Medici, unfortunately lost.[12] The elaboration of a *hortus siccus* entails two main epistemological issues. In line with Ghini's study of botany, the first point is the idea that a book of plants should be made with actual specimens that have been dried and pressed onto paper, while the representation of plants in printing is inefficient if not misleading.[13] Second, botanical knowledge should therefore derive from the observation of plants in nature. A science of plants thus consisted in the direct observation of specimens and their cultivation, something favored by the work in a botanical garden, the laboratory of botany. Contrasting the textual accounts of specimens, for Cesalpino the knowledge of plants primarily is a knowledge of actual bodies derived from a direct and practical experience with plants (see Figure 7.1 and Figure 7.2).

Yet, the observation of plants is one side of botanical knowledge; the second is their systematization. The herbarium connects these two aspects, as it resulted from both his work at the botanical garden and from several travels in Northern and Central Italy, where he collected several specimens. He utilized his experience to attempt to order specimens systematically. The herbarium collects 768 specimens, corresponding to 760 species (while *De plantis* mentions around 1500 plants), which he named in Greek, Latin, and sometimes in the vernacular; references to Theophrastus, Dioscorides, or Pliny surface in the text (see Figure 7.3).[14] In making actual plants visible, and not their mere appearance,[15] the herbarium reveals an epistemological value, as it favored botanical knowledge, connecting the knowledge inherited by ancient texts with the

Figure 7.1 [On the left] 157. Lupus salictarius. Pli: Lupulo (Humulus Lupulus L). [On the right] 158. Κάνναβις: Cannabis sativa: Canapa (Cannabis sativa L). Andrea Cesalpino, *Herbarium*, fol. 63. Courtesy of Sistema Museale di Ateneo, Museo di Storia Naturale (Botanica) of the Università di Firenze.

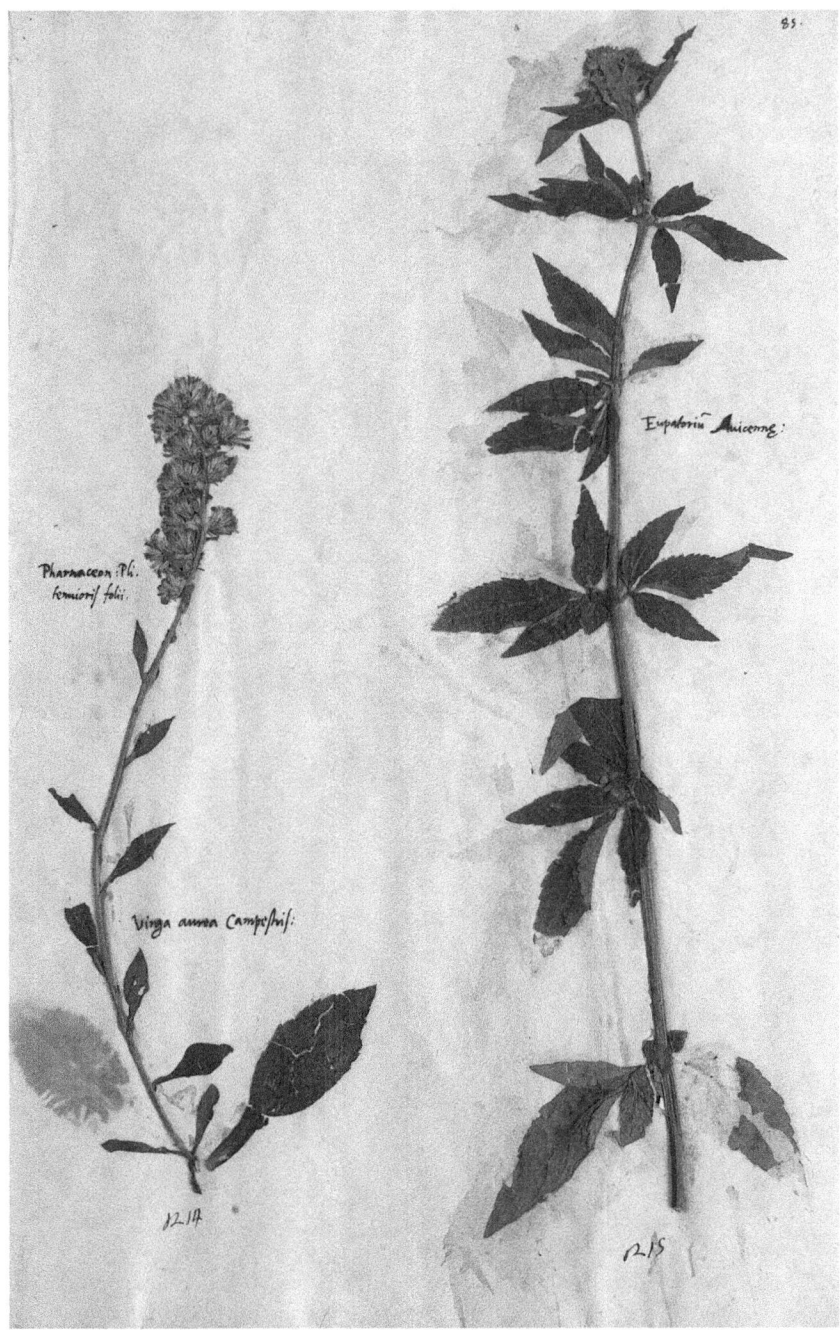

Figure 7.2 [On the left] 214. Pharnaceon. Pli. tenuioris folii: Virga aurea Campestris (Solidago Virgaurea L). [On the right] 215. Eupatorium Avicennae (Eupatorium cannabinum L). Cesalpino, *Herbarium*, fol. 85. Courtesy of Sistema Museale di Ateneo, Museo di Storia Naturale (Botanica) of the Università di Firenze.

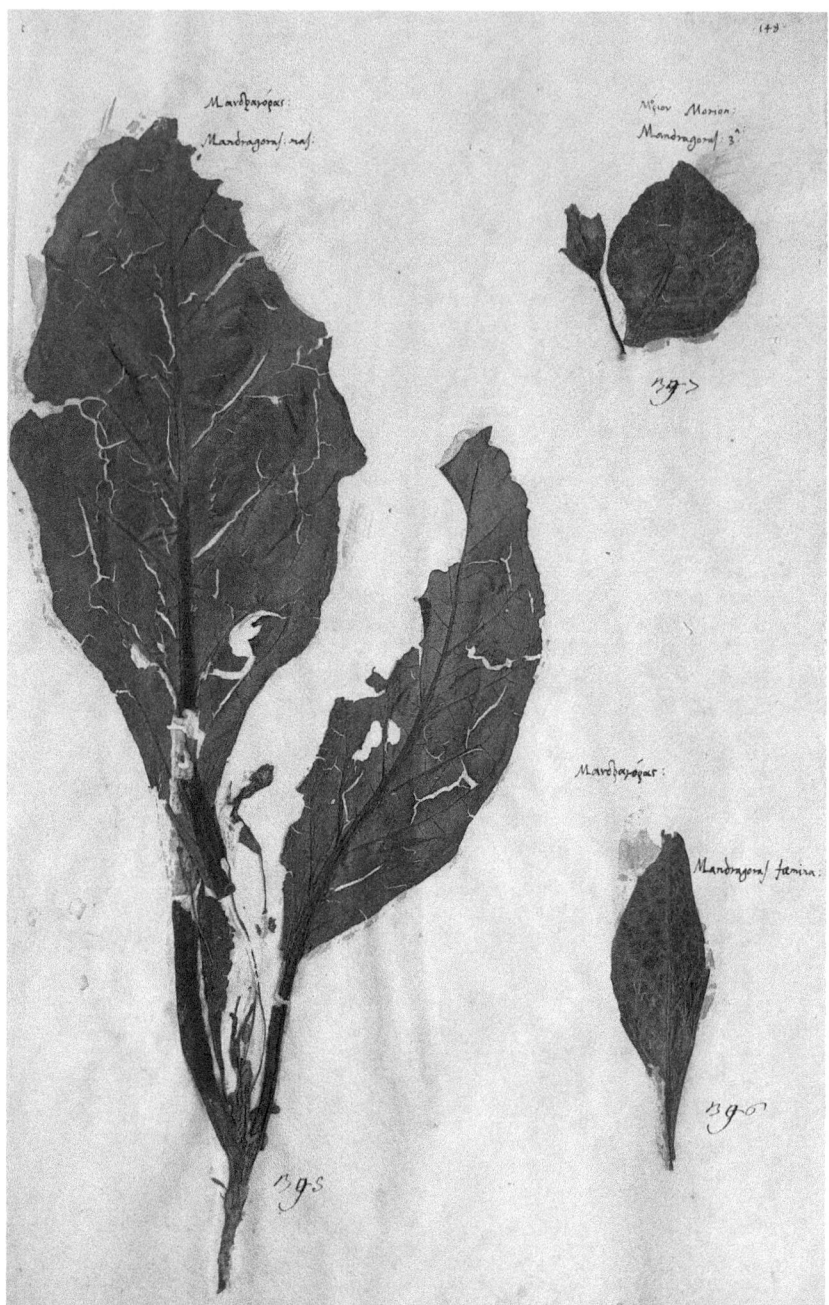

Figure 7.3 [On the left] 395. Μανδραγόρας: Mandragoras mas (Mandragora veralis B). [On the bottom right] 396. Μανδραγόρας: Mandragoras foemina (Mandragorae microcarpae B). [On the top right] 397. Μόριον: Morion: Mandragoras 3° (Mandragora officinarum L). Cesalpino, *Herbarium*, fol. 148. Courtesy of Sistema Museale di Ateneo, Museo di Storia Naturale (Botanica) of the Università di Firenze.

direct observation of specimens. The second point is to use the herbarium as a way to test the theoretical systematization of plants. Indeed, the order he followed in collecting specimens mirrored the one used in *DP*, as the systematization of plants is homogeneous to his later text, and his investigation is triggered by the same theoretical aspects, as I discuss in the next paragraph. As a result, the herbarium offers a bridge between the collection and identification of specimens and their theoretical systematization.

Cesalpino's broad interest in plants surfaces in a few surviving letters, in which he either identified specimens or discussed their healing power. For example, in a October 2, 1541, letter to Baccio Valori, Cesalpino identified some vines as being "*Cuscuta* as it is named in *spetierie*, which is a plant that *grows only on tall herbs*, or shrub (*frutex*), or trees, and with some long threads it intertwines and curls up little branches, as if almost choking [them] dry them out, for what reason, Theophrastus called it *Orobanche*, as it strangles the Orobo."[16] In a letter from 1586, he also discussed plants coming from Africa and Asia, such as the balsam, possessed by "a physician from Vicenza [i.e., Prospero Alpini] [who has] one pound and a half of true Balsam from Arabia Felix."[17] In the same year, Cesalpino sent a sample of such Balsam contained in a vial to Belisario Vita, with the result of his examination of its nature. He claimed that

> from the marks [*contrassegni*] written by Dioscorides and others, this is the true Balsam: because, more than the suavity of smell and its pungent taste, in pouring a little drop of water on it makes it enlarge in a white and very thin veil; this is unlike other oils that collect in round drops, or with the shape of stars, on the water, as Dioscorides claimed; and it is unlike white spirits that fell to the bottom.[18]

As it appears, Cesalpino possibly performed some experiments with it.

He also expected to receive plants of cinnamon from the Indies, likely from Filippo Sassetti, a former student of Cesalpino, who had written a treatise on it, *Discorso sopra il cinnamomo*.[19] Cesalpino received a sheet with the story of "Cadira Tree [*Albero Cadira*], whose juice is called Catu, and had been judged [to be] the *Lycium indicum* of Dioscorides," claiming that if he could receive a specimen he would be able "to say his opinion regarding the Lycium."[20] Later, he proclaimed to have used Catu to heal ophthalmic inflammations and restore the eye.[21] And he studied the powers of white hellebores, which provide him the occasion to discuss plants' toxicity (for example in "Aconitus," "Epimenidia," "giunco," and so on). In 1602, he discussed melons and similar fruits, such as cucumbers and pumpkins, *pepon* and *melopepon*, and quinces.[22] Besides the collection of plants in the herbarium, Cesalpino's investigation of botany surpassed the strictures of a theoretical approach, as he engaged in examining exotic plants to recapture the references of Dioscorides, and to determine the medicinal (both healing or toxic) powers of plants, ultimately revealing the breath of his studies. Besides the issue of classification, a broad attention to plants surfaces in Cesalpino's correspondence, as he investigated different areas, such as materia medica, exotics, philology, and the physical properties of specimens. A discussion of these cases was included in the *Appendix to De plantis*, posthumously published in 1603, which contained sections on eastern balsam, cinnamon, Lycium indicum, pepons, and cucumbers, and other plants that did not find any space in the 1583 version of *DP*.[23]

From his study of plants in the field and in the botanical garden, his fabrication of a herbarium, and his later discussion of particular plants such as exotics of different kinds, what emerges is that Cesalpino's botanical aims were not purely philosophical, theoretical, or speculative. While his epistemological attention to plant systematization undoubtedly played a major role in the elaboration of *De plantis*, Cesalpino observed plants at different levels, performing experiments on them to test their powers and virtues, and used them for therapeutic purposes, uncovering a wide spectrum of what he intended for botanical science. In the next sections, I focus more on Cesalpino's methodology in botany.

2. From the Herbarium to *De plantis*: A Methodology in Botany

Cesalpino prefaced the Herbarium with a long letter to Alfonso Tornabuoni (1506-77), dated September 14, 1563 (see Figure 7.4). Here, Cesalpino provided an explanation of the reasons underlying the preparation of the herbarium and the methodology he followed in collecting the specimens. Accordingly, "while the number of plants [...] keeps growing constantly, and this cannot be comprehended by the human intellect, by gathering them according to their similarities, and reducing to a small number, it would be easy to have the knowledge of them we expect."[24] In the Italian text, supposedly the original, Cesalpino's claim is more specific, as he wrote that the number of plants grows *in infinito*, suggesting that the number of plants circulating at the time, and likely brought from the West Indies, was growing without any limitation. If, on the one hand, this condition makes any science of plants impossible, according to Cesalpino, on the other hand it is possible to reduce plants to a smaller number by gathering them by means of their similarities. This point is crucial. Cesalpino was aware, in 1563, of the different attempts of his fellow naturalists to gather and catalogue the variety of plants, and for this reason, his claim of the scientific inadequacy of their efforts is striking.[25] In contrast to these efforts, Cesalpino proposed his own way of collecting plants according to their similarities. So far, the reason for creating a herbarium is to favor the knowledge of plants and deal with their variety.

Then, Cesalpino reconstructed a history of botanical science. In going back to the ancients who attempted to perform a systematic reduction of plants, Cesalpino mentioned Theophrastus, who had very carefully [*con gran' diligentia*] examined trees, crops, and vegetables, but neglected medicinal herbs, and Dioscorides, who gathered plants according to the similarities in medical virtues.[26] A difference between the two scholars surfaces, according to Cesalpino. In *Historia plantarum*, Theophrastus concentrated on plants in general, using particular plants as example to clarify his system, as his goal was to define the vegetable kingdom as a whole. In *Materia medica*, Dioscorides discussed 600 medicinal plants, specifying their singular properties, as this system would be useful to physicians for treating diseases. At this stage, Cesalpino adopted the role of the physician, voicing a common accusation against Theophrastus's

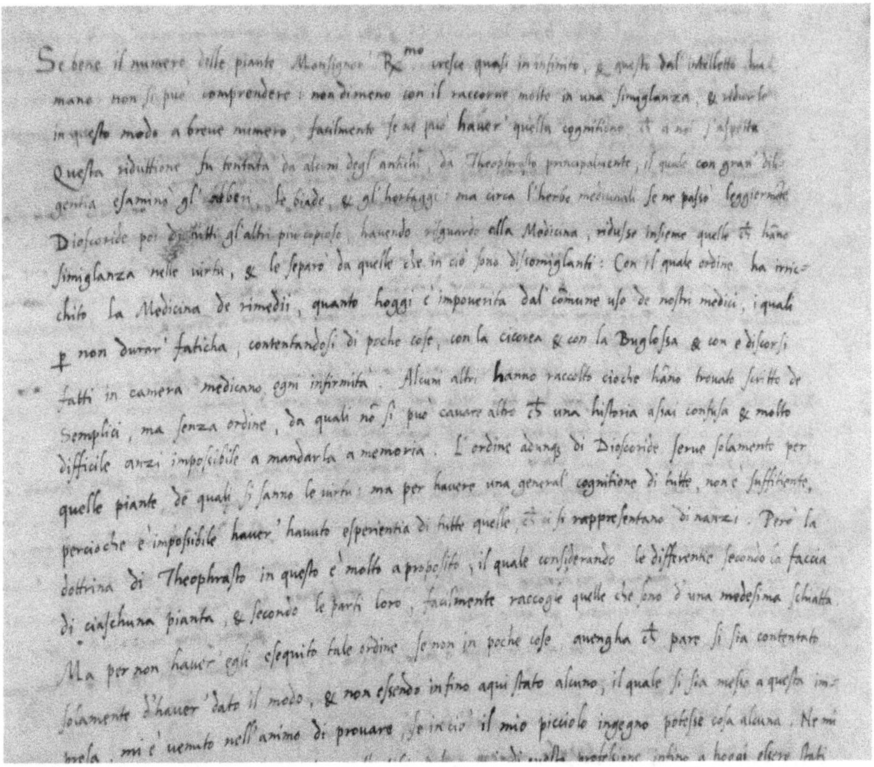
Se bene il numero delle piante Monsignor R.mo cresce quasi in infinito, & questo dal intelletto hu-
mano non si può comprendere: nondimeno con il raccorne molte in una simiglanza, & ridurle
in questo modo a breve numero, facilmente se ne può haver quella cognitione che a noi s'aspetta.
Questa riduttione fu tentata da alcuni degl'antichi, da Theophrasto principalmente, il quale con gran' diligentia esaminò gl'arberi, le biade, & gl'herbaggi: ma circa l'herbe medicinali se ne passò leggiermente.
Dioscoride poi di tutti gl'altri più copioso, havendo riguardo alla Medicina, ridusse insieme quelle che hanno
simiglanza nelle virtù, & le separò da quelle che in ciò sono dissomiglianti: Con il quale ordine ha arric-
chito la Medicina de rimedii, quanto hoggi è impoverita dal comune uso de nostri medici, i quali
per non durar' faticha, contentandosi di poche cose, con la cicorea & con la Buglossa & con e discorsi
fatti in camera medicano ogni infirmità. Alcuni altri hanno raccolto cioche hanno trovato scritto de
Semplici, ma senza ordine, da quali non si può cavare altro che una historia assai confusa & molto
difficile anzi impossibile a mandarla a memoria. L'ordine adunque di Dioscoride serve solamente per
quelle piante de quali si sanno le virtù: ma per havere una general' cognitione di tutte, non è sufficiente,
perciochè è impossibile haver' havuto esperientia di tutte quelle, che ci si rappresentano dinanzi. Però la
dottrina di Theophrasto in questo è molto a proposito, il quale considerando le differentie secondo la faccia
di ciaschuna pianta, & secondo le parti loro, facilmente raccoglie quelle che sono d'una medesima schiatta.
Ma per non haver' egli esequito tale ordine se non in poche cose, avengha che pare si sia contentato
solamente d'haver' dato il modo, & non essendo infino aqui stato alcuno, il quale si sia messo a questa impresa, mi è venuto nell'animo di provare, se in ciò il mio picciolo ingegno potesse cosa alcuna. Ne mi

Figure 7.4 Cesalpino, section of the letter to Bishop Tornabuoni used as a preface to the herbarium. Courtesy of Sistema Museale di Ateneo, Museo di Storia Naturale (Botanica) of the Università di Firenze.

systematization of plants, as the latter had very rarely discussed the healing powers of plants, and suggesting, in contrast, the importance of Dioscorides' work, whose system had enriched medicine with many remedies.

Cesalpino continued claiming that contemporary physicians had instead depleted the knowledge inherited by Dioscorides, as they tended to use the same two remedies, namely chicory [*cichorea*] and bugloss [*buglossa*],[27] while other scholars had more generally gathered the books of simples without any order, therefore deriving an incoherent history of plants. Here, he suggested that, while contemporary physicians had revealed no interest in Dioscorides' rich systematization of medicinal herbs by similarities and dissimilarities, other naturalists and botanists had gathered what they found in the study of simples without any order, producing very confusing and disordered histories of plants.

Besides his appreciation of Dioscorides' clear system of gathering plants by similarities and dissimilarities, Cesalpino then raised a criticism against the Greek naturalist. Accordingly, "Dioscorides' systematization only operates for those plants about which one already knows the virtues, while this is ineffective for acquiring a general knowledge of all [plants], as it is impossible to have experience of all of them."[28] This point is epistemologically meaningful. Cesalpino claimed that, insofar as Dioscorides' system is based on the experience one has of plants, one could draw some knowledge of that specific plant. Two features develop from this point. The first is that within Dioscorides' system it is difficult to know new plants. This is a relevant aspect, especially because, as the letter begins, Cesalpino claimed that an infinite number of new plants have penetrated Europe and need to be identified. In this sense, Dioscorides' botany has effectively provided a crucial system to medical knowledge, but has little effectiveness in accommodating and identifying new items, and it is not fit to serve for a general theory of plants. The second point is that Dioscorides' system favors a knowledge of particularities, of which one could have a direct experience, while a general framework falls beyond its goal. In challenging Dioscorides, Cesalpino thus combined two perspectives. The first is that of the prefect of the botanical garden who deals with simples and particular plants, but who also needed to accommodate and identify new specimens unknown in the ancient times. The second is that of the philosopher, aiming at constructing a general framework, universally valid. According to Cesalpino, a philosophical framework is therefore necessary to ground a science of botany.

At this point, Theophrastus resurfaces in Cesalpino's letter as a crucial point of reference. Accordingly, Theophrastus had ordered plants following the differences between plant *facies*, that is, shapes or figures, and parts, "therefore differentiating plants pursuant morphological differences."[29] However, Theophrastus did not develop a system of classification, but applied his methodology to few cases, as this consisted of comparing plants according to their similarities and differences. Still, few scholars have followed Theophrastus's methodology.

Cesalpino thus continued his history of botany by claiming that botanists or pharmacists [*semplicisti*] have paid no philosophical attention to nature, without which one cannot expect any fruit from knowledge; while only very few philosophers have studied particular things such as plants, for "the entire power [*nervus*] of philosophy consists in [such a knowledge of particular bodies]."[30] To embark in the enterprise of making Theophrastus's methodology operative, Cesalpino knew he needed to combine the botanic observation of particulars nature with a philosophical perspective.

Apparently, the herbarium is a first attempt and a crucial medium to see whether Cesalpino's methodology of dividing plants could work. First, he set out all plants and divided them into different sections, "for the first time approximatively, according to his own resolution."[31] In this way, experience has a primary role. Yet, one should add a philosophical theory to experience, defining a criterion to ground classification for all cases. Cesalpino thus claimed he did not classify plants following "the similarities between leaves, flowers, seeds, roots, nor the similarities of other parts," for several plants with different leaves are of the same group.[32] In contrast to this external way of classifying plants, Cesalpino focused on their internal functioning, claiming that "the perfection of plants, from which depends their existence and their life for generation does not proceed from those parts (though these make plants living), but proceeds from that sort of soul called vegetative, whose task is to preserve life and the species."[33] According to Cesalpino, what makes a plant is the Aristotelian vegetative soul, the principle accounting for the faculties of nutrition and reproduction.[34] These activities develop in the roots, which do not present enough differences to provide a basis for taxonomy, and in the rest of the plant, which constructs the seeds needed for reproduction, according to Cesalpino.[35] Comparing "the ways of producing seeds, or the proportion between seeds and genitals, and the similarities between seeds,"[36] Cesalpino drew the similarities to group plants in genres and families.

Although he refrained from specifying too many details here, he however indicated the division he had followed in the herbarium—while he would provide a more detailed classification later on. That is, the first group is constituted of trees and shrubs; the second group of those plants whose seeds are without any cover; the third of the plants whose seeds are enclosed in channels or vases; the fourth of the plants that do not produce any seed. This division echoes Theophrastus's text.

Cesalpino's main goal for the study of plants emerges, that is, to make botany a systematic discipline by embedding the observation of specimens within a philosophical framework. On the one hand, he rejected any systematization of plants based on outward differences, which had led to haphazard and inconsistent classifications of plants; on the other hand, he reduced the physical features of plants to nutrition and generation, that is, to the operations of the vegetative soul, "through which all [plants] have their existence."[37] In collecting plants in the herbarium, Cesalpino followed a system grounded on the idea that plants principally are living bodies endowed with a vegetative soul, and therefore able to perform nutrition and reproduction. In isolating a characteristic related to generation, Cesalpino thus grounded the differentiation of plants in genres and families on the vegetative soul.

Although the dedicatory letter contains several crucial issues, it nuances his attempt to combine a direct observation of plants with a philosophical ground, which has no conclusiveness at this stage, as he both suggested that the herbarium is a rough division of specimens and asked Tornabouni not to circulate the herbarium.[38] A more refined fruit of his botany was published twenty years later.

3. Cesalpino's Philosophy of Plants in *De plantis*

In 1583, Cesalpino published *DP*, where he laid down the principles of his philosophy of plants. These principles surface especially in Book 1, in which the criteria of such a methodology for classification are discussed, while in the remaining fifteen books, he grouped the varieties of vegetation.[39] In the dedicatory letter to the Duke Francesco I de' Medici, Cesalpino repeated some of the claims of the letter to Tornabuoni analyzed above, while adding several important clarifications. The first argument pertains to the difficulty in dealing with the vastness of the vegetal kingdom (which parallels the difficulties in dealing with the mineral and animals reigns); yet, Cesalpino claimed that this does not depend on the fact that "nature produces new forms [nor] produces new plants [...], but because new ones of their incredible number is shown to us every day."[40] New specimens circulating in Europe constituted the wide array of the vegetal world, which arrived in Pisa thanks to the travels of several naturalists.

Then, Cesalpino reconstructed a history of botanical studies, from the ancients to contemporary scholars, which is mostly a history of the therapeutic powers of plants. Yet, epistemological shortfalls had characterized this history. Cesalpino claimed that the study of plants presented several pitfalls, "not only as [botany] remained unfinished [*imperfecta*], but it is also found to be suffused with darkness [*caligine*]: [on the one hand], it is imperfect for the number of plants seems to increase day by day ..."[41] and, on the other hand, because of a certain confusion and ambiguity concerning it. A main issue regards the nomenclature of plants, as it was difficult to relate the name of plants in ancient texts with the actual specimen. After medieval obscurity, this linguistic issue had recently attracted the attention of scholars such as "[Jean] Ruel, Ermolao [Barbaro] [and] [Antonio Musa] Brasavola," who had dealt with the identification of plants. More recently, Cesalpino continued, "[Pietro Andrea] Mattioli and Luca Ghini [and] Luigi Anguillara" had exhaustively commented the ancient texts, and several exotic plants from the West and East Indies had been described in the works of Garcia de Orta and Nicolás Monardes.[42]

Despite the important work of his predecessors, botany lagged in a deplorable state, as Cesalpino wrote:

What with such an immense number of plants, I feel the want of that which one normally aspires to in any other unstructured mass. For it is inevitable that all things will be thrown into unstable disorder, unless they are collected into ranks and divided into their proper classes .... This is particularly relevant for the world of plants, where the vastness and intricacy of the disorder appall the mind and result in endless controversies over insoluble errors. For if the genus is not known, no description of a plant, however carefully propounded, will enable one to undisputedly identify it, and such descriptions are apt to mislead; for if the genera are confused all is necessarily confusion.[43]

This passage represents Cesalpino's view of the state of botany in his time. Accordingly, botany presented several problems, reducible to the issue of identification (both linguistic and physical), and to the question of classification. As scholars have focused on plants from a medical perspective, accommodating new plants for therapeutic goals, they have overlooked the general rule of any botanical science, namely the identification of correct genera and species, according to Cesalpino. Indeed, "all science consists in gathering the similar together and in differentiating the dissimilar, and this division is into genera and species, that is, into classes based on the characters, which describe the nature of the subject matter according to its differences, I tried to do this in my universal history of plants."[44] Constituting a universal history of botany, Cesalpino's program consists of dividing plants into classes and genera according to their similarities and dissimilarities.[45]

A similar methodology for the study of plants was "pointed out" by Theophrastus, "but few scholars followed him," claimed Cesalpino, "and among the contemporaries, Ruel indeed attempted [to follow it], but besides those few things he took from Theophrastus's methodology, there was no further progress."[46] Moreover, Theophrastus seldom applied his methodology, and did not make it a system grounded on an a priori principle, according to Cesalpino. Although Theophrastus identified the correct way of proceeding, he only concentrated on external criteria, like Dioscorides, who ordered plants according to their medical properties. According to Cesalpino, however, "the most fallacious [system], and the furthest from nature"[47] is the one of scholars ordering plants according to their names, such as Leonhart Fuchs did. In contrast, Cesalpino's method for finding the essential *differentiae* in plants and dividing them in genres should be grounded in nature [*secundum naturam*].

As he spelled out in the dedicatory letter, his own criteria of classification are the easiest to recognize, memorize, and use to contemplate plants; and they are not subject to changes, thereby excluding any attention to external variety. Moreover, these criteria develop an easier, shorter, more practical and more precise system, because there is no need to repeat the identifying feature of a genre, as it belongs to the plants of the same group. For this reason, he continued, there is no need for pictures of plants, as the differences between species are better conveyed by words.[48] Finally, he claimed his methodology to be predictive, as it is able to place previously unknown plants within this system and give them a name and a genre, although this may not always be the case as often only parts of exotic plants were shipped, and he could not examine the whole plant.[49]

Yet, what is this natural system? After having praised it, Cesalpino fleshed it out in book 1. He followed a philosophical path, starting from defining the nature of plants and then inferring a classification from this definition. Within this philosophical framework, the principle of classification is psychological, as he grounded it on the faculties of the vegetative soul. Then, Cesalpino provided a physical investigation of these activities, claiming that plant differences reside specifically in these aspects. Let us follow his path.

At the very beginning of the book, Cesalpino claims that:

> The nature of plants has only that genre of soul through which they nurture, grow, and generate their like, whereas they lack the power of feeling and of movement, in which consist the nature of animals. Therefore, plants require an apparatus with fewer instruments than animals do.

While the latter have a multiplicity of organs, plants are very dissimilar to animals, and many animal operations are denied to them. Therefore, plants only need "nutriment for the conservation of the individual and the seed for the perpetuation of the species."[50] In other words, the essence of the plant is the vegetative soul and its faculties, namely, nutrition, conservation, and procreation; these activities allow him to differentiate between the accidental and essential aspects of vegetation. He thus discarded the accidental aspects, dealing with external varieties, and concentrated on the vegetative operations. Since the vegetative soul is the principle of the living activities of plants, it helps specify the operations that construct and characterize plants. In this way, Cesalpino isolated the essential nature of vegetation. One should note that Cesalpino here claimed that plants only possess vegetative faculties, and were therefore deprived of sensation and motions, an issue that had already surfaced in *Quaestionum peripateticarum libri V* (1571), and that was debated in Scaliger.[51]

Not only does this philosophical premise entail a formal definition of plants as bodies essentially nurturing, growing, and reproducing, but it also entails a physical knowledge and classification of vegetal bodies. In other terms, the *differentiae* through which one constructs the classes and genres should be related to these activities principled by the vegetative soul. He started from investigating the structure of plants that perform these activities. Accordingly, there are two organs [*partes*] necessary to perform them: "the one is the roots, which draw nutrition. The other is the stalk (for herbs) or trunk (in trees) that carries the fruit and the progeny [*foetum*] for the propagation of the species."[52]

Then, following his psychological framework, Cesalpino first provided a physical description of the structure of plants (chapters 1–11); and he then set out the principles of his classification (chapters 12–14). Let us follow the chapters of Book 1.

At the end of chapter 1, he explored the soul of plants and its location, not an easy task.[53] As he stressed, if one locates it in roots, then some plants that grow from grafting appear excluded. Cesalpino also followed the ancients, who defined the inner part of plants as either a heart [*cor*], a cerebellum [*cerebrum*] or a matrix [*matricem*], as if the principle of reproduction lies there. However, Cesalpino claimed that the point of conjunction between the root and the shoot is the suitable location for the heart of plants, that is, the seat of their soul.[54] A specific substance lies here (which is edible, according to Cesalpino), and like the marrow in animals, goes from the brain, which in plants are the roots, to the stalk, distributing the vital humor [*humorem vitalem*] in branches and so on. This body is the pith.[55]

From chapters 2 to 5, Cesalpino discussed nutrition, while fructification and reproduction is the subject of chapters 6 to 10. Let us examine chapter 2. As the previous chapter, this one reveals Cesalpino's observations of plants—first negative, "in plants, we observe neither veins nor other channels visible [*manifestos*], nor perceive [*sentimus*] any heat,"[56] then positive, especially as he referred to several specific cases (such as Euphorbias, figs, fir trees, among others). He then claimed that an imperceptible heat dwells within plants, which cause nutrients to move within the plants' very little channels [*meatuum*] and nerves [*nervorum*] and climb to their top. In the middle of these channels, the pith [*medulla*] transforms the liquid of nutrients.[57] Cesalpino's physiology of plants appears an outstanding aspect to ground his knowledge.

Still, how plants draw nutrients from the soil appears problematic. Indeed, plants do not attract food, according to Cesalpino, as they lack sensation (i.e., taste); and "since plants lack sensation, they do not choose the kind of aliment, but draw the humor mixed to the earth for another reason, which is difficult to understand."[58] In order to help the reader, Cesalpino sought an example. The widely used example of magnetism, however, does not work correctly, as the smaller body (the plant) cannot attract the largest (the earth). The same occurs for the void in plants to be filled, as not only nutrients, but air would enter plants—to confirm this point, Cesalpino performed the experiment with a cupping-glass [*cucurbitula*], which he applied to the ground as they draw air and moisture. A more suitable analogy is that of linen, sponge, or powder, as roots absorb nutrients as these bodies absorb water.[59] The roots then are not continuous vessels, like veins, but have a hairy substance, as observed by Cesalpino, and their very porous nature constantly draws food from the earth to the center of the plant, where the internal heat transforms the food and carries it to the top of plants.

This chapter reveals Cesalpino's theory-laden observation of the functioning of plants. He grounded his investigation on the notion of the vegetative soul, which is the principle of plant life, as it draws food, transforms it in the pith, and carries it through the channels to the extreme parts of the plant, ultimately forming flowers and seeds. Yet, he investigated these activities in a physical exploration and observation of the internal structures and functioning of plants. Ultimately, Cesalpino's plant morphology is an investigation of the physical manifestation of the faculties of the vegetative soul in the physiological activities of the plant.

This investigation appears crucial, as in chapter 4, for example, he acknowledged that there is a correspondence between the arrangements of buds and leaves [*ordo autem quidam germinum spectator ut foliorum*], as buds are not produced in all leaves. While differences emerge between plants, Cesalpino individuated a harmony in the arrangement of branches and leaves and described various cases. However, he noted that the arrangement of parts of plants, from the roots to the extreme shoots, parallels the differences of germination and in the structure of the seeds. In this sense, the characters of plants (included those more external such as the disposition and structure of leaves, and the characteristics of flowers) are linked with the development of plants aiming at reproduction, the final causes of vegetation. This is the ultimate difference, on which he grounded the classification of plants. In other words, while several differences arise in plants, these may be reduced to reproduction, namely, on seeds, which emerge as the most important standpoint to specify plants differences.

He discussed this point in chapters 13 and 14, where he claimed that nutrition and reproduction (or fructification) are the basis for establishing genres and species in plants.[60] More precisely, since plants' perfection resides in fructification,[61] the seeds surface as the most important element in Cesalpino's system of classification.[62] Finally, he discarded the accidental differences of plants (which change according to the cultivation, or the diversity of place, as in was in Theophrastus) and cannot be accounted as criteria for classifying plants, and specified three essential differences: the number of seeds, the position, and the shape (*numerus, situs et figura*). Changes in this last case reveal diverse species. Cesalpino grounded his system of classification on these essential differences in the organs of reproduction, that is, on the seed.

By concentrating on morphology, Cesalpino's classification distanced itself from sixteenth-century taxonomies, and opened up to a science of botany.[63] Yet, he encompassed his botany within a rather philosophical framework. Not only did he ground his study of plants on the vegetative soul, which per se would be insufficient to define morphological diversities, as he claimed, but also investigated the operations principled by the vegetative soul, focusing on the physical manifestations of these activities.[64] In this sense, he made the philosophical framework operative. He was not content to refer to a philosophical theory, but he made this theory operating in the science of plants, ultimately combining Aristotle's philosophy (the vegetative soul of Pseudo-Aristotelian *De plantis*) with Theophrastus (the classification of *De causis plantarum*), systematizing the knowledge of plants and producing an Aristotelian botany in the Renaissance.

4. Conclusion: The Reception of Cesalpino

As Alan Morton has claimed, Cesalpino "was the first who tried to define the principles [with] which a comprehensive natural classification of plants could be constructed, and the first to publish a classification which, however imperfectly, reflected the relationship within the plant kingdom."[65] This relationship reveals some important traits. First, Cesalpino grounded his classification on characters arising from the nature of plants, connecting plant morphology to physiology as he had observed, and experimented on these features in the botanical garden. Second, he established botany on a rational system, grounding these characters in Aristotelian psychology, the principle of vegetal life, and differentiation between bodies. Third, he investigated the diverse powers of plants, included therapeutic virtues. What resulted is the construction of a science of plants, grounded in psychology, developing through morphology and physiology, and ultimately dealing with therapeutics. Accordingly, he approached the subject from a philosophical lens, explicitly providing a great deal of discussion on his methodology. Cesalpino thus inverted the traditional relationship between plants and medicine, making medical botany a (final) subsection of a science of plants philosophically (and thus theoretically) grounded. In this sense, Cesalpino's botany appears as an autonomous science, in which the systematization of plants and the knowledge of their healing powers are embedded within a theoretical framework. This confirms his claim to combine the work of *simplicisti* (pharmacists) with philosophical knowledge. The ultimate result is a philosophy of plants of Book 1 of *DP*.

Yet, Cesalpino's botany was rooted in Aristotelian philosophy, as he grounded it on both Aristotelian psychology and Aristotelian matter theory. As Carlo Colombero has pointed out, Cesalpino's interpretation of matter as an extended body, *quantum* and *substantia* at the same time, reveals his Aristotelianism as the one of physics, that is, an exploration of the natural reality of bodies, which he achieved through reasoning and experimentation.[66] His matter theory thus played a major role in his botanical knowledge, as it underlay both the experience of corporeal nature and the reduction of psychology as a principle operating in the physiology of bodies, ultimately resulting in the morphology of the seeds, fructification, and reproduction, the final cause of plant life. In this sense, encompassed within an Aristotelian framework (comprising both a theory of matter and a psychology), Cesalpino's attempt to develop an autonomous science of plants ultimately aimed to fill the lacuna of the Aristotelian corpus, bridging the fracture between the philosophical interpretation of living nature and vegetal bodies that affected Western thought.

Yet, despite Cesalpino's efforts in providing botany with a rational systematization, embedding it within a philosophical system, and defining it as a scientific enterprise, his system received little appreciation in his time. On the one hand, a classification based on the capacity to reproduce that surfaces in morphological differences was not utterly innovative in the Renaissance, as scholars such as Conrad Gessner (1516–65) or Lobel had tried to provide a systematic classification of living nature on either reproduction or the shape and figure of leaves. In his *Methodi herbariae libri tres* (1592), Adam Zalužansky (c.1538–1613), for example, discussed the sex of plants.⁶⁷ Nor was his appeal to the vegetative soul entirely original, as both Giovanni Costeo (1528–1603) and Franz Tidike (1554–1617), in *De universali stirpium natura libri duo* (1578) and *Phytologia generalis* (1582), respectively, provided examples of a theoretical and Aristotelian account to botany.

On the other hand, naturalists such as Caspar Bauhin (1560–1624) referred to Cesalpino's *DP* as "a learned and most obscure" text, as reported by Karen Reeds.⁶⁸ Scholars thus tended to overlook *DP*, probably because it was fashioned in a less interesting shape for the time, being without images. However, as Ogilvie has stressed, Cesalpino "attempted to find a rational basis for this sense of affinity …. In this he was unusual, most Renaissance naturalists did not see any need to go beyond common sense when they organized their histories of plants. … Cesalpino was ahead of his time; from his contemporaries' point of view, he was imagining problems that did not really exist."⁶⁹ More than a century later, scholars such as John Ray and Carolus Linnaeus significantly praised Cesalpino's botany.⁷⁰ Both ultimately acknowledged the importance of the Italian botanist and philosopher who established a rational and philosophical systematization of plants.

In sum, Cesalpino's botany appears as a fruitful combination of the naturalistic observation and cultivation of specimens, the medical knowledge of plant virtues, and the systematization of plants established within a theoretical framework. The central point of his enterprise is the definition of vegetal life, by means of Aristotelian psychology, and to chart out the different manifestations of the vegetative soul. Principled in the vegetative soul, the knowledge of the functions of plants paved the ground to understand the ways plants are formed and, ultimately, diversified, a knowledge established on his Aristotelian matter theory. Cesalpino's philosophical ground thus shaped a science of plants in their own right, and for this reasons, it remained unparalleled and archetypical in Renaissance botany.

Notes

1 See also for bibliography, Fabrizio Baldassarri, "The Seed, the Tree, the Fruit, the Juice: Plants in Early Modern knowledge," *Nuncius* 37, no. 2 (2022): 243–53. Fabrizio Baldassarri, "The World of Plants in Pre-Modern Medical Knowledge," in *Plants in 16th and 17th Century: Botany between Medicine and Science*, ed. Fabrizio Baldassarri (Berlin: De Gruyter, 2023), 3–17.

2 Brian W. Ogilvie, *The Science of Describing: Natural History in Renaissance Europe* (Chicago: University of Chicago Press, 2006), 29.

3 Guido Moggi, "La conoscenza del mondo vegetale prima e dopo Andrea Cesalpino," in *Le monde végétal (XIIe–XVIIe siècles). Savoirs et usages sociaux*, ed. Allen J. Grieco, Odile Redon and Lucia Tongiorgi Tomasi (Saint-Denis: Presses universitaires de Vincennes, 1993), 123–40.

4 Iolanda Ventura, "Changing Representations of Botany in Encyclopaedias from the Middle Ages to the Renaissance," in *Collectors' Knowledge: What Is Kept, What Is Discarded*, ed. Anja-Silvia Goeing, Anthony T. Grafton, and Paul Michel (Leiden: Brill, 2013), 97–144, at 130–31.

5   See, for example, Guido Giglioni, "Girolamo Cardano e Giulio Cesare Scaligero. Il dibattito sul ruolo dell'anima vegetativa," in *Girolamo Cardano, Le opere, le fonti, la vita*, ed. Marialuisa Baldi and Guido Canziani (Milano: FrancoAngeli, 1999), 313-39. Stefano Perfetti, "Giulio Cesare Scaligero commentatore e filosofo naturale tra Padova e Francia," in *La presenza dell'aristotelismo padovano nella filosofia della prima modernità*, ed. Gregorio Piaia (Padova: Antenore, 2002), 3-31. Andreas Blank, "Julius Caesar Scaliger on Plants, Species, and the Ordained Power of God," *Science in Context* 25, no. 4 (2012): 503-23. Guido Giglioni, "Scaliger versus Cardano versus Scaliger," in *Forms of Conflict and Rivalries in Renaissance Europe*, ed. David A. Lines, Marc Laureys, and Jill Kraye (Bonn: Bonn University Press, 2015), 109-30. Guido Giglioni, "La vita oscura delle piante e la natura appetitiva della materia. Nodi di filosofia aristotelica nel Commento al *De plantis* di Giulio Cesare Scaligero," in *Peri phyton. Trattati greci di botanica in Occidente e in Oriente*, ed. Maria Fernanda Ferrini and Guido Giglioni (Macerata: EUM, 2020), 215-36.
6   Luciana Repici, "Andrea Cesalpino e la botanica antica," *Rinascimento* 45 (2005): 47-87.
7   Sandra Tugnoli Pattaro, *La formazione scientifica e il "Discorso naturale" di Ulisse Aldrovandi* (Trento: Unicoop, 1977), 40-4.
8   An indirect exchange reveals that Cesalpino's botanical knowledge was renowned at the time and taken in high consideration by Aldrovandi. See Alessandro Grifoni to Ulisse Aldrovani, December 27, 1569: "concerning what you asked me to contact the excellent Mr Andrea Cesalpino, I did it; and you have the testimony in attachment, with this that I send you a letter of this Mr Andrea [Cesalpino] with some more seeds provided by him, as I know you will appreciate this, and so on *di mano in mano* on the occasion that we will exchange more seeds [between] him and me" (in Alessandro Tosi, ed., *Ulisse Aldrovandi e la Toscana. Carteggio e testimonianze documentarie* (Firenze: Olschki, 1989), 64. For more mentions in Aldrovandi's correspondence, see Tosi, *Ulisse Aldrovandi*, 124, 125, 126, 133, 134, 135, 443). According to Oreste Mattirolo, Aldrovandi's criteria for classification comply with Cesalpino's *DP*, see Oreste Mattirolo, *L'opera botanica di Ulisse Aldrovandi (1549-1605)* (Bologna: Merlani, 1897), 79. This point remains speculative. In her work on Aldrovandi's method, Sandra Tugnoli Pattaro stresses that in 1556 Aldrovandi started developing "a botany on a biological ground, based on the organs devoted to reproduction, therefore anticipating a thread developed by Cesalpino" (Sandra Tugnoli Pattaro, *Metodo e sistema delle scienze nel pensiero di Ulisse Aldrovandi* (Bologna: Clueb, 1981), 150,) but a connection between the two scholars appears difficult to be disclosed, for they ultimately aimed at diverse goals.
9   See Fabio Garbari and Lucia Tongiorgi Tomasi, "Il giardino dei Semplici," in *Storia dell'Università di Pisa, 1343-1737*, vol. 1. (Pisa: Pacini, 1993), 363-76.
10 Cf. Paula Findlen, "The Death of a Naturalist: Knowledge and Community in Late Renaissance Italy," in *Professors, Physicians and Practices in the History of Medicine. Essays in Honor of Nancy Siraisi*, ed. Cynthia Klestinec and Gideon Manning (Cham: Springer, 2017), 155-96.
11 Cf. Pierre Belon, *De neglecta cultura stirpium* (Antwerp: Plantin, 1589), 20. Matthias de Lobel, *Nova stirpium adversaria* (Antwerp: Plantin, 1576), 38-9. See Paolo Galluzzi, *Firenze e la Toscana dei Medici nell'Europa del Cinquecento* (Firenze: Olschki, 1983).
12 Cesalpino, *DP*, fol. 5r: "Tibi autem Serenissime Francisce munusculum hoc, quodcumque fit, nuncupo: tibi enim iure debetur, apud quem extat eius rudimentum ex plantis libro agglutinatis utcumque à me multo antea iussu Cosmi patris tui

compositum cum pollicitatione .... Eiusdem alterum extat exemplum apud clarissima familiam Tornabonam Reverendiss. Alphonso ..." For a study of the science under Cosimo I de' Medici, see Sheila Barker, "Cosimo I de' Medici and the Renaissance Sciences: 'To Measure and to See'," in *A Companion to Cosimo I de' Medici*, ed. Alessio Assonitis and Henk Th. van Veen (Leiden: Brill, 2022), 520–80.

13 Cf. Dietrich von Engelhardt, "Luca Ghini (um 1490–1556) und die Botanik des 16. Jahrunderts: Leben, Initiativen, Kontakte, Resonanz," *Medizinhistorisches Journal* 30, no. 1 (1995): 3–49.

14 Theodore Caruel, *Illustratio in Hortum Siccum Andreae Caesalpini* (Florence: Le Monnier, 1858). On the herbarium, its contents and history, see Guido Moggi, "L'erbario di Andrea Cesalpino," in *Gli erbari aretini, da Andrea Cesalpino ai giorni nostri*, ed. Chiara Nepi and Enrico Gusmeroli (Firenze: Firenze University Press, 2008), 3–20.

15 Although Cesalpino's *De plantis* does not contain any images of plants, both in the dedicatory letter and a 1579 letter to Belisario Vita the author's willingness to have some figures collided with the cost of such work: "la promessa fatta a voce ... in Pisa di fare intaglare in rame a un suo intaglatore le piante per darle alla stampa. Et perché intendo essere in grande spesa, quali gli stampatori di Firenze dicono non posser fare et io manco, veggio senza qualche aiuto di S.A. Serenissima non si possere mandare a esectuione cosa alcuna. ... Caso che no, io vedrò di far stampare l'opera senza le figure, come fu il primo mio disegno perché tale è l'ordine et dichiaratione di ciascuna pianta, che non ha bisogno di figura, ma solo serebbe a maggior vaghezza appresso e più" (Cesalpino to Belisario Vita, June 25, 1579, in Ugo Viviani, *Vita e opere di Andrea Cesalpino* (Arezzo: Bennatu, 1922), 86–7).

16 Cesalpino to Baccio Valori, October 2, 1541, in Viviani, *Vita*, 82.
17 Cesalpino to Belisario Vita, July 2, 1586, in Viviani, *Vita*, 92.
18 Cesalpino to Belisario Vita, September 17, 1586, in Viviani, *Vita*, 94.
19 Cesalpino to Baccio Valori, June 19, 1588, in Viviani, *Vita*, 98–9. Cf. Cesalpino to Baccio Valori, November 8, 1602, in Viviani, *Vita*, 115–17.
20 Cesalpino to Baccio Valori, June 14, 1589, in Viviani, *Vita*, 99.
21 Cf. Cesalpino to Baccio Valori, October 4, 1589, in Viviani, *Vita*, 100–1.
22 See Cesalpino to Baccio Valori, September 12, 1602, in Viviani, *Vita*, 113–14. Cesalpino to Baccio Valori, September 27, 1602, in Viviani, *Vita*, 115.
23 Andrea Cesalpino, *Appendix ad libros de plantis et quaestiones peripateticas* (Rome: Zannetti, 1603).
24 Andrea Cesalpino, "Al Rmo Monsignore il Sor Alfonso veschovo de Tornabuoni," in *Illustratio in Hortum Siccum Adreae Caesalpini*, 1. A Latin translation of this letter is in Andrea Cesalpino, "Lettera inedita di Andrea Cesalpino e notizie intorno al suo erbario che si conserva in Firenze in casa Nencini," *Biblioteca Italiana ossia Giornale di letteratura scienza ed arti* 10 (1818): 211–15. The letter is collected with the herbarium, but I was unable to see it during my visit to Florence, as the letter was part of a temporary exhibition.
25 See Giuseppe Olmi, *L'inventario del mondo. Catalogazione della natura e luoghi del sapere nella prima età moderna* (Bologna: il Mulino, 1992).
26 Cesalpino, "Lettera al Tornabuoni," 1: "da Theophrasto principalmente, il quale con gran' diligentia esaminò gl'alberi, le biade, ed gli ortaggi: ma circa l'herbe medicinali se ne passò leggiermente. Dioscoride poi di tutti gl'altri piu copioso, havendo risguardo alla Medicina, ridusse insieme quelle che hanno simiglanza nelle virtu, ed le separò da quelle che in ciò sono dissomiglanti."

27 Ibid., "quanto hoggi è impoverita dal' comune use de nostri medici, i quali per non durar' fatica, contentandosi di poche cose, con la cicorea ed con la Buglossa ed con e discorsi fatti in camera medicano ogni infirmità."

28 Ibid., 1–2: "l'ordine adunque di Dioscoride serve solamente per quelle piante, de quali si sanno le virtu: ma per havere una general' cognitione di tutte, non è sufficiente, percioche è impossibile haver'havuto esperientia di tutte quelle, che si rappresentano di nanzi."

29 Repici, "Andrea Cesalpino e la botanica antica," 61.

30 Cesalpino, "Lettera al Tornabuoni," 2: "fra i Semplicisti pochissimi sono quelli che habbino congiunto questa professione con li studi di Philosophia, senza la quale non è possibile farvi frutto alcuno: ed fra e Philosophi di qualche conditione, pochissimi sono che habbino messo e loro studii nelle cose particolari, come sono e Semplici, anchorche tutto il nervo della Philosophia consista in quelli."

31 Ibid., 2–3: "Però essendomi messo innanzi tutti e semplici, quali infino a qui mi sono venuti alle mani, gli ho distribuiti per questa prima volta grossamente, facendone le schiatte separate l'una dall'altra secondo il mio proponimento."

32 Ibid., 3: "non secondo la simiglianza delle fogle, né de fiori, né de semi, né delle radici, né d'altre simili parti sono le piante d'una medesima schiatta: … il che facilmente si può vedere, avengha che grandissima dissomiglianza è fra le fogle dell'Elleboro nero, ed le fogle del bianco, similmente infra le fogle della lattuga domenista ed quelle della selvativa, nondimeno sono d'una medesima schiatta."

33 Ibid.: "La perfettion' delle piante d'onde dipende l'essere di ciaschuna, ed d'onde procedono varie generationi, anchorche non sia senza le dette parti, non però è in quelle, ma in quella sorte d'anima, qual' chiamo Vegetativa, la quale non ha altro offitio, che dar' la vita, ed mantenere la spetie."

34 One should note that the concept of the vegetative soul is drawn from Aristotle, *De anima* and, likely, from Pseudo-Aristotle *De plantis*, while Theophrastus never mentions the vegetative soul. See Fabrizio Baldassarri, "Early Modern Philosophy of Plants and the Unwelcome Guest: Pseudo-Aristotle's *De plantis*," in *Peri Phyton*, ed. Ferrini and Giglioni, 237–64. On the powers of the vegetative soul throughout the centuries, see Fabrizio Baldassarri and Andreas Blank, ed., *Vegetative Powers: The Roots of Life in Ancient, Medieval, and Early Modern Natural Philosophy* (Cham: Springer, 2021). On the connection between Cesalpino's *De plantis* and Pseudo-Aristotle's *De plantis*, see Hiernaux and Tresnie in this volume.

35 Cesalpino, "Lettera al Tornabuoni," 4: "d'intorno alle radici non posseva molto variare, percioche … non hanno avuto bisogno di molti instrumenti per preparare il cibo …. Ma gl' artifitii mirabili ed varii instrumenti appariscono in quella parte che serve alla generatione."

36 Ibid., 5: "da e modi varii del produrre e semi, o quello che ha proportione con e semi genitali, ed dalla simiglianza di quelli ho rintracciato e generi ed le spetie delle Piante."

37 Ibid.: "quelli più propinquamente mi dinotano la virtù dell'anima, per la quale tutte hanno l'esser' loro."

38 Ibid., 6: "la voglo preghare ed quanto posso astrignere che facci che questo libro resti sempre in casa."

39 Alan G. Morton, *History of Botanical Science, an Account of the Development of Botany from Ancient Times to the Present Day* (London: Academic Press, 1981), 128–45, at 135: "the task of establishing a rational classification of plants."

40 Cesalpino, *DP*, fol. 2v: "non quod natura novas edat formas, aut novas rerum pulchritudines effingat, sed quod ob numerum immensum nobis in dies novae ostendantur."

41 Ibid.: "adhuc tamen eadem non solum imperfecta, sed et multa caligine suffusa deprehenditur: imperfecta quidem, nam et plantarum numerus quasi in immensum novis in dies repertis augeri videtur."
42 Ibid., fol. 3r–v.
43 Ibid., fol. 3v. [Translation is an adaptation of Kristian Jensen, "Description, Division, Definition—Caesalpinus and the Study of Plants as an Independent Discipline," in *Renaissance Reading of the Corpus aristotelicum*, ed. Marianne Pade (Copenhagen: Museum Tusculanum Press, 2000), 185–206, at 193. Cf. Edward Lee Greene, *Landmarks of Botanical History*, ed. Frank N. Egerton (Stanford, CA: Stanford University Press, 1983), 2: 816.]
44 Cesalpino, *DP*, fol. 3v.
45 On the epistemology underlying this program, see Marco Sgarbi in this volume. On classes in Renaissance botany, see Philippe Selosse, "Peut-on parler de classification à la Renaissance: les concepts d''ordre' et de 'classe' dans les ouvrages sur les plantes," *Seizième siècle* 8 (2012): 39–56.
46 Cesalpino, *DP*, fol. 3v: "Apud nostros autem Ruellius tentavit quidem sed praeter ea, quae a Theophrasto excerpsit circa rationem communem, ulterius nequaquam est progressus."
47 Ibid., fol. 4r.
48 Ibid.
49 Ibid., fol. 5r. This point is, undoubtedly, a very modern claim, suggesting that Cesalpino here devised an inductive methodology.
50 Cesalpino, *DP*, I.1. An English translation of this text is forthcoming by Hiernaux and Tresnie.
51 On the connection between sensitive and vegetative powers, see Guido Giglioni, "Plantanimal Imagination: Life and Perception in Early Modern Discussions of Vegetative Power," in *Vegetative Powers*, 325–45, at 332. See Eva Del Soldato and Andreas Blank in this volume. In *QP*, Cesalpino deprived plants of all sensitive and cognitive power, see Cesalpino, *QP* (1571), fols. 19r, 44r, a point that is ultimately confirmed in *DP*.
52 Cesalpino, *DP*, I.1.
53 Ibid., I.2: "Verum enimvero difficile fuerit in plantis huiusmodi partem invenire, in qua sit animae principatus."
54 Ibid., I.3: "duae autem sunt partes plantarum maxime conspicuae radix scilicet, et id totum, quod sursum attollitur, merito in intermedio, qua scilicet radix germini coniungitur, locus videatur cordi plantarum oportunissimus."
55 Ibid., I.3: "in animalibus cerebri medulla in capite est, unde spinalis medulla exoritur in totam spinae longitudinem diducta, sic in plantis cerebrum in radice tamquam in capite sedens per totum caulem quasi per spinam dorsi medullam deducit ad vitalem humorem ramis et extremis surculis distribuendum."
56 Ibid.
57 Ibid., I.4: "sed satis fuit alterari humorem tactu medullae cordis, ut in animalibus cerebri medulla, aut iecoris caro facit."
58 Ibid.: "Cum igitur plantae omni sensu careant, genus alimenti non seligunt, sed humorem in terra mixtum alia ratione trahunt, quae autem ista fuerit, difficile est videre."
59 Ibid.: "ut lintea, spongiae, pulveres …. Ex huiusmodi igitur natura partes illas in plantis constare putandum est, quibus utitut anima altrix ad trahendum alimentum."

60 Ibid., I.28: "Sed quoniam duobus praedictis absolvitur plantarum operatio, idcirco in illis tantum versabitur genetum collectio et partitio. Et merito ex modo fructificandi multa emerserunt plantarum genera. In nullis enim aliis partibus tantam organorum multitudinem et distinctionem natura molita est, quanta in fructibus condendis spectatur."

61 Ibid.: "quemadmodum enim animalia ex sensuum, aut motuum instrumentis plerasque et praecipuas differentias sortita sunt; ultra enim sensum et motum alias operationes non habent. Sic plantae in fructificatione, tamquam ultima perfectione admirabilem varietatem ostendunt."

62 Ibid., I.29: "Cum ad organorum constitutionem tria maxime faciant, scilicet, partium numerus, situs, et figura, (magnitudo enim non videtur speciem organi immutare, nisi simul figuram immutet. Solutio autem continui, aut unio ad numerum pertinent: durities, mollities, color, et reliquae qualitates ad similares partes referuntur) natura secundum illorum differentias in fructibus condendis multis modis lusit, ex quibus varia plantarum generra constituta sunt."

63 See Ogilvie, *Science of Describing*.

64 Cesalpino, *DP*, I.27: "Alii differentias secundum formam ex anima tantum colligi oportere putantes, coguntur fateri omnes plantas unius speciei esse, cum unicam animae partem, quae vegetativa appellatur, sortitae sint omnes. At ostendum illud quoque est, differentias formam constituentes etiam ex materia, quae illius gratia data est, colligi oportere, si igitur in plantis indifferentes essent partes ad operationes secundum illam animae partem praestandas, una esset omnium plantarum species."

65 Morton, *History of Botanical Science*, 137.

66 Carlo Colombero, "Il pensiero filosofico di Andrea Cesalpino," *Rivista critica di storia della filosofia* 32, no. 3 (1977): 269–84.

67 Holger Funk, "Adam Zalužanskỳ's 'De sexu plantarum' (1592): An Early Pioneering Chapter on Plant Sexuality," *Archives of Natural History* 40, no. 2 (2013): 244–56.

68 Karen Reeds, *Botany in Medieval and Renaissance Universities* (New York: Garland, 1991), 19.

69 Ogilvie, *Science of Describing*, 225–6.

70 Bremekamp has provided a diagram for Cesalpino's classification of plants. See Cornelis Eliza Bertus Bremekamp, "A Re-Examination of Cesalpino's Classification," *Acta Botanica Neerlandica* 1, no. 4 (1952): 580–93.

Bibliography

Primary Sources

Belon, Pierre. *De neglecta cultura stirpium*. Antwerp: Plantin, 1589.

Cesalpino, Andrea. "Al Rmo Monsignore il Sor Alfonso veschovo de Tornabuoni." In *Illustratio in Hortum Siccum Andreae Caesalpini*, edited by Teodoro Caruel and Andrea Cesalpino, 1–7. Florence: Le Monnier, 1858.

Cesalpino, Andrea. *Appendix ad libros De plantis et Quaestiones peripateticas*. Rome: Zannetti, 1603.

Cesalpino, Andrea. *De plantis libri XVI*. Florence: Marescotti, 1583.

Cesalpino, Andrea. *De Plantis Libri XVI (1583) and the Transformation of Medical Botany in the 16th Century. Edition, Translation, and Commentary on Book I*, edited by Quentin Hiernaux and Corentin Tresnie. Berlin: De Gruyter, forthcoming.

Cesalpino, Andrea. "Lettera inedita di Andrea Cesalpino e notizie intorno al suo erbario che si conserva in Firenze in casa Nencini." *Biblioteca Italiana ossia Giornale di letteratura scienza ed arti* 10 (1818): 211–15.
Lobel, Matthias de. *Nova stirpium adversaria*. Antwerp: Plantin, 1576.

Secondary Sources

Baldassarri, Fabrizio. "Early Modern Philosophy of Plants and the Unwelcome Guest: Pseudo-Aristotle's *De Plantis*." In *Peri phyton. Trattati greci di botanica in Occidente e in Oriente*, edited by Maria Fernanda Ferrini and Guido Giglioni, 237–64. Macerata: EUM, 2020.
Baldassarri, Fabrizio. "The Seed, the Tree, the Fruit, the Juice: Plants in Early Modern Knowledge." *Nuncius* 37, no. 2 (2022): 243–53.
Baldassarri, Fabrizio. "The World of Plants in Pre-Modern Medical Knowledge." In *Plants in 16th and 17th Century: Botany between Medicine and Science*, edited by Fabrizio Baldassarri, 3–17. Berlin: De Gruyter, 2023.
Baldassarri, Fabrizio, and Andreas Blank, eds. *Vegetative Powers: The Roots of Life in Ancient, Medieval, and Early Modern Natural Philosophy*. Cham: Springer, 2021.
Barker, Sheila. "Cosimo I de' Medici and the Renaissance Sciences: 'To Measure and to See.'" In *A Companion to Cosimo I de' Medici*, edited by Alessio Assonitis and Henk Th. van Veen, 520–80. Boston: Brill, 2022.
Blank, Andreas. "Julius Caesar Scaliger on Plants, Species, and the Ordained Power of God." *Science in Context* 25, no. 4 (2012): 503–23.
Bremekamp, Cornelis Eliza Bertus. "A Re-Examination of Cesalpino's Classification." *Acta Botanica Neerlandica* 1, no. 4 (1952): 580–93.
Caruel, Theodore. *Illustratio in Hortum Siccum Andreae Caesalpini*. Florence: Le Monnier, 1858.
Colombero, Carlo. "Il pensiero filosofico di Cesalpino." *Rivista critica di storia della filosofia* 32, no. 3 (1977): 269–84.
Findlen, Paula. "The Death of a Naturalist: Knowledge and Community in Late Renaissance Italy." In *Professors, Physicians and Practices in the History of Medicine*, edited by Cynthia Klestinec and Gideon Manning, 155–95. Cham: Springer, 2018.
Funk, Holger. "Adam Zalužanský's 'De sexu plantarum' (1592): An Early Pioneering Chapter on Plant Sexuality." *Archives of Natural History* 40, no. 2 (2013): 244–56.
Galluzzi, Paolo. *Firenze e la Toscana dei Medici nell'Europa del Cinquecento*. Firenze: Olschki, 1983.
Garbari, Fabio, and Lucia Tongiorgi Tomasi. "Il giardino dei Semplici." In *Storia dell'Università di Pisa, 1343–1737*, 1:363–76. Pisa: Pacini, 1993.
Giglioni, Guido. "Girolamo Cardano e Giulio Cesare Scaligero. Il dibattito sul ruolo dell'anima vegetativa." In *Girolamo Cardano, Le opere, le fonti, la vita*, edited by Marialuisa Baldi and Guido Canziani, 313–39. Milano: FrancoAngeli, 1999.
Giglioni, Guido. "La vita oscura delle piante e la natura appetitiva della materia. Nodi di filosofia aristotelica nel Commento al *De plantis* di Giulio Cesare Scaligero." In *Peri phyton. Trattati greci di botanica in Occidente e in Oriente*, edited by Maria Fernanda Ferrini and Guido Giglioni, 215–36. Macerata: EUM, 2020.
Giglioni, Guido. "Plantanimal Imagination: Life and Perception in Early Modern Discussions of Vegetative Power." In *Vegetative Powers: The Roots of Life in Ancient, Medieval and Early Modern Natural Philosophy*, edited by Fabrizio Baldassarri and Andreas Blank, 325–45. Cham: Springer, 2021.

Giglioni, Guido. "Scaliger versus Cardano versus Scaliger." In *Forms of Conflict and Rivalries in Renaissance Europe*, edited by David A. Lines, Marc Laureys, and Jill Kraye, 109–30. Bonn: Bonn University Press, 2015.

Greene, Edward Lee. *Landmarks of Botanical History*, edited by Frank N. Egerton. 2 vols. Stanford: Stanford University Press, 1983.

Jensen, Kristian. "Description, Division, Definition—Caesalpinus and the Study of Plants as an Independent Discipline." In *Renaissance Reading of the Corpus aristotelicum*, edited by Marianne Pade, 185–206. Copenhagen: Museum Tusculanum Press, 2000.

Mattirolo, Oreste. *L'opera botanica di Ulisse Aldrovandi (1549–1605)*. Bologna: Merlani, 1897.

Moggi, Guido. "La conoscenza del mondo vegetale prima e dopo Andrea Cesalpino." In *Le monde végétal (XIIe–XVIIe siècles). Savoirs et usages sociaux*, edited by Allen J. Grieco, Odile Redon, and Lucia Tongiorgi Tomasi, 123–40. Saint-Denis: Presses universitaires de Vincennes, 1993.

Moggi, Guido. "L'erbario di Andrea Cesalpino." *Gli erbari aretini da Andrea Cesalpino ai giorni nostri*, edited by Chiara Nepi and Enrico Gusmeroli, 3–20. Florence: Firenze University Press, 2008.

Morton, Alan G. *History of Botanical Science: An Account of the Development of Botany from Ancient Times to the Present Day*. London: Academic Press, 1981.

Ogilvie, Brian W. *The Science of Describing: Natural History in Renaissance Europe*. Chicago: University of Chicago Press, 2006.

Olmi, Giuseppe. *L'inventario del mondo. Catalogazione della natura e luoghi del sapere nella prima età moderna*. Bologna: il Mulino, 1992.

Perfetti, Stefano. "Giulio Cesare Scaligero commentatore e filosofo naturale tra Padova e Francia." In *La presenza dell'aristotelismo padovano nella filosofia della prima modernità*, edited by Gregorio Piaia, 3–31. Padua: Editrice Antenore, 2002.

Reeds, Karen. *Botany in Medieval and Renaissance Universities*. New York: Garland, 1991.

Repici, Luciana. "Cesalpino e la botanica antica." *Rinascimento* 45 (2005): 47–87.

Selosse, Philippe. "Peut-on parler de classification à la Renaissance: les concepts d''ordre' et de 'classe' dans les ouvrages sur les plantes." *Seizième siècle* 8 (2012): 39–56.

Tosi, Alessandro, ed. *Ulisse Aldrovandi e la Toscana. Carteggio e testimonianze documentarie*. Firenze: Olschki, 1989.

Tugnoli Pattaro, Sandra. *La formazione scientifica e il "Discorso naturale" di Ulisse Aldrovandi*. Trento: Unicoop, 1977.

Tugnoli Pattaro, Sandra. *Metodo e sistema delle scienze nel pensiero di Ulisse Aldrovandi*. Bologna: Clueb, 1981.

Ventura, Iolanda. "Changing Representations of Botany in Encyclopaedias from the Middle Ages to the Renaissance." In *Collectors' Knowledge: What Is Kept, What Is Discarded*, edited by Anja-Silvia Goeing, Anthony T. Grafton, and Paul Michel, 97–144. Leiden: Brill, 2013.

Viviani, Ugo. *Vita e opere di Andrea Cesalpino*. Arezzo: Bennati, 1922.

von Engelhardt, Dietrich. "Luca Ghini (1490–1556) il padre fondatore della botanica moderna nel contesto dei rapporti scientifici europei del sedicesimo secolo." *Annali del Museo Civico di Rovereto, Sezione: Archeologia, Storia, Scienze naturali* 27 (2011): 227–46.

von Engelhardt, Dietrich. "Luca Ghini (um 1490–1556) und die Botanik des 16. Jahrunderts: Leben, Initiativen, Kontakte, Resonanz." *Medizinhistorisches Journal* 30, no. 1 (1995): 3–49.

8

Aristotelian Metaphysics of the Vegetative Soul and Early Modern Plant Physiology: A Comparison of Plant Functions in Aristotle, Pseudo-Aristotle, and Cesalpino

Quentin Hiernaux and Corentin Tresnie

Andrea Cesalpino was a major scholar of botany during the Renaissance, known for being the first systematist and for developing accurate observations of plant morphology and anatomy.[1] As a philosopher, he endorsed Aristotelianism. In the first book *De plantis libri XVI* (1583),[2] Cesalpino presented his theses on the anatomy and physiology of plants. He mixed new considerations of the functions of plants, based on his observations, while trying to remain faithful to the Aristotelian doctrine of the vegetative soul. In this chapter, we aim to answer the following questions. To what extent do Cesalpino's theses on the growth, nutrition, reproduction, movement, and sensation of plants agree with or differ from those of Aristotle, Theophrastus, and Pseudo-Aristotle—author of the apocryphal treatise *De plantis*—whose texts were authoritative for Aristotelianism at the time?[3] How does Aristotelianism influence Cesalpino's botanical theses, and conversely, how do certain botanical theses defended by Cesalpino challenge Aristotelian ideas? To find solutions to these questions, we show how Cesalpino problematized and attempted to resolve discrepancies between the metaphysical and the scientific dimensions concerning the vegetative functions of plants.

1. Context

Aristotle's treatise on plants is not extant.[4] Nevertheless, Aristotle's ideas about plants can be partially reconstructed from passages in other works. Although there are some brief botanical remarks in his other treatises, it is mainly in *De anima* that Aristotle discussed plants in a theoretical perspective, although plants are not the main focus of Aristotle's *De anima*, which deals with the nature, location, properties, and the faculties of the soul of all living beings, especially animals and humans. Theophrastus, a disciple of Aristotle, wrote two of the most important ancient treatises on botany: *Historia plantarum* and

De causis plantarum. These treatises were only rediscovered in the West during the Renaissance. Because of the absence of a Latin translation of Theophrastus, Pseudo-Aristotle's *De plantis* served as the primary botanical reference throughout the Middle Ages in the Latin West and in the Islamicate world. This treatise is not by Aristotle, and historians today usually attribute it to Nicolaus of Damascus (Damascenus, *c.* 64 BC—after AD 14). The text was probably written with much inspiration from Aristotle's genuine treatise on plants and from Theophrastus's works however, and the text of Pseudo-Aristotle's *De plantis* has been deeply altered by the successive translations that have brought it to us (first in Syriac, then in Arabic, then in Hebrew, finally in Latin and again in Greek), making it inconsistent and difficult to interpret.[5] Nevertheless, medieval scholars relied on this text in the West thanks to the first Latin translation by Alfred of Shareshel (*c.* 1160–after 1220)[6] which was used, for example, by Albertus Magnus and Vincent de Beauvais.[7]

Cesalpino, when writing *DP*, was aware of this treatise, at the time attributed to Aristotle, although he may have doubted his authenticity.[8] Moreover, he had access to the work of Theophrastus rediscovered in the West from 1483 thanks to the printing of the Latin translation by Theodore Gaza (*c.* 1410–*c.* 1476).[9] It is not clear, however, exactly where the Aristotelian influences on Cesalpino's botany came from. They might be from Nicolaus Damascenus as well as directly from Aristotle and Theophrastus. Indeed, the first part of Nicolaus Damascenus's *De plantis* draws from all of Aristotle's naturalist treatises and mainly from *De anima*, while the second part of book I is inspired, as for it, especially by Theophrastus's *Historia plantarum*, of which it paraphrases entire passages. Finally, book II, less structured and less clear, borrows from Aristotle's *Meteorology*.[10] In the rest of this chapter, we explain first the positions of Aristotle, Theophrastus, and Pseudo-Aristotle (or Nicolaus Damascenus) on the functions of plants and then compare them with Cesalpino's views. Indeed, the history of botany has commented extensively on Cesalpino's morphological observations and especially on his famous classification, while the history of science and the history of philosophy have shown little interest in the Italian botanist's Aristotelian-tinged physiological ideas.

2. Plants, Their Functions, and Their Soul in Aristotle and Nicolaus Damascenus

In Aristotle's *De anima*, plants are repeatedly used as examples or counterexamples in discussions of the faculties of the soul. Most notably, the case of plants provides both the motivation for and the first application of the famous definition of the soul as the first actuality of a natural body that has organs. Aristotle wrote:

> Even the parts of plants are organs, although extremely simple ones, e.g., the leaf is a covering for the pod, and the pod for the fruit; while roots are analogous to the mouth, for both take in food. If then we are to speak of something common to every soul, it will be the first actuality of a natural body which has organs.[11]

If plants are to be considered alive in the same sense as humans are, the definition of the soul must equally fit both.[12] Plants, along with insects, provide an important objection to attempts to locate the soul in a specific place of the body. As plants and some insects can survive—and even grow and reproduce—after being cut into parts, Aristotle argued that each of these parts must retain the whole of the plant's or the insect's soul and all its functions, such as nutrition and reproduction.[13]

1.1. Nutrition in the Aristotelian Tradition

Everything that lives must possess the ability to grow.[14] Any kind of growth (and, for that matter, of maturation and of decay) implies the presence of food and hence of a nutritive power (θρεπτική δύναμις); therefore, every living being must have such a power.[15] In other words, to count as an ensouled or living being, it is enough to use food to fuel growth or maturation. When this power exists in a soul without any other psychic faculty, Aristotle called this soul and its body a plant. This most elementary power of the soul, namely the nutritive power, fulfills two functions (ἔργα). The first is nutrition strictly speaking, that is, obtaining and processing food. The second is "generation" (γένεσις), often translated as "reproduction," by which a living being produces another being, similar to it.[16] This generative power does not complement the nutritive one but is another *function* of the very same *power*.[17] It has been remarked that Aristotle told neither how it is possible for the same power of the soul to have two functions, nor why these two functions are attached to the nutritive power.[18] It might be because the seed (of both plant and animal) is a residue of the food after it has been used to feed the body, rendering nutrition and seed production two steps of the same process.[19] Aristotle's successors, including Cesalpino, shed light on the close relation between nutrition and generation through the study of plants. Nonetheless, what Aristotle wrote in *De anima* is that nutrition and reproduction allow for the survival of the living being: as an individual for the former, as a species for the latter.[20] Both explanations are compatible, the former focusing on the material side of these functions, the latter on their teleological side.[21] Cesalpino accepted the attribution of both operations to the nutritive soul and the teleological argument.[22]

Aristotle's followers slightly altered his views. Nicolaus Damascenus departed from Aristotle on several points. For example, Aristotle believed that no locomotion could be attributed to plants and their souls; Nicolaus Damascenus considered nutrition to be locomotion within the plant.[23] He wrote, "but within plants motion is easy, because dryness, which is one of the powers of earth, draws moisture."[24] This movement is understood to be earth moving inside the plant, which attracts moisture. According to Nicolaus Damascenus, the heat contained in the plant allows the moisture to flow. He wrote:

> It is not in the nature of moisture to rise upwards, but the heat draws that moisture into the extremities of the plant, so that the food will get to all its parts, while that which is superfluous is secreted.[25]

Indeed, contrary to Aristotle's assertion,[26] plants are not made up of only elemental earth, but also of water and fire:

> Plants have three properties: the first is derived from earth, the second from water, the third from fire. From earth, the plant receives a fixed position; from water, the coagulation of its parts; from fire, the cohesion of its fixed position.[27]

Unlike Aristotle in *De anima*, Nicolaus Damascenus sought to explain more precisely the practical workings of plant nutrition and growth on the basis of the theory of the elements and the principle of concoction (concoction being a process involving heat and moisture).[28] It seems that Nicolaus Damascenus altered Aristotelian physical and metaphysical doctrines to allow for solutions to botanical problems, drawing very freely on Aristotle's explanations in the *Meteorology* about the formation of salt water, sand, and earthquakes, which he sought to transpose analogously to the functioning of plants. However, his physiological accounts are hard to follow. For example, he wrote:

> And so grasses and herbs are only formed by a process of composition, not from a simple element, as in the case of the salination of sea-water and the production of sand. For when the ascending vapors coagulate, grasses can be formed, while dew is falling and the place is rarefied. From it the forms of the seed will come forth in accordance with the powers of the stars. As to the matter—I mean the matter of water—it is one and the same; for even if there exist many different kinds, from water nothing else will ascend than fresh water. Accordingly, salt water is heavier; and accordingly that which arises from water is finer than water. When, therefore, the air draws it up, it will become fine and rise upwards.[29]

This passage seems to take up the Aristotelian idea that the formation of plants and their growth are intimately linked to species growth, that is, its reproduction through the formation of seeds. However, it remains unclear how this process works. Cesalpino was unsatisfied by these elemental explanations and tried to return to a stricter Aristotelian interpretation of plant physiology.

1.2. Generation in the Aristotelian Tradition

In Aristotelianism, nutrition allows for the growth and the reproduction of the organism. If Aristotle did not develop precise ideas on plant reproduction in *De anima*, Nicolaus Damascenus, inspired by Theophrastus and other passages from Aristotle's diverse treatises, explicitly addressed the subject. This passage from Theophrastus played an important role in Nicolaus Damascenus's theory:

> The ways in which trees and plants in general originate are these: spontaneous growth, growth from seed, from a root, from a piece torn off, from a branch or twig, from the trunk itself; or again from small pieces into which the wood is cut up (for some trees can be produced even in this manner).[30]

Theophrastus enumerated seven types of generation for plants' growth, without giving special status to any of them. Although Nicolaus Damascenus's *De plantis* (§113-31) is based on this text, the author's interpretation significantly deviates, as he conceives of three or sometimes five modes of reproduction. He wrote:

> Some plants grow when they are planted, others when they are sown, while others grow spontaneously. Plants that are planted are cut off, either from the root to be planted, or from the trunk, from branches [or from the seed],[31] either from all of it, or when tiny cuttings are torn from it. Some are planted in the earth and others are planted in other trees, such as those which are engrafted.[32]

Nicolaus Damascenus suggested three main types of plant reproduction: planting (which includes grafting and any type of vegetative reproduction), sowing of seeds, and spontaneous generation. Emphasis was placed on how plants reproduced, which means that spontaneous generation and sowing were given special status, while all other modes are gathered under the heading of planting, where they are subsequently organized. The distinction between vegetative and seed reproduction was probably based on Aristotle's comparison of the seed of the plant to the embryo of a fertilized egg that contains both the power to engender the chick and the material for its nutrition.[33] This comparison with the egg was taken up by Nicolaus Damascenus.[34] In contrast to seed reproduction, vegetative reproduction was conceived as being closer to growth since it does not imply the mixing of a male and female principle. In this sense, plants, more than animals, allow us to understand how the growth of individuals and the reproduction of species are two sides of the same nutritive faculty, as *De anima* posits. Moreover, we should not necessarily project the idea of sexual reproduction onto reproduction by means of seeds. Indeed, the question of plant sexuality was very problematic for the ancients.

Theophrastus seemed to consider the presence of separate sexes in plants, male and female, as symbolic rather than a biological property.[35] Following Theophrastus, Nicolaus Damascenus explained:

> For in every kind of plant the male is what is coarse, hard and rigid, and the female what is tender, weak and full of fruit.[36]

And further on, still using Theophrastus, he wrote:

> Some people assert that the differences between cultivated and wild plants are known by the character of masculinity and femininity, whenever the existence of each of them is distinguished by their features. For the male is denser than the female, has more branches, is harder and has less moisture, whereas the fruits are smaller and less liable to reach maturity. The leaves too and likewise the twigs are different.[37]

Already in Aristotle, we find the idea that, for certain species like the fig tree, some trees bear fruit, while others do not but favor the fruiting of the first. However, in Aristotle, this usage of sex is strictly analogical, as he wrote:

> The creatures which cannot move about ... are in their essence similar to plants, and therefore, as in plants, so also in them, male and female are not found, although they are called male and female just by way of similarity and analogy.[38]

Aristotle thus seems to be closer to Empedocles, who conceived (according to Nicolaus Damascenus) the idea that there must be a mixture of male and female sex in each plant, writing:

> Now in plants the female is not separate from the male; in certain of the animals, however, it is separate, and here, in addition, it has need of the male.[39]

This thesis (at least the version of Empedocles reported in *De plantis* asserting the reunion of the male and female sexes in each plant)[40] is rejected by Nicolaus Damascenus, notably on the grounds that the resulting capacity for self-fertilization would make the plant superior to the animal in its autonomy. This possibility of self-fertilization does not seem coherent to Nicolaus Damascenus for metaphysical reasons, because a substance cannot be both agent and patient, but also for empirical reasons. He considered the development and growth of plants to be heteronomous: they depend on external circumstances such as the earth, the sun, the temperature, and the seasons. It must therefore be the same for their generation, the earth providing the female nutritive principle and the sun the male generative principle in the fruit.[41]

The fact that Nicolaus Damascenus explicitly distinguished reproduction by seed from vegetative reproduction should not let us think he was on the track of true sexual reproduction in plants. Yet Theophrastus had already observed that the reproduction of plants from their fruits produced plants of inferior quality to those obtained by vegetative reproduction.[42] Nicolaus Damascenus agreed with this analysis and noted the consequences of sexual reproduction, namely a potential adulteration of the variety. He simply stated that reproduction from seeds is not always reliable, because sometimes a seed is of inferior quality to the plant from which it is derived, and vice versa.[43]

Nicolaus Damascenus also repeated an anecdote from Theophrastus about the fertilization of female palm trees which allows their fruiting through the use of some parts of male palm trees. While Theophrastus clearly explained that the powder of the male inflorescences must be shaken onto the female inflorescences in order to obtain viable fruit,[44] the Latin version of *De plantis* reads:

> In the case of palms, if leaves, leaf powder or bark of a male palm are applied to the leaves of a female palm, so that they are in good contact, this will cause the fruit to ripen quickly and prevent it from falling.[45]

The method of fertilization here is therefore quite different, less precise (and inefficient) than the one described by Theophrastus.[46] The text also adds:

> Sometimes a heavy wind blows and bears the odour of the male to the female, so that its fruits are concocted.[47]

However, this mentioning of a kind of wind might be an addition from the Arabic tradition, inspired by Pliny the Elder.[48]

Among the ancients, the use of the terms male and female for plants is therefore mostly analogical. The characteristics associated with the sex of plants are more symbolic than biological. Consequently, *De plantis* leaves a great deal of room for spontaneous generation compared to the other modes of generation. Contrary to the three modes of reproduction mentioned in §113, in §205 (827a3–7), Nicolaus Damascenus tells us that there are five principles of plant generation: seed, planting, putrefaction, water moisture, or parasitization of another plant. In reality, this is not contradictory insofar as the last three cases are in fact three modalities of spontaneous generation. Thus, he specified that some organisms "proceed from earth or from trees."[49]

Those ideas about plant spontaneous generation are directly borrowed from Aristotle. He wrote:

> The same holds good also in plants, some coming into being from seed and others, as it were, by the spontaneous action of Nature, arising either from decomposition of the earth or of some parts in other plants, for some are not formed by themselves separately but are produced upon other trees, as the mistletoe.[50]

Similar conceptions are found in Theophrastus from which Nicolaus Damascenus took the example of the dodder.[51] However, Theophrastus was more circumspect about the generality of spontaneous generation, and even about its existence and called for more studies on the subject.[52] The § 187–8 of *De plantis* explain the supposed functioning of spontaneous generation:

> Sometimes, however, putrefactions are set up in damp ground and in sand, due to enclosed air. When there has been much rain and wind, the sun causes these putrefactions to appear, and owing to the dryness of the earth their roots will dry up and harden, and then mushrooms and the like will be produced. Some plants are produced in places that are exceedingly hot, because the heat concocts what is inside the earth and the heat of the sun is retained, so that vapor is formed and suckers come from it. And so palm trees are suddenly produced in all hot places.[53]

This explanation makes it possible again to account for the Aristotelian proximity of generation and growth. Nicolaus Damascenus then explained that the same thing happens in cold places in opposite ways and that "the ground opens up and a plant comes out," as well as in the generation of aquatic plants on the surface of water and even in sulfurous waters or on the surface of rocks that generate plants by their internal concoction.[54] More specifically, §203 discussed the appearance of specific plants on wet soil:

> The plants which grow in damp places will appear like patches of verdure on the surface of the earth. In such a place there is, in my opinion, little rarity, and when the sun stands over it, it draws that dampness and the place will grow warm through the resulting motion and the heat which is retained within the earth. So

the plants have no nutriment to stimulate their growth, but the moisture helps them with their expansion. Accordingly, they trail along on the surface of the earth like a green mantle. They have no leaves but grow like the kind of plants which appear on the surface of the water, but they are smaller than those on the water because they are related to earthiness and neither go upwards nor expand.[55]

This passage probably describes the growth of moss. The plants that appear on the surface of the water are algae. This passage can be compared with one in the Pseudo-Aristotelian treatise *De coloribus*, that reads:[56]

This happens logically, and in all growing things this [green] is the first colour that obtains. For all water that stands for a long time is green originally, being mixed with the rays of the sun, but it gradually grows black, but becomes green again when mixed with fresh water.[57]

The idea is that the element "water" tends naturally toward the color green under the action of heat; since water is partly the material of plants, it tends to take the green color when it is exposed to the action of the sun. On this question of plant color left unaddressed by Aristotle, Nicolaus Damascenus combined Aristotle's and Theophrastus's observations with his own reflections to build a descriptive model independent from classical metaphysical reasoning. It is not always clear how these can fit in the framework of *De anima*.

3. Cesalpino on Plant Nutrition and Generation

Nicolaus Damascenus tried to expand on Aristotle's model of plant nutrition by introducing explanations based on the Aristotelian theory of elements. Cesalpino, as a careful reader of Aristotle, was unsatisfied with such innovations. He therefore proposed his own ideas on nutrition. Thus, Cesalpino did not assert in *DP* that plant nutrition is a simple attraction of moisture due to the nature of elements. He distanced himself from theories of the properties and affinities of the four elements. Rather, he sought to better understand the physical mechanism of plant nutrition.[58] As an Aristotelian, Cesalpino confronted an aporia that results from Aristotle's methodological zoocentrism that systematically explains plants and their organs by analogy with animals and posits that plant roots are like animal veins.

According to Cesalpino, both roots and veins serve to transport food from an organ of nutrition to a principle that extracts vital heat from it. The earth plays the same role for plants as the abdomen for an animal because the roots are connected to the entrails like veins. However, the analogy is imperfect, since it does not account for the selection of food by plants insofar as this function is carried out by sensation (taste, touch, etc.) in animals. Since plants lack the sensitive part of the soul, Cesalpino undertook to find an explanation for such a selection within the nutritive faculty. The models of the selective attraction of nutrients that he favors belong to the inanimate and artificial realm: the force of attraction of a magnet, of the vacuum of a gourd or a sucker (*utriculus*), the absorption of a sponge, and finally the filtration by capillarity of oil lamps, which he finally retains.

Once again, the general spirit of this inquiry might be inspired from Nicolaus Damascenus's treatise. Just like him, Cesalpino attempted to explain nutrition on the basis of properties of the plant's constituents. The Aristotelian method and psychology led to the description of plants from animals; their limitations lead Cesalpino to complete this description from the physical world and from craft objects. This could be seen as a first step toward a mechanistic conception of plants. However, Cesalpino still considered his explanation as falling within the scope of Aristotelian psychology: capillarity is but the means (*ratio, ingenium*) used by nature to fulfill the nutritive function. Indeed, the keystone of his physiology remains the soul and the principle of heat that allows growth, movement, and sensation.[59]

Concerning plant reproduction, it should be noted that the Italian naturalist recognized, like Nicolaus Damascenus, three distinct modes: by seeds, by sobols (vegetative reproduction), and by spontaneous generation.[60] This last mode of reproduction is, however, mentioned only in a single sentence:

> The first stage of a plant's development happens from the root, as this is what is born first—either from the seed, or from putrefaction.[61]

Cesalpino did not bring any real development to the hypothesis of spontaneous generation in this work, although he discussed it in depth in *Quaestiones peripateticae*, where he contended that all animals including humans can be generated out of putrefaction.[62] At most, one can see in Chapter 7 an indirect echo of the passage of the theory of colors of Nicolaus Damascenus mentioned above, without associating it clearly with the spontaneous generation of algae:

> The color of the leaves is the same as grass because the liquid of plants, once it is exposed to the sun, takes on this color, just as we can see in stagnant water, when it is dried up by the sun.[63]

The fact that Cesalpino did not develop any explanation of the functioning of spontaneous generation, while his mention of putrefaction might be referring to it, is strange. Here, maybe he shared Theophrastus's carefulness about the phenomenon of the spontaneous generation of plants.

Cesalpino, unlike his predecessors, theorized more explicitly the difference between vegetative reproduction and reproduction by seeds:

> The sobole differs from the seed as the fetus does from the egg: the seed is like an egg which contains a principle of life, but by no means life itself, whereas the sobole has life of its own; albeit near and like a shoot from its parent, before it is able to draw its liquid from the soil by itself with its own roots. Previously, the sobole, when it is big enough to be visible, is either an incomplete root, or a shoot,

or both. The principle of these produces the seed within the bark. As a result, plants are not able to nourish too many offspring, whereas they have no problem in bearing many seeds, as can viviparous and oviparous animals. On the other hand, the generation of the sobole is simpler, since it consists of a release, while the formation of seed requires several stages.[64]

Cesalpino took up the Aristotelian analogy of the seed and the egg and clarified that vegetative reproduction, by sobole, is more akin to growth than to the more complex generation that takes place from seeds.

The Italian botanist also compared animal and plant growth. However, he emphasized the peculiarity of the development or budding (*germinatio*) of plants capable of generating new essential organs, whereas this is only possible during embryogenesis in animals:

> It is only in the uterus, in viviparous animals, that we can observe a true "budding" (*germinatio*). The fetus, in fact, which sprouts like a sort of shoot in its own way, survives thanks to the food that is provided, in the same way that a shoot does. There is a difference, however, in that in animals, the principle [of development] comes from the outside, that is by the semen of the male, although the food comes from the uterus. In plants, on the other hand, both the matter and the principle come from within. Of course, in oviparous animals, the eggs grow, but those that are deprived of the male semen are infertile. Indeed, without the contact of the male, they do not have the sensitive soul by which animals are defined. As for the plant, it has no need for this principle; as if it is up to it alone to release the shoot from itself.[65]

Once again, we can recognize the Aristotelian comparison of the seed and the egg, which Cesalpino made explicit. In the seed, both the "male" principle and the "female" matter come from the mother plant. Thus, the egg is an imperfect analogy for the development of the seed, since without external fertilization the embryo does not develop, likely indicating that Cesalpino did not recognize the sexuality of plants and preferred the thesis of self-reproduction. He also distanced himself from the thesis, relayed by Nicolaus Damascenus,[66] of an external female principle brought by the earth and an external male principle brought by the Sun. The following passage goes in the direction of a self-reproduction not involving sexuality:

> On the other hand, in plants, we have not needed to consider that the task of generation is carried out by anything other than matter, in contrast to animals which are divided into males and females: the sperm of the male gives form to matter in the female by using her corporeality (*corpulentia*), as we explained in *Quaestiones peripateticae*. But as plants do not need a great differentiation of their organs and use less breath, they organize their matter thanks to the breath of life conceived as in the case of an egg. This is why the male/female distinction is not something they would need but lack, even if we do name them as male and female in accordance with some comparison.[67]

Although Cesalpino claimed to rely on the Aristotelian position by referring to his own *Peripatetic questions*, his position on plant sexuality is in fact more complex and nuanced. Other observations on the sexes of certain plants are indeed more precise and closer to the truth than that of the Ancients. Thus, in Chapter 7 of *DP* devoted to flowers, he wrote:

> Certain [plants] are completely sterile, including the Amentaceous plants, which are born without any hope of producing fruit. As for [sterile plants] which do bear fruit, they do not flower, such as cade, yew and in the herbs' genus, mercury, nettle and hemp. In all these species, sterile plants are called male and those that fruit female. This is for the reason that the female's plant matter is more tepid and the male's hotter; because what should have passed into the fruit vanishes in flowering due to the excessive heat. However, it is said that in this type [of plant], females grow better and are more fertile if they are planted near males. It is noticeable in the case of the date palm, for example, that a sort of breath emitted from the male plant compensates for the lack of heat in the female for fructification.[68]

In this passage, Cesalpino associated the idea of sexes in plants only with dioecious species (nettle, mercurial, hemp, cade, date palm, and yew), that is, species whose male plants bear inflorescences that do not fruit, while the female plants do. Cesalpino based his conception of life, as we have said, on the (metaphysical) principle of heat. His hypothesis is that in dioecious plants, the male's excessive heat is entirely transferred to the development of flowers, so that there is not enough left to fructify in the manner of female plants, whose flowers require less heat. In this same passage, he took up the famous example of date palms, relying on Pliny's thesis of the fertilizing wind in a version that is once again more metaphysical than empirical. These observations do not, therefore, lead to the recognition of a theory of plant sexuality in Cesalpino as has sometimes been asserted.[69] The theory, inherited from antiquity, which still prevailed during the Renaissance, is notably recounted by Jean Ruel.[70] Cesalpino quoted Ruel in *DP* and maybe shared his ideas on the subject. According to this theory, seeds that fall into the earth are sterile before a breath manifesting itself as a wind called *Favonius* or *spiritus genitalis* fertilizes them.[71] This fertilizing breath would also be at work between the male and female plants of dioecious species as Cesalpino suggests.[72]

Despite his fidelity to Aristotle's interpretation of plant reproduction, Cesalpino contributed to the history of the discovery of plant sexuality insofar as he was a precursor of flower morphology, whose different parts he distinguished in Chapter 7: sepals, petals, stamens and anthers (and pollen), ovary (receptacle), and pistil. This step of differentiation and description was essential to recognize the organs of flowers, to describe them precisely, to contemplate about their function, and to demonstrate their respective roles in reproduction, as Rudolf Jacob Camerarius did in 1694. His contribution was a repetition neither from Aristotle nor from Theophrastus or Nicolaus Damascenus, as he himself freely combined their respective takes with his own empirical observations to propose a new model. He remained careful, probably much more than Nicolaus Damascenus, to make this model compatible with the metaphysical organization of psychic faculties found in *De anima*.

4. Sensation, Motion, and Desire in Plants: From Aristotle to Cesalpino

In addition to questions of nutrition and reproduction in plants, Cesalpino dealt with a long-standing problem within Aristotelian tradition, asking whether plants can be said to perceive, move, or desire. Aristotle defined plants by their nutritive and reproductive power. He distinguished them from animals by their lack of any kind of cognition or local motion, which are essential features of animal souls rather than of every soul.[73] These distinctions regarding cognition, desire, and motion converge, since, for Aristotle, local movement presupposes a desire that sets the aim of the motion, otherwise plants would be able to move in space.[74] Souls only set their bodies in motion when they long for something, which is why animals move and plants do not.

In turn, desire requires cognition: the soul must be able to differentiate between what it wants and does not want. In the most basic case, animals will choose one pleasant thing (typically: one kind of food) over another painful or less pleasant one. The ability to choose food entails a sense of pain and pleasure, which rests upon having a nutritive power, in order for the body to be fortified, and a sensitive power, in order to be able to feel it. Feeling pain and pleasure entails having the sense of touch, which is common to all animals. Therefore, both nutrition and sensation are needed for cognition, desire, and motion. As plants only possess the former, they cannot desire or move.[75]

According to Aristotle, plants are affected by the material world and its qualities such as heat and cold. However, they lack an intermediary state (or "a mean", μεσότης) between these determinations, which could serve as a reference, or as a judging principle.[76] More specifically, the sense of touch consists in a variation of the equilibrium of the four fundamental qualities: dry, wet, hot, and cold.[77] Plants in their natural state are, according to Aristotle, constituted exclusively of earth, which is cold and dry, making them unable to gauge the variations in the qualities they do not naturally have (namely hot and wet), as neither can our bones and hair, also made of earth.[78] The mono-elemental nature of the body of plants is thus the reason why their soul is unable to have sensation as well as desire and locomotion. In turn, this inability constitutes the difference between plants and animals. Cesalpino knew this doctrine very well and approvingly referred to it.[79]

The fact that Nicolaus Damascenus considered plants to be made up of three elements (water, fire, earth) rather than just earth could have led him to different conclusions about their sensations and movement. However, he adopted a reasoning quite similar to Aristotle's. He wrote that "plants have no motion of their own because they are attached to the earth, and the earth is motionless."[80] This argument probably appeals to Aristotle's theory of affinities between elements.[81] The idea is that entities composed of a particular element or having one element with which they are in affinity, like plants with the earth, share characteristics of that element. As the earth is immobile, so are plants. The Latin version of §135 quoted above also went in this direction by stating that plants take their fixed position from the earth. Nicolaus Damascenus then asserted, like

Aristotle, that plants have no movement of their own and no voluntary movement, no sensation, and that their parts have no defined limits.[82] Plants are indeed endowed with a soul, because they possess a part of it (vegetative), but they do not possess sensation like animals.

Logically, Cesalpino envisaged that plants, especially for their nutrition, are conditioned by external physical causes. But at the same time, fidelity to Aristotelian psychology imposed an explanatory role for the soul, since only inanimate entities, devoid of soul, are subject to physical causality alone. This explains the further elaboration and qualification of the Aristotelian model Cesalpino developed to explain plant nutrition, as well as the greater importance he attached to plants' particular environment.

At that level, he could also have been influenced by some passages of Theophrastus. For example, at least in one place in *De causis plantarum*, Theophrastus seemed to attribute a form of sensation to plants, as a mediating operator between plants and the physical causes that influence their reversible movements. He wrote:

> The closing and opening of the flowers is a less difficult matter and easier to solve, since it is brought about by cold and heat, the flowers being cold and weak. Thus, they close up when their fluid condenses and (as it were) freezes (since at this time their heat leaves them too), and open when the fluid dissolves again and thaws, this being done by the sun. The plants that sink under the water and emerge above it to a greater extent are evidently colder and weaker than the flowers, and for this reason more affected by the changes. That a plant under water should be so keenly sensitive[83] is not unreasonable, especially in a torrid region of fiery heat.[84]

Another difficulty is that Cesalpino, like Theophrastus and contrary to Aristotle and Nicolaus Damascenus, observed the local movements of certain plants, in particular climbing plants, which adopt a behavior similar to the voluntary movement of animals. Indeed, he wrote that thanks to their tendrils or hooks, they cling with "hands, so to speak, with which they catch the neighboring plants" to support their weight.[85] From this he deduced "a kind of sensation" of climbing plants. Unfortunately, this sentence is the only place in *DP* where Cesalpino mentions sensation in plants. He did not elaborate any theoretical ideas on the subject, and we are therefore reduced to hypotheses.

As *DP* is not explicit, we can look at its influences. In this respect, Nicolaus Damascenus stated that the plant "possesses a soul [and sensation]. For a thing that is nourished is not without a soul."[86] The Arabic version and the Latin translation of Nicolaus Damascenus's *De plantis*, on which Cesalpino relied, adds the word for sensation, which is nowadays considered an interpolation.[87] Consequently, if Cesalpino attributed this ambiguous position on the sensation of plants to Aristotle, this could explain his tendency to recognize a "quasi sensation" in plants, in particular in climbing plants which would need it to perform their movements. This would allow him to account for what he observed while giving a coherent Aristotelian interpretation to this ambiguous passage of *De plantis*. Of course, Aristotle himself did *not* attribute sensation to plants, as this suggestion was only hinted to in Therophrastus, then more explicitly added by Nicolaus Damascenus, or rather by whoever might be the author of the interpolation. Cesalpino knew Nicolaus Damascenus's text well enough to keep (consciously or not) the idea that, after all, sensation could serve plants' nutrition.[88] Assuming he did consider the passage genuinely Aristotelian, the consequence of this attribution of a quasi sensation is that climbing plants could express a "quasi desire." Cesalpino did not write this explicitly, but hinted at this consequence of which he was aware as an Aristotelian. In no text did Aristotle accept any kind of desire in plants, but it is precisely because (as we have seen) desire is grounded in sensation. Therefore, if we allow for sensation, it could open the way for desire. And Cesalpino explained that these climbing plants:

> climb by wrapping themselves around their neighbors [...] as if they possessed a kind of sensation (*quasi sensus quiddam*) of the body next to them, since they creep until they find it, and having found it, grab onto it.[89]

They crawl "until" they find, that is to say that they seek (even desire) a support "to" catch it. Their vegetal "hands" would allow them to touch, to feel, and to locate the desirable supports. What we are witnessing here is a case of Cesalpino accepting a proposition (plants have sensation) which is not in the model found in *De anima*, perhaps under the combined pressure of Nicolaus Damascenus's treatise and Theophrastus suggestion, added to his own observation. But in doing so, he immediately injected it back in Aristotle framework, as he draws another conclusion (plants have desire) which only makes sense if we have the argument of the *De anima* in mind. His way of tackling botanical problems clearly involves the continuous attempt to keep together both Aristotelian metaphysical theses and empirical botanical observations.

Finally, let us add that Aristotle and Nicolaus Damascenus affirmed that plants do not breathe and are not characterized by the alternation of wakefulness and sleep, because the latter is a diminution of sensation. On these faculties, Cesalpino wrote nothing.

5. Conclusion

Aristotle's characterization of plants and their faculties, albeit scanty, remained a pervasive framework for ancient and early modern botany. His theory of the soul structured the ways in which research about plants might be conducted. He kept his remarks about plants consistent with *De anima*: plants feed and reproduce through one faculty, common with animals, but they can't feel, desire, or move, as they essentially lack the required internal diversity.

Theophrastus, Nicolaus Damascenus, and Cesalpino all took Aristotle's *De anima* as a starting point and an undisputable authority. Yet it did not prevent either of them to somehow innovate, for the Stagirite left many a question unanswered. This is especially appreciable concerning plants' reproduction as well as their ability to desire and obtain food. Nicolaus Damascenus introduced several theses that go beyond the scope of Aristotle's treatises. These were sometimes at odds with Aristotelian orthodoxy, notably in the case of plants' elemental composition. The many headed tradition of

De plantis treatise, whether we call it Pseudo-Aristotle or Nicolaus Damascenus, was in any case ready to depart from (or at least qualify) Aristotle's theoretical model in order to account for otherwise unexplained phenomena, even at the cost of creating some confusion within the Aristotelian frame of research. In *De plantis*, plants seem to have reproductive and sensitive capacities that are not allowed by a faithful reading of *De anima*. The metaphysical and psychological theses are even altered in order to stay somehow consistent with the observed phenomena, sacrificing broader philosophical systematicity. It might be a deliberate effort of innovation as well as the mere effect of mistranslation or clumsy interpolation from Aristotle's original text, or anything in between.

Cesalpino certainly tackled important problems unsettled by Aristotle himself, like the modalities of plants' generation or the possibility for them to have a kind of sexuality or sensation. On this latter point, he might have integrated suggestions from Nicolaus Damascenus or Theophrastus. Yet Cesalpino was more cautious and conservative than them. He kept claiming faithfulness to Aristotle's thought and indeed took care of staying consistent with its main lines, principally using concepts and arguments similar to what can be found in his treatises. Reforming the main tenets of *De anima* (or for that matter of any of Aristotle's theoretical treatises) is out of question. Plants can only have one power, although with two functions, they do not have sensitive soul as animals do. Still, there are empirical facts that hardly fit this framework. What made Cesalpino innovative was the attentiveness of his observations, which enabled him to integrate new distinctions and data from within the (slightly augmented) Aristotelian psychological and biological framework, without losing too much coherence. One important goal of *DP* was to accommodate the Aristotelian metaphysical framework to new, finer observation about plants' ability to move and reproduce. At least concerning the faculties of the soul, Cesalpino answered questions left understudied by Aristotle rather than enforcing his own theoretical point of departure.

Notes

1   Julius von Sachs, *History of Botany (1530–1560)*, trans. H. E. F. Garnesey (Oxford: Clarendon Press, 1890); Alan G. Morton, *History of Botanical Science: An Account of the Development of Botany from Ancient Times to the Present Day* (London: Academic Press, 1981); Edward Lee Greene, *Landmarks of Botanical History. Part II*, ed. Frank N. Egerton (Stanford: Stanford University Press, 1983); Brian W. Ogilvie, *The Science of Describing: Natural History in the Renaissance* (Chicago: University of Chicago Press, 2006), 222–6.

2   Page numbers refers to the *editio princeps* of Andrea Cesalpino, *De plantis libri XVI* (Florence: Marescotti, 1583). We first add the book and the chapter, then the number of the page. For the sake of precision, we add paragraph numbers from our forthcoming English translation of Book I: Quentin Hiernaux and Corentin Tresnie, eds., *Andrea Cesalpino's De Plantis Libri XVI (1583) and the Transformation of Medical Botany in the 16th Century. Edition, Translation, and Commentary on Book I* (Boston: De Gruyter, 2023 forthcoming). All translations from Cesalpino's *De plantis libri XVI* (abbreviated by *DP*) are our own.

3   Fabrizio Baldassarri, "Early Modern Philosophy of Plants and the Unwelcome Guest: Pseudo-Aristotle's De plantis," in *Peri phyton. Greek Botanical Treatises in the West and the East*, ed. Maria Fernanda Ferrini and Guido Giglioni (Macerata: EUM, 2020), 237–64.
4   For example, in Aristotle, *Gen. an.* 1.1.716a1–2: "Still, plants will have to be considered independently all by themselves" (trans. A. L. Peck).
5   According to Galen's testimony (*De indolentia*, 17), Aristotle's true treatise on plants disappeared at the end of the second century, when one of its last manuscripts was burned in a fire in Rome. Alexander of Aphrodisias presents the loss of the original treatise as an established fact at about the same time (*In librum de sensu commentarium*, 87, 11–12) (Marwan Rashed, "Aristote à Rome au IIe siècle: Galien, *De indolentia*, §§15–18," *Elenchos* 32, no. 1 (2011): 55–77; Michel Federspiel, Jean-Pierre Levet and Marie Cronier, eds., *Pseudo-Aristote. Du Monde. Positions et dénominations des vents. Des plantes* (Paris: Belles Lettres, 2018), 40). However, it was not until the sixteenth century that the authorship of the surviving treatise was questioned. It was the historian of botany Ernst Heinrich Friedrich Meyer, *Nicolai Damasceni De plantis libri duo Aristoteli vulgo adscripti* (Leipzig: Voss, 1841), who first proposed Nicolaus Damascenus as the author.
6   The current reference translation in French (Federspiel, Levet and Cronier, *Des plantes*) is therefore based mainly on this Latin version of the text, because of its completeness and influence. The English reference translations (H. J. Drossaart Lulofs and E. L. J. Poortman, eds., *Nicolaus Damascenus. De Plantis: Five Translations* (Leiden: Brill, 1989)) are based on the Syriac fragments, and the Hebrew and Arabic versions.
7   On the influence of Pseudo-Aristotle on Albertus Magnus's botany, see Marilena Panarelli, "Albert the Great's *De vegetabilibus* and its Unique Position among the Medieval Commentaries on *De plantis*," in Ferrini and Giglioni, *Peri phyton*, 137–62.
8   Julius Caesar Scaliger (1484–1558) rejected the authorship of Aristotle on *De plantis*. See Julius Caesar Scaliger, *In libros duos, qui inscribuntur De plantis, Aristotele autore, libri duo* (Paris: Vascosan, 1556), 38. It continued to circulate among Renaissance thinkers with less influence and remained a source for Aristotelian botanists such as Cesalpino. Luciana Repici, "Andrea Cesalpino e la botanica antica," *Rinascimento* 45 (2005): 47–87. Karen Reeds, *Botany in medieval and Renaissance universities* (London: Garland, 1991), 19. Fabrizio Baldassarri, "Early Modern Philosophy of Plants and the Unwelcome Guest."
9   Cesalpino mentions explicitly Gaza and Theophrastus.
10 Federspiel, Levet, and Cronier, *Des plantes*, 49.
11 Aristotle, *De an.* 2.1.412a29–b6 (trans. D. W. Hamlyn). See also Aristotle, *Part. an.* 2.10.655b32–656a2.
12 The question of why exactly plants are substances is a noteworthy problem of Aristotelian exegesis, see for example Rosamond Kent Sprague, "Plants as Aristotelian Substances," *Illinois Classical Studies* 16, no. 1 (1991): 221–9.
13 Aristotle, *De an.* 1.4.410a9–10; 1.5.411b19–21; 2.2.413b16–22.
14 Aristotle, *De an.* 2.2.413a27–b1.
15 Aristotle, *De an.* 2.2.413b6–9; 2.4.415b25–28; 3.12.434a22–27.
16 Aristotle, *De an.* 2.4.415a22–415b1.
17 This precision has raised challenging issues about how the same power may accomplish so different things. We can only sketch them in this chapter. See for example the discussion by David Lefebvre, "Looking for the Formative Power

in Aristotle's Nutritive Soul," in *Nutrition and Nutritive Soul in Aristotle and Aristotelianism*, ed. Giouli Korobili and Roberto Lo Presti (Berlin: De Gruyter, 2021), 101–25, as well as Klaus Corcilius, "Soul, Parts of the Soul, and the Definition of the Vegetative Capacity in Aristotle's *De anima*," in *Vegetative Powers: The Roots of Life in Ancient, Medieval and Early Modern Natural Philosophy*, ed. Fabrizio Baldassarri and Andreas Blank (Cham: Springer, 2021), 13–34.

18   See, for example, David Walter Hamlyn, *Aristotle's De anima Books II, III* (Oxford: Clarendon Press, 1968), 95.
19   See Aristotle, *Gen. an.* 2.3.736b26–27 and 2.4.740b29–37, as proposed by Pierre Thillet, *Aristote. De l'âme* (Paris: Gallimard, 2005), 113, n. 202.
20   Aristotle, *De an.* 2.4.415b1–7. This is true of all living beings: Aristotle, *Gen. an.* 2.1.731b31–732a1 and *Gen. corr.* 2.10.336b25–337a4.
21   Georges Rodier, *Aristote. Traité de l'Âme* (Paris: Belles Lettres, 1900), 2:227, already suggests the simple interpretation that nutrition *stricto sensu* and reproduction are the two possible results of the food's processing, which therefore remains one power.
22   Cesalpino, *DP* 1.1, p. 1; Hiernaux-Tresnie §5.
23   Federspiel, Levet and Cronier, *Des plantes*, 220 associate this movement with the *elxis* of Aristotle, *Ph.* 7.2.243a17ff. which is a movement that goes towards the motor.
24   Translation borrowed from Drossaart Lullofs and Poortman, *De plantis*, 174, §142, 822b1–2.
25   Ibid., 176, §147, 822b18–19.
26   Aristotle, *De an.* 3.13.435a21–b4.
27   *De plantis*, §135, 822a12–14. This quotation is a personal translation from the Latin version of the text (cf. the French translation of Federspiel, Levet and Cronier, *Des plantes*, 107) because the Arabic version and its English translation (Drossaart-Lulofs and Poortman, *De plantis*, 172–3) are significantly different: "Plants have three powers: earthy, watery and fiery. The earthy power is the subsistence of plants, the watery one makes them grow and the fiery one consolidates them." Instead of stating that plants are fixed by virtue of their proximity to the earth, the Arabic version and the English translation simply state that plants get their food from the earth. This interpretation seems to us to be less consistent with the argument of §135 which we comment on below.
28   Ibid., §253, 829b29–32.
29   Ibid., 184, §171–173, 824b4–16.
30   Theophrastus, *Hist. pl.* 2.1.1.
31   We put or from the seed in square brackets because according to Federspiel, Levet, and Cronier (*Des plantes*, 207), this part would constitute an apocryphal addition, which is consistent with the idea that Nicolaus does distinguish three modes of reproduction and does not equate sowing with vegetative reproduction. "Pour pousser, certains arbres ont besoin d'être plantés; d'autres naissent d'une graine; d'autres enfin naissent par génération spontanée. Ceux qui sont plantés sont détachés de la racine ou du tronc, ou des branches, [ou de la graine], ou bien sont entièrement transplantés; certains sont légèrement brisés. Certains sont replantés dans la terre, d'autres dans les arbres, c'est-à-dire greffés" (*Des plantes*, 103–4 §113–114, 820b30–35). Drossaart-Lulofs and Poortman already marked it with a cross, noting (*De plantis*, 299) that these words are "puzzling."
32   *De plantis*, 162, §113–114, 820b30–35.
33   Aristotle, *Gen. an.* 1.23.731a5ff.
34   *De plantis*, §39–47, 817a10–40.

35 Theophrastus, *Hist. pl.* 3.8.1; 5.4.1.
36 *De plantis*, 138, §38, 817a8-9.
37 *De plantis*, 168, §130, 821b21-27.
38 Aristotle, *Gen. an.* 1.1.715b17-21.
39 Aristotle, *Gen. an.* 2.4.741a4-6.
40 *De plantis*, §36; §39, 817a.
41 *De plantis*, §36-49, 817a1-b6.
42 Theophrastus, *Hist. pl.* 2.2.4.
43 *De plantis*, §116, 821a3-6.
44 Theophrastus, *Caus. Pl.* 2.9; 3.18.1 and Theophrastus, *Hist. pl.* 2.8.4.
45 *De plantis*, §119, 821a14-16. Here we propose a personal translation from the text of the Latin edition, as the Arabic version is quite different in content, see the next footnote.
46 The Arabic version used for the English translation (Drossaart-Lulofs and Poortmann, *De plantis*, 164-5) makes better sense and is more faithful to Theophrastus: "As regards the palm tree, when over its spathe something from the male spathe with its bloom and its dust is sprinkled, it ripens the fruit and prevents it from being shed." This version of the text clearly, and only, mentions "dust" of "the spathe," which is the pollen of the inflorescence. Cesalpino had only the Latin version.
47 *De plantis*, 164 §120, 821a20-21.
48 According to Federspiel, Levet and Cronier, *Des plantes*, 210, referring to Pliny, *HN* 12.35.
49 *De plantis*, 132, §20, 816a20-21.
50 Aristotle, *Gen. An.* 2.1.716a10. See also Aristotle, *Hist. an.* 5.1.539a22ff. and 5.19.551a5.
51 Compare Theophrastus, *Caus. pl.* 2.17 with Pseudo-Aristotle, *De plantis*, §204.
52 Theophrastus, *Caus. pl.* 4.15.4.
53 *De plantis*, 190, §187-188, 825b13-24.
54 *De plantis*, §190-195, 825b29-826a27.
55 *De plantis*, §196, §203, 826b20-32.
56 It is unlikely that the same author wrote *De coloribus* and *De plantis*.
57 [*Col.*] 5.794b24-29. The translation is taken from W. S. Hett, *Aristotle Minor Works* (Cambridge, MA: Harvard University Press, 1936). We add "[green]" as it is clearly implied in the original context.
58 Cesalpino, *DP* 2.2, 4-5; Hiernaux-Tresnie §20-25.
59 In Book I of *DP*, this notion of heat is itself ambiguous, sometimes considered in its physical sense of heat production, sometimes as a metaphysical vital principle. We can therefore see a trace of the elemental theory of the ancient philosophers.
60 Cesalpino, *DP* 1.3-6, 5-13; Hiernaux-Tresnie §27-63.
61 Cesalpino, *DP* 1.4, 8; Hiernaux-Tresnie §38.
62 At least in his botany. However, he discusses spontaneous generation in his *Quaestiones peripateticae* 5.1, 92-7.
63 Cesalpino, *DP* 1.7, 14; Hiernaux-Tresnie §69.
64 Cesalpino, *DP*, 1.5, 11; Hiernaux-Tresnie §53.
65 Cesalpino, *DP*, 1.3, 5-6; Hiernaux-Tresnie §28.
66 Pseudo-Aristotle, *De plantis* §36-49, 817a1-b6, summarized in the section about generation above.
67 Cesalpino, *DP* 1.6, 11-12; Hiernaux-Tresnie §57.

68 Cesalpino, *DP* 1.7, 15; Hiernaux-Tresnie §73.
69 For example, by Augustin-Pyramus de Candolle, *Physiologie végétale, ou expositions des forces et des fonctions vitales des végétaux* (Paris: Béchet Jeune, 1832, 48).
70 See Jean Ruel, *De natura stirpium libri tres* (Paris: Simon de Colines, 1536, 28–33).
71 Greene, *Landmarks of Botanical History. Part II*, 648–52.
72 Cesalpino, *DP* 1.7, 15; Hiernaux-Tresnie §73.
73 Aristotle, *De an.* 1.5.410b22–27. See Aristotle, *De an.* 2.2.413b1–4; 2.3.414a29–b7; Aristotle, *Gen. an.* 2.5.741a9–10; Aristotle, *Sens.* 436b8–12.
74 Aristotle, *De an.* 3.9.432b14–18. This does naturally not preclude other kinds of movement or change: generation, growth, and alteration.
75 Aristotle, *De an.* 2.3.414a34–b15.
76 Aristotle, *De an.* 2.12, 424a32–b2.
77 Aristotle, *De an.* 2.11.423b27–424a6. On these qualities and their link with the four elements, see Aristotle, *Gen. corr.* 2.3.330a30–b12.
78 Aristotle, *De an.* 3.13.435a21–b4. Aristotle adds that all the other senses require touch, see also Aristotle, *Part. an.* 2.1.647a14–19.
79 Cesalpino, *QP* (1593), fol. 135v, citing the second book of Aristotle's *De anima*.
80 Pseudo-Aristotle, *De plantis*, 134, §22, 816a26–27.
81 Aristotle, *Mete.* 4.4.382a3–21; 4.5.382b2–10; 4.6.382b28–383a26; 4.7.383b18–384a20, and 384a3b25.
82 Pseudo-Aristotle, *De plantis*, §52, 817b22–24.
83 The Greek could also be read as saying "such a sensation" (Ἡ δὲ αἴσθησις οὕτως).
84 Theophrastus, *Caus. pl.* 2.19.3.6—4.519, 3,6–4,5; trans. Benedict Einarson and George K. K. Link, 357–9.
85 Cesalpino, *DP*, 1.11, 23; Hiernaux-Tresnie §114.
86 Pseudo-Aristotle, *De plantis*, 134, §27, 816b4–5.
87 Droossaart Lulofs and Poortman, *De plantis*, 261.
88 On this link between nutrition and a vegetative sensation see Guido Giglioni, "Plantanimal Imagination: Life and Perception in Early Modern Discussions of Vegetative Power," in *Vegetative Powers: The Roots of Life in Ancient, Medieval and Early Modern Natural Philosophy*, ed. Fabrizio Baldassarri and Andreas Blank (Cham: Springer, 2021), 325–45.
89 Cesalpino, *DP* 1.11, 23; Hiernaux-Tresnie §114.

Bibliography

Primary Sources

Aristotle. *Generation of Animals*, translated by A. L. Peck. Cambridge, MA: Harvard University Press, 1943.
Aristotle. *Minor Works*, translated by Walter Stanley Hett. Cambridge, MA: Harvard University Press, 1936.
Aristotle. *The Complete Works of Aristotle*, edited by Jonathan Barnes. 2 vols. Princeton: Princeton University Press, 1984.
Candolle, Augustin-Pyramus de. *Physiologie végétale, ou expositions des forces et des fonctions vitales des végétaux*. Paris: Béchet Jeune, 1832.
Cesalpino, Andrea. *De plantis libri XVI*. Florence: Marescotti, 1583.

Cesalpino, Andrea. *De Plantis Libri XVI (1583) and the Transformation of Medical Botany in the 16th Century. Edition, Translation, and Commentary on Book I*, edited by Quentin Hiernaux and Corentin Tresnie. Boston: De Gruyter, 2023 forthcoming.
Cesalpino, Andrea. *Quaestionum peripateticarum libri quinque*. Venice: Giunta, 1593.
Drossaart Lulofs, H. J., and E. L. J. Poortman, eds. *Nicolaus Damascenus. De Plantis: Five Translations*. Leiden: Brill, 1989.
Federspiel, Michel, Jean-Pierre Levet, and Marie Cronier, eds. *Pseudo-Aristote. Du Monde. Positions et dénominations des vents. Des plantes*. Paris: Belles Lettres, 2018.
Galen. *Opera omnia*, edited by Karl Gottlob Kühn. 20 vols. Leipzig: Karl Knobloch, 1821–33.
Hamlyn, David Walter. *Aristotle's De anima Books II, III*. Oxford: Clarendon Press, 1968.
Meyer, Ernst Heinrich Friedrich. *Nicolai Damasceni De plantis libri duo Aristoteli vulgo adscripti*. Leipzig: Voss, 1841.
Ruel, Jean. *De natura stirpium libri tres*. Paris: Simon de Colines, 1536.
Scaliger, Julius Caesar. *In libros duos, qui inscribuntur De plantis, Aristotele autore, libri duo*. Paris: Vascosan, 1556.
Theophrastus. *De causis plantarum*, translated by Benedict Einarson and George K. K. Link. 3 vols. Cambridge, MA: Harvard University Press, 1976–90.
Theophrastus. *Enquiry into Plants and Minor Works on Odour and Weather Signs*, translated by Arthur Hort. 2 vols. Cambridge, MA: Harvard University Press, 1961.
Thillet, Pierre. *Aristote. De l'âme*. Paris: Gallimard, 2005.

Secondary Sources

Baldassarri, Fabrizio. "Early Modern Philosophy of Plants and the Unwelcome Guest: Pseudo-Aristotle's *De Plantis*." In *Peri phyton. Trattati greci di botanica in Occidente e in Oriente*, edited by Maria Fernanda Ferrini and Guido Giglioni, 237–64. Macerata: EUM, 2020.
Corcilius, Klaus. "Soul, Parts of the Soul, and the Definition of the Vegetative Capacity in Aristotle's *De anima*." In *Vegetative Powers: The Roots of Life in Ancient, Medieval and Early Modern Natural Philosophy*, edited by Fabrizio Baldassarri and Andreas Blank, 13–34. Cham: Springer, 2021.
Giglioni, Guido. "Plantanimal Imagination: Life and Perception in Early Modern Discussions of Vegetative Power." In *Vegetative Powers: The Roots of Life in Ancient, Medieval and Early Modern Natural Philosophy*, edited by Fabrizio Baldassarri and Andreas Blank, 325–45. Cham: Springer, 2021.
Greene, Edward Lee. *Landmarks of Botanical History*, edited by Frank N. Egerton. 2 vols. Stanford: Stanford University Press, 1983.
Lefebvre, David. "Looking for the Formative Power in Aristotle's Nutritive Soul." In *Nutrition and Nutritive Soul in Aristotle and Aristotelianism*, edited by Giouli Korobili and Roberto Lo Presti, 101–25. Berlin: De Gruyter, 2021.
Morton, Alan G. *History of Botanical Science: An Account of the Development of Botany from Ancient Times to the Present Day*. London: Academic Press, 1981.
Ogilvie, Brian W. *The Science of Describing: Natural History in Renaissance Europe*. Chicago: University of Chicago Press, 2006.
Panarelli, Marilena. "Albert the Great's *De vegetabilibus* and its Unique Position among the Medieval Commentaries on *De plantis*." In Ferrini and Giglioni, *Peri phyton*, 137–62.

Rashed, Marwan. "Aristote à Rome au IIe siècle: Galien, *De indolentia*, §§15–18." *Elenchos* 32, no. 1 (2011): 55–77.

Reeds, Karen. *Botany in Medieval and Renaissance Universities*. New York: Garland, 1991.

Repici, Luciana. "Cesalpino e la botanica antica." *Rinascimento* 45 (2005): 47–87.

Sprague, Rosamond Kent. "Plants as Aristotelian Substances." *Illinois Classical Studies* 16, no. 1 (1991): 221–9.

von Sachs, Julius. *History of Botany (1530–1560)*, translated by H. E. F. Garnesey. Oxford: Clarendon Press, 1890.

9

Paratextual Debates in *De plantis* (1583): On the Best Form of Botanical Prose, Garden and Things, and the Author-Figure of Cesalpino

Julia Heideklang

When Andrea Cesalpino (1524/25–1603)[1] wrote his masterpiece, the botanical treatise *De plantis libri XVI (Sixteen Books on Plants)* in 1583, he was well aware that the field of botanical studies was competitive and that he had to position himself within a long, well-established, and increasingly crowded line of tradition. To this end, like earlier herbals and botanical print works, Cesalpino's *De plantis* contains a paratextual apparatus.[2] Paratexts, such as title pages, dedicatory letters, and dedicatory poems, allow each author to position himself within this long tradition as well as to participate in the self-fashioning of the scientific community and in its debates on botanical practices and literary form.

For early modern botanical prints, these paratexts were central literary tools in negotiating important epistemic aspects of the botanical science, hereby shaping this particular field of research, its community, and its practices. Title pages with their pictorial and textual presentation of the work, dedicatory epistles, and the complementary dedicatory poems address central and highly debated issues, such as the question of how book and garden as spaces of knowledge are related to one another, how botanical print works should be read, and what should be considered the best form of writing (*ratio tractandi*) of such a work. At the same time, these paratexts allow the botanical scholar to present himself, not only as a botanical author but also as an author-persona amidst his fellow colleagues, which is achieved by style and tone displayed within these paratexts, by the way contributions and errors of others are noted, acknowledged, reprimanded, or ignored and the overall construction of the field of botanical studies. For this purpose, an enumeration, a kind of catalog of ancient and contemporary contributors and fellow botanical scholars, is usually included within the dedicatory epistle.

In the following chapter, I shed light on how Cesalpino presented and framed his work by means of his dedicatory epistle and particularly one of the dedicatory poems written by his pupil, Cristoforo Paganelli (1551–91). Out of the many aspects that are debated throughout the paratexts of sixteenth-century botanical prints, I will focus on two very central aspects that to this day remain powerful key points as to how we perceive the botanical science and its history. First, the form of writing in relation to the debate on how the spaces of book and garden relate to one another. Second, who is considered part of the scientific community and whose contributions emphasized in the paratextual stories on the history of botany. For this purpose, I will compare Cesalpino's paratextual strategies with those of other sixteenth-century botanical scholars, and especially Pietro Andrea Mattioli (1501–77).

1. A Garden without Boundaries and Limitations

A central aspect of sixteenth-century herbals is the debate on epistemic implications of printing a herbal, and consequently, the question on what is the most appropriate form for botanical prose works. For this purpose, a garden metaphor is often deployed to signify each author's individual approach.

For a long time, the connection between book and garden has been recognized as an essential relation for developments within early modern botany. The complex and twofold meaning of the garden as a real as well as metaphorical space of knowledge are held to be the central link between botany and literature.[3] In her groundbreaking monograph on herbals in 1938, Agnes Arber recognized the continuing importance of garden metaphors and analogies in early modern herbals.[4] Accordingly, this interrelation has been explored in subsequent studies and ultimately has been coined "the salient characteristic of sixteenth-century *res herbaria*."[5] However, it is worthwhile to take a closer look at this relationship once more, by considering in detail the chosen garden metaphors and their epistemic implications: Otto Brunfels (1488–1534), for instance, envisioned his *Herbarum vivae eicones* (1530) as *horti* and the image of a newly collected and arranged garden out of different seeds is created through its paratexts and connected to the writing-technique of a cento.[6] While Leonhart Fuchs (1501–66) too referred to scholarly collecting practices with his garden metaphor, the garden form[7] of *viridarium* implies notable differences that manifest in the resulting textual form of Fuchs's *De historia stirpium commentarii insignes* (1542): Not only does the *viridarium*, a private greenery with its "novel display of well-arranged plants, particularly those that are imported, skillfully pruned, or propagated"[8] advertise the print work to his noble addressee,[9] but it also implies a more skillfully achieved form, a "novel display of well-arranged" plant-chapters—and in Fuchs's case so skillfully pruned that the scholarly practices used in composing the herbal are concealed by the coherent textual form presented, with the original excerpts no longer visibly recognizable nor attributed to its source.[10] Turning away from the specific textual form achieved, Mattioli strongly advertised his herbal as a paper garden, superior to physical gardens; whereas the real physical garden space is inherently characterized by its changeability making continuous efforts of cultivation necessary to preserve its form and affecting the (range of) plants available for closer observation, the printed paper garden is available to its readers all the time, presenting knowledge seemingly secured for eternity and not subjected to the influences of time.[11]

In the case of Cesalpino's *De plantis*, the reader encounters a dedicatory letter by Cesalpino himself, followed by four dedicatory poems. These four poems are closely connected to Cesalpino's *epistula nuncupatoria*, sometimes echoing *topoi* from the epistle and building upon its concepts, and sometimes inverting its *topoi* due to the differences of form and function between dedicatory epistle and dedicatory poem.[12] Three poems are written by the aforementioned Cristoforo Paganelli, a former student of Cesalpino's at the University of Pisa, and later renowned Italian poet,[13] followed by a fourth poem written by another pupil, Antonio Pellicini of Empoli.[14]

Poems 1, 2, and 4 are epigrams as indicated by their headings and stylize Cesalpino in his relation to *Natura*, the plant world, and preceding botanical prose works.[15] All three poems—maybe even including the fourth written by Pellicini—form a coherent poem cycle. But in context of this paper, I will focus solely on the third poem *Hortum si libet*, which gains extraordinary meaning due to its central position, considerable length, and different meter (see **Table 9.1**). In contrast to the surrounding poems, it can be understood as programmatic to the overall approach of *De plantis* regarding its concepts of garden, book, and plant specimens:

Hortum si libet ingredi viator	1	If it pleases a traveler to walk into the garden
Securus potes: aspice, ut reclusi		You can be carefree; see, how unlocked
Cunctis sint aditus, patensque limen.		the entrance is for all and open the border.
Non est qui vetet huc iter, Priapus		There is not ugly Priapus, who denies the way in here
Turpis, falce minax, et impudicus:	5	Threatening with his sickle (and) without shame:
Non latrans Canis, aut Puella custos,		No barking hound, or maiden ward,
Iratus neque Villicus, neque Agger		Neither a furious custodian, nor a blockade
Obstat saepibus, horridisque spinis.		Stands in the way, with hedges and horrid thorns.
Miraris, loca quid vides aperta		You may wonder, what an open space you see
Non ullae timor imminet rapinae;		With no imminent danger of predation;
Totum nam licet hunc vores ocellis,	10	For you may devour this whole (sc. garden) with your eyes
Intactus tamen usquequaque fiet:		And it will still be unscathed everywhere:
Qui tot muneribus scatet frequenter,		It is frequently filled with so many gifts,
Ut ipsi Aonidum queant sororum		That (even) the beautiful hills of the Aeonid Sisters
Formosi merito invidere colles,		May rightfully lament their envy,
Nec non quicquid habet suavioris	15	And not anything sweeter than this field
Agri dives Arabs odore multo		Does possess the Arab, rich with strong aroma.
Quod si tu semel hic vades parumper		If ever once you walked here for a little while
Siue poma legens, virentis horti,		Whether picking up a fruit of the greening garden,
seu herbas, seu bene flosculos olentes		or herbs, or pleasantly smelling flowers,
Nil est, quod cupias minus, quam abire.[16]	20	there is nothing you will want less than to leave.

Table 9.1 Overview of paratexts in Cesalpino's *De plantis*, discussed in this chapter. © Julia Heideklang.

Paratext	Position in *DP*	Author	Language	Meter
Epistula nuncupatoria	a2r–b1r	Cesalpino	Latin	n/a
HOC opus egregium	b1v	Paganelli	Latin	elegiac distich
HORTUM si libet	b1v–b2r	Paganelli	Latin	elegiac distich
RURSUS ad aethereas	b2r	Paganelli	Latin	Phalaecian
QUAS Texi formas	b2v	Pellicini	Latin	elegiac distich

At first glance, the poem depicts an imaginary garden (*hortum*), into which anyone who wants to (*si libet*) can enter. This description incorporates three very intriguing aspects relating to garden spaces. First, we can observe the movement of the *viator* in and through that imagined space of a garden as a fundamental aspect of the poem. Hereby, the first line (*si libet ingredi uiator*) together with the very last frames the description (*nil est, quod cupias minus quam abire*). Whereas at the beginning the visitor (*viator*) voluntarily enters the garden, at its end, he is so engulfed in the sensorial experience[17] of the garden and its objects that he wants nothing less than to leave. Therefore, while the two lines connect and frame the imaginary space, the anticipated mindset of the visitor changes fundamentally throughout the poem and is nearly antithetical to the beginning. Overall, the garden is described as a true *locus amoenus*,[18] in which "aesthetic and emotional pleasure arises from knowledge."[19]

Secondly, the image of a visitor moving back and forth within this space is accompanied by the emphasized absence of any obstacles, hindrances, or barriers potentially limiting movement and experience. Within the lines 5–8, possible barriers and obstructive figures are enumerated which could have prevented the viator from his journey (*iter*) through the garden. At the same time, they seem to embody different forms of gardens that are excluded from the described concept and as apt candidates for the metaphor, such as the private garden or the *hortus conclusus* of any kind. Additionally, another kind of artificially created boundary is mentioned that could limit the accessibility of the space but is equally absent: a wall with awful thorny bushes (*agger … saepibus, horridisque spinis*).

Aside from having neither natural or artificially created borders nor guards which could impair the integrity of the observations made and experiences gained within the garden, there is nearly a paradoxical atmosphere of safety and integrity expressed in connection with the movements and missing hindrances. This double-edged paradox of the limitlessness of the garden on the one hand and its implicit completeness on the other, as well as its missing protection as opposed to its seemingly innate security and integrity depict this garden as an ideal space of knowledge, a *locus amoenus scientiae*, wherein there are no such limits and boundaries as there are inevitably in a physical garden space.

Finally, the visitor needs his senses to fully grasp the experience and to gain the knowledge that the metaphorical garden as an archive and site of collection, observation, and demonstration is offering. Throughout the description the focus is laid on the sensorial perception, especially the visual sense: *aspice* (l. 2), *quid vides* (l. 9), (*totum ... hunc*) *vores ocellis* (l. 11), *non quicquid suavioris* (l. 16), *odore multo* (l. 17). Particularly in the four closing lines (ll. 18–21), the sensorial experience culminates. Simultaneously, the visitor or flaneur (*viator*) is directly identified with the reader of the poem, and thus, anticipated future reader of *De plantis*: *tu ... hic vades ... legens ... cupias*. Within the lines 19–20, the activities of the reader-*viator* are defined through a participial construction that further emphasizes the simultaneously operating senses: *sive poma legens* indicates a visual as well as tactile sensation (of touching the fruit), the object (*virentis horti*) points to the visual perception of colors, and *seu herbas seu flosculos olentes* finally refers to the olfactorial senses. Whereas *legens* in the context of the poem primarily means "picking up," it also implies the epistemologically fundamental practices of "collecting" and—understanding the poem as a metaphor for *De plantis*—"reading."[20]

Throughout all poems written by Paganelli that are included in this printed work, natural things and the practices of collecting, writing, and reading are interlocked, but only in the third poem to such extent. It can probably be understood as programmatic for the overall approach of *De plantis*, and, like the other poems, it is deeply linked to the *epistula nuncupatoria* written by Cesalpino himself. Taking a closer look at Cesalpino's dedicatory letter, therefore, might answer what kind of garden he envisioned his printed work to be.

Cesalpino wrote his printed work against the background of his experience as a prefect of the botanical garden and "in proximity of a well-stocked garden."[21] This background is emphasized at the beginning of his dedicatory epistle addressed to Francesco I de' Medici. In contrast to his predecessors, Cesalpino focused on the botanical garden as an already established institution of the scientific network stating: "supported ... by the abundance of gardens, which founded for the common good preserve foreign plants, collected from everywhere even the most remote regions."[22] In this regard, Cesalpino himself wrote about the importance of the *copia hortorum* and their contribution as institutions for collecting and preserving plants (*plantas undique advectas ... conservant*), and accordingly, the knowledge that comes with it. These two functions of the botanical garden as scientific institution point at two inherent problems of medico-botanical research that concern Cesalpino throughout his dedicatory letter: a) the need to protect and preserve the knowledge already gained from falling into oblivion (again) on the one hand, and b) finding an effective form of writing about plants to ensure the first point, on the other hand.[23] Naturally, this desire presents a challenge due to the seemingly infinite number of plants. And although Cesalpino recognizes the contributions of his predecessors, he simultaneously criticizes their lack of completeness (*imperfecta*) and clarity (*multa caligine suffusa*).[24]

After evaluating the contributions and contributors to botanical studies, therefore, Cesalpino turns his attention toward the form of writing (*ratio tractandi*)—of course, the titles of his works already indicate to the reader that he will probably position himself within the Theophrastean-Aristotelian tradition of scientific prose writing. He wrote: "Theophrastus of the ancient writers had suggested this form of treatise, but it was pursued in only a few (writings); of the contemporary (writers) Ruel tried indeed, but apart from those [sc. excerpts], which he extracted from Theophrastus, he nowhere applied (this form)."[25]

Cesalpino then criticized all forms of botanical prose in the tradition of Dioscorides' *De materia medica*. As a physician, Cesalpino himself valued the plants' faculties and includes them in his plant chapters as well, but his criticism points toward the orientation of plant description primarily focusing on medical faculties: "Dioscorides, though, like a physician solely assumed community with regard to the medical virtues, which he deals with sequentially as saps, resins, roots, seeds, and other plant parts."[26]

Furthermore, Cesalpino even more strongly rejected all works with an alphabetical structure (*ordo qui secundum nominis incipientes literas datus est*), which refers to the encyclopedic tradition in a more general sense as well as the herbal tradition, including the works of Brunfels and Fuchs.[27] Not surprisingly, in a third step Cesalpino then finally arrives at the form of botanical prose writing he deems most apt and designates Theophrastus as his role model:

> Qui autem [sc. plantas] secundum naturarum societatem assignatur, omnium facillimus reperitur, tutissimus, utilissimusque tum ad memoriam, tum ad facultates contemplandas. ... In persequenda autem secundum hunc ordinem plantarum historia sit, ut brevior descriptio satisfaciat, non enim cogimur in singulis ea repetere, quae communiter generibus conveniunt; atque adeo certa ex hac brevi descriptione paratur notitia ut pictura certiorem efficere non possit.[28]

> He, however, who allocates (sc. the plants) according to their communities of nature, finds them among all most easily, and most securely, and most useful for remembering as well as for the consideration of their virtues ... The history of plants has to be pursued but according to this system, so that a shorter description is sufficient, for as we are not forced to repeat for the single (plant), what is common for the whole group; and out of that short description is gained such certain knowledge that a picture could not produce a more certain one.

Hereby, Cesalpino emphasized as others had before, *brevitas* as a standard for botanical prose writing. Like Brunfels, Fuchs, and others, he tried to tackle the balancing act of brevity and completeness in the context of the information overload and the material limitations of the book as a three-dimensional physical container of knowledge experienced by sixteenth-century naturalists.[29] And since his predecessors failed to contain the mass of plants through their approaches, Cesalpino suggested another form for organizing knowledge about plants in accordance with their shared features to avoid repetitions lastingly. Therefore, he refuted the medico-botanical tradition of *materia medica* for their one-sided perspective as leading to a flawed organization of knowledge. When repudiating the writings artificially organized in an alphabetical order, Cesalpino stresses that they only seem to serve the purpose of easily memorizing botanical knowledge when in fact they are not (*tamquam maxime fallax*). In contrast, his approach is *utilissimusque tum ad memoriam*, leading to reliable and constantly available botanical knowledge (*certa ex hac brevi descriptione paratur notitia*).³⁰

With this analysis of Cesalpino's dedicatory epistle, we may finally understand what kind of garden his pupil Paganelli was describing: a memory garden. At first glance, particularly considering Cesalpino's background as professor and director of the botanical garden, one might think the description, so cleverly refuting other forms of gardens, such as the *hortus conclusus* or the private garden,³¹ might aim at the botanical garden as the ideal space. However, there are certain hints indicating that this is not the case, such as the missing borders or the explicit exhortation to pick up the *naturalia* contained and displayed within it,³² which then come into interplay with Cesalpino's concerns regarding stability of knowledge and *memoria*. Hereby, *legere* even gains another semantic layer indicating the recollection of stored knowledge.³³

Like all physical gardens, even a botanical garden is subdued by the changeability of living vegetation and the circle of seasons—something Mattioli pondered in his *Discorsi*. Whereas Mattioli chose to contrast this imagery of the ever-changing garden in need of constant cultivation efforts to his herbal as a seemingly everlasting and unchanging paper garden, Cesalpino suggested the memory garden as the ideal space of knowledge.³⁴ His botanical treatise in presenting descriptions as short as possible in a systematic order then were meant for the reader as a threshold in creating his own memory garden where herbs, flowers, fruits, and plants of all kinds could be "plucked" from memory. An approach that, just as all other areas of botanical study and research, was characterized and based on re-iteration of scholarly and botanical practices—re-reading, re-arranging, and re-collecting.

Additionally, as Fabrizio Baldassarri and Craig Martin have pointed out in the introduction to this volume, Cesalpino's own print work was fundamentally connected to the herbarium he collected beforehand, which is mentioned in the dedicatory epistle as well. Finally, considering Marco Sgarbi's analysis of Cesalpino's *Quaestionum peripateticarum libri V* (1571), it becomes clear that the predominance and centrality of sensorial experiences as celebrated in Paganelli's poem in dialogue with the *ordo* and mode of description proposed by Cesalpino in his dedicatory letter, build upon Cesalpino's very own epistemology.³⁵

2. The Few and the Many: The Paratextual Strategies of Cesalpino and Mattioli

As we have seen, the paratexts of early modern herbals were central tools in shaping the notion of the botanical science as well as debating in a century-long discourse its appropriate form and its relation to book, garden, and plants.

In addition to the paratexts working together like a network in representing and shaping the idea of the botanical science, the representation of the scientific community and its network within the paratexts is equally important for shaping a shared community as well as for the self-positioning of each author. By assembling a catalogue of authorities whom they excerpted or quoted for their own compositions of botanical prose, the authors narrated different histories of botanical knowledge. As Paula Findlen already observed for the formation of the community in the field of natural history more broadly, the authors of such printed works were very well aware that they were on the verge of change in the institutionalization of botanical practices, particularly related to the impact of printed works in those processes.[36]

Mapping the written histories of sixteenth-century herbals allows us to observe how those authors did not only write herbals, but simultaneously set out to both write and shape the history and to define the community of the emerging botanical discipline.[37]

A fundamental part of the self-positioning of all authors is based on enumerating the authorities they rely on and include in their own works, both earlier as well as contemporary authors[38]—a catalog of these authorities often forms part of paratexts and particularly dedicatory letters.

These artfully woven networks of names show notable differences regarding the number of enumerated authorities (see **Figure 9.1**), and they reflect different paratextual strategies that are deployed by each botanical author.

For that purpose, I want to briefly compare Cesalpino' *De plantis* and Mattioli's *Discorsi/Commentarii*—an especially intriguing comparison, since their contrast in number of paratexts as well as listed authorities shows very great differences.[39] We may also note that the vernacular printed works usually invoke a significantly smaller number of authorities in comparison with their Latin counterparts. In this context, Cesalpino is quite singular in his minimal approach for his Latin printed work. Other works printed at the end of the sixteenth century also tend to incorporate a lot more names and paratexts, as for instance with Caspar Bauhin's *Phytopinax* (1596) or John Gerard's *The Herball or General Historie of Plantes* (1597).

Both Cesalpino and Mattioli (see **Figure 9.2**) identified a group of authorities (Ruel, Barbaro, Brasavola, Dioscorides) that can be considered a core group in the sixteenth-century herbals and additionally both agreed that Theophrastus was an essential authority—although the extent to which he becomes central differs. Moreover, both additionally list their fellow countrymen Luigi Anguillara (c. 1512–70) and Luca Ghini (c. 1490–1556).[40]

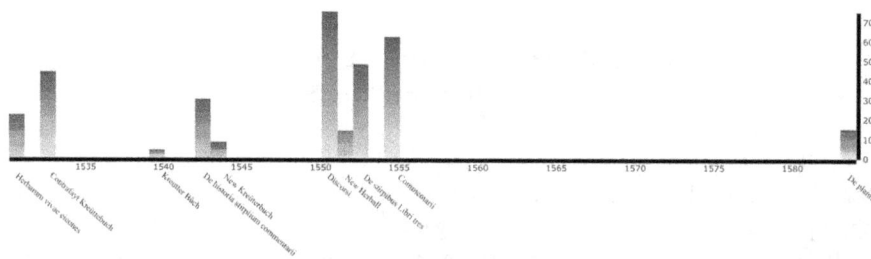

Figure 9.1 Number of listed authorities within the paratexts of sixteenth-century printed herbals in relation to each first print edition (For Mattioli's *Discorsi* the first print edition by Vincenzo Valgrisi is considered). [©Julia Heideklang]

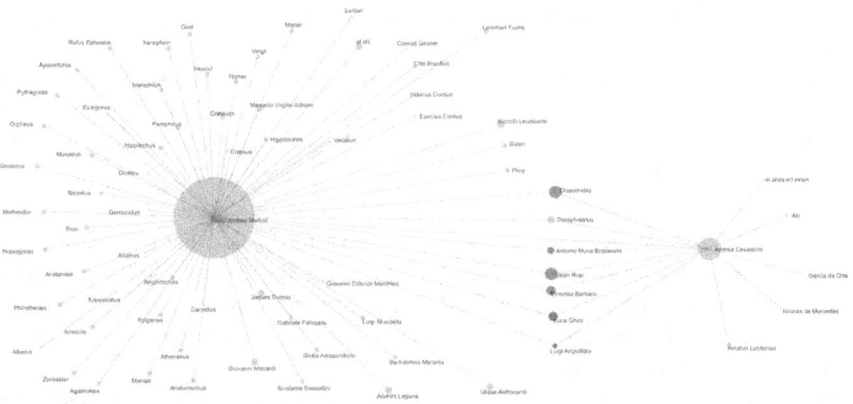

Figure 9.2 Comparison of the Authorities listed by Andrea Cesalpino and Mattioli: authorities constituting a core group of continuously invoked authors in sixteenth-century print herbals; Theophrastus as additionally shared ancient authority; southern European authorities who are quoted by both or Cesalpino only. [©Julia Heideklang]

It is striking how Mattioli's node is immersed in invoked authorities and designated contributors, whereas Cesalpino names exactly just four additional authorities (aside from Mattioli himself, represented by a direct line in Figure 9.1): Amatus Lusitanus (1512–70), Garcia de Orta (1495–1568), Nicolás Monardes (1493–1588), and a summarizing, yet intriguingly concealing *et aliique exteri*.[41] Cesalpino's additionally selected authorities are not chosen randomly. Monardes, de Orta, and Lusitanus each brought new knowledge into the scientific discourse, writing about regions largely unknown to the ancient writers, while Anguillara was chosen for his condensation and brief form of writing without loss of quality.[42]

Whereas Mattioli accumulated authorities in an expansive way, Cesalpino seems to tend to the opposite and to reduce the representative authorities strictly to a few botanical scholars, hereby particularly distinguishing the selected few within the field simply by naming them. At the same time, this strategy allows him to conveniently exclude many others from the disciplinary historiography. Mattioli's strategy on the other hand gives even more significance to individual authorities he decided not to mention at all, as for instance his silence on Amatus Lusitanus in his enumeration.[43] Overall, Mattioli followed a three-step-system, as most herbalists did.[44] All contemporary authorities enumerated above are grouped together under the label *alcuni preclarissimi ingegni dei tempi nostri diligentissimi investigatori*, and we may note, how Mattioli did not deploy a particular order in his enumeration and closed with a more general "together with some others, but to keep it short, I will not mention them"[45]—at first glance similar to Cesalpino, but in fact giving quite a comprehensive catalog instead. This verbalization, then, furthers the impression of a large group of authorities in the field of natural history on the one hand, while posing the question why certain persons might have been dismissed on the other. We also should consider the effect of reading such a long and crowded history, which then reaches new heights with Mattioli's work, according to his storytelling.

Mattioli's closing remark brings us back to the group subsumed so surprisingly vaguely by Cesalpino, in contrast to his very specific list of names: the *aliique exteri*. Somehow, Cesalpino managed to write a very southern European history of the field of botany, that is, additionally, largely based on the achievements of Italians. Of course, we could claim that the several northern European writers fall under the various points Cesalpino criticized so emphatically, but those criticisms could be at least partly also attributed to Italian botanical authors. Moreover, his reflections about knowledge and the form of botanical prose implicitly refer to discourses on books and garden which were established prominently in the earlier botanical works such as those of the German authors Brunfels and Fuchs.[46]

Finally, the criticism voiced by Cesalpino against herbals following in their *ratio tractandi* of Dioscorides' approach also implicitly criticizes Mattioli. This implicit criticism does not only become apparent when considering a direct mention of Mattioli in Cesalpino's list of contributors to the botanical science,[47] but even more so regarding the self-fashioning of Mattioli and the reception of his *Commentarii*, which were soon awaited as "the new Mattioli." In a later edition, a woodcut was added to Mattioli's voluminous work together with an elegiac distich by his pupil and successor Georg Handsch (1529–c. 1578), explicitly putting Mattioli and Dioscorides on the same level with one another.[48]

In this context, Cesalpino's criticism against Dioscorides' form of writing together with his overall paratextual strategy of invoking a selected corpus of authorities can be understood as two different parts of an interlocking strategy to promote the Italian achievements on the one hand and simultaneously undermining the overwhelmingly powerful position of Mattioli and his commentary on the other.[49]

3. Conclusion

Drawing the threads together, we are able to observe how self-fashioning and self-positioning of sixteenth-century botanical scholars were enabled by the printed herbal's paratexts through their multi-directional references spanning a whole range of concepts, authorities, and *topoi*. And it is precisely the heterogeneity of the various paratextual forms—dedicatory poems, dedicatory letters, preface to the reader, etc.—that allows this effective and effectful communication and construction of shared conceptualizations.

The dedicatory poem by Cristoforo Paganelli can be understood as programmatic. Read together with the dedicatory epistle and in light of complementary observations made by Sgarbi in this very volume, it becomes clear that it is a means to convey Cesalpino's epistemological approach regarding botanical knowledge. Hereby, the central importance of sensorial experiences is obvious and deeply connected to Cesalpino's deliberations on the best system (*ordo*) and the best form of writing (*ratio tractandi*) enabling readers to create their very own memory garden.

In the case of Cesalpino, we have a comparatively minimal yet refined set of paratexts in *De plantis*, not only in the number and forms of paratexts but also with regard to the number of authorities invoked within the paratext that portray the history and development of botanical knowledge. In contrast to his colleague Mattioli, Cesalpino chose a minimal approach, listing only a few selected botanical scholars, which made his selection of names all the more meaningful. He also displayed a much more restricted authorial persona. Mattioli accumulated authorities and contributors of all kinds, depicted his herbals as an idealized paper garden for all those who are in want of a teacher, and used the margins of the main text to point aggressively to every error seemingly made by fellow naturalists.[50] Cesalpino's whole display underlines the contrast to Mattioli by the way he presents himself as a scientific authorial persona, by the garden metaphor deployed, and by the ideal form of writing he proposes.

However, the construction of disciplinary concepts, histories, and communities does not conclude with the work being printed. In this context, the question arises whether Cesalpino was successful in his (paratextual) communicative effort to his intended readership. His botanical treatise was printed in one edition only, and it was never published in a vernacular edition like so many other herbals were. Regarding Cesalpino's strong emphasis on brief descriptions for a better and less repetitive arrangement of plant species and the importance of plant specimens for gaining botanical knowledge, it might come as surprising that in contrast to other printed works, we only find very sparse annotations and, so far, only one instant of plant findings, probably preserved unintentionally.

Maybe the botanical treatise as a form indeed did not motivate (or in some cases, agitate) the readership in the same way Fuchs's *Commentarii insignes* or Mattioli's *Discorsi* and *Commentarii* did—or maybe not the same broad array of readers. Right from the start publishing in Latin excluded readership not able to partake in the Latin scientific discourse. Another hypothesis could be that writing from his position as a professor and prefect of the botanical garden at Pisa, Cesalpino did indeed have his own students in mind, therefore enforcing the memory garden probably going hand in hand with the regular exercises in plant identification usually performed in botanical gardens.[51]

Notes

1   On the debate surrounding his biographical data see Guido Moggi, "L'erbario di Andrea Cesalpino," in *Gli erbari aretini da Andrea Cesalpino ai giorni nostri*, ed. Chiara Nepi and Enrico Gusmeroli (Florence: Firenze University Press, 2008), 1–20; and see the introduction to this volume.

2   This term is sometimes already in use, although without definition and seemingly chosen more intuitively in respect to the paratext theory laid out by Gérard Genette, *Paratexts: Thresholds of Interpretation*, trans. Jane E. Lewin (Cambridge: Cambridge University Press 1997). Even more so this term is very promising, when defined more clearly, to describe the mechanisms through which the different paratexts work together as literary forms by means of collaboration and interference taking advantage of their heterogeneity in direct proximity to one another.

3   See Benjamin Bühler, "Botanik," in *Literatur und Wissen, Ein interdisziplinäres Handbuch*, ed. Roland Borgards, Harald Neumeyer, Nicolas Pethes, and Yvonne Wübben (Stuttgart: J.B. Metzler, 2013), 64–9, at 65.
4   See Agnes Arber, *Herbals, Their Origin and Evolution, a Chapter in the History of Botany 1470–1670*, 3rd ed. (Cambridge: Cambridge University Press, 1986), 18. See also Andrew Cunningham, "The Culture of Gardens," in *Cultures of Natural History*, ed. Nicolas Jardine, James A. Secord, and Emma C. Spary (Cambridge: Cambridge University Press 1996), 38–56, at 50. Lea Knight, *On Books and Botany in Early Modern England, Sixteenth-Century Plants and Print Culture* (London: Routledge, 2009), 49 sees this as an "all-purpose solution adopted by printers … to characterize herbal works, … by botanical metaphors that construed books as gardens … The ensuing popularity of printed herbals in the sixteenth century may, in turn, have led to a more vigorous exploitation of that same metaphor by more literary publishers." Certainly, economic strategies played a role, but this explanation—even with the extension on the usage of actual images—might fall short, particularly when looking at the collaborations of printer, artist(s), and author throughout the sixteenth century.
5   Knight, *On Books and Botany*, 15.
6   On Brunfels's herbals and his concept of cento and garden see Julia Heideklang, "*Hos Centones*: Brunfels' *Herbarum vivae eicones* (1530) and *Contrafayt Krëutterbuch* (1532)," in *Cento-texts in the Making, Aesthetics and Poetics from Homer to Zong!*, ed. Manuel Baumbach (Trier: Wissenschaftlicher Verlag, 2022), 63–88.
7   On the term "types" and the different garden forms in the Renaissance see Raffaella Fabiani Giannetto, "Types of Gardens," in *A Cultural History of Gardens in the Renaissance*, ed. Elisabeth Hyde (London: Bloomsbury, 2016), 43–72.
8   Kathryn Gleason, "Design," in *The Cultural History of Gardens in Antiquity*, ed. Kathryn Gleason (London: Bloomsbury, 2016), 1–40, at 16. On *viridarium* and its connection to the *ars topiaria* and an increasing professionalization of gardening art, see Lena Landgren, "Plantings," in *A Cultural History of Gardens in Antiquity* (London: Bloomsbury, 2016), 75–89, at 81. For the metaphor see Leonhart Fuchs, *De historia stirpium commentarii insignes* (Basel: Isengrin, 1542), title page.
9   Fuchs is presenting his "plant collections" as a gift to the dedicatee Joachim II, Margrave of Brandenburg (1505–71) and therefore advertises his "garden" in reference to the private gardens of the nobility while skillfully linking the two spaces book and *viridarium* through their epistemological and spatial qualities; see also Fuchs, *De historia stirpium commentarii*, sig. β2v.
10 Although the learned reader would certainly recognize them as nearly *verbatim* excerpts from source authorities such as Pliny and Dioscorides.
11 See Pietro Andrea Mattioli, *Il Dioscoride. Con li suoi discorsi* Venice: Valgrisi, 1550), sig. α4v; Pietro Andrea Mattioli, *Commentarii, in libros sex Pedacii Dioscoridis Anazarbei, de materia medica* (Venice: Valgrisi, 1554), sig. α4v. A short comparison of Fuchs's, Mattioli's, and Cesalpino's metaphors will be published in Julia Heideklang, "Leaf: The Twofold Materiality of Early Modern Herbals," in *Natural Things in Early Modern Worlds*, ed. Mackenzie Cooley, Anna Toledano, and Dyugu Yıldırım (London: Routledge, 2023), 265–90.
12 In the scope of this paper it would be too far-reaching to analyze their interplays in detail, so one example of deliberate inversion may suffice. In his *epistula nuncupatoria*, Cesalpino displays topical humility in calling his work "this little work" (*hoc munusculum*, [sig. b1r]), but in the dedicatory poems, of course, his

pupil Paganelli celebrates his work as "this excellent work" (*HOC opus egregium*, [sig. b1v])—it takes only the turning of a page to turn from one to the other.

13 Cristoforo Paganelli was Cesalpino's pupil studying medicine at the University of Pisa. Only scarce information about him is found in primary sources. For his work as a poet, see for instance in Pietro Paolo Ginnani, *Memorie storico-critiche degli scrittori ravennati* (Faenza: Archi, 1769), 2:127. He seems to have been quite acquainted with Roman poetry, such as the works of Catullus and Horace. In 1587, for instance, he published a *Carmen pium*—printed by the same print house of Giorgio Marescotti (1563–1601/2) as Cesalpino's *De plantis*—that reportedly begins with: *Fert animus noster CLAVI miranda referre / Unius illorum, (veterum si fama superstes) / Qui sacros Christi foderunt saeviter artus*. See Pier Francesco Cateni, *Notizie della reliquia insigne del scaro chiodo* (Colle: Pacini, 1821), 34.

14 Unfortunately, there are no sources pertaining to the figure of Antonio Pellicini or Antonio Pellegrini. However, considering that he is characterized as *Emporiensis*, his dedicatory poem might give us an answer as to the origin of one of the two copies of Cesalpino's *De plantis*, which, according to book plates and catalogs, were held at the Convento di Santo Stefano a Empoli, namely the copy with signature R.i. 19, Biblioteca Marucelliana, Florence, which seems to have been used actively in the garden or in nature by a sixteenth-century reader.

15 On the broad field of Latin and even more so the Neo-Latin epigram, see Victoria Moul, "Lyric Poetry," in *The Oxford Handbook of Neo-Latin*, ed. Sarah Knight and Stefan Tilg (Oxford: Oxford University Press 2015), 41–56. See also Karl A. E. Enenkel, "Introduction. The Neo-Latin Epigram: Humanist Self-Definition in a Learned and Witty Discourse," in *The Neo-Latin Epigram, A Learned and Witty Genre*, ed. Susanna de Beer, Karl A. E. Enenkel, and David Rijser (Leuven: Leuven University Press 2009), 1–24. Although the epigram is often treated together with other forms of occasional poetry, the dedicatory poems of the sixteenth-century botanical prints show for the main part a highly erudite and elaborate prowess and are additionally very involved in the epistemic and literary discourse of botanical writings.

16 Andrea Cesalpino, *De plantis libri XVI* (Florence: Marescotti, 1583), sig. b2r. All following transcripts, translations, and figures are based on the copy Andrea Cesalpino, *De plantis libri XVI* (Florence: Marescotti, 1583) digitized by Bayerische Staatsbibliothek München: Augsburg, Staats- und Stadtbibliothek 4 Nat 54; urn:nbn:de:bvb:12-bsb11220346-2, unless noted otherwise. All translations are my own.

17 It should be noted that Paganelli playfully intertwines possible readings of the sensorial with the sensual by starting his list of hindrances with Priapus as well as a *puella[e] custos* he lays the grounds for reading the *timor rapinae* and the phrase *hunc vores ocellis* against the background of various sexual contexts and their literary traditions, particularly regarding garden spaces.

18 On the long literary tradition of the *locus amoenus* as motif in ancient literature see the detailed study of Petra Hass, *Der locus amoenus in der antiken Literatur: Zu Theorie und Geschichte eines literarischen Motivs* (Bamberg: Wissenschaftlicher Verlag Bamberg, 1998). On the garden as *locus amoenus* in concepts of the Renaissance see the Alexander Samson, "Introduction," in *Locus amoenus, Gardens and Horticulture in the Renaissance*, ed. Alexander Samson (Chichester: Wiley-Blackwell, 2012), 1–11.

19 Alessandro Tosi, "Botanical Illustration and the Idea of the Garden in the Sixteenth Century between Imitation and Imagination," in *Gardens, Knowledge and the Sciences*

in the Early Modern Period, ed. Hubertus Fischer, Volker R. Remmert, and Joachim Wolschke-Bulmahn (Berlin: Birkhäuser, 2016), 183–210, at 191.

20   Peter G. W. Glare, ed., *Oxford Latin Dictionary* (Oxford: Oxford University Press, 1997).

21   Tosi, "Botanical Illustration," 198.

22   Cesalpino, *DP*, sig. a2v: "adiutus … atque hortorum copia, qui ad publicam utilitatem consiti peregrinas plantas undique vel ex remotissimis regionibus advectas conservant …"

23   Both the narrative of the botanical knowledge rescued and now in need of diligent preservation as well as the debate on an apt form of botanical prose writing had a prominent place in printed botanical paratexts throughout the sixteenth century.

24   As in other fields of scholarly writing, botanical texts made necessary a balancing act, deploying an apt *brevitas* while avoiding *obscuritas*. See Baldassarri in this volume.

25   Cesalpino, *DP*, sig. a3v: "Hanc vero tractandi rationem Theophrastus inter antiquos indicavit, sed in paucis est persecutus. Apud nostros autem Ruellius tentavit quidem, sed praeter ea, quae a Theophrasto excerpsit circa rationem commune, ulterius nequaquam est progressus."

26   Ibid., sig. a4r: "At Dioscorides tamquam medicus solum communionem circa facultates medicas accepit, quo ordine succos, lachrymas, radices, semina et alias plantarum partes persecutus est."

27   Ibid.: "Aliis, quo facilius memoriae mandarentur, placuit eo ordine digere, qui secundum nominis incipientes literas datus est. Sed hic tamquam maxime fallax, et longissime a rei natura discedens a gravioribus huius scientiae authoribus reprobatus est." [My translation: "Others again decided, to make it more easily to remember, divide them in such order that is written down corresponding to the first letter of the name: but this form was rejected at the same time as most misleading and furthest from the nature of things by the more influential writers of this knowledge."]

28   Ibid.

29   See Brain W. Ogilvie, "The Many Books of Nature: Renaissance Naturalists and Information Overload," *Journal of the History of Ideas* 64, no. 1 (2003): 29–40.

30   On the debate regarding the epistemic value of pictures in contrast to words see Sachiko Kusukawa, *Picturing the Book of Nature. Image, Text, and Argument in Sixteenth-Century Human Anatomy and Medical Botany* (Chicago: University of Chicago Press, 2012), 98–177; Dominic Olariu, "'Kräuterautopsie' im Jahr 1487," *Geschichte der Pharmazie* 70 no. 3 (2018): 29–51. It has to be noted, however, that Cesalpino did not take a clear stance in his *De plantis*, suggesting, if funding were to be provided that a luxury edition with woodcuts might be printed.

31   Cesalpino, *DP*, sig. b2r, ll.5–8. It is noteworthy that these have been garden forms chosen before in other metaphors, as we have seen before, and therefore may be implied here too.

32   On the rules in botanical gardens see Paula Findlen, "Anatomy Theaters, Botanical Gardens, and Natural History Collections," in *The Cambridge History of Science, vol. 3: Early Modern Science*, ed. Katharine Park and Lorraine Daston (New York: Cambridge University Press, 2006), 272–89 and Gregory Grämiger, "Reconstructing Order: The Spatial Arrangement of Plants in the Hortus Botanicus of Leiden University in Its First Years," in *Gardens, Knowledge and the Sciences*, ed. Hubertus Fischer et al. (Berlin: Birkhäuser, 2016), 235–51.

33   On ἀναγιγνώσκειν and *legere* in this specific context, see Mary Carruthers, *The Book of Memory. A Study of Memory in Medieval Culture*, 2nd ed. (Cambridge: Cambridge University Press, 2010), 34.

34 On gardens as popular devices for the architectonic *ars memorandi* following Cicero's *De oratore*, see Mary Carruthers, *The Book of Memory*, 22; John Dixon Hunt, *Garden and Grove: The Italian Renaissance Garden in the English Imagination 1600–1750*, 2nd ed. (Philadelphia: University of Pennsylvania Press, 1996), 68–100.
35 See the contribution of Marco Sgarbi to this volume.
36 Paula Findlen, "The Formation of a Scientific Community: Natural History in Sixteenth-Century Italy," in *Natural Particulars, Nature and the Disciplines in Renaissance Europe*, ed. Anthony Grafton and Nancy Siraisi (Cambridge, MA: MIT Press, 1999), 369–400, at 372.
37 Of course, botanical knowledge was important prior to the sixteenth century and outside of Europe as well, the notion of an "emerging" discipline is meant solely in contrast to the later emancipated and institutionalized discipline to which we refer today as botany.
38 See Brian W. Ogilvie, *The Science of Describing. Natural History in Renaissance Europe* (Chicago: University of Chicago Press, 2006), 87–93 for the invention of natural history.
39 Pietro Andrea Mattioli wrote his commentary on Dioscorides' work first in Italian and it was printed in 1544; in 1554 a Latin edition was printed. In this very case, the paratexts were translated from Italian to Latin almost word by word, making every slight change all the more noticeable.
40 For Luigi Anguillara, see Florike Egmond, "Into the Wild: Botanical Fieldwork in the Sixteenth Century," in *Naturalists in the Field: Collecting, Recording and Preserving the Natural World from the Fifteenth to the Twenty-First Century*, ed. Arthur MacGregor (Leiden: Brill, 2018), 166–211, at 174 and 181. For Luca Ghini, see Paula Findlen, "The Death of a Naturalist: Knowledge and Community in Late Renaissance Italy," in *Professors, Physicians and Practices in the History of Medicine. Essays in Honor of Nancy Siraisi*, ed. Cynthia Klestinec and Gideon Manning (Cham: Springer, 2017), 155–95.
41 See Cesalpino, *DP*, sig. a3r.
42 Ibid., sig. a3r-v.
43 On Lusitanus and Mattioli, see Richard Palmer, "Medical Botany in Northern Italy in the Renaissance," *Journal of the Royal Society of Medicine* 78 (1985): 149–57, at 150.
44 Even Cesalpino did, although he omits the ancient authorities as stylized "first generation" of scholars in the timeline of his storytelling and instead focused on the two contemporary groups and their achievements.
45 Mattioli, *Discorsi*, sig. α3v: "Al che havendo pur finalmente avertito alcuni preclarissimi ingegni de i tempi nostri diligentissimi investigatori della materia medicinale, ed parimente peritissimi tanto nella lingua Greca, quanto nella latina, dico Hermolao Barbaro, il Leoniceno, il Manardo da Ferrara, il Ruellio, Marcello Vergilio, il Brunfelsio, il Brasavola, il Fuchsio, il Silvio, il Mondella, ed l'uno, ed l'altro Cordo, insieme con alcuni altri, che per brevità trapasso." Mattioli constructs that group in a similar manner as the group of ancient authorities shortly before: "Del che ce ne fanno amplissima fede Pittagora, Aristotele, Theophrasto, Democrito, … Dioscoride fra tutti gli altri celeberrimo, Galeno, Plinio, ed altri infiniti antichi, i nomi de i quali per brevità trapasso."
46 They were first published in Latin and were later published in vernacular editions too. Both Otto Brunfels's *Herbarum vivae eicones* (1530) and Leonhart Fuchs's *De historia stirpium commentarii insignes* (1542) were widely known and distributed.
47 Cesalpino, *DP*, sig. a3r.

48 See Pietro Andrea Mattioli, *I Discorsi nelli sei libri di Pedacio Dioscoride Anazarbeo della materia medicinale* (Venice: Valgrisi 1568), sig. m8v.
49 On Mattioli's central importance, see Findlen, "Death of a Naturalist," 160; Findlen, "The Formation of a Scientific Community."
50 As already observed by Palmer, "Medical Botany," 149–57.
51 See for instance the printed forms used in the botanical garden at Leiden, presented in Grämiger, "Reconstructing Order."

Bibliography

Primary Sources

Cesalpino, Andrea. *De plantis libri XVI*. Florence: Marescotti, 1583. Notes consulted from copy R.i. 19, Biblioteca Marucelliana, Florence.
Fuchs, Leonhart. *De historia stirpium commentarii insignes*. Basel: Isengrin, 1542.
Mattioli, Pietro Andrea. *Commentarii, in libros sex Pedacii Dioscoridis Anazarbei, de materia medica*. Venice: Vincenzo Valgrisi, 1554.
Mattioli, Pietro Andrea. *Il Dioscoride. Con li suoi discorsi*. Venice: Valgrisi, 1550.

Secondary Sources

Arber, Agnes. *Herbals, Their Origin and Evolution, a Chapter in the History of Botany 1470–1670*, 3rd ed. Cambridge: Cambridge University Press, 1986.
Bühler, Benjamin. "Botanik." In *Literatur und Wissen, Ein interdisziplinäres Handbuch*, edited by Roland Borgards, Harald Neumeyer, Nicolas Pethes, and Yvonne Wübben, 64–9. Stuttgart: J.B. Metzler, 2013.
Carruthers, Mary. *The Book of Memory. A Study of Memory in Medieval Culture*. Cambridge: Cambridge University Press, 2010.
Cateni, Pier Francesco. *Notizie della reliquia insigne del sacro chiodo*. Colle: Pacini, 1821.
Cunningham, Andrew. "The Culture of Gardens." In *Cultures of Natural History*, edited by Nicolas Jardine, James A. Secord, and Emma C. Spary, 38–56. Cambridge: Cambridge University Press 1996.
Egmond, Florike. "Into the Wild: Botanical Fieldwork in the Sixteenth Century." In *Naturalists in the Field: Collecting, Recording and Preserving the Natural World from the Fifteenth to the Twenty-First Century*, edited by Arthur MacGregor, 166–211. Leiden: Brill, 2018.
Enenkel, Karl A. E. "Introduction. The Neo-Latin Epigram: Humanist Self-Definition in a Learned and Witty Discourse." In *The Neo-Latin Epigram, A Learned and Witty Genre*, edited by Susanna de Beer, Karl A. E. Enenkel, and David Rijser, 1–24. Leuven: Leuven University Press, 2009.
Fabiani Giannetto, Raffaella. "Types of Gardens." In *A Cultural History of Gardens in the Renaissance*, edited by Elisabeth Hyde, 43–72. London: Bloomsbury, 2016.
Findlen, Paula. "Anatomy Theaters, Botanical Gardens, and Natural History Collections." In *The Cambridge History of Science, vol. 3: Early Modern Science*, edited by Katharine Park and Lorraine Daston, 272–89. New York: Cambridge University Press, 2006.
Findlen, Paula. "The Death of a Naturalist: Knowledge and Community in Late Renaissance Italy." In *Professors, Physicians and Practices in the History of Medicine*, edited by Cynthia Klestinec and Gideon Manning, 155–95. Cham: Springer, 2018.

Findlen, Paula. "The Formation of a Scientific Community: Natural History in Sixteenth-Century Italy." In *Natural Particulars: Nature and the Disciplines in Renaissance Europe*, edited by Anthony Grafton and Nancy Siraisi, 369–400. Cambridge, MA: MIT Press, 1999.
Genette, Gérard. *Paratexts: Thresholds of Interpretation*, translated by Jane E. Lewin. Cambridge: Cambridge University Press, 1997.
Ginnani, Pietro Paolo. *Memorie Storico-critiche degli scrittori*. Faenza: G.A. Archi, 1769.
Glare, Peter G. W., ed. *Oxford Latin Dictionary*. Oxford: Oxford University Press, 1997.
Gleason, Kathryn. "Design." In *The Cultural History of Gardens in Antiquity*, edited by Kathryn Gleason, 1–40. London: Bloomsbury, 2016.
Grämiger, Gregory. "Reconstructing Order: The Spatial Arrangement of Plants in the Hortus Botanicus of Leiden University in Its First Years." In Gardens, Knowledge and the Sciences, edited by Hubertus Fischer et al., 235–51. Berlin: Birkhäuser, 2016.
Hass, Petra. *Der locus amoenus in der antiken Literatur: Zu Theorie und Geschichte eines literarischen Motivs*. Bamberg: Wissenschaftlicher Verlag Bamberg, 1998.
Heideklang, Julia. "*Hos Centones*: Brunfels' *Herbarum vivae eicones* (1530) and *Contrafayt Kreütterbuch* (1532)." In *Cento-texts in the Making, Aesthetics and Poetics from Homer to Zong!*, edited by Manuel Baumbach, 63–88. Trier: Wissenschaftlicher Verlag, 2022.
Heideklang, Julia. "Leaf: The Twofold Materiality of Early Modern Herbals." In *Natural Things in Early Modern Worlds*, edited by Mackenzie Cooley, Anna Toledano, and Dyugu Yıldırım, 265–90. London: Routledge, 2023.
Hunt, John Dixon. *Garden and Grove: The Italian Renaissance Garden in the English Imagination 1600–1750*, 2nd ed. Philadelphia: University of Pennsylvania Press, 1996.
Knight, Lea. *On Books and Botany in Early Modern England, Sixteenth-Century Plants and Print Culture*. London: Routledge, 2009.
Kusukawa, Sachiko. *Picturing the Book of Nature. Image, Text, and Argument in Sixteenth-Century Human Anatomy and Medical Botany*. Chicago: University of Chicago Press, 2012.
Landgren, Lena. "Plantings." In *A Cultural History of Gardens in Antiquity*, edited by Kathryn Gleason, 75–89. London: Bloomsbury, 2016.
Moggi, Guido. "L'erbario di Andrea Cesalpino." *Gli erbari aretini da Andrea Cesalpino ai giorni nostri*, edited by Chiara Nepi and Enrico Gusmeroli, 3–20. Florence: Firenze University Press, 2008.
Moul, Victoria. "Lyric Poetry." In *The Oxford Handbook of Neo-Latin*, edited by Sarah Knight and Stefan Tilg, 41–56. Oxford: Oxford University Press, 2015.
Ogilvie, Brian W. "The Many Books of Nature: Renaissance Naturalists and Information Overload." *Journal of the History of Ideas* 64, no. 1 (2003): 29–40.
Ogilvie, Brian W. *The Science of Describing: Natural History in Renaissance Europe*. Chicago: University of Chicago Press, 2006.
Olariu, Dominic. "'Kräuterautopsie' im Jahr 1487." *Geschichte der Pharmazie* 70, no. 3 (2018): 29–51.
Palmer, Richard. "Medical Botany in Northern Italy in the Renaissance." *Journal of the Royal Society of Medicine* 78 (1985): 149–57.
Samson, Alexander. "Introduction." In *Locus amoenus, Gardens and Horticulture in the Renaissance*, edited by Alexander Samson, 1–11. Chichester: Wiley-Blackwell, 2012.
Tosi, Alessandro. "Botanical Illustration and the Idea of the Garden in the Sixteenth Century between Imitation and Imagination." In *Gardens, Knowledge and the Sciences in the Early Modern Period*, edited by Hubertus Fischer, Volker R. Remmert and Joachim Wolschke-Bulmahn, 183–210. Berlin: Birkhäuser, 2016.

10

Cesalpino's Mineralogy between Meteorology and Chymistry

Hiro Hirai

In 1592 Andrea Cesalpino (1524/5–1603) was called to Rome by Pope Clement VIII (1536–1605) and became a professor of medicine at *La Sapienza*.[1] Upon his arrival, he found his former student, Michele Mercati (1541–93), in charge of cataloging the Vatican's mineral collection. But Mercati soon passed away, leaving the manuscript of his *Metallotheca* incomplete.[2] Hoping to complement its missing parts, Cesalpino devoted himself to the study of mineralogy. His efforts crystalized in the publication of his treatise *On Metallic Bodies* (*De metallicis*) (1596).[3]

According to Cesalpino's own words, this treatise is a "compendium" useful for those who cannot dedicate a considerable amount of time to reading specialized literature. Nevertheless, it bears witness to his remarkable erudition regarding the mineralogical writings of ancient and medieval authors such as Theophrastus, Dioscorides, Pliny, Galen, Avicenna, Marbode, and Albertus Magnus. Among the writers of his time, Cesalpino especially used the works of the German physician and naturalist, Georg Agricola (1494–1555), without mentioning his name.[4] Although there is no mineralogical work of the sixteenth century that can rival those of Agricola, Cesalpino's treatise from a rigorous Aristotelian perspective can be considered a critical response. What were the criteria on which he established his mineralogy? Why did he find Agricola's system problematic? What was his attitude toward "chymical" (alchemical/chemical) doctrines in vogue in his time?[5] How did he perceive the difference of minerals from living beings? Exploring these questions, I aim to place Cesalpino's mineralogical work in its historical and intellectual context. Largely relying on Aristotle's *Meteorology*, he even tried to reinterpret major chymical doctrines while rejecting vitalistic understandings of the mineral kingdom.

1. Mineral Classification

Distributed in three books, Cesalpino's *De metallicis* addresses over 450 names of minerals. The first book is devoted to earths, salts, sulfur, and bitumen while the second deals with stones, further divided in four groups: rocks, marbles, gems, and other stones. Agricola's influence is visible in this fourfold division of stones. The third and last book then explores metals and related substances. Cesalpino's descriptions focus on the names of mineral species and the places of their production. Comparing to those of Agricola, they are shorter and often consist of comparisons of information gathered from the works of three major ancients: Dioscorides, Pliny, and Galen.

In the first book Cesalpino clearly shows his standpoint for mineral classification as he paraphrases Aristotle's essential passage in his *Meteorology*:

> As Aristotle at the end of his *Meteorology*, book 3, establishes their double matter, that is, double exhalation, one vaporous and the other smoky (the former draws its origin from water, the latter from earth), two kinds of bodies are also produced inside the earth. Those called *fossilia* since they are obtained by quarrying, like non-liquefiable stones and all that is rendered into powders, [come] from the dry exhalation. By contrast, those from the humid exhalation are properly called *metallica* since they require transmutation after mining so that a liquid of metal melted by fire is cleansed of slags.[6]

The elusive notion of "exhalation" (*anathumiasis* in Greek and *exhalatio* in Latin) was key to understanding Aristotle's meteorology.[7] Divided into two kinds, the vaporous or humid exhalation was said to come from water while the smoky or dry exhalation from earth. At the end of his *Meteorology*, 3.6, Aristotle briefly explained the formation of minerals and metals on the basis of this theory.[8] Since he did not leave his own classification of mineral substances, one major possibility of its reconstruction was to follow this line of reasoning. Thus, upon Aristotle's theory of double exhalations, Cesalpino tried to establish his twofold system of mineral classification: *fossilia* and *metallica*.

In his text Cesalpino addresses the terminology of *fossilia* and *metallica* as the first problem to be clarified. According to him, physicians following Galen applied the term *metallica* to all the medicines coming from mines, furnaces, or other related operations while Dioscorides used it for subterraneous bodies.[9] As for his contemporaries, Cesalpino continues by arguing that they call these substances "minerals" (*mineralia*) because the ground pit for their extraction is called a "mine" (*mina*). For him *metallica* are humid and fusible while *fossilia* are dry and non-fusible; humid bodies are aqueous while dry bodies are of an earthy nature.

Cesalpino praises the superiority of his twofold system by criticizing the fourfold system (stones, metals, sulfurs and salts) of Avicenna and the threefold one (stones, metals and intermediates) of Albertus Magnus. Among his contemporaries, Cesalpino blames those who hold the fourfold system by adding earths and "solidified juices" (*succi concreti*) to stones and metals. His criticism is especially directed to the class of solidified juices. Although he does not mention any particular name, it is not very difficult to imagine that Agricola is his principal target. Indeed, the class of solidified juices was the distinctive feature of the latter's "Neptunian" position. Based on the idea that all minerals resulted from a liquid state, this position had a great affinity with the daily observation and experience of practical miners. Cesalpino himself adopts the very notion of solidified juices. What he finds problematic is the ambiguity of its classification by Agricola.[10]

Cesalpino also acknowledges the notion of "lapidifying juice" (*succus lapidescens*) which was the crucial idea of Agricola's mineralogy.[11] Indeed this notion enjoyed considerable success during the late sixteenth and seventeenth centuries. It was celebrated as "gur" by the mining town preacher, Johann Mathesius (1504-65) of Joachimstahl, and culminated in the notion of "bur" for the Flemish chymist, Jan Baptist Van Helmont (1579-1644). Even Robert Boyle (1627-1691) was fascinated by their discussions on the growth and eventual regeneration of mineral ores in nearly exhausted mines.[12] As for Cesalpino, he explains the nature of this mysterious juice as follows: waters containing the lapidifying juice are much denser and earthier than simple waters; if someone drinks them, that person can be killed or become seriously ill due to the production of stones in the kidneys and bladder; these waters are distinguished by their places of origin and passages since they leave stony sedimentations on other bodies.[13]

Boasting his twofold system as the best solution, Cesalpino knows, however, that it does not represent the wide diversity of *fossilia* among which some are soluble and others are not. To remedy this shortcoming, he arranges his treatise in three books, each of which addresses soluble minerals, stones, and metallic substances, respectively.

Cesalpino then divides *fossilia* into two categories by solubility. One of these categories comprises stones, and the other receives bodies which can dissolve or be rendered into powders by humidity. Soluble *fossilia* are further divided into two groups: some are dissolved in aqueous solvents and the others not. The first group is subdivided into two classes: earths and salts. Other soluble *fossilia* such as sulfurs and bitumens, which dissolve in oily solvents, form another class. Since Cesalpino does not provide them a specific name, let us call them "unctuous minerals" for ease of discussion. Finally, insoluble *fossilia* form the class of stones.

As for *metallica*, Cesalpino also divides them into two categories by ductility. Ductile *metallica* fall in the class of metals. Non-ductile *metallica* such as glasses and slags form the last class. Cesalpino thus establishes six classes in total for the mineral kingdom on the bases of the twofold division of *fossilia* and *metallica*:

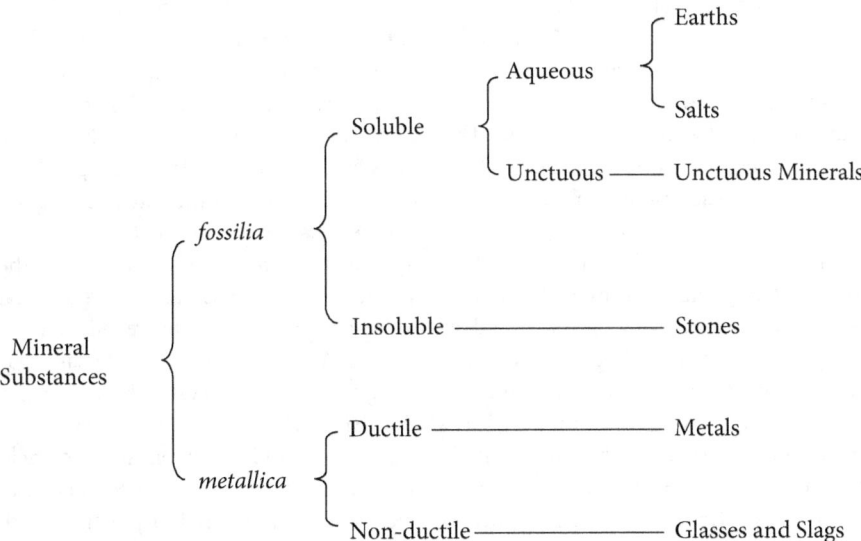

2. Exhalations

Cesalpino's twofold system of minerals and metals is based on the double mode of their formation. Unlike Agricola who preferred the line of Aristotle's *Meteorology*, book 4, he closely follows the theory of double exhalations expounded in *Meteorology*, 3.6.[14] Thus, for him *fossilia* result from the dry exhalation while *metalla* are produced from the humid exhalation. The humid exhalation is a "vapor" (*vapor*) which is water in potentiality. By contrast, the dry exhalation comes from the ardent part of the bowel of the earth. Cesalpino argues:

> The generation of the [dry] exhalation is perpetual because of the movement of the heavens. That which is caught by water turns salty while that which reaches the [region of] air produces diverse fiery impressions high above the ground. Inside the earth it is solidified into diverse bodies or ignited by catching the origin of fire. Thus, once inflamed, fire will last as long as the abundance of the exhalation allows it. The material is provided longer in the underground places than in the air for comets since the exhalation is not dispersed in a confined space.[15]

This explanation reconstructs ideas expounded by Aristotle in his *Meteorology*. But the double nature of exhalations is not enough to explain the diversity of minerals. Although *fossilia* are produced from the dry exhalation, the cause of different solubility between salts and unctuous minerals remains inexplicable. That is why Cesalpino introduces the subspecies of the dry exhalation: meager and fatty. This division allows him to explain the difference between aqueous *fossilia* (earths and salts) and unctuous ones. Cesalpino goes even further by subdividing the fatty exhalation into two kinds: bituminous and sulfurous. For him the bituminous one is inoffensive and used in the steam baths of Italy. The sulfurous one is rather harmful since it kills living beings if it is abundantly enclosed in a confined space. Rarefied and diffused in a vast space, the sulfurous exhalation loses its harmfulness. Cesalpino adds that it can be observed in the mines of orpiment, mercury, and other metallic bodies. Indeed, the subdivision of the dry exhalation into bituminous and sulfurous on the basis of the newly acquired chymical knowledge from observations and experiences in laboratories and mines was a remarkable tendency in the meteorological literature of the period.[16] Cesalpino thus adhered to this trend and even preceded key figures such as Daniel Sennert (1572–1637), the renowned professor of medicine at the Protestant University of Wittenberg.[17]

In his text Cesalpino also regards the sulfurous exhalation as the cause of plagues. Note that the most popular explanation for their genesis was a "putrefied air" (*miasma* in Greek) in the late Renaissance.[18] The notion of *miasma* was often linked to the idea of "bad exhalation" by meteorological writers. In his text Cesalpino argues that what is produced from putrefied cadavers during wars or from putrefied swamps does not affect vast regions but only nearby places. Although a more universal cause is required to explain the wide diffusion of plagues, he finds celestial influences far too remote. He thus opts for "terrestrial dispositions" (*dispositiones terrestres*) as their immediate causes. Indeed, in an important chapter of his *Canon*, Avicenna held celestial influences as remote causes and terrestrial dispositions as immediate causes for plagues.[19] Cesalpino goes even further to identify the terrestrial dispositions with the harmful subterranean emanation, that is, the sulfurous exhalation. For him an excessive amount of this exhalation is produced by the agitations of the ground, namely during earthquakes.[20]

3. The Nature and Production of Minerals

Now let us turn to the production of minerals. According to Cesalpino, earths are the simplest of all minerals. They are dry bodies resulting from the dry exhalation. Tending to be pulverized, their parts cannot achieve cohesion in one mass without humidity. Their mode of production is twofold. One is the cooling of the dry exhalation which is directly converted from a gaseous state into powders. The other is the "putrefaction" of other mixed bodies. For example, if stones receive greater changes in their nature by the action of violent fire, they can dissolve in rainwater. Even mountains can imperceptibly dissolve and turn into earths.[21]

Cesalpino applies the term "salt" to minerals such as alum, niter, and sodium. They are produced from the dry exhalation and dissolve in aqueous solvents. They differ from earths since they receive fewer changes by the action of heat than earths. Each species of salts has its particular taste. Their mode of production is also twofold. One is the cooling of the dry exhalation. The other is the combustion of substances as in the residue of burned wine.[22]

Cesalpino's unctuous minerals also result from the dry exhalation. They dissolve in oily solvents. Sulfur and bitumen are typical species of this class. Along with salts, Agricola placed them in the class of solidified juices. Without mentioning his name, Cesalpino contests this "confusion" since they cannot dissolve in aqueous solvents. That is why he separates them from salts. As has been seen, there are in his system two kinds of dry exhalation: meager and fatty. Since unctuous minerals come from the fatty one, they are inflammable and contain volatile humidity like oils.[23]

Cesalpino's stones are the dry and earthy bodies which occupy the entirety of the second book of his *De metallicis*. Being insoluble and non-liquefiable, they are distinguished from other minerals. Cesalpino argues that their production requires coagulation by which they receive remarkable hardness. Note that stones were believed to be produced by the mixture of earth and water according to Aristotle and Theophrastus.[24] Taking the humid exhalation as a sort of water and the dry exhalation as a sort of earth, Cesalpino adopts the same perspective: heat achieves the mixture of water and earth while coldness solidifies it.

As for the transparency of gems, there was a traditional belief according to which this property was due to the character of water. Thus, their production was often confused with that of ice. Gems were regarded as a kind of water frozen by the action of intense coldness. This belief can be traced back to the ancient Greeks. Many authors contributed to establish its intellectual basis. Plato says in his *Timaeus*:

> Take now the water that is mixed with fire. It is fine and liquid and on account of its mobility and the way it rolls over the ground, it is called liquid. It is soft, moreover, in that its faces, being less firm than those of earth, give way to it. When this water is separated from its fire and air and is isolated, it becomes more uniform, and it

is pressed together into itself by the things that leave it. So compacted, the water above the earth which is most affected by this change turns to hail, while that on earth turns to ice.[25]

Aristotle also argued that "ice" (*krystallos* in Greek) is produced from water by the removal of heat alone.[26] Then Pliny wrote that crystal was solidified from the aqueous material frozen by the action of intense coldness. Seneca followed this line of reasoning. Thus, Marbode sang in his poem *On Stones*: "Crystal is ice through countless ages grown."[27] Albertus in his turn spoke of the rainwater that turned into stones in the Pyrenees. For him the material of transparent stones was water mixed with a little amount of "very subtle earth."[28] As for Cesalpino, he explains the cause of this confusion by the fact that the term "ice" in Greek meant bodies frozen by coldness. For him the coagulation of stones differs from the transformation of water into ice. Nevertheless, he concludes with an opinion close to Albertus: the material cause of stones is water mixed with "meager earth."[29]

The production of stones is also twofold for Cesalpino. One is the fusion of the mixture of earth and water by the action of fire just as earthenware is produced by the cooking of earth in the furnaces. The other mode is the solution of burnt earth in water. Some stones are solidified by dryness from this solution. The production of stalactites is its typical example. The same mode applies to the formation of gems since they are produced by the filtration of juices through rocks. It is also observed in the production of calculus within the bodies of living beings.

Agricola criticized Aristotle for having regarded the dry exhalation as the material cause of stones. His principal objections were as follows: If this theory were correct, 1) the parts of the material for stones could achieve cohesion without humidity; 2) stones could be produced in the sky just as comets and shooting stars are formed by the dry exhalation; 3) stones rather than ashes and ponce stones could be produced in underground fires.[30] To these objections Cesalpino in his turn counters: 1) humidity is provided since the dry exhalation does not produce stones directly from a gaseous state but by an intermediary solution; 2) the dry exhalation does not stay thick enough in the sky for the production of stones; 3) the dry exhalation does not produce only aches and ponce stones but also other *fossilia* in the bowel of the earth.

On the cause determining the species of minerals, Cesalpino uses quantitative factors of materials. The diversity of species depends on the proportion of humidity and dryness in the mixture of earth and water, and especially the purity and fattiness of the dry exhalation which is dissolved in the mixture. Foreign substances such as sands, diverse stones, and parts of plants and animals can also be mixed in the production of stones, which explains the existence of fossil shellfish in rocks.[31]

4. Metals and Sulfur as Their Seed

Next let us turn to Cesalpino's *metallica*. For him they are humid bodies produced from the humid exhalation. Since the element of water dominates their composition, they are fusible. They are liquid in potentiality and solid in actuality.

Cesalpino first divides *metallica* into two categories: metals and other fusible bodies such as glasses and slags.[32] The essential factor of this division is ductility caused by the internal humidity of each body. For Cesalpino *metallica* possess properties such as gravity, solidness, and dryness resulting from the element of earth. In their production the humid exhalation obtains some features of the element of earth from the coexisting dry exhalation. Although glasses also possess their humidity in potentiality and are fusible, they are not placed among metals since they are not ductile. Likewise, slags do not belong to metals.

On the production of metals, Cesalpino begins with a review of a chymical doctrine, which he considers widely diffused in his time:

> The opinion of chymists is known everywhere: all metals are coagulated from sulfur as masculine seed and from quicksilver as menstruum. Diverse metals are produced because of the difference of these principles, partly by the purity and impurity of quicksilver, partly by the coagulation of sulfur. [Chymists] posit a certain incombustible sulfur, white and red, which they claim produces silver and gold that resists fire and a certain combustible sulfur which produces the other imperfect metals.[33]

According to Cesalpino, some chymists consider that there are mines of these special sulfur and quicksilver and that these principles of metals are first converted into a certain earthy substance which will be transformed into metals after it is sublimed by heat and washed by water. But Cesalpino confesses that he finds none of either principle inside the metallic bodies.[34]

To better grasp Cesalpino's perception of chymical sulfur, which is the "seminal principle" of metals for those chymists, let us look at his description of sulfur in the group of *fossilia*:

> Chymists proclaim many things about sulfur: it is the principle of metals like masculine seed to coagulate quicksilver according to various conditions. The incombustible sulfur, white or red, is required for the generation of gold and silver since that which is combustible blackens everything being consumed by fire. But the kind of sulfur which is not consumed and gives a metallic fusion is known only to chymists in their secrets.[35]

According to Cesalpino, chymists try to convert the ordinary combustible sulfur into this special species of incombustible nature by diverse operations. But for him they are all in error because the total elimination of its combustible fattiness is impossible. Unfortunately, these words do not offer much more than what was reported by Vannoccio Biringuccio (c. 1480–c. 1539) on the sulfur of chymists in his famous treatise *De la pirotechnia* (Venice, 1540):

> [Sulfur] is produced from an unctuous earthy and powerfully hot substance so that it is considered among experienced workers to bear a resemblance to the element of fire. This is called by them "masculine seed" and "prime agent of nature" in

the composition of metals [...]. What I have already told you about quicksilver (contrary to the opinion of philosophic chymists concerning the generation of metals), I now repeat to you concerning sulfur because I do not believe that either of these really occurs except in similar elemental substances. I say this because I have never seen sulfur found in any metal mine, or metal near any sulfur or mercury ore.[36]

Pietro Andrea Mattioli (1501–77) adopted almost *verbatim* Biringuccio's description of sulfur in his commentary on Dioscorides' *De materia medica* (Venice, 1554): "[...] therefore the authors of chymistry say that sulfur is similar to fire by nature. They call it 'masculine seed' and 'prime agent of nature' to procreate all metals."[37] Like Biringuccio and Mattioli, Cesalpino does not interpret the idea of metallic seeds in line with the concept of seeds, stemming from the tradition of Renaissance Platonism and influential among the followers of the Swiss physician Paracelsus (1493/94–1541) at the turn of the sixteenth and seventeenth centuries.[38]

Interestingly enough, Cesalpino argues that thunder and lightning possess a smell of sulfur due to the presence of sulfur in the sky while earthquakes and subterraneous fires or volcanos are produced by sulfur inside the earth.[39] Indeed these characteristics were not frequently attributed to the mysterious sulfur of chymists but to the dry exhalation in the perspective of Aristotle's *Meteorology*. Cesalpino's effort to reinterpret chymical ideas on the basis of Aristotle's teachings thus led him to a position close to the theory of "aerial niter." This famous theory was promoted by leading Paracelsians such as Gerard Dorn (fl. 1566–84), Petrus Severinus (1540/42–1602), and Joseph Du Chesne (1546–1609) for the cause of thunder, lightning, and earthquakes.[40] Most likely, Cesalpino himself did not read their works; rather they shared the common source in the commentary tradition of Aristotle's *Meteorology*, following the *Meteora* of Albertus.[41]

As for the transmutation of metals, which is the heart of the chymical art, Cesalpino's text reveals his skepticism. Indeed, he is convinced of the limit of human arts.[42] Like his forerunners such as Biringuccio and Agricola, Cesalpino thinks that human beings cannot achieve the works that nature perfects with the enormous amount of time and the concourse of diverse conditions.

Cesalpino also criticized another chymical doctrine, namely the "unctuous moisture" (*humor pinguis*) advanced by Albertus and his followers.[43] According to this doctrine, just like the incombustible sulfur of chymists, the "radical moisture" (*humidum radicale*) of all metals cannot be destroyed by fire but is converted into metals by the slow cooking of heat. Indeed, this doctrine is a modified version of the traditional theory of chymical sulfur. Both have remarkable incombustibility in common. But Cesalpino considers it false since anything fatty is combustible. He then tries to reinterpret it by relying on Aristotle's *Meteorology*, 4.8: all mixed bodies are composed of earth and water.[44] Thus, for Cesalpino the mysterious radical moisture of all metals must be understood as a mixture of earth and water, which can logically be frozen by coldness. But he observes no aqueous moisture which, solidified by coldness, becomes as ductile as metals. Thus, he contests Albertus by arguing that this kind of moisture is not found anywhere in the underground mines.[45]

After refuting the chymical doctrines mainly taken from Albertus's work, his major source for chymical knowledge, Cesalpino reveals his own opinion. For him there is only one solution provided by Aristotle at the end of his *Meteorology*, 3.6:

> All these [metals] originate from the imprisonment of the vaporous exhalation in the earth, and especially among stones. Their dryness compresses it, and it congeals just as dew or snow does when it has been separated off, though in the present case the metals are generated before that separation occurs.[46]

Cesalpino regrets that his contemporaries do not sufficiently understand the real meaning of this crucial passage. According to him, the humid exhalation is imprisoned in the earth, especially near the stones whose dryness helps its coagulation. This dryness results from these stones or from the dry exhalation enclosed together with the humid one. Since stones are produced from the dry exhalation, they potentially have a similar nature in common. With the contact of the dry exhalation or stones, the humid exhalation is compressed and coagulated into a mass. This scheme explains the production of dew and snow in the atmospheric region. Cesalpino applies the same reasoning to the formation of metals:

> The mode of their generation is as follows: the subterraneous vapor enclosed especially among stones, due to their dryness, that is, the dry exhalation going upwards, is compacted into a mass and coagulated into tiny parts (*minima*), that is, drops like dew and snow. Surely, this does not take place without coldness. But here is a difference. This dryness going upward is separated in the production of dew and snow while the separation does not occur in the origin of metals. The dry exhalation remains together [with the humid exhalation].[47]

The production of metals does not require only the vapor or humid exhalation but also the dry exhalation. By the action of coldness, the humid exhalation turns into solid state, either into metals or into dew and snow. What is the factor differentiating the terrestrial bodies from the meteorological ones? Indeed, the dry exhalation plays a significant role. If it does not stay enough with the humid exhalation, their product will be dew and snow in the atmospheric region. By contrast, metals are produced in the bowel of the earth since the dry exhalation can stay long enough with the humid one, both being confined together in closed spaces.[48]

After establishing his own theory of the formation of metals, Cesalpino returns to the chymical doctrines. For him when chymists argue that "quicksilver is coagulated by the smell of sulfur," quicksilver must be understood as the humid exhalation and the smell of sulfur as the dry exhalation. Since Cesalpino divides the dry exhalation into two kinds (bituminous and sulfurous), his reinterpretation is not very surprising. As has been seen, chymists similarly distinguish two subspecies of sulfur: combustible and incombustible. Cesalpino replaces these subspecies of sulfur by those of the dry exhalation. For example, copper, iron, silver, and gold cannot easily melt since they contain more abundantly incombustible exhalation. While iron encloses the most incombustible one, copper possesses more combustible type of exhalation, which explains the fusibility and inflammability of copper. Silver and gold contain much less combustible exhalation while glasses and slags possess more.[49]

Cesalpino applies the same line of reasoning to the external figure of metallic ores. The condensation of the humid exhalation into metals takes place just as in the case of dew and snow. That is why metals are not found in large masses inside the mines but often in the form of small grains or thin and unbound layers.[50] However, considerations on the formal cause do not play a significant role in the preoccupations of Cesalpino just as in the case of Agricola.

5. Life in the Mineral Kingdom?

As has been shown, Cesalpino established his theory of the formation of minerals and metals in line with Aristotle's *Meteorology*, which had been the intellectual basis of two traditional currents of interpretation, either based on double exhalations (*Meteorology*, 3.6) or the mixture of earth and water (*Meteorology*, 4.8). Preferring the first current, Cesalpino did not particularly embrace Agricola's new theory of lapidifying juice and tried to reinterpret the chymical doctrine of the double principles (sulfur and quicksilver).

Rejecting vitalistic ideas such as the animation of minerals and metals, Agricola was very careful to replace the term "generation" (*generatio*) with "origin" (*ortus*) from the second edition of his mineralogical dialogue, *Bermannus* (Basel, 1546).[51] Although Cesalpino did not adopt any kind of biological analogy in his discussion on the mineral kingdom, he seemed free from the same concern. Despite its biological connotations, he kept using the term *generatio* for the production of subterraneous bodies.

To better understand the basis of Cesalpino's attitude, let us now examine how he handled the difference of minerals from living beings in terms of generation. Relying on Aristotle's *Meteorology*, 4.10, Cesalpino argues in his text that the "similar parts" of living beings result from the coagulation of the elements, water, and earth.[52] This coagulation takes place by the action of heat and coldness, two active agents in the system of Aristotle. For Cesalpino minerals share the same material causes and efficient causes with living beings although living beings possess the highly complex structures due to "organs" (*organa*) composed of similar parts.[53]

More importantly, Cesalpino advances that minerals do not participate in the activities of life. He enumerates three major points in this connection. Firstly, for him no living being consumes minerals as foods. Some would object that plants draw nutriment from earth and that some animals ingest mud. Cesalpino responds that plants draw only moisture from earth and do not directly take minerals. For him even if minerals are found in the bodies of living beings, they are not absorbed as foods but as medicines.[54] Remember that nutrition is one of the three fundamental activities of the most rudimentary life along with growth and reproduction, and these three functions are governed by the nutritive or vegetative soul according to Aristotle.[55] Indeed, the theory of the vegetative soul plays a crucial role in Cesalpino's plant physiology. Here in his mineralogy, he argues that minerals are not suitable for nutrition since they are too heavy and earthy. The innate heat of living bodies as the instrument of nutrition resides in the blood and physiological spirits.[56] Since it requires something light and volatile, spirits extracted from the heavy and earthy bodies of minerals have no affinity with this heat of life. Cesalpino adds that even the radical moisture of metals, which he identifies with the quicksilver of chymists, is too heavy and too earthy.[57] For him even if a certain spirit is extracted from metals by the innate heat of living beings, it will be totally harmful for their activities of life. When metallic spirits flow in the mines or emanate from furnaces, they destroy living beings. By contrast, the humid exhalation can heal diseases as is seen in the steam bathes of Italy since it is much milder than metallic spirits although it can also kill plants and animals when it is provided too abundantly in a confined space.[58]

Secondly, for Cesalpino minerals do not contribute to the growth of living beings as their matter. Remember that growth is the second function of the nutritive soul according to Aristotle. Cesalpino argues that no animal can grow from the putrefaction of minerals. Indeed, no living being is found inside stones and metals like worms observed in the corrupted bodies of plants and animals. Cesalpino firmly holds the belief in spontaneous generation not only for worms and insects but also for mushrooms, mosses, and even corals.[59] However, he does not apply this belief to minerals and seeks a reason elsewhere. For him worms are born in the mud due to the putrefied water mixed with it. Small worms are observed, he adds, in the interstices of rocks on the shore but never in the mines of metals. This argument leads Cesalpino to consider the origin of stones bearing figures of animals or plants. He says:

> Although the shells of oysters and the rests of other shellfish are sometimes found in the cut [of stones], they turned into stones after they were abandoned there by the retreat of sea and the ground was petrified. Aristotle witnesses that there exited a sea in all places now dry. It is thus more reasonable to judge in this way than to think that a certain animal force produced the rudiments of animals and plants inside the stones just as some people do.[60]

According to Cesalpino, fossilized things were first born as living beings in the sea. By the retreat of sea, they were left behind in the place where they are now observed. Being dried up, they were petrified into stones. Cesalpino relies on Aristotle's teachings about the retreat of seas in his *Meteorology*.[61] For him there is no need to call upon unusual ideas such as a certain "animal force" (*vis animalis*) or "mineral power" (*virtus mineralis*) advanced by Avicenna, Albertus and their followers for the production of stones possessing the shape of animals or plants.[62]

Thirdly, Cesalpino enumerates four possible modes for reproduction, which is also the fundamental function of the nutritive soul according to Aristotle: 1) sexual reproduction for animals; 2) spontaneous generation for worms and insects; 3) reproduction by seeds for plants; and 4) spontaneous generation for mushrooms and mosses. Arguing that these four modes are never observed among metallic substances, Cesalpino concludes:

> Their difference is also very remarkable. Living beings generate beings similar to themselves. It is the work of the nutritive soul as it converts food into their

nature. But metallic [bodies] cannot procreate beings similar to themselves or grow themselves.[63]

After examining these three issues (nutrition, growth, and reproduction), Cesalpino rejects the participation of minerals and metals in the activities of life. He then returns to the chymical doctrine of metallic seeds as follows: "Chymists affirm that there exist the seeds of gold by which gold is infinitely multiplied. This remains rather a rumor than a certified fact to this day."[64] Cesalpino closes his discussion without mercy. It is true that he concedes the transmutation of metals to the extent that the natural philosophy of Aristotle allows it. But when he does not find any intellectual support in his master's teachings, he does not easily accept even traditional, widely held views.

6. Conclusion

Cesalpino's mineral kingdom was totally devoid of vitalistic ideas enthusiastically promoted by influential figures such as Paracelsus and Girolamo Cardano (1501–76).[65] Likewise, he did not embrace the chymical doctrines in vogue among his contemporaries. What he presented as the doctrines of chymists was largely dependent on the ideas presented by Albertus Magnus in his *On Minerals*, one of the fundamental literatures for the knowledge of minerals and metals even in the sixteenth century. Cesalpino's mineralogical system was strictly based on the natural philosophy of Aristotle. Indeed, Agricola before him also tried to render the mineral kingdom the most "mechanistic" possible by eliminating the intervention of mysterious forces and adopting the "Neptunian" position based on the notion of mineral juices akin to the daily observations and experiences of practical miners. Unlike Agricola, Cesalpino preferred Aristotle's meteorological theory of double exhalations and even tried to reinterpret the chymical doctrines in the framework of this theory. These two systems advanced by Agricola and Cesalpino represented two dominant currents of the Aristotelian perspective on the formation of minerals and metals at the threshold of the Scientific Revolution.

Notes

1   On Cesalpino, see Lynn Thorndike, *A History of Magic and Experimental Science* (New York: Columbia University Press, 1941), 6: 325–38. Paula Findlen, *Possessing Nature: Museums, Collecting, and Scientific Culture in Early Modern Italy* (Berkeley: University of California Press, 1994), 58–61, passim. My warmest thanks go to Clare Hirai, Craig Martin, and Fabrizio Baldassarri for the preparation of this chapter.
2   Michele Mercati, *Metallotheca* (Rome: Salvioni, 1717). See also Bruno Accordi, "Michele Mercati (1541–1593) e la *Metallotheca*," *Geologica romana* 19 (1980): 1–50; Findlen, *Possessing Nature*, passim.
3   The text I have used is the first edition: Andrea Cesalpino, *De metallicis libri tres* (Rome: Zannetti, 1596). On this work, see also John R. Partington, *A History of*

Chemistry (London: Macmillan, 1961), 2: 89–92; François Ellenberger, *Histoire de la géologie* (Paris: Lavoisier, 1988), 1: 149–50, 1:175–8.

4   On Agricola, see Robert Halleux, "La nature et la formation des métaux selon Agricola et ses contemporains," *Revue d'histoire des sciences* 27 (1974): 211–22; Hiro Hirai, *Le concept de semence dans les théories de la matière à la Renaissance, de Marsile Ficin à Pierre Gassendi* (Turnhout: Brepols, 2005), 111–34.

5   I have adopted the term "chymistry" to avoid any arbitrary distinction between chemistry and alchemy, which did not exist in his time. See William R. Newman and Lawrence M. Principe, "Alchemy vs. Chemistry: The Etymological Origins of a Historiographic Mistake," *Early Science and Medicine* 3 (1998): 32–65; idem, "Some Problems with the Historiography of Alchemy," in *Secrets of Nature: Astrology and Alchemy in Early Modern Europe*, ed. William R. Newman and Anthony Grafton (Cambridge, MA: MIT Press, 2001), 385–431.

6   Cesalpino, *De metallicis*, 1.3, 6–7: "Cum duplex eorum materia statuatur ab Aristotele 3. Meteo. in fine: scilicet duplex exhalatio, haec quidem vaporosa, haec autem fumosa, illa quidem ex aqua ortum ducens, haec autem ex terra, etiam duo genera corporum intra terram fieri; ex sicca quidem exhalatione fossila ideo dicta, quia fodiendo inveniuntur ut illiquabilia lapidum genera, et quaecumque in pulverem solvuntur. Ex humida autem, quae proprie metallica vocantur, quia post effossionem transmutatione egent, ut liquor metalli igne fundente a recrementis expurgetur."

7   Aristotle, *Mete.* 1.3.340b27–29. Cf. Philoponus, *In Aristotelis meteorologicorum librum primum commentarium*, ed. Michael Hayduck (Berlin: Akademie, 1901), 1.3, 36 = Philoponus, *On Aristotle Meteorology 1.1–3* (London: Bloomsbury, 2011), 66. See also Paul Lettinck, *Aristotle's Meteorology and Its Reception in the Arab World* (Leiden: Brill, 1999), 32–9; Vaios Argyrakis, "The Evolution of Wind Theory and the Concept of Exhalation in the Context of Ancient Greek Thought," *Almagest* 4 (2013): 122–36.

8   Aristotle, *Mete.* 3.6.378a18–b8.

9   Cesalpino, *De metallicis*, 1.3, 7. Cf. Galen, *Simple Drugs*, 9.3 (12:208–10K). See also Ludwig Israelson, *Die* materia medica *des Klaudios Galenos* (University of Dörpat, 1894), 159–74; Robert Halleux, *Le problème des métaux dans la science antique* (Paris: Les Belles Lettres, 1974), 42–3, 134–7.

10 Cesalpino, *De metallicis*, 1.3, 7. On the detail of his criticism, see below.

11 On the notion of lapidifying juice, see Georg Agricola, *De ortu et causis subterraneorum* (Basel: Froben, 1546), 4.1, 51–2, 56–7. See also Hirai, *Le concept de semence*, 120–3, passim.

12 See Hirai, *Le concept de semence*, 459–61; Hiro Hirai and Hideyuki Yoshimoto, "Anatomizing the Sceptical Chymist: Robert Boyle and the Secret of His Early Sources on the Growth of Metals," *Early Science and Medicine* 10, no. 4 (2005): 453–77; John A. Norris, "Early Theories of Aqueous Mineral Genesis in the Sixteenth Century," *Ambix* 54, no. 1 (2007): 69–86; idem, "*Auß Quecksilber und Schwefel Rein*: Johann Mathesius (1504–65) and *Sulfur-Mercurius* in the Silver Mines of Joachimstahl," *Osiris* 29 (2014): 35–48; Warren A. Dym, "Alchemy and Mining: Metallogenesis and Prospecting in Early Mining Books," *Ambix* 55, no. 3 (2008): 232–54.

13 Cesalpino, *De metallicis*, 1.7, 20–1; 1.8, 21.

14 On Aristotle's theory, see D. E. Eichholz, "Aristotle's Theory of the Formation of Metals and Minerals," *Classical Quarterly* 43, nos. 3–4 (1949): 141–6; Robert Halleux, *Le problème des métaux*, 97–113. On its influence, see John A. Norris, "The Mineral

Exhalation Theory of Metallogenesis in Pre-Modern Mineral Science," *Ambix* 53, no. 1 (2006): 43–65.

15 Cesalpino, *De metallicis*, 1.7, 19–20: "Perpetua est enim exhalationis generatio ob coeli motum. Quae igitur ab aqua appraehenditur, in salsedinem vertitur, quae autem ad aerem venit, supra terram quidem in sublimi varias impressiones ignitas facit: intra terram autem condensatur in varia corpora, aut ignis principio assumpto exardescit, ubi igitur semel contigerit accendi, tamdiu perseverabit ignis, quamdiu exhalationis copia suppeditabitur: diutius autem in subterraneis materia suppeditatur, quam in aere ad cometas, quia in loco angusto non disperditur exhalatio."

16 See Craig Martin, *Renaissance Meteorology: Pomponazzi to Descartes* (Baltimore: Johns Hopkins University Press, 2011), 80–105.

17 On Sennert's case, see Martin, *Renaissance Meteorology*, 99–104. On Sennert in general, see Hiro Hirai, *Medical Humanism and Natural Philosophy: Renaissance Debates on Matter, Life and the Soul* (Leiden: Brill, 2011), 151–72; idem "Daniel Sennert, Chymistry and Theological Debates," *Ambix* 68, nos. 2–3 (2021): 198–213.

18 See Jacques Jouanna, "Miasme, maladie et semence de la maladie: Galien lecteur d'Hippocrate," in *Studi su Galeno*, ed. Daniela Manetti (Florence: Università di Firenze, 2000), 59–92; Jacques Jouanna, "Air, Miasma and Contagion in the Time of Hippocrates and the Survival of Miasmas in Post-Hippocratic Medicine (Rufus of Ephesus, Galen and Palladius)," in Jacques Jouanna, *Greek Medicine from Hippocrates to Galen*, ed. Philip van der Eijk (Leiden: Brill, 2012), 119–36.

19 Avicenna, *Canon*, 4.1.4.1. See also Jon Arrizabalaga, "Facing the Black Death: Perceptions and Reactions of University Medical Practitioners," in *Practical Medicine from Salerno to the Black Death*, ed. Luis García-Ballester et al. (Cambridge: Cambridge University Press, 1994), 237–88, at 252–4; Girolamo Mercuriale, *On Pestilence: A Renaissance Treatise on Plague*, trans. Craig Martin (Philadelphia: University of Pennsylvania Press, 2022), 13–14, 42, 44–7, 63–4, 70.

20 Cesalpino, *De metallicis*, 1.4, 12. On earthquakes and plagues, see Arrizabalaga, "Facing the Black Death," 254–6; Rienk Vermij, *Thinking on Earthquakes in Early Modern Europe* (London: Routledge, 2020), 53–4; Mercuriale, *On Pestilence*, 39–40, 46. See also Albertus Magnus, *Meteora*, 3.2.12, relying on Seneca, *QNat*. 6.27.2. Cf. Albertus Magnus, *Meteora*, 3.3.19.

21 Cesalpino, *De metallicis*, 1.9, 25.

22 Ibid., 1.16, 40–1.

23 Ibid., 1.27, 62.

24 Aristotle, *Mete*. 4.8.384b30–34; Theophrastus, *De lapidibus*, 1–3 = Earle R. Caley and John F. C. Richards, *Theophrastus: On Stones* (Columbus: Ohio State University, 1956), 45.

25 Plato, *Ti*. 59d–e. See also Frank D. Adams, *The Birth and Development of the Geological Sciences* (London: Dover, 1954), 472–4.

26 Aristotle, *Mete*. 4.10.388b16–17.

27 See Pliny, *HN* 37.9.23; Seneca, *QNat*. 3.25.12; Marbode, *De lapidibus*, 1.41 = John M. Riddle, *Marbode of Rennes' (1035–1123) De lapidibus* (Wiesbaden: Steiner, 1977), 77–8.

28 Albertus Magnus, *De mineralibus*, 1.1.3; 1.1.7 = Dorothy Wyckoff, *Albertus Magnus: Book of Minerals* (Oxford: Clarendon, 1967), 16, 28.

29 Cesalpino, *De metallicis*, 2.1, 75.

30 Agricola, *De ortu et causis*, 4.1, 47; 5.1, 61, rejected the production of minerals in the air. On the belief in underground fires, see Adams, *The Birth and Development*, 279–82; Rienk Vermij, "Subterraneous Fire: Changing Theories of the Earth during the Renaissance," *Early Science and Medicine* 3, no. 4 (1998): 328–47.
31 Cesalpino, *De metallicis*, 2.3, 80.
32 Ibid., 3.2, 171. Cf. Aristotle, *Mete.* 4.9.386b18–25.
33 Cesalpino, *De metallicis*, 3.1, 166: "Vulgata est chimistarum sententia: metalla omnia ex sulphure tanquam semine maris et ex argento vivo tanquam menstruo coagulari. Pro differentia autem istorum principiorum diversa oriri metalla, partim quidem ex argenti vivi puritate et impuritate, partim vero ex sulphure coagulante: quoddam enim ponunt incombustibile album vel rubeum, unde argentum vel aurum fieri asserunt, quae igni resistunt: quoddam combustibile unde fiant caetera metalla imperfecta."
34 Ibid., 167, finds this idea not far from the one attributed to "Democritus." His source is Albertus Magnus, *De mineralibus*, 3.1.4 (Wyckoff, 162). On the discussion of Albertus, see Robert Halleux, "Albert le Grand et l'alchimie," *Revue des sciences philosophiques et théologiques* 66, no. 1 (1982): 57–80, at 71. On Pseudo-Democritus, see Matteo Martelli, *Pseudo-Democrito: Scritti alchimici con il commentaria di Sinesio* (Paris: SEHA, 2011); Matteo Martelli, *The* Four Books *of Pseudo-Democritus* (London: Maney, 2013).
35 Cesalpino, *De metallicis*, 1.28, 64: "De sulphure multa chymistae praedicant esse metallorum principium tanquam semen masculi ad argentum vivum coagulandum secundum varias conditiones. Nam ad auri et argenti generationem requiri sulphur incombustibile album vel rubeum, quod enim combustibile est, omnia denigrare, et in igne absumi. At id genus sulphuris, quod non comburitur, et fusionem praestat metallicam ipsis solis notum est inter eorum arcana."
36 Vannoccio Biringuccio, *De la pirotechnia* (Venice: Navò, 1540), 2.2, fols. 25v–26r = Cyril S. Smith and Martha T. Gnudi, *The Pirotechnia of Vannoccio Biringuccio* (Cambridge, MA: MIT Press, 1942), 86–7.
37 Pietro Andrea Mattioli, *Commentarii in libros sex Dioscoridis de medica materia* (Venice: Valgrisi, 1554), 618: "a chymistarum authoribus igni natura simile sulphur dicantur. Vocant id ii masculum semen, et primum naturae agens ad omia metalla procreanda." Cf. Dioscorides, *De materia medica*, 5.83.
38 On Renaissance concept of seeds, see Hirai, *Le concept de semence*; Hiro Hirai, "Bodies and Their Internal Powers: Natural Philosophy, Medicine and Alchemy," in *The Routledge Companion to Sixteenth Century Philosophy*, ed. Henrik Lagerlund et al. (London: Routledge, 2017), 394–410, at 405–8.
39 Cesalpino, *De metallicis*, 1.28, 63. On exhalations and earthquakes, see Martin, *Renaissance Meteorology*, 60–79; Vermij, *Thinking on Earthquakes*, 26, 32, 56–7, 116–17.
40 On the aerial niter, see Allen G. Debus, "The Paracelsian Aerial Niter," *Isis* 55, no. 1 (1964): 43–61; Robert G. Frank, *Harvey and the Oxford Physiologists* (Berkeley: University of California Press, 1980), 115–39, 221–45. See also Didier Kahn and Hiro Hirai, eds., *Pseudo-Paracelsus: Forgery and Early Modern Alchemy, Medicine and Natural Philosophy* (Leiden: Brill, 2022).
41 Albertus Magnus, *Meteora*, 3.2.6. Cf. Seneca's *QNat*, 2.21.2. See also Martin, *Renaissance Meteorology*, 88.

42 Cesalpino, *De metallicis*, 3.1, 167; 3.2, 172. On nature/art debates, see William R. Newman, *Promethean Ambitions: Alchemy and the Quest to Perfect Nature* (Chicago: University of Chicago Press, 2004).

43 Cf. Albertus Magnus, *De mineralibus*, 3.1.2 (Wyckoff, 156–7). See also Gad Freudenthal, "The Problem of Cohesion between Alchemy and Natural Philosophy: From Unctuous Moisture to Phlogiston," in *Alchemy Revisited*, ed. Zweder R. W. M. von Martels (Leiden: Brill, 1990), 107–16; Hirai, *Le concept de semence*, 117–18. On the medical and chymical notion of radical moisture, see Chiara Crisciani and Giovanna Ferrari, "Introduzione," in Arnald of Villanova, *Opera omnia medica, 5.2: Tractatus de humido radicali*, ed. Michael R. McVaugh (Barcelona: Universitat de Barcelona, 2010), 319–608.

44 Aristotle, *Mete.* 4.8.384b30–34.

45 Cesalpino, *De metallicis*, 3.1, 168.

46 Aristotle, *Mete.* 3.6.378a27–33.

47 Cesalpino, *De metallicis*, 3.1, 168: "Modum autem generationis hunc esse ut vapor subterraneus inclusus praesertim in lapidibus, propter siccitatem, id est, siccam exhalationem, quae sursum ducebat, coarctetur in unum et coaguletur veluti ros et pruina in minimas scilicet guttas: quod profecto sine frigitate non fit, sed haec differentia est, quod in roris et pruinae generatione, separatur dicta siccitas, quae sursum ducebat, at in metallorum ortu, segregatio illa non fit, simul enim compraehenditur sicca exhalatio."

48 Ibid.

49 Ibid., 3.1, 169.

50 Ibid., 3.1, 168–9.

51 Along with his treatise *De ortu et causis*, the revised edition of Agricola's *Bermannus* was published by the Froben press of Basel in 1546. See Robert Halleux and Albert Yans, *Georg Agricola, Bermannus (Le mineur)* (Paris: Les Belles Lettres, 1990), 148, n. 10.

52 Aristotle, *Mete.* 4.10.388a22–26.

53 Cesalpino, *De metallicis*, 1.2, 4.

54 Ibid., 1.2, 5.

55 Aristotle, *De an.* 2.4.415a14–416b31. On the vegetative soul in the Renaissance, see Dennis Des Chene, *Life's Form: Late Aristotelian Conceptions of the Soul* (Ithaca: Cornell University Press, 2000), 133–8. See also Giouli Korobili and Roberto Lo Presti, eds., *Nutrition and Nutritive Soul in Aristotle and Aristotelianism* (Berlin: De Gruyter, 2020); Fabrizio Baldassarri and Andreas Blank, eds., *Vegetative Powers: The Roots of Life in Ancient, Medieval and Early Modern Natural Philosophy* (Cham: Springer, 2021).

56 Cesalpino, *De metallicis*, 1.2, 5. On the medical and chymical notion of spirit, see Hirai, *Le concept de semence*; Hirai, *Medical Humanism and Natural Philosophy*. On the spirit in Renaissance Platonism, see Hiro Hirai, "The World Soul in the Renaissance from Ficino to Campanella and Lipsius," in *The World Soul: A History*, ed. James Wilberding (Oxford: Oxford University Press, 2021), 151–76.

57 Cesalpino, *De metallicis*, 1.2, 5–6.

58 Ibid., 1.2, 6. On his notion of spirit, see also Mark Edward Clark and Kirk M. Summers, "Hippocratic Medicine and Aristotelian Science in the *Daemonum investigatio peripatetica* of Andrea Cesalpino," *Bulletin of the History of Medicine* 69, no. 4 (1995): 527–41.

59 Cesalpino, *De metallicis*, 1.2, 5. On the belief of spontaneous generation in the Renaissance, see Hirai, *Medical Humanism*, 121–47, 162–71.
60 Cesalpino, *De metallicis*, 1.2, 5: "Etsi enim aliquando in eorum caesura ostrearum testae, aut caetera conchilia reperta sint, haec recedente mari, et lapidescente solo inibi derelicta in lapides concreverunt. Ubique enim ubi nunc est arida, aliquando affuisse mare testatur Aristoteles. Hoc enim modo censere magis consonum est rationi, quam putare vim animalem intra lapides rudimenta animalium ac plantarum gignere, ut quidam putant."
61 Aristotle, *Mete.* 1.14.351a19–353a28.
62 See Avicenna, *De congelatione et conglutinatione lapidum*, ed. Eric J. Holmyard et al. (Paris: Geuthner, 1927), 22, 48–9. See also Hirai, *Le concept de semence*, 122–32.
63 Cesalpino, *De metallicis*, 1.2, 6: "Est quoque valde conspicua differentia. Viventia enim gignunt sibi simile, quod est opus animae altricis, ut alimentum in sui naturam convertat. At metallica nec procreant sibi similia neque se ipsa augere possunt."
64 Ibid.: "Et quod chimistae asserunt, semina esse auri, quibus multiplicetur in infinitum, adhuc famosum est magis quam compertum."
65 On the case of Paracelsus, see Hirai, *Le concept de semence*, 179–216; Hiro Hirai, "*Logoi spermatikoi* and the Concept of Seeds in the Mineralogy and Cosmogony of Paracelsus," *Revue d'histoire des sciences* 61, no. 2 (2008): 245–64. For the case of Cardano, see Hirai, *Le concept de semence*, 135–56.

Bibliography

Primary Sources

Agricola, Georg. *De ortu et causis subterraneorum*. Basel: Froben, 1546.
Albertus Magnus, *Book of Minerals*, translated by Dorothy Wyckoff. Oxford: Clarendon, 1967.
Aristotle. *The Complete Works of Aristotle*, edited by Jonathan Barnes. 2 vols. Princeton: Princeton University Press, 1984.
Avicenna. *De congelatione et conglutinatione lapidum*, edited by Eric J. Holmyard et al. Paris: Geuthner, 1927.
Avicenna. *Liber canonis*. Basel: Herwagen. 1556.
Biringuccio, Vannoccio. *De la pirotechnia*. Venice: Navò, 1540.
Biringuccio, Vannoccio. *The Pirotechnia of Vannoccio Biringuccio*, translated by Cyril S. Smith and Martha T. Gnudi. Cambridge, MA: MIT Press, 1942.
Cesalpino, Andrea. *De metallicis libri tres*. Rome: Zannetti, 1596.
Galen. *Opera omnia*, edited by Karl Gottlob Kühn. 20 vols. Leipzig: Karl Knobloch, 1821–33.
Marbode, *De lapidibus*. In John M. Riddle, *Marbode of Rennes' (1035–1123) De lapidibus*. Wiesbaden: Steiner, 1977.
Mattioli, Pietro Andrea. *Commentarii, in libros sex Pedacii Dioscoridis* Anazarbei, *de materia medica*. Venice: Valgrisi, 1554.
Mercati, Michele. *Metallotheca*. Rome: Salvioni, 1717.
Mercuriale, Girolamo. *De pestilentia*. Padua: Mietti, 1577.
Mercuriale, Girolamo. *On Pestilence: A Renaissance Treatise on Plague*, translated by Craig Martin. Philadelphia: University of Pennsylvania Press, 2022.

Philoponus. *In Aristotelis meteorologicorum librum primum commentarium*, edited by Michael Hayduck. Volume 14.1 of *Commentaria Aristotelem Graeca*. Berlin: Akademie, 1901.

Philoponus. *On Aristotle Meteorology 1.1-3*, translated by Inna Kupreeva. London: Bloomsbury, 2011.

Pliny. *The Natural History of Pliny*, translated by John Bostock and H. T. Riley. London: H.G. Bohn, 1855-7.

Seneca. *Natural Questions*, translated by Harry M. Hine. Chicago and London: University of Chicago Press, 2010.

Theophrastus. *On Stones*, edited and translated by Earle R. Caley and John F. C. Richards. Columbus: Ohio State University, 1956.

Secondary Sources

Accordi, Bruno. "Michele Mercati (1541-1593) e la *Metallotheca*." *Geologica romana* 19 (1980): 1-50.

Adams, Frank D. *The Birth and Development of the Geological Sciences*. London: Dover, 1954.

Argyrakis, Vaios. "The Evolution of Wind Theory and the Concept of Exhalation in the Context of Ancient Greek Thought." *Almagest* 4 (2013): 122-36.

Arrizabalaga, Jon. "Facing the Black Death: Perceptions and Reactions of University Medical Practitioners." In *Practical Medicine from Salerno to the Black Death*, edited by Luis García-Ballester et al., 237-88. Cambridge: Cambridge University Press, 1994.

Baldassarri, Fabrizio and Andreas Blank, eds. *Vegetative Powers: The Roots of Life in Ancient, Medieval, and Early Modern Natural Philosophy*. Cham: Springer, 2021.

Clark, Mark E., and Kirk M. Summers. "Hippocratic Medicine and Aristotelian Science in the *Daemonum investigatio peripatetica* of Andrea Cesalpino." *Bulletin of the History of Medicine* 69, no. 4 (1995): 527-41.

Crisciani, Chiara, and Giovanna Ferrari. "Introduzione." In Arnald of Villanova, *Opera omnia medica, 5.2: Tractatus de humido radicali*, edited by Michael R. McVaugh, 319-608. Barcelona: Universitat de Barcelona, 2010.

Debus, Allen G. "The Paracelsian Aerial Niter." *Isis* 55, no. §1 (1964): 43-61.

Des Chene, Dennis. *Life's Form: Late Aristotelian Conceptions of the Soul*. Ithaca: Cornell University Press, 2000.

Dym, Warren A. "Alchemy and Mining: Metallogenesis and Prospecting in Early Mining Books." *Ambix* 55, no. 3 (2008): 232-54.

Eichholz, D. E. "Aristotle's Theory of the Formation of Metals and Minerals." *Classical Quarterly* 43, nos. 3-4 (1949): 141-6.

Ellenberger, François. *Histoire de la géologie*. Paris: Lavoisier, 1988.

Findlen, Paula. *Possessing Nature: Museums, Collecting, and Scientific Culture in Early Modern Italy*. Berkeley: University of California Press, 1994.

Freudenthal, Gad. "The Problem of Cohesion between Alchemy and Natural Philosophy: From Unctuous Moisture to Phlogiston." In *Alchemy Revisited*, edited by Zweder R. W. M. von Martels, 107-16. Leiden: Brill, 1990.

Halleux, Robert. "La nature et la formation des métaux selon Agricola et ses contemporains." *Revue d'histoire des sciences* 27 (1974): 211-22.

Halleux, Robert. *Le problème des métaux dans la science antique*. Paris: Les Belles Lettres, 1974.

Halleux, Robert, and Albert Yans. *Georg Agricola, Bermannus (Le mineur)*. Paris: Les Belles Lettres, 1990.
Hirai, Hiro. "Bodies and Their Internal Powers: Natural Philosophy, Medicine and Alchemy." In *The Routledge Companion to Sixteenth Century Philosophy*, edited by Henrik Lagerlund et al., 394–410. London: Routledge, 2017.
Hirai, Hiro. "Daniel Sennert, Chymistry and Theological Debates," *Ambix* 68, nos. 2–3 (2021): 198–213.
Hirai, Hiro. *Le concept de semence dans les théories de la matière à la Renaissance, de Marsile Ficin à Pierre Gassendi*. Turnhout: Brepols, 2005.
Hirai, Hiro. "*Logoi spermatikoi* and the Concept of Seeds in the Mineralogy and Cosmogony of Paracelsus." *Revue d'histoire des sciences* 61, no. 2 (2008): 245–64.
Hirai, Hiro. *Medical Humanism and Natural Philosophy: Renaissance Debates on Matter, Life and the Soul*. Leiden: Brill, 2011.
Hirai, Hiro. "The World Soul in the Renaissance from Ficino to Campanella and Lipsius." In *The World Soul: A History*, edited by James Wilberding, 151–76. Oxford: Oxford University Press, 2021.
Hirai, Hiro, and Hideyuki Yoshimoto, "Anatomizing the Sceptical Chymist: Robert Boyle and the Secret of His Early Sources on the Growth of Metals." *Early Science and Medicine* 10, no. 4 (2005): 453–77.
Israelson, Ludwig. *Die materia medica des Klaudios Galenos*. University of Dörpat, 1894.
Jouanna, Jacques. "Air, Miasma and Contagion in the Time of Hippocrates and the Survival of Miasmas in Post-Hippocratic Medicine (Rufus of Ephesus, Galen and Palladius)." In Jacques Jouanna, *Greek Medicine from Hippocrates to Galen*, edited by Philip van der Eijk, 119–36. Leiden: Brill, 2012.
Jouanna, Jacques. "Miasme, maladie et semence de la maladie: Galien lecteur d'Hippocrate." In *Studi su Galeno*, edited by Daniela Manetti, 59–92. Florence: Università di Firenze, 2000.
Kahn, Didier, and Hiro Hirai, eds. *Pseudo-Paracelsus: Forgery and Early Modern Alchemy, Medicine and Natural Philosophy*. Leiden: Brill, 2022.
Korobili, Giouli, and Roberto Lo Presti, eds. *Nutrition and Nutritive Soul in Aristotle and Aristotelianism*. Berlin: De Gruyter, 2020.
Lettinck, Paul. *Aristotle's Meteorology and Its Reception in the Arab World*. Leiden: Brill, 1999.
Martelli, Matteo. *Pseudo-Democrito: Scritti alchimici con il commentaria di Sinesio*. Paris: SEHA, 2011.
Martelli, Matteo. *The Four Books of Pseudo-Democritus*. London: Maney, 2013.
Martin, Craig. *Renaissance Meteorology: Pomponazzi to Descartes*. Baltimore: Johns Hopkins University Press, 2011.
Newman, William R. *Promethean Ambitions: Alchemy and the Quest to Perfect Nature*. Chicago: University of Chicago Press, 2004.
Newman, William R., and Lawrence M. Principe. "Alchemy vs. Chemistry: The Etymological Origins of a Historiographic Mistake." *Early Science and Medicine* 3, no. 1 (1998): 32–65.
Newman, William R., and Lawrence M. Principe. "Some Problems with the Historiography of Alchemy." In *Secrets of Nature: Astrology and Alchemy in Early Modern Europe*, edited by William R. Newman and Anthony Grafton, 385–431. Cambridge, MA: MIT Press, 2001.
Norris, John A. "*Auß Quecksilber und Schwefel Rein*: Johann Mathesius (1504–65) and *Sulfur-Mercurius* in the Silver Mines of Joachimsthal." *Osiris* 29 (2014): 35–48.

Norris, John A. "Early Theories of Aqueous Mineral Genesis in the Sixteenth Century." *Ambix* 54, no. 1 (2007): 69–86.

Norris, John A. "The Mineral Exhalation Theory of Metallogenesis in Pre-Modern Mineral Science." *Ambix* 53, no. 1 (2006): 43–65.

Partington, John R. *A History of Chemistry*. London: Macmillan, 1961.

Thorndike, Lynn. *A History of Magic and Experimental Science*, vol. 6. New York: Columbia University Press, 1941.

Vermij, Rienk. "Subterraneous Fire: Changing Theories of the Earth during the Renaissance." *Early Science and Medicine* 3, no. 4 (1998): 328–47.

Vermij, Rienk. *Thinking on Earthquakes in Early Modern Europe*. London: Routledge, 2020.

Part Three

Medicine

11

Anatomy and Practice: Andrea Cesalpino's *Praxis universae artis medicae*

R. Allen Shotwell

This chapter examines the anatomical content of Andrea Cesalpino's *Praxis universae artis medicae* with two purposes in mind. The first is to explore Cesalpino's own anatomical ideas. Studies of Cesalpino's anatomy have largely focused on their relations to the later discovery concerning the circulation of blood by William Harvey and have made only passing use of the *Praxis*. From the perspective of precursors to Harvey, Cesalpino's views appear contradictory.[1] For example, while he made very little reference to contemporary developments in anatomical structures, Cesalpino advanced novel ideas about the way the body worked. But the *Praxis* was devoted to explaining diseases and their cures, and Cesalpino ideas were often concerned with pathological conditions in addition to normal bodies.

The second purpose of this chapter is to demonstrate the value of interpreting anatomical thinking in the context of medical practice like the one found in the *Praxis*. Cesalpino's book was just one example of the way medical practice incorporated anatomical thinking in early modern period. Recent work has shown a deep connection between anatomy and practice, especially in the sixteenth century and demonstrated the rich but largely unstudied influence of books about medical practice on the developments of renaissance medicine. Cesalpino's *Praxis* was part of a long tradition extending into the Middle Ages of works devoted to practice that revealed details about the author's understanding of anatomy in the context of understanding disease.[2]

1. The Practica Tradition

In this chapter, I have used the term *practica* to refer to books devoted to medical diagnostics and treatment that were generally intended for learned physicians rather than surgeons or lay healers, although obviously their actual readership is a separate question. They were organized by the parts of the body, in order from head to the toe, listing the ailments and cures for each, and the material came from a wide range of sources. By the later sixteenth century, books on practice were increasingly based on classical authorities, especially Galen, rather than on medieval authors. Well-known examples of medieval *practica* included Bernard of Gordon's *Lilly of Medicine,* Niccolò Falcucci's *Medical Sermons,* and Michele Savonarola's *Practica medicinae*.[3]

Practica circulated widely in late medieval and early modern medical worlds, and their value for physicians was manifest. A book that contained the information about identifying and treating all known diseases and organized in a way that made it easy to immediately locate by the part of the body affected was clearly useful to anyone treating patients. By the fifteenth century, some versions of *practica* had become the most commonly owned work on medicine for physicians. With the coming of print late in the fifteenth century and well into the next, works on medical practice in general (which included *practica* as well as other books with a similar purpose) composed some 60 percent of all medical books printed.[4]

In the fifteenth century, writers of medical *practica* also began to argue that practice and theory were equivalent, denying the traditional hierarchy that placed theory at the top. Some even suggested that the practice genre, at least in the form of Galen's *Methodus medendi,* was superior to other sources for knowledge of theory as well as of practice. Fifteenth-century *practica* were certainly important sources of anatomical information. Each section of a *practica,* devoted to a different part of the body, began with a discussion of the anatomy of the body part in question. These discussions used anatomical material drawn from a variety of sources and, in at least some case, reflected contemporary ideas and ongoing debates. The anatomical ideas in fifteenth-century *practica* made them important sources for authors of anatomy texts early in the sixteenth century. For example, Matteo Ferrari da Grado's fifteenth-century book was repeatedly cited alongside more traditional sources like Galen and Avicenna in Berengario da Carpi's 1521 book on anatomy.[5]

Berengario turned out to be unique in his use of medieval *practica* as sources for writing about anatomy in the sixteenth century. As the century progressed and books devoted exclusively to anatomy became more and more common and especially after the appearance of Vesalius's *Fabrica* in the 1540s, anatomical works developed a strongly humanist approach that ignored or derided medieval precedents and consequently ignored medieval *practica*.[6]

New *practica* continued to be written in the sixteenth century however, and earlier *practica* were often reprinted. Matteo Ferrari da Grado's book went through at least five editions in the sixteenth century, including a Giunta edition in 1560. An edition of Michele Savonarola's book on practice, most likely written in the 1440s, also appeared in 1560, and even Bernard of Gordon's fourteenth-century *Lilly of Medicine* was printed at least twice in the sixteenth century. In the middle of the sixteenth century, Giambattista Da Monte wrote a new commentary on the so-called Ninth Book of *Almansor,* the Arabic work that had served as the basis for Ferrari da Grado's fifteenth-century work. New works on practice by Cesalpino's contemporaries included Girolamo Mercuriale's *Medicina practica* printed in 1601, Domenico Leoni's *Ars medendi humanos* printed in 1576, and Felix Platter's *Praxeos medicae* printed in 1602. As we shall see, the newer generation of *practica* discussed the same diseases as the older one, with the addition of the *morbus gallicus* which had only arrived in Europe in the late fifteenth century, but the way they discussed those diseases shifted. Doubtless the changes came from a number of motivations, but one factor, especially in the work of Cesalpino, involved new ways of thinking about how the body worked.[7]

Cesalpino's *Praxis* had a varied publishing history. It first appeared in the early seventeenth century in two, incomplete parts. The first four books, covering general topics like fever rather than diseases specific to particular parts of the body (or *morbi universales* according to the title) plus the *morbus gallicus* were printed by Luigi Zanetti in Rome in 1602. In a note to the reader, Cesalpino dedicated the book to newly trained physicians for whom, he said, he wrote the handbook in his old age, so that "it may supply the labors which my age denies."[8]

Books 7 and 8 were printed in a second volume by Zanetti in 1603, although the title page referred only to Book 7. These two books covered diseases of the stomach and the genitals. Concluding, Cesalpino warned his readers (imagined, again, to be newly trained physicians) against novel and experimental cures that could endanger the patient. He advised them that if they read anything in his book that seemed to deviate from the decrees of the ancients to not believe it. Zanetti's two editions made it clear, by the numbering of the books, that he was aware of, and presumably in possession of, Books 5 and 6 but he never printed them.[9]

The complete work with all eight books was first printed in Frankfurt as *Κάτοπτρον, sive speculum artis medicae Hippocraticum* in 1605 and in Italy as *Praxis universae artis medicae* in Treviso in 1606. The previously unprinted Books 5 and 6 which covered diseases of the head and the thorax were included with both. The Frankfurt edition included a dedication from Adamus Bruxius who was responsible for having it printed and who claimed the work had not been widely circulated in Germany because most copies were in Italy and Cesalpino's heirs did want to make them available, a possible reason for Zanetti never printing the remaining books given that Cesalpino died shortly after the second part appeared. The two complete editions both omitted Cesalpino's introductory and concluding remarks, but otherwise their content did not vary in any substantial way from the material found in the earlier, partial versions by Zanetti. I have used the Treviso edition and its title, *Praxis,* for what follows.[10]

2. Cesalpino's Anatomy in the Context of the Late Sixteenth Century

Cesalpino's *Praxis* appeared when new anatomical concepts, especially those related to structure, were routinely being introduced and debated. Beginning early in the sixteenth century, several basic structures of the body identified by Galen were called in question. In the 1540s, Andreas Vesalius pointed out more of Galen's mistakes, especially those that arose from confusions between animal and human anatomy.[11] Vesalius's claims sparked reactions, both in support of and in denial of Galen, and subsequent anatomists identified additional structural issues and began to dismiss or modify longstanding conceptions of how the body worked.[12]

In keeping with his advice at the end of his *Praxis* about avoiding novelties, Cesalpino made almost no reference to these new developments and he rarely mentioned his contemporaries when discussing anatomy. While this was not necessarily unusual, it makes it more difficult to trace the influences on his anatomical thought. The only contemporary anatomist referred to by Cesalpino in the *Praxis* that I found was Gabriele Falloppio who Cesalpino credited as the discoverer of the *chorda tympani*, the nerve that runs through the inner ear. Cesalpino mentioned Falloppio a second time in his discussion of pleurisy, but this time merely as one of in a list of authors.[13]

Much of Cesalpino's anatomy in the *Praxis* was as silent about the developments of the sixteenth century as it was about the people who contributed to them. For example, the early sixteenth century saw the denial of the existence of the *rete mirabile* in humans, a network of arteries at the base of the brain described by Galen as the part of the body responsible for concocting *pneuma* from arterial blood. The existence of the *rete* had been denied as early as 1521 by Berengario and was subsequently also identified as a mistake by Vesalius who rightly determined that the *rete* was found in some animals but not in humans. Yet, in the *Praxis*, Cesalpino reported the *rete* as a structure in the head without comment, ignoring any contemporary claims to the contrary.[14] Similarly, Cesalpino's description of the heart in the *Praxis* included a permeable septum through which blood passed from one side to another, another idea of Galen's that been refuted by sixteenth-century anatomists. Realdo Colombo denied the existence of pores in the septum in the 1560s, but their existence had already been cast into doubt before then, including by Vesalius. Denial of a permeated interventricular septum and the existence of the *rete mirabile* were not universal in the late sixteenth century, but those who did not accept those ideas tended be staunch defenders of Galen whereas Cesalpino seemed quite willing to depart from Galen's authority in other ways.[15]

When it came to the organs of reproduction, Cesalpino's account was also not particularly innovative although here he mixed together newer and older ideas about structure. Following Aristotle, Cesalpino drew an analogy between the shape of male and female organs but did not repeat Aristotle's claims about a woman's body being an underdeveloped version of a man's body. He described some structures that were questioned by others of his time, like the cotyledons in the uterus, but denied others like the existence of two "horns" in the uterus, which was more in keeping with later sixteenth-century opinions.[16]

Despite its lack of references to contemporary anatomical works, the *Praxis* contained some new content. When it came to the eye, Cesalpino's description, which was admittedly brief, seemed to follow Vesalius when he described the position of the crystalline humor. Early sixteenth-century anatomists from Alessandro Benedetti and Gabriele Zerbi to Berengario placed the crystalline humor near the front of the eye. Although a couple of other sixteenth-century authors made no comment on its location at all, only Vesalius placed it squarely in the middle of the eye, making Cesalpino's reference to the same idea a good indication that he got the idea from Vesalius.[17]

In the early decades of the seventeenth century, some new ideas about anatomical structure informed innovative conceptions about the way body worked, most famously William Harvey's theory of circulation. A large amount of twentieth-century scholarship focused on tracing the sources that may have influenced or predated Harvey including Cesalpino. Cesalpino's lack of engagement with sixteenth-century anatomical discoveries proved an impediment for many who sought to label him a precursor of Harvey. Nevertheless, it is possible to find original ideas about the operations of the body in Cesalpino's work. The literature on the subject is extensive, and I have only drawn from some its conclusions here. I will emphasize how Cesalpino's thinking was tied to practice rather than links to Harvey.[18]

Looking at anatomy as tied to practice, especially over time, shows that new ideas about the body were developed in the early seventeenth century within a traditional framework. Cesalpino looked at questions of disease from a different perspective than Ferrari da Grado or Berengario did. For example, one key idea associated with accounts of Cesalpino's ideas on circulation was the role of anastomoses, in the sense of interconnections between the veins and arteries that allowed for blood to pass from one to the other. The concept of anastomoses goes back to Galen, who made repeated references to them as normal structures in his *De usu partium* and in his *De naturalibus facultatibus*.[19] Walter Pagel argued that Cesalpino understood blood movement through anastomoses to be a normal aspect of human anatomy, rather than something "exceptional and pathological" even though the contexts of Cesalpino's various remarks on the subject were specific scenarios involving medical conditions. Pagel pointed to Cesalpino's use of words like "accustomed" and "natural" as indications of this acceptance of anastomoses, and it certainly seemed that Cesalpino understood them as a normal part of anatomy.[20]

Another definition of anastomoses, however, existed in Galenic medicine, one that is more closely related to disease, and Cesalpino made use of this definition as well. In addition to "unexceptional" connections between veins and arteries, anastomoses were also understood to be pathological conditions. Galen made references to this version of anastomoses in his *Methodus medendi*, for example, describing anastomoses as ruptures or splits in blood vessels, caused either by a massive influx of blood or by an actual puncture from a sharp object.[21] This understanding of anastomoses was also in use in the sixteenth and seventeenth centuries. For example, the 1555 edition of Ambrogio Calepino's Latin dictionary defined an anastomosis specifically in these terms, citing Galen's *Methodus medendi*, and made no mention of the non-pathological version of the idea. Anastomosis was also used in this sense in the early seventeenth century by Felix Platter in his work on medical practice. As we shall see below Cesalpino used anastomoses in the same way in the *Praxis* although not in the passages examined by Pagel.[22]

Another finding from the scholarship on Cesalpino's circulation work was that he seemed to have advocated against the free flow of blood in organs, maintaining that blood was confined to vessels, arteries or veins, except in the case of the heart. Galen endorsed the concept of blood existing in organs in a manner like a sponge, and Cesalpino's insistence on blood containment by vessels reflected the influence of Aristotle. This too had important ramifications for the causes of disease.[23]

3. Anastomoses as Ruptures: The Kidney and Urine in the Blood

The structure of the kidney and how it performed its basic task of filtering urine from blood was a matter of debate in the fifteenth and sixteenth centuries. Galen relied on the idea of natural faculty to explain the process, suggesting that the kidney attracted the mixture of urine and blood and that its density prevented the blood from passing through while allowing the urine to continue and eventually enter the bladder. But in the fourteenth century, the anatomist Mondino de' Liuzzi offered a more concrete explanation by describing a filtering membrane in the kidney by which the urine and blood were separated. Mondino's view was disputed in fifteenth century, particularly in *practica*, and ultimately denied in the sixteenth century.[24]

For fifteenth-century authors of *practica*, like Matteo Ferrari da Grado, and for the early sixteenth-century anatomists, like Berengario, who followed them, Mondino's argument for a filtering membrane was flawed not only because it was not supported by any other authority but also because it conflicted with a general understanding of the diseases of the kidney, particularly with the condition of blood in the urine. For Ferrari da Grado and Berengario, if the kidney had a simple filtering membrane, then blood in the urine must be the result of a rupture or tear in that membrane. This rupture, a presumably grave condition, hardly accorded with the relatively light treatment assigned to the condition in *practica*, which typically prescribed a simple decoction of mallow. Consequently, Mondino's filtering membrane conflicted with medical practice in addition to violating Galen's basic conception of the kidney's functioning.[25]

The presence of blood in the urine involved another anatomical question beside the issue of whether the kidney contained a filtering membrane. The kidney, like every other organ in the Galenic system, was nourished by blood delivered by the veins. In the kidney's case, the venous blood also contained urine, which was separated out, but the blood still performed its basic nourishing function. Just as he did not provide a detailed account of the separation of urine from blood in the kidney, Galen also did not detail how the nourishing venous blood was absorbed by the kidney, although it involved the kidney's dense, fleshy substance. Berengario's account referred to the blood urine mixture "bathing" the kidney, which absorbed blood in the process for nourishment. That perspective contended blood would pass through with the urine if the kidney was somehow debilitated by a disease that caused it to fail in this absorption process, but it implied that the internal structure of the kidney was not composed of separated blood vessels containing the blood but was more like a sponge.[26]

Vesalius condemned Mondino's version of the kidney, claiming it was held by all unnamed anatomists before him. Instead, he offered a careful description (and illustration, which was subsequently copied by Platter, see Figure 11.1) of the actual internal structure of the kidney formed by branches of the veins and arteries, contrasting it with an illustration of the wrong description of the kidney given by Mondino where the kidney was largely an empty cavity with a single filtering membrane across its middle. While Vesalius retained the basic Galenic account of how the kidney worked, he did not address the question of urine in the blood.[27]

Works on practice following Vesalius differed in their account of blood in the urine from those of the late fifteenth and early sixteenth centuries in part because they were based on Galen's *De locis affectis* (*On the Affected Parts*) and written without reference to medieval Latin or Arabic traditions found in Ferrari da Grado and Berengario. Galen described identifying the diseases of the kidney by examining what appeared in the discharged urine—for example, sand or gravel in the urine was an indication of stones, and pieces of tissue an indication of ulceration of the kidney.

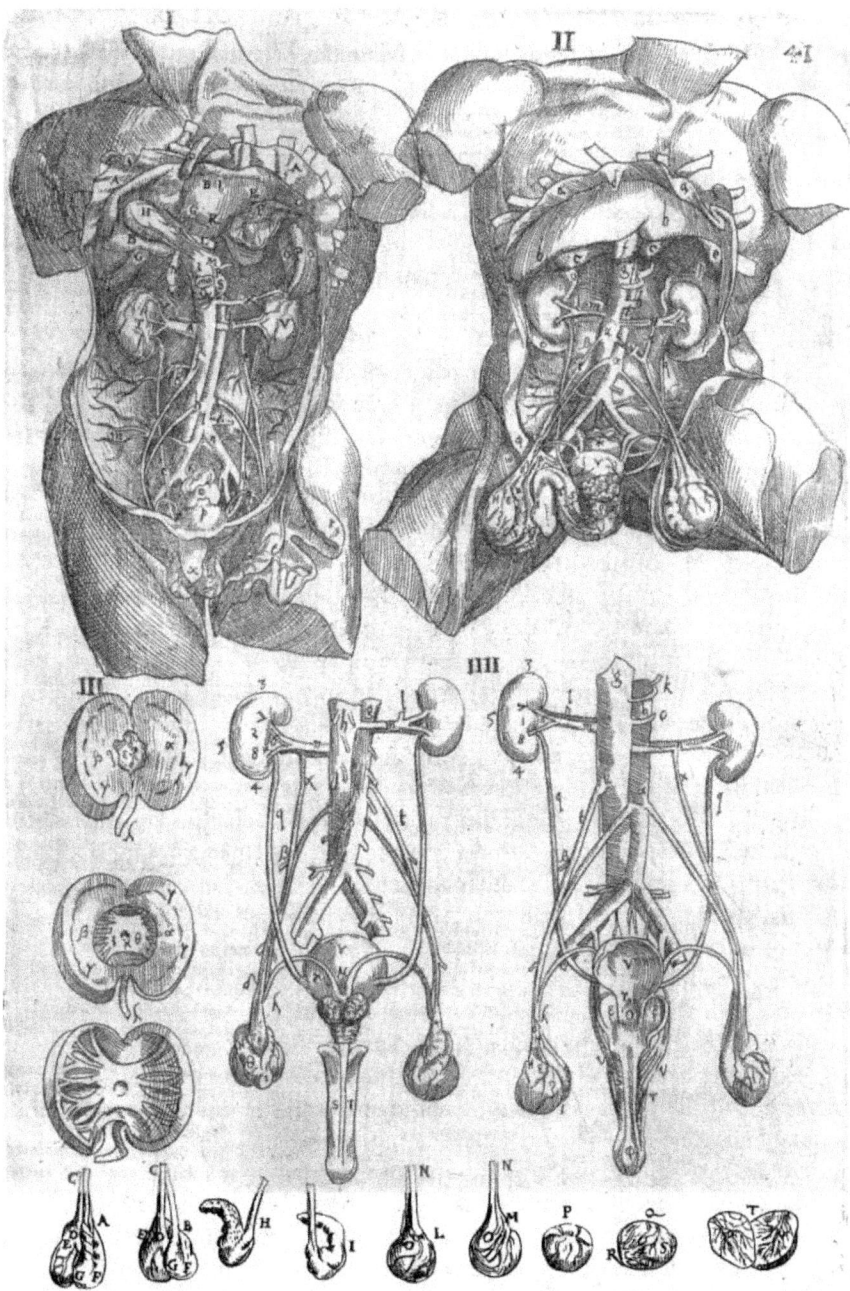

Figure 11.1 Illustration of the internal structure of the kidney (III) from Felix Platter *De corporis humani structura et usu* (Basel: Froben 1583), 41. Platter copied Vesalius's illustration which contradicted the medieval view of the kidney containing a filtering membrane that was abandoned by Berengario earlier in the sixteenth century partly because of matters of practice. Public Domain.

A large amount of blood in the urine indicated a rupture of a blood vessel from a blow or a fall or from a plethora of blood, while a small amount of blood discharged slowly was a sign of a "dilation of the openings which filter the urine from the vena cava into the kidney."[28]

Galen's description of blood in the urine changed the nature of the discussion surrounding that condition since it allowed for both physical damage to the kidney in the form of a rupture as well as for a "weakening" of its power of separation, the difference being the amount of blood discharged. The difference also translated into differences in cures. Early seventeenth-century authors looked to venesection or cupping to treat the heavy flux of blood and medication to treat the lesser, slower effusion.

In the *Praxis*, for example, Cesalpino retained Vesalius's basic account of the kidney's internal structure, describing it as formed by the scattering of the small vessels that entered into it and avoiding any concept of a filtering membrane. He also identified three possibilities for blood in the urine. Following Galen, he noted that blood flowing freely and strongly was a sign of a rupture in the vessels of the kidney caused by a violent blow as might occur in a fall from a great height. On the other hand, if the blood passed with difficulty and was accompanied by pain then it was a sign of stones or mordent humors. Cesalpino's third possibility was that "sometimes" blood was also passed gradually "through an anastomosis" rather than suddenly as in the case of a ruptured vessel.[29]

Cesalpino did not elaborate on this last possible source of blood in the urine, leaving the reader to speculate on its exact nature. That an anastomosis in the kidney caused blood in the urine was also described by Felix Platter in his *Praxeos* (*The Practice of Medicine*) first printed in 1602 the same time as the first books of Cesalpino's *Praxis*. For Platter, an anastomosis in the kidney referred to the pathological condition that led to damage, caused by a forceful purging of blood from the emulgent vein which burst the veins. In other words, it was a condition akin to Galen's plethora of blood described in *On the Affected Parts*.[30] Also, like Galen, Platter associated ruptures with excessive flow of blood rather than the gradual flow Cesalpino championed.[31]

Since he described the amount of blood flow arising from anastomoses in the kidney differently than Platter, Cesalpino's conception of them may not have been the same. Further clues to what Cesalpino might have meant are found in his next remark, where he noted that Galen insisted that the mixture of blood with a large amount of urine or other lighter liquids happens quickly. This argument seemed focused on a recombining of blood and urine rather than a failure in initially separating them and, therefore, to a process that happened *after* the two were separated by the kidney. Possibly the anastomosis Cesalpino had in mind was located somewhere past the kidney.[32]

Regardless of the exact nature of the anastomoses involved in producing blood in the urine, Cesalpino was almost certainly referring to them in the form of damaged or ruptured veins rather than to the normal structures of the body that connected veins and arteries. The discussion of the kidney was the only place in the *Praxis* when he did so. Other discussions of disease, like those related to the stomach and food production, invoked anastomoses as normal, rather than pathological arrangements.

4. Anastomoses as Normal Structures: The Mesentery and *Picrocholi*

Anastomoses also play a role in Cesalpino's account of nourishment of the stomach and associated organs, the intestines, this time as an integral part of the normal operations of the body related to the production of chyle and nourishment. As Jerome Bylebyl has perceptively observed, Cesalpino's account of that process resonates with broader questions related to his ideas on circulation since it represents another example of Cesalpino's willingness to depart from standard Galenic accounts of blood flow; and it is similar to later remarks by Harvey. But it is also true that, like his discussion of the kidney, Cesalpino's ideas about the mesentery were connected to questions of diseases and their cures.[33]

In the Galenic system, blood was produced from food through an intermediary substance called chyle. The stomach converted food to chyle, which was carried by the mesentery veins to the liver where it was converted to blood. There was a problem with this account, however, because if venous blood nourishes all the parts of the body, then how was the stomach nourished? The mesentery veins were supposed to be carrying chyle *to* the liver not blood *from* it to the stomach. The problem was compounded by the observation that the mesentery examined in bodies always contained blood, not chyle.

Galen hinted at one possible solution to the question. He referred to a bidirectional flow in the mesentery with chyle traveling *to* the liver and blood traveling *from* the liver back to the stomach, but Galen's description indicated the process was infrequent and, as such, could not be reconciled with the experience of regularly finding blood in the mesentery. As Bylebyl pointed out, finding blood in the mesentery was common enough for Vesalius to ask one audience at a dissection if anyone had ever seen anything else.[34]

Cesalpino's solution involved the arteries as well as the veins of the mesentery. According to him, the reason why blood was always found in the mesentery veins was that arteries transmitted blood into them through anastomoses and that blood mixed with the chyle which was turned into blood "as wine makes a mixture of water." In other words, the blood found in the mesentery was actually a mixture of blood and chyle, but the chyle was not visible. Using Cesalpino's system, the nourishment problem was solved. Blood mixed with chyle nourished the stomach (and intestines) as it did with all the other parts of the body. Also, the unidirectional flow of venal and arterial blood was preserved. "Blood is continually borne upwards through the mesentery veins to the liver, and perfected blood downward through the arteries."[35] The mixing of blood and chyle in the mesentery described by Cesalpino was similar to his ideas concerning blood and urine discharged from the kidneys. In both cases, the blood quickly mixed with another material, although the white chyle became imperceptible in the blood while the red blood was readily visible in the urine. Also, the anastomoses of the mesentery were part of their normal anatomy, while the anastomoses of the kidney were pathological.

Cesalpino's solution to the issue of nourishment for the stomach through anastomoses between the veins and arteries had ramifications for medical practice. After his description of the process in the *Praxis*, he turned to various ailments in the stomach. Many pains in the stomach itself depended upon the presence or absence of food, and Cesalpino described different scenarios where pain was present before eating or after eating and analyzed whether eating made the pain go away.[36] According to Cesalpino, some patients were seized with a stomach pain caused by *picrocholi* due to bile effusing during fasting. He wrote "for when the mesentery veins suck, and do not find food, they are filled with bile, which they transmit into the stomach, whence comes the pain."[37] This brief description seemed contradictory to an account of the mesentery veins that did not allow for bidirectional flow since it implied that bile flowed back into the stomach from the mesentery. Once again, however, Platter described something similar that helped to clarify Cesalpino's meaning.

Like Cesalpino, Platter described the mesentery as "sucking" chyle from the stomach, although he did not follow Cesalpino in the mixing of blood from arteries. Platter's discussion of the cause of *picrocholi* also came close to Cesalpino's. The stomach was irritated by bile which led to pain, but to Platter that bile was sent into the stomach from "the gut called duodenum."[38] In other words, for Platter, the sucking property of the mesentery *pulled* bile into the stomach from the duodenum. The mesentery did not deliver bile to the stomach. Cesalpino's description was probably suggesting something similar to Platter[39]

Much was left unsaid in Cesalpino's description of *picrocholi*. If the arteries were supplying blood into the mesentery veins through anastomoses, then what happened when chyle was absent and the mesentery drew bile into itself instead? Galenic theories allowed for the possible presence of two materials in the same vessel since the attractive powers of various organs were able to separate them out, as was the case with blood and urine in the kidneys. But the "sucking" of bile into the mesentery complicated that picture by suggesting their attractive powers extended to bile and chyle. Also, as Bylebyl pointed out, Galen had described something similar in *On Natural Faculties* when he said the mesentery sucked nourishing blood from the liver in periods of fasting when it could not get chyle. This, however, was part of the idea of bidirectional flow rejected by Cesalpino, although it might have helped his thinking about the presence of bile.[40]

5. Blood Repletion

In addition to reinterpreting traditional ideas like anastomoses to explain disease, Cesalpino also worked within standard accounts of disease, while reframing them by refocusing the argument, an approach that was apparent in his emphasis on repletion in diseases of the heart. Repletion, in the sense of excessive amounts of blood, was closely related to rupturing veins as described above. In Platter's account of blood in the urine, an excessive amount of blood overfilled the veins and led to a rupture, but too much blood could also produce stasis when the influx occluded the flow of blood and blocked the delivery of nutrients without bursting the vessel. Excessive blood posed other problems as well. Fluid surrounding or overfilling the heart or lungs could dampen or even stop their motion, leading to an erratic pulse, suffocation, and death. Cesalpino made special use of the idea of repletion to explain two medical conditions—angina and palpitations.[41]

Both angina and palpitation were complex subjects that involved multiple causes. In describing angina, Matteo Ferrari da Grado, using the word quinsy (in Latin, *squinantia*), identified the basic condition as a swelling in the throat that made it difficult to breath and to swallow. The extrinsic cause might be one of a range of things—a blow to the neck or eating or drinking something that caused swelling for example, but the "bodily" (*corporalis*) cause was the swelling itself which might be filled with blood or other humors, either separated or mixed together.[42]

In his discussion of palpitations (heart tremors), Ferrari da Grado first described an overarching idea that the cause must ultimately be an effect on the heart itself. Specifically, bodily causes included matter communicated to the heart, fluid in the pericardium, or complexions. The most contentious cause for Ferrari da Grado was *apostemata*, which depending on the source may or may not actually be found in the heart and which several authorities associated with a quick death.[43]

Cesalpino discussed both angina and palpitation a decade before the appearance of the *Praxis* in Question 17 and Question 20 of Book 2 of his *Quaestionum medicarum libri II* (1593). In Question 17 he explored the idea that the overfilling of the jugular veins (rather than the constriction of larynx) might be the cause of suffocation in the case of angina. As Pagel pointed out, Cesalpino's arguments provided important hints about how he understood the flow of blood, but for our purposes three key concepts related to repletion stand out. The first was the idea that overfilling of the jugular veins could lead to stasis that stopped blood flow. The second was the idea that blood preventing from flowing normally could be regurgitated to the heart and lungs, overfilling them and impeding or stopping their movement altogether. The third was the idea that blocking the veins could also prevent the flow of the essential "virtue of the heart" to the brain, causing all bodily motion to stop.[44]

In Question 20, Cesalpino looked at the possible causes of palpitation. He began with the observation that there were two types of motion of the heart—its natural movement (the pulse) and the preternatural movement caused by disease. Motion from disease had a number of possible causes as described by various authors—cold according to Aristotle, heat (from fever) according to Actuarius, copious blood in the heart according to Paul of Aegina, and fluid in the pericardium according to Galen. But ultimately all palpitations came either in the form of heat when the repletion of the vital spirit obstructed somewhere beyond the heart or in the form of cold when fluid in the pericardium or tubers near the heart impeded its motion.[45]

Cesalpino returned to these two topics in his *Praxis*. He discussed angina in Book 5, Chapter 5, where he repeated the basic premise in the *Medical Questions*, noting that the cause of suffocation in the case of angina was not always the compression of the larynx (as Galen had said) but sometimes repletion of blood. By taking this approach, Cesalpino changed the fundamental question about its causes as found in Ferrari da Grado. While Ferrari da Grado described the causes of the swelling, Cesalpino focused on the cause of the suffocation. This analysis, based on a careful thinking out of the direction of blood flow, expanded the number of possible causes and also had complex repercussions for understanding other disease conditions and Galen's interpretation of them, particularly apoplexy which Galen described based on motor activity.[46]

In his discussion of palpitations in the *Praxis*, Cesalpino returned to the question of causes found in his *Medical Questions*, where his discussion more closely mirrored Ferrari da Grado's approach, focusing on the immediate and remote causes of the condition. In Chapter 20 "On the Diseases of the Heart and Palpitations," Cesalpino identified the proximate causes of palpitation as overeating, lack of evacuation of humors, and rapid breathing. One remote cause was the overfilling of the veins with blood which caused occlusion and intercepted the flow of the vital spirit. He had already identified this same process in *Medical Question* 17 in relation to angina and suffocation, revealing the connections between his understandings of different conditions. Cesalpino identified other causes also found in Medical Question 20, such as fluid in the pericardium and copious blood as shown by Paul of Aegina.[47] Cesalpino had added a potential cause, namely repletion, to the standard list for palpitations, one that apparently arose from his consideration of angina. He was not alone in suggesting it. Platter also described the idea that palpitation might be caused by repletion, specifically by the overfilling of the arteries, which, unlike the veins, needed "room for the vital spirits." Platter's overall account, however, differed from Cesalpino's. Like Ferrari da Grado, he focused on the heart together with the arteries as the ultimate source of changes in the pulse "because no other parts beat."[48]

6. Conclusion

Although Cesalpino largely ignored the new anatomical ideas of the sixteenth century, he still developed innovative conceptions about the body. He was able to do so, at least in part, because his ideas were often developed in the context of diseases and their cures rather than in the context of explaining the normal functioning of the body. Cesalpino posited new ideas for how the body worked, but because many of them were in specific contexts, they lacked any sort of comprehensive anatomical account, like Harvey's theory of circulation. This context of practical medicine was certainly one reason why Cesalpino's ideas seemed conflicted to scholars trying to interpret them through a Harverian lens.

Especially in his *Praxis*, the ideas Cesalpino proposed fit better into the tradition of writing about disease than of writing about anatomy. His approach represented a change from the approaches of a century before. Writing in the early seventeenth century, his sources were Galenic rather than Arab or medieval, change in his approach that resulted was often one of interpretation or addition rather than complete replacement. It involved positing new causes for well-known diseases, shifting the focus of causes from the source of a condition to the way it produced certain effects on the body and highlighting key conditions like repletion. These ideas mixed together anatomy and pathology in an era where clear separations between the two were still not commonplace.

Notes

1 The most comprehensive treatment of Cesalpino's anatomy is Walter Pagel, *William Harvey's Biological Ideas. Selected Aspects and Historical Background* (New York: Karger, 1967), 169–208. See also John P. Arcieri, *The Circulation of the Blood and Andrea Cesalpino of Arezzo* (New York: Vanni, 1945).
2 See, for example, Michael Stolberg, "Empiricism in Sixteenth-Century Medical Practice," *Early Science and Medicine* 18, no. 6 (2013), 487–516; R. Allen Shotwell, "The Anatomical Injections of Berengario da Carpi," in *Scientiae in the History of Medicine*, ed. Fabrizio Baldassarri and Fabio Zampieri (Rome: L'Erma di Bretschneider, 2021), 153–69; Sabrina Minuzzi, "15th-Century Practical Medicine in Print. Beyond the Profession towards the miscere utile dulci," *Nuncius* 36, no. 2 (2021): 199–263.
3 For the structure of medical *practica* and their history see Luke Demaitre, *Medieval Medicine: The Art of Healing, from Head to Toe* (Oxford: Prager, 2013), ix–xiv.
4 For the popularity of that genre see Minuzzi, "15th-Century Practical Medicine in Print," 213; Katharine Park, *Doctors and Medicine in Early Renaissance Florence* (Princeton: Princeton University Press, 1985), 191–8.
5 On the *practica* tradition see Jerome Bylebyl, "Teaching Methodus Medendi in the Renaissance," in *Galen's Method of Healing*, ed. Fridolf Kudlein and Richard Durling (Leiden: Brill, 1982), 157–89; Ian Maclean, *Logic, Signs and Nature* (Cambridge: Cambridge University Press, 2002), 68–72. For Berengario and Ferrari da Grado, see Shotwell, "Injection Experiments," 155–6.
6 See R. Allen Shotwell, "The Great Pox and the Surgeon's Role in the Sixteenth Century," *Journal of the History of Medicine and Allied Sciences* 72, no. 1 (2017): 21–33.
7 Giambattista Da Monte, *In nonum librum Rhasis ad Mansorem regem arabum expositio* (Venice: Costantini, 1554); Girolamo Mercuriale, *Medicina practica* (Frankfurt: Schönwetter, 1602); Felix Platter, *Praxeos seu de cognoscendis, praedicendis, praecavendis curandisque affectibus homini incommondantibus tractatus tres* (Basel: Waldkirch, 1602); Domenico Leoni, *Ars medendi humanos, particularesque morbos a capite, usque ad pedes* (Bologna: Rossi, 1576). For sixteenth-century editions of earlier *practica* I relied on WorldCat searches. I have made use of a seventeenth-century English translation of Platter's work in the references below.
8 Andrea Cesalpino, *Artis medicae pars prima, de morbis universalibus* (Rome: Zannetti, 1602), 4: "ut laboribus, quos aetas negat."
9 Andrea Cesalpino, *Artis medicae liber VII, De morbis ventris* (Rome: Zannetti, 1603), 454–5.
10 Andrea Cesalpino, *Κάτοπτρον, sive Speculum artis medicae Hippocraticum* (Frankfurt: Becker, 1605); Andrea Cesalpino, *Praxis universae Artis medicae* (Treviso: Deuchino, 1606).
11 Vesalius visited Pisa where Cesalpino taught in 1543. See Rosalba Ciranni, "Andrea Vesalio a Pisa," *Medicina nei secoli*, 22 (2010): 143–62.
12 Pagel, *William Harvey's Biological Ideas*, 169–208; Arcieri, *The Circulation of the Blood*; Jerome Bylebyl, "Cesalpino and Harvey on the Portal Circulation," in *Science, Medicine and Society in the Renaissance. Essays to Honor Walter Pagel*, vol. 2, ed. Allen G. Debus (New York: Heinemann, 1972), 39–52.
13 Cesalpino, *Praxis*, 425, 546.

14 Ibid., 299. For a history of the *rete* see John Forrester, "The Marvelous Network and the History of Enquiry into Its Function," *Journal of the History of Medicine and Allied Sciences* 57, no. 2 (2002): 198–217.
15 The problem of the septum was key to the development of circulation. See L. G. Wilson, "The Problem of the Discovery of the Pulmonary Circulation," *Journal of the History of Medicine and Allied Sciences* 7, no. 2 (1962): 229–44. Cesalpino's neglect of it was an issue for scholars who wished to assign him an important role in the discovery of circulation as described by Harvey. See Pagel, *William Harvey's Biological Ideas*, 171.
16 Cesalpino, *Praxis*, 621–2. For the cotyledons see Katharine Park, *Secrets of Women. Gender, Generation, and the Origins of Human Dissection* (New York: Zone Books, 2006), 184. For details about the "horns" see R. Allen Shotwell, "Alessandro Achillini and the 1502 Galen Opera Omnia: The Influence of Pseudo-Galenic Sources in Early Sixteenth-Century Anatomy," in *Pseudo-Galenica: The Formation of the Galenic Corpus from Antiquity to the Renaissance*, ed. Caroline Petit, Simon Swain, and Klaus-Dietrich Fischer (London: University of London Press, 2020), 167–72.
17 Cesalpino, *Praxis*, 408. For details on sixteenth-century writing about the eye in Vesalius and others see Tawrin Baker, "Dissection, Instruction, and Debate: Visual Theory at the Anatomy Theatre in the Sixteenth Century," in *Perspective as Practice: Renaissance Cultures of Optics*, ed. Sven Dupré (Turnhout: Brepols, 2019), 123–47.
18 Pagel, *William Harvey's Biological Ideas*, 169.
19 Galen, *De usu partium* 1.6 (3.455K); Galen, *Nat. fac.* 3.15 (2.208K).
20 Pagel, *William Harvey's Biological Ideas*, 181.
21 Galen, *Methodus medendi* 5.2 (10.311K).
22 Ambrogio Calepino, *Dictionarium* (Venice: Griffio, 1555), fol. 30v.
23 Pagel, *William Harvey's Biological Ideas*, 183.
24 Michael McVaugh, "Losing Ground. The Disappearance of Attraction from the Kidneys," in *Blood, Sweat and Tears—The Changing Concepts of Physiology from Antiquity into Early Modern Europe*, ed. Manfred Horstmanshoff, Helen King, and Claus Zittel (Leiden: Brill, 2012), 103–38. Jacopo Berengario da Carpi, *Commentaria cum amplissimis additionibus super anatomia Mundini* (Bologna: Benedetti, 1521), fols.177v–180v.
25 Berengario, *Commentaria*, fol. 178r–v.
26 Berengario, *Commentaria*, fol. 178r.
27 McVaugh, "Losing," 113–16; Andreas Vesalius, *De humani corporis fabrica libri septem* (Basel: Oporinus, 1543), 515; Giovanni Matteo Ferrari da Grado, *Practica, seu, Commentaria in nonum Rasis ad Almansorem* (Venice: Giunta, 1560), 319–50.
28 Galen, *On the Affected Parts. Translation from the Greek Text with Explanatory Notes*, trans. Rudolph E. Siegel (New York: Karger, 1976), 173.
29 Cesalpino, *Praxis*, 606: "Aliquando sanguis egreditur per anastomosim, quod paulatim incipit, non repente."
30 Galen, *De loc. aff.* 6.3 (8.394K).
31 Felix Platter, *Platerus Golden Practice of Physick* (London: Cole, 1664), 653.
32 Cesalpino, *Praxis*, 606. See Pagel, *William Harvey's Biological Ideas*, 84 for Cesalpino and the free flow of blood in organs.
33 Bylebyl, "Cesalpino," 39.
34 Ibid., 41.
35 Cesalpino, *Praxis*, 522. Translation given in Bylebyl, "Cesalpino," 43.
36 Cesalpino, *Praxis*, 523–4.

37 Ibid., 524: "Cum enim venae meseraicae sugant, nec cibum inveniant, replentur bile, quam transfundunt in ventriculum unde dolor."
38 Platter, *Platerus golden practice*, 279.
39 Ibid., 156.
40 Bylebyl, "Cesalpino," 41.
41 Cesalpino, *Praxis*, chapters 20–3. Cesalpino, *QM*, questions 17 and 20.
42 Ferrari da Grado, *Practica*, 239–41.
43 Ibid., 188–9.
44 Cesalpino, *QM*, fol. 234v. Pagel, *William Harvey's Biological Ideas*, 172.
45 Cesalpino, *QM*, fol. 236v.
46 Cesalpino, *Praxis*, 447. Pagel, *William Harvey's Biological Ideas*, 172.
47 Cesalpino, *Praxis*, 504.
48 Platter, *Platerus Golden Practice*, 152–3.

Bibliography

Primary Sources

Berengario da Carpi, Jacopo. *Commentaria cum amplissimis additionibus super anatomia Mundini*. Bologna: Benedetti, 1521.

Calepino, Ambrogio. *Dictionarium*. Venice: Griffio, 1555.

Cesalpino, Andrea. *Artis medicae pars prima, de morbis universalibus*. Rome: Zannetti, 1602.

Cesalpino, Andrea. *Artis medicae pars II. De morbis particularibus internarum partium*. Rome: Zannetti, 1603.

Cesalpino, Andrea. Κάτοπτρον, *sive Speculum artis medicae Hippocraticum*. Frankfurt: Becker, 1605.

Cesalpino, Andrea. *Praxis universae artis medicae*. Treviso: Deuchino 1606.

Da Monte, Giambattista. *In nonum librum Rhasis ad Mansorem regem arabum expositio*. Venice: Costantini, 1554.

Ferrari da Grado, Giovanni Matteo. *Practica seu Commentaria in nonum Rasis ad Almansorem*. Venice: Giunti, 1560.

Galen. *On the Affected Parts. Translation from the Greek Text with Explanatory Notes*, translated by Rudolph E. Siegel. New York: Karger, 1976.

Galen. *Opera omnia*, edited by Karl Gottlob Kühn. 20 vols. Leipzig: Karl Knobloch, 1821–33.

Leoni, Domenico. *Ars medendi humanos, particularesque morbos a capite, usque ad pedes*. Bologna: Rossi, 1576.

Mercuriale, Girolamo. *Medicina practica*. Frankfurt: Schönwetter, 1602.

Platter, Felix. *Platerus Golden Practice of Physick*. London: Cole, 1664.

Platter, Felix. *Praxeos seu de cognoscendis, praedicendis, praecavendis curandisque affectibus homini incommondantibus tractatus tres*. Basel: Waldkirch, 1602.

Platter, Felix. *De corporis humani structura et usu*. Basel: Froben 1583.

Vesalius, Andreas. *De humani corporis fabrica libri septem*. Basel: Oporinus, 1543.

Secondary Sources

Arcieri, John P. *The Circulation of Blood and Andrea Cesalpino of Arezzo*. New York: Vanni, 1945.

Baker, Tawrin. "Dissection, Instruction, and Debate: Visual Theory at the Anatomy Theatre in the Sixteenth Century." In *Perspective as Practice: Renaissance Cultures of Optics*, edited by Sven Dupré, 123–47. Turnhout: Brepols, 2019.

Bylebyl, Jerome J. "Cesalpino and Harvey on Portal Circulation." In *Medicine and Society in the Renaissance. Essays to Honor Walter Pagel*, edited by Allen G. Debus, 1: 39–52. New York: Science History Publications, 1972.

Bylebyl, Jerome J. "Teaching Methodus Medendi in the Renaissance." In *Galen's Method of Healing*, edited by Fridolf Kudlein and Richard Durling, 157–89. Leiden: Brill, 1982.

Ciranni, Rosalba. "Andrea Vesalio a Pisa." *Medicina nei secoli* 22 (2010): 143–62.

Demaitre, Luke. *Medieval Medicine: The Art of Healing, from Head to Toe*. Oxford: Prager, 2013.

Forrester, John. "The Marvelous Network and the History of Enquiry into Its Function." *Journal of the History of Medicine* 57, no. 2 (2002): 198–217.

Maclean, Ian. *Logic, Signs and Nature*. Cambridge: Cambridge University Press, 2002.

McVaugh, Michael. "Losing Ground. The Disappearance of Attraction from the Kidneys." In *Blood, Sweat and Tears—The Changing Concepts of Physiology from Antiquity into Early Modern Europe*, edited by Manfred Horstmanshoff, Helen King, and Claus Zittel, 103–38. Leiden: Brill, 2012.

Minuzzi, Sabrina. "15th-Century Practical Medicine in Print. Beyond the Profession towards the miscere utile dulci." *Nuncius* 36, no. 2 (2021): 199–263.

Pagel, Walter. *William Harvey's Biological Ideas. Selected Aspects and Historical Background*. New York: Karger, 1967.

Park, Katharine. *Doctors and Medicine in Early Renaissance Florence*. Princeton: Princeton University Press, 1985.

Park, Katharine. *Secrets of Women. Gender, Generation, and the Origins of Human Dissection*. New York: Zone Books, 2006.

Shotwell, R. Allen. "Alessandro Achillini and the 1502 Galen Opera Omnia: The Influence of Pseudo-Galenic Sources in Early Sixteenth-Century Anatomy." In *Pseudo-Galenica: The Formation of the Galenic Corpus from Antiquity to the Renaissance*, edited by Caroline Petit, Simon Swain, and Klaus-Dietrich Fischer, 167–72. London: University of London Press, 2020.

Shotwell, R. Allen. "The Anatomical Injections of Berengario da Carpi." In *Scientiae in the History of Medicine*, edited by Fabrizio Baldassarri and Fabio Zampieri, 153–69. Rome-Bristol: L'Erma di Bretschneider, 2021.

Shotwell, R. Allen. "The Great Pox and the Surgeon's Role in the Sixteenth Century." *Journal of the History of Medicine and Allied Sciences* 72, no. 1 (2017): 21–33.

Stolberg, Michael. "Empiricism in Sixteenth-Century Medical Practice." *Early Science and Medicine* 18, no. 6 (2013), 487–516.

Wilson, L. G. "The Problem of the Discovery of the Pulmonary Circulation." *Journal of the History of Medicine and Allied Sciences* 7, no. 2 (1962): 229–44.

12

Simple and Compound Drugs in Late Renaissance Medicine: The Pharmacology of Andrea Cesalpino (1593)

Elisabeth Moreau

From antiquity, Galenic physicians extensively discussed the active powers of simple and compound drugs. In their views, simple drugs, that is, single ingredients, acted according to their material qualities and the properties of their substance. As for compound drugs, their efficacy resulted from the mutual interaction of their ingredients and their modes of preparation. In the late Renaissance, Galenic physicians and naturalists, such as Leonhart Fuchs and Pietro Andrea Mattioli, attempted to explain these pharmacological properties or "faculties" at the intersection of medicine, botany, and natural philosophy. This chapter examines the case of the Italian physician and botanist Andrea Cesalpino. His pharmacological treatise *De medicamentorum facultatibus* [*On the Faculties of Drugs*, 1593] was particularly significant for its reception of ancient and medieval medical texts on drug properties, *materia medica*, and the role of the senses in the knowledge of bodies.[1]

Appended to the second editions of his *Quaestiones peripateticae* [*Peripatetic Questions*] and *Daemonum investigatio* [*Investigation on Demons*] and the first edition of *Quaestiones medicae* [*Medical Questions*], Cesalpino's pharmacological treatise has passed unnoticed among historians of early modern science, whereas his *Quaestiones peripateticae* and *Investigatio* have raised more attention.[2] Indeed, his works were first devoted to Aristotelian natural philosophy and botany. It was in a later phase that he wrote on medicine, mostly therapy. In this regard, the *Quaestiones medicae* (1593) shows his interest in disease and treatment.[3] The first part of this treatise addresses a series of questions on the efficacy of drugs and poisons, as well as the types of fevers. The second part discusses various questions, such as phlebotomy, purgative drugs, sleep, and diet. In 1601, Cesalpino published a textbook on the art of healing, the Κάτοπτρον, *sive Speculum artis medicae Hippocraticum* [*Hippocratic Mirror of the Medical Art*].[4] This treatise systematically studies the general principles of therapy, fevers, poisons, syphilis, and skin diseases, before examining diseases in the traditional order from head to toe.

Among Cesalpino's medical works, *De medicamentorum facultatibus* is particularly important in bridging his medical training with his research on botany and mineralogy, as found in *De plantis* (1583) and the subsequent *De metallicis* (1596). In *De medicamentorum facultatibus*, instead of taking the viewpoint of a naturalist, Cesalpino discussed the powers and properties of substances as a learned physician trained in Galenic medicine.[5] It was from this angle that he offered his account of the medicinal powers of bodies, that is, "faculties" in relation to their nature, as well as their modes of preparation. Cesalpino's account referred as much to the tradition of *materia medica* and pharmacology as to Aristotelian natural philosophy. For Cesalpino, defining the active powers of drugs related to the components of bodies, their modes of transformation, and their relationship with the physician's sensory experience. By examining these questions, this chapter aims to provide an outline of Cesalpino's pharmacological theory at the crossroads of ancient, medieval, and Renaissance medical philosophy.

1. The Properties of Simple Drugs

The first part of Cesalpino's *De medicamentorum facultatibus* is centered on "simple" drugs, that is, single medicinal ingredients including food, minerals, and parts of plants and animals. To present their pharmacological properties, Cesalpino embraced the ethos of Renaissance humanism by referring to the ancient medical sources that were printed in Greek and translated into Latin in the Renaissance. The main reference in pharmacology was Galen's *On Simple Drugs*.[6] Following this treatise, early physicians framed the properties of drugs according to a determined scheme: the types of drug powers or "faculties" (*facultates*) according to their nature or temperament, their material structure, and their substance. While referring to the Galenic account of simple drugs and their faculties, Cesalpino also relied on the description and classification of drugs in ancient treatises of botany and pharmacy, overall, Theophrastus's *On the Causes of Plants* and Dioscorides' *Materia medica*.

Cesalpino followed the ancient pharmacological tradition by discussing several types of faculties of drugs.[7] The first faculties of drugs came from their temperament, that is, their constitution coming from the mixture of the four primary qualities—hot, cold, dry, and moist. These qualities resulted from the proportion of the four elements that composed bodies—air, fire, water, and earth. In addition, the second faculties of drugs came from the material texture of simple drugs, for instance, soft or hard, dense or loose, rough or smooth. The third and fourth faculties of drugs were associated with their substance. While the third had the capacity to attract, digest, or glue the body parts, the fourth acted on vital organs.

Such a typology of drug properties followed the principle of "curing by contraries," which was central to Galenic medicine. In humoral medicine, the patient was attributed a certain bodily temperament that came from the proportion of qualities. When the patient was sick due to a lack or an excess of these qualities, the physician prescribed a "contrary" remedy, which had an opposite temperament. For instance, an excessively moist temperament was cured by a dry remedy, and a thick body part was healed by a thin remedy. Cesalpino adopted this Galenic framework to explain the properties of simple drugs, for instance, their cleansing, digestive, or cicatrizing powers coming from their temperament, that is, the proportion of their elemental qualities.

Cesalpino's conception of simple drugs highlighted the physician's task of determining the physical properties of bodies through the senses. To this purpose, he mostly summarized the fourth book of Galen's *On Simple Drugs* on the taste, odor, and color of drugs.[8] In his view, discussing the medicinal powers of plants, minerals, and animals required identifying their sensible properties, overall flavors, and, to a lesser extent, odors and colors. In particular, Cesalpino envisaged the list of seven flavors established by Galen and Aristotle.[9] The list comprised sweet, bitter, astringent, sour, acidic, salty, and acrid flavors. This classification was flexible as physicians tended to consider additional flavors. In this regard, Cesalpino expanded on the so-called "insipid" (*insipidus*), "fatty" (*pinguis*), and "nitrous" (*nitrosus*) flavors throughout his medical works.

It was mostly in considering the flavors of drugs that Cesalpino revealed his obedience to Aristotelian physics. Indeed, he aimed to show that the sensory properties of bodies came from the mixture of elements and qualities. Each flavor was characterized by a certain temperament, namely, a proportion of hot, cold, dry, and moist qualities, as well as a corresponding texture made of thick or thin parts. Such a framework, in turn, allowed the physician to infer the temperament and materiality of drugs through their very taste.

Remarkably, Cesalpino's gustative approach to drug powers also involved the properties related to the substance of bodies. In the Galenic tradition, drugs acting through their total substance included strong ingredients with poisonous or purgative effects. Whereas their effects were remarkable, they were difficult to explain through the action of the four qualities and were hence associated to their whole substance.[10] An influential interpretation that had emerged in the late medieval pharmacology, through works incorrectly attributed to the Persian physician Mesue (ibn Masawaiyh), was that such a substance had a celestial origin coming from their essence or "specific form."[11] Cesalpino, however, adopted a different standpoint. Whereas he related the strong properties of the total substance to the substantial form of drugs, he refuted any celestial nature for these powers. For Cesalpino, these powers came from the only material constitution and temperament of bodies, most notably, the complexity of their overall arrangement with respect to elements and qualities. This position meant that taste could be used too for assessing the properties of the total substance.[12] Such a stance about the role of the senses and the elemental nature of the total substance can be found across Cesalpino's medical works and it reflects, overall, his Aristotelian viewpoint on the nature and materiality of bodies. Following Aristotle, Cesalpino viewed drugs as tangible bodies made of elements, whose mixture defined their nature, that is, their primary and secondary qualities.

So far, we have seen that Cesalpino examined the role of the flavors to assay the constitution of simple drugs, that is their primary qualities and texture, and their related medicinal powers. Besides flavors, other sensory properties, such as odors and colors, were discussed in his pharmacology according to Galen's account in *On Simple Drugs*. Although odors did not allow the physician to fully distinguish the properties of drugs in the same way that flavors did, Cesalpino examined them for their effects on the body.[13] Along the lines of Aristotle's *De sensu*, he broadly divided odors in pleasant and unpleasant types, with each having the same categories as flavors.[14] Most importantly, for Cesalpino, some odors had medicinal properties, as testified by the fragrance of flowers, ointments, and aromatic herbs. These types of odors were characterized by the proportion of the primary qualities, which could cure the constitution of the brain and the physiological spirits. Unpleasant odors could express medicinal powers, for instance, fumigations made of mineral bodies like sulfur and mercury, whose toxicity was beforehand mitigated by a careful preparation.[15]

As for colors, they hardly provided any clear indication of temperament because of their presence in each type of constitution.[16] Still, Cesalpino considered them according to the Aristotelian account of seven colors by including white (*albus*), yellow (*flavus*), purple (*puniceus*), red (*purpureus*), green (*viridis*), blue (*cyaneus*), grey (*fuscus*), and black (*niger*).[17] Each of them encompassed countless declinations and names. If these colors did not have specific medicinal properties, Cesalpino mentioned their role in theoretical and practical medicine.[18] In this regard, the color spectrum of urine was fundamental in uroscopy for diagnosing the patient, as shown by the Byzantine physician Actuarius (*c.* 1275–*c.* 1328) in *De urinis*.[19] In addition, Galenic physiology established different types of healthy and morbid humors with corresponding colors and flavors, mostly, variations of phlegm, bile, and melancholy. Furthermore, Cesalpino, as a Peripatetic physician, referred to the Aristotelian *De coloribus* to expand on the chromatic change of bodies in the physical world.[20] According to this treatise, colors were due to the reception of light on a surface rather than the mixture of primary qualities.

In emphasizing the various flavors, colors, and odors of many ingredients, Cesalpino pointed to the need for considering a series of natural factors, from climate, soil, and time to inner transformations such as combustion and coagulation. The vegetal realm, in particular, inspired two major arguments in his explanation. The ripening of fruits—from insipid, acidic, astringent, or sour to sweet—and wine production emphasized the role of taste in assessing the powers of simple drugs. On this point, Cesalpino drew on Galen's accent on the gradual transformation of grape into verjuice, ripe grape, and wine with its residual lees and flower, as well its transformation into alcohol and vinegar. These materials were the most obvious examples of how a same body might change in taste and texture, and how this process reflected the inner alteration in its very elements and qualities.[21]

In addition to the transformation of plants, mineral and metallic bodies raised the attention of Cesalpino, especially alkaline minerals, such as potash (*lixivium*) and saltpeter (*salnitrum*), which were used as detergent and fertilizer.[22] In examining their nitrous and acrid flavors, Cesalpino envisaged the formation of oils, acids, and combustible materials, either of natural origin, such as bitumen, or obtained through the art of distillation.[23] The ways of their formation mirrored Aristotle's account of terrestrial and aerial exhalations in the *Meteorology*.[24] This question also appealed for the mineralogical theory expounded in Cesalpino's 1596 *De metallicis*, where he explained the formation and therapeutic use of numerous mineral and metallic ingredients in reference to Dioscorides' *Materia medica*. As we will see in this chapter, the strong powers of mineral and metallic drugs related to methods of drug preparation. Before examining this question, I shall now explore Cesalpino's account of compound drugs.

2. The Art of Drug Composition

Whereas a huge number of simple drugs could be used individually to cure simple diseases, Renaissance physicians and apothecaries combined simples in some cases. Usually, such compound drugs were used when the disease was complex in its symptoms or when the simple drug needed to be "corrected," that is, adjusted through a mixture with other simples. As Cesalpino underlined, the art of mixing ingredients into compound drugs was a longstanding practice among physicians, especially in Greek and Arabic pharmacy.[25] Galenic medicine celebrated theriac and mithridate as the most famous examples of how the pharmaceutical art of composition could produce powerful remedies and antidotes.[26]

Such a traditional line of thought underlay the second book of Cesalpino's *De medicamentorum facultatibus* on the properties of compound drugs.[27] The treatise was dedicated to the qualities and dosage of compounds, as well as their types of preparation. Throughout his exposition of compound drugs, Cesalpino mostly related to Galen's *On the Composition of Drugs According to Kind* and *Method of Healing*. In what follows, I examine Cesalpino's explanation of drug composition, including his general views on the mixture of their qualities and their transformation during diverse types of preparation.

Cesalpino first discussed the specificity and benefit of compound drugs in comparison with simple drugs. As he pointed out, "ostentation" (*pompa*) often motivated physicians and their rich patients to prefer sophisticated compounds based on a myriad of expensive ingredients, such as spices, gems, and precious metals. Yet, for Cesalpino, composing drugs was a useful pharmaceutical practice for therapy. According to Galen's *Method of Healing*, the art of drug composition was based on the general method of treatment, that is, on both reason and experience. Following this principle, physicians needed to determine the temperament of the patient to adjust his pharmacological treatment.[28] By combining different ingredients, they could adjust the qualitative balance of the resulting compound drug, for instance, by composing a hot and dry compound to cure a cold and moist disease.

The main simple drug, which was used as a basis (*radix*), might be mixed with additional ingredients to counterbalance its excessively strong, weak, noxious, or unpleasant nature.[29] Ingredients could also be harmonized by various types of preparation based on specific materials such as sugar and oil. One typical example came from Galen's recommendation for curing wounds.[30] While oil, wax, and verdigris as individual ingredients caused the infection of wounds, they produced an efficacious compound if mixed up into a plaster. Such a happy formula required the physician's knowledge of nature and temperament as a balanced mixture of qualities.

Compound drugs also offered the advantage of releasing the powers of their respective ingredients.[31] As Cesalpino explained, they were particularly efficacious to cure diseases with secondary infections following a certain order in their therapeutic effects. This reasoning was anchored in Galen's conception of *epikrasis*, namely the method of progressively replacing the noxious substance by a salutary one.[32] Following this method, Cesalpino expanded on the interaction of the ingredients according to their respective natures and relationships—"similar," "dissimilar," or "opposite"—in order to avoid their antagonism during their assimilation by the patient.[33] Such an approach offered the advantage of providing a progressive treatment of complex diseases with multiple causes and symptoms so to avoid the exhaustion of the patient.

For that purpose, physicians might mix similar ingredients, that is, simple drugs with the same temperament, in order to consolidate their powers or to heal several imbalanced conditions. The same reasoning went for the composition of dissimilar drugs to cure simultaneous diseases of different kinds. Opposite drugs followed the same path. As they did not act at the same time, they did not "cancel" each other. For instance, "attenuating" drugs operated before astringent drugs. It was in that very case that physicians could adjust the compound to the very constitution of the patient. Indeed, the temperament of the respective ingredients would balance and moderate each other, as Galen illustrated with the verdigris-based plaster. During this process, the respective qualities reached a medium so that the most intense qualities would be blunted.

The improvement or "correction" of drugs was another reason for combining simples. As Cesalpino noted, it was the treatise *De consolatione medicinarum* [*On the Consolation of Drugs*] attributed to Mesue that established the correction of drugs, yet only in the case of purgatives.[34] From this, Cesalpino set up six ways of correcting drugs. The first two ways consisted of correcting ingredients whose qualities were excessively strong or week. In this regard, the strengthening of drugs should follow the rule of affinity (*affinitas*), in reference to Pseudo-Mesue. For instance, agaric was corrected by ginger, aloe by cinnamon, and more broadly, by using sharp drugs with a hot and thin texture. The third way consisted of taming toxic ingredients, such as scammony. The fourth way aimed to improve the sensory features of drugs in order to make them more appealing, such as enhancing their taste by means of sugar, honey and wine, their color, and smell. The fifth way consisted of preparing the ingredient to facilitate its ingestion or application, for instance, through a mixture with a greasy substance in the case of ointments or with a beverage in the case of potions. The sixth way aimed to preserve drugs through a series of preparations within vinegar, salt, honey, and sugar, in the forms of preserves, electuaries, and syrups.[35]

While each of the ingredients of compounds acted with their own timing, they were also efficacious due to their mixing with other ingredients. In this regard, the powers of the total substance were typical of sophisticated compound drugs as they stemmed from the balance of all their ingredients. For instance, Cesalpino explained, theriac and antidotes were powerful because of their many ingredients, whose powers were slightly transformed by their mutual mixture. While their most toxic ingredients were tamed, the others retained some of their powers within the compound. This explained the efficacy of the compound to repel numerous ailments without injuring the patient.[36]

In order to combine simples in a way that would be efficient and safe, the constitution of each simple, in particular the intensity of its primary qualities, needed to be considered too. As Cesalpino pointed out, Galen and Dioscorides both emphasized that each quality could be either obscure, manifest, intense, or extreme to the senses. But it was the medieval Arabic-Latin texts provided by Al-Kindi, Averroes, and Arnald of Villanova that expounded on these levels of intensity, according to a gradual scale.[37] Following their views, Cesalpino comprised the level of intensity of each quality in a declination of four degrees, which the medical tradition called the "latitude" of temperament. His appraisal of the conception of degrees followed the idea that the qualities of bodies were relative to a scale between two extremes (hot and cold). Such a scale involved Galen's idea of a latitude of qualities through four degrees. Each degree corresponded to sensible variations that the human body could perceive, from almost imperceptible (first degree), to moderate (second degree), to harmful (third degree), to corrupted (fourth degree). Following this reasoning, Cesalpino established a latitude of eight parts between the extreme degrees of qualities, whose middle point (*medium*) was a temperate state.[38]

The knowledge of temperament and qualitative degrees was also important in the order of combination of simple drugs. Ingredients with the same qualities and similar degrees should be combined first.[39] Most importantly, the dosage of simple drugs within compounds should be smaller so to avoid toxic dosage of drugs with similar temperament and effects, especially in the case of psychoactive drugs and purgatives.[40] For instance, a purgative compound with cassia (whose dosage was twelve drachms) and rhubarb (whose dosage was two drachms) should combine six drachms of cassia with one drachm of rhubarb. The combination of simples with other ingredients was also an important aspect of their preparation, which Cesalpino expounded in a series of dedicated chapters.

3. The Types of Preparation

The last part of Cesalpino's book on compound drugs addressed a series of preparations that aimed to cleanse or transform the initial components. These included two main processes: filtration ("separation") and transformation ("alteration").[41]

The preparation of drugs by separation aimed to separate their "earthy," that is, their consistent part through washing or extraction. Washing (*ablutio*) removed the useless parts of an ingredient, for instance, ash from a burnt substance, fat from a greasy substance, or sand from minerals, in order to keep its main part and retain its powers. The typical ingredients subject to washing were hot and dry, with an acrid, bitter, or salty flavor. The resulting drug was more temperate, with a thicker and colder nature, since its thinner and hotter part remained in the washing liquid. Another type of separation included the extraction (*extractio*) of juices and oils from fruits, herbs, bulbs, and gums. Pressed oil was typically used for healing wounds through plasters and poultices, and to cure dry throat through "eclegmas."

Alteration aimed to transform the powers of drugs by fire through two main processes: decoction (*decoctio*) and distillation (*distillatio*).[42] As Cesalpino explained, decoction in water, called *elixatio* (boiling), liquefied substances by loosening their parts. In the process, some powers disappeared, such as purgative properties and smell, while other remained, such as astringent properties.[43] The transformation of drugs by decoction also depended on the duration and the intensity of the fire. Mild decoctions included using a bain-marie (*in balneo*) and steam (*vapor*).

Preparation by alteration could also consist of cooking simple drugs with additional ingredients into liquid (rob, syrup, julep) or solid drugs (lozenges, pills).[44] For instance, syrups were made of an ingredient cooked with sugar or honey, robs through the cooking of fruit juice. These sweet ingredients offered the advantage to thicken these drugs and soften their powers, as well as to improve their taste and prolong their preservation time. Otherwise, simple drugs could be cooked with non-sweet substances. In this regard, purgatives like hellebore required slow cooking in combination with mastic in order to preserve their medicinal powers.[45]

Distillation both transformed and separated drugs. Cesalpino called "distillation" (*distillatio*) the separation of liquor, and "sublimation" (*sublimation*) the separation of a dry exhalation from a substance.[46] It was through these specific processes that Cesalpino expressed his position toward alchemy. In his view, alchemists (*chimisti*) considered distillation a technical art capable of purifying the elements of bodies in order to prevent them from putrefying, a phenomenon that had been confirmed by the conservation of distilled waters. Such a process, Cesalpino went on, aimed to obtain liquors, powders, and "ashes," as well as to introduce a golden or silver tincture into metals for their transmutation. As Cesalpino deplored, alchemists attempted to apply this process to medicine through the making of elixir and quintessence. Whereas he considered these materials as vain panaceas, he still proposed to examine what was useful for pharmacy in the alchemical art.[47]

Along the lines of the physicians and naturalists of his time, Cesalpino was attentive to the nature of the different phases of distillation. First, he noted, a thin part, made of air and water, evaporated, then thicker parts made of earth were separated under a longer and more intense fire. In the case of wine, the distilled liquor was a thin and airy, highly combustible, substance, namely *aqua ardens* (brandy). The residues of the distilled material provided a liquor made of earth and fire, whose caustic powers were comparable to lime. From this account, we see that Cesalpino considered the phases of distillation according to the Aristotelian physics of elements and qualities, rather than the alchemical notions of mercury, sulfur, and salt that were proposed by followers of Paracelsus.[48]

For Cesalpino, the first liquor extracted by distillation had medicinal properties because of its spirituous and fragrant substance. Made of very thin parts, it could easily penetrate the body and revive its physiological spirits, which had the same subtle constitution.[49] Distilled rose water was an example of aqueous humor with some aerial fragrant part. Cesalpino explained the formation of distilled waters through the case of cinnamon: its fragrant and fiery part was extracted in the form of an ascending vapor in the upper part of the cucurbit, which condensed into water by cooling down in the alembic.

The oil coming from the second phase of distillation was more difficult to execute. It came from the separation of an aerial and viscous part that surfaced from water, in the example of the distilled oil of lavender seeds and anise. As Cesalpino noted, distilled oils were thinner and hotter than pressed oils. He also specified that pressed oils could be distilled but needed to be mingled with pieces of marble, glass, or sand in the cucurbit, to regulate the process of boiling. Following Pseudo-Mesue, he added the example of distilled oil of tiles (a similar material to oil of bricks), whose acrid substance was comparable to naphtha. Bitumen as well as resinous materials such as amber, pitch, and myrrh were also involved in the distillation of oils.[50]

Overall, Cesalpino's discussion on distillation reflected the common knowledge of plant distillation (flowers, woods, and seeds) for pharmaceutical purposes.[51] What was at stake was the possible preservation of sensory properties in distilled waters and oils. For instance, roses, lavender seeds, and cinnamon provided fragrant distillates that could heal the bodily spirits. In addition, distilled oils such as balsam were prescribed for their fatty and hot properties calming neuro-inflammation. The distilled waters of plants retained the powers of their initial ingredients only if they preserved their aerial part, which was responsible for their fragrant or acrid properties, or their aqueous part. The aerial substance could easily disappear during distillation, and hence it was required to heat up materials in a bain-marie. Cesalpino found distilled waters better to cure putrid fevers than decoctions and juices, because of their incorruptible nature. Distilling waters also offered the advantage of removing the astringent properties of plants, which remained in the thick part of the plant. At any rate, the distillation apparatus should be devoid of lead vessels, which would imbue distilled waters with a toxic led-based substance in the example of ceruse. Moreover, "circulatory" vessels (pelicans) could also be used to extract thicker waters within a single crucible through the circulation of steam.[52]

Outside of plants, minerals, such as alum, chalcanthite, and antimony, also provided medicinal waters and oils extracted by distillation. Indeed, mineral and metallic materials produced an acrid water as well as a thick liquor under a strong fire. Such distillates required special apparatus: namely, small glass cucurbits buried in mud to support a long fire, whose fumes descended into larger vessels. From a therapeutic angle, metallic distillates provided caustic oils that were useful to halt gangrene.[53] Nonetheless, Cesalpino insisted that most of the time plant decoctions and juices were enough to cure diseases.[54]

Not only did minerals provide distilled waters and oils, they also supplied powders and salts through the alchemical process of sublimation.[55] As Cesalpino explained, sublimation consisted of extracting dry exhalations in the form of some "ashes," namely transforming solid materials into fumes. This process was immediately followed by their condensation into a whitish powder as they cooled down on the lid of the crucible. According to Cesalpino, sublimation had been known since Dioscorides, who mentioned the processing of pitch and resin ashes, as well as burnt pyrites.[56] Indeed, sublimation allowed to obtain the dry and earthy part of materials. Their exhalation (fumes) cooled down into some earthy substance with hot and bitter properties, which had been observed since Galen. In the case of silver and bronze, the earthy substance ascended in the form of yellowish or white slags (*cadmia*) on the upper side of the oven. These slags, in turn, were the basis for making pompholyx and spodium, whose washing would leave out their caustic properties and allowed physicians to use them safely as desiccants.[57]

Sublimation could also be used for softening the toxic powers of sulfur, orpiment, and quicksilver.[58] For instance, quicksilver could be sublimed with sal ammoniac into a "sugar" (*saccharum*) called "sublimate" (*sublimatum*), that is, mercury bichloride. In late Renaissance medicine, such "corrosive sublimate" was used as a "caustic" topical remedy to cure wounds. For Cesalpino, these properties were due to its very hot and thin properties. Orpiment could also be sublimed as realgar into some white arsenic, with a translucent and crystalline texture. As for sulfur, it could be sublimed with quicksilver into cinnabar (mercury sulfide), a corrosive substance. In sum, for Cesalpino, sublimation offered the advantage of separating the exhalations of materials by increasing the degree of their heat, hence producing caustic drugs.[59] Following Galen, he broadly agreed on the preparation by fire (per ignem) as a way to improve certain ingredients by giving them new properties and by taming their strength and taste with a view of further medicinal preparations.[60]

4. Conclusion

Cesalpino's discussion of drug properties provides a striking example of how late Renaissance medical humanism was applied to pharmacology. At first, his discussion on the "faculties" of drugs confirms the appeal for the ancient Greek sources of pharmacology, overall, Galen. Nonetheless, Cesalpino's exposition of compound drugs also reveals his deep interest in medieval medicine. He was aware of the critical reception of the scholastic framework of pharmacological degrees in his own time. Nonetheless, Cesalpino believed the discussion necessary given the difficulty of predicting the qualities of compound drugs. In this way, he proved that the authority of Arabic–Latin texts was still strong in late sixteenth-century pharmacology.

In addition, Cesalpino discussed the art of separating body parts by the fire, that is, alchemy. Whereas he considered as vain the promises of immortality brought by medicinal elixir and quintessence, he acknowledged the usefulness of distillation and sublimation for drug making. For Cesalpino, distillation pointed to the relationship between the three phases of bodies and the "faculties" that he put forward in the first part of his treatise on simple drugs: elemental qualities, texture, and sensory properties. Following the Aristotelian physics of elements and qualities, the aqueous phase of distillation consisted of an aerial and thin body, the solid phase corresponded to a terrestrial and thick body, and the oily phase was a hot and thin body.

Within this Galenic and Aristotelian frameworks, Cesalpino put forward the role of the senses to appraise the active powers of drugs. Indeed, it was according to the sensorial world of physicians and botanists, namely in relation to taste, odor, and color, that he framed the types of physical and medicinal qualities. However, whereas it would be tempting to recollect a definite set of qualities for each medicinal ingredient, Cesalpino's treatise suggested the opposite reasoning for its in-depth discussion of their possible variations depending on their provenance or type of transformation. Beyond the extended classifications that existed in both pharmacological and botanical literature, Cesalpino blurred the boundaries between medicinal, physical, and sensible properties by taking the example of a select number of substances from vegetal, mineral, and (more rarely) animal realms. Similarly, his discussion of the theoretical models for the composition of simple drugs emphasized the tension between the qualitative approach to bodies in view of their infinite variety within nature.

Notes

1 Andrea Cesalpino, *De medicamentorum facultatibus libri duo* (Venice: Giunta, 1593), fols. 242r–291v. I will refer to this treatise as *DMF* in the subsequent notes.
2 See for instance Andrea Strazzoni, "Cesalpino, Andrea," in *Encyclopedia of Renaissance Philosophy*, ed. Marco Sgarbi (Cham: Springer, 2022), 1:689–91; Carlo Colombero, "Andrea Cesalpino e la polemica anti-Aristotelica e anti-Spinoziana," *Rivista Critica di Storia della Filosofia* 35 (1980): 343–56; Mark E. Clark and Kirk Summers, "Hippocratic Medicine and Aristotelian Science in the *Daemonum investigatio peripatetica* of Andrea Cesalpino," *Bulletin of the History of Medicine* 69, no. 4 (1995): 527–41.
3 Andrea Cesalpino, *Quaestionum medicarum libri duo* (Venice: Giunta, 1593), fols. 170r–241v.
4 This treatise was also published as *Praxis universae artis medicae* [*Practice of the Whole Medical Art*], a systematic study on disease and treatment, which was reprinted in 1602-6, 1666, and 1670. On this text, see R. Allen Shotwell's contribution to this volume.
5 On Cesalpino's pharmacological theory, see Frederick W. Gibbs, *Poison, Medicine, and Disease in Late Medieval and Early Modern Europe* (New York: Routledge, 2019), 208–9. On his botanical works, see Brian W. Ogilvie, *The Science of Describing: Natural History in Renaissance Europe* (Chicago: Chicago University Press, 2006), 223–6. See also Fabrizio Baldassarri's, and Quentin Hiernaux's and Corentin Tresnie's contributions to this volume.
6 Galen, *De simplicium medicamentorum temperamentis et facultatibus*, 11:379–892K, 12:1–377K.
7 Cesalpino, *DMF*, fol. 242r: "Cum autem facultates vel in primis qualitatibus consistant, ut calefaciendi, refrigerandi, humectandi, et siccandi; vel in secundis, ut emolliendi, indurandi, rarefaciendi, condensandi, et aliis huiusmodi; vel in tertiis, ut glutinandi, concoquendi, abstergendi, repellendi, et tandem quae opera magis particularia et partes peculiares respiciunt, quae inter quartas facultates recenseri possunt, ut gignendi lac, et semen, ex obstruendi, hepar, lienem: aut roborandi cor, cerebrum, ventriculum, unde hepatica medicamenta, cephalica, stomachica, cordialia, et alia huiusmodi dicuntur."
8 Galen, *De simplicium medicamentorum temperamentis et facultatibus* 4.1–23 (11:619–703K).
9 See Galen, *De simplicium medicamentorum temperamentis et facultatibus* 4.1–4.13 (11:619–62K); Aristotle, *Sens.* 4.442a15–20.
10 See Linda Deer Richardson, "The Generation of Disease: Occult Causes and Diseases of the 'Total Substance,'" in *The Medical Renaissance of the Sixteenth Century*, ed. Andrew Wear, Roger K. French, and Iain M. Lonie (Cambridge: Cambridge University Press, 1985), 175–94; Gibbs, *Poison, Medicine, and Disease*, 195–204.
11 Pseudo-Mesue, *De consolatione et electione simplicium medicinarum, seu Canones universales*, 1.1, in *Opera omnia* (Venice: Valgrisi, 1562), fol. 2r. Paula De Vos, *Compound Remedies: Galenic Pharmacy from the Ancient Mediterranean to New*

Spain (Pittsburgh: University of Pittsburgh Press, 2021), 71–8. On Pseudo-Mesue, see also Dag Nikolaus Hasse, *Success and Suppression: Arabic Sciences and Philosophy in the Renaissance* (Cambridge : London, 2016), 10, 391–6.

12 Cesalpino, *DMF*, fol. 243r: "Soli autem sapores certius et propinquius non solum temperamentum ostendunt in calido frigido humido et sicco sed et reliquas facultates longe efficaciores tum ad morbos gignendos, tum sanandos."
13 Ibid., fols. 255v–260r.
14 Aristotle, *Sens.* 5.443b19–444a8.
15 Cesalpino, *DMF*, fol. 260r: "Alii ad morbum gallicum suffumigia parant sudatoria ex cinnabrio factitio, quod ex argento vivo et sulphure fit, quamvis genere sit deleterium. Praeparatio enim vitia corrigit."
16 Ibid., fols. 260v–261r: "Ex coloribus incertam esse temperamenti significationem … quod in unoquoque colore et calida et frigida et humida et sicca reperiuntur."
17 Ibid., fols. 261r–266r.
18 Ibid., fol. 261r: "Scientiam de coloribus in medicina ad multa alia utilem habebimus. Quod tanto libentius efficiam, quanto ab aliis hanc partem alioqui difficillimam, minus elaboratam perspicio."
19 See for instance Cesalpino, *DMF*, fol. 261r: "Albi igitur differentiae sex notantur ab Actuario in urinis: chrystalleus, niveus, aqueus, lacteus, glaucus, et charopus."
20 Ibid., fols. 263v–264v.
21 Ibid., fols. 249r–250r.
22 Ibid., fols. 252v–254v.
23 Ibid., fol. 253r: "Nitrosum iure in medio est; nam non omnino eius salsugo ab exhalatione combustibili absolvitur, ut patet in terrae salsugine, ex qua salnitrum extrahitur, ardet enim. Reliqua tamen genera nitri ad naturam salis magis accedunt, nam et inodora sunt et sine pinguedine, at carent astrictione."
24 See Aristotle, *Mete.* 1.4.341b6–18.
25 Cesalpino, *DMF*, fols. 267v–268r: "Quod si compositiones a clarissimis medicis non sine ratione excogitatas esse credendum est. Celebrantur enim a Galeno innumerae et a se inventae et ab antiquioribus. Arabes quoque multas in usum invexerunt, quibus frequenter hodie utimur felicissimo successu."
26 On theriac and mithridate in early modern medicine, see Alisha Rankin, *The Poison Trials: Wonder Drugs, Experiment, and the Battle for Authority in Renaissance Science* (Chicago: University of Chicago Press, 2021), 23–50.
27 See Cesalpino, *DMF*, fols. 266v–291v.
28 Galen, *Methodus medendi* 2.3 (10:85–93K).
29 Cesalpino, *DMF*, fols. 269v–271r.
30 Galen, *De compositione medicatorum per genera* 1.1 (13:362–67K); Galen, *Methodus medendi* 3.2 (10:162–73K).
31 Cesalpino, *DMF*, fols. 268r–269v.
32 Galen, *Methodus medendi* 9.10 (10:635–40K).
33 Cesalpino, *DMF*, fol. 268v: "Si igitur similes fuerint affectus, similia videntur exposcere remedia, si dissimiles dissimilia, si contrarii etiam contraria, seu plures morbi, seu plures causae, seu symptomata affuerint, quae sigillatim remedia exposcant, unde compositio tum similium, tum dissimilium, aut contrariorum necessaria esse videtur."
34 Pseudo-Mesue, *De consolatione*, fols. 1v–44r; De Vos, *Compound Remedies*, 91–8; Cesalpino, *DMF*, fol. 269v: "De hac re diligentissime egit Mesues … at solum de medicamentis purgantibus locutus est."

35 Ibid., fols. 269v–271r.
36 Ibid., fol. 269v: "Fieri tamen posse credendum est, ut etiam mixtum ratione componentium agat eas operationes, quae non ratione primarum qualitatum, sed secundarum et sequentium, et quae a tota substantia dicuntur, fiunt. Cum enim in mixtione non corrumpantur miscibilia, sed alterentur tantum, multas facultates eorum servari credendum est, quae permanent integra, cum praesertim ars non perfecte misceat. Sic theriacae compositio extat remedium ad omnia venena, quia in ea acervata sunt omnia, quae ad singula faciunt. Huiusmodi sunt et alia antidota a Graecis Polychresta appellata, quia ad diversos usu accommodantur propter multorum simplicium receptionem."
37 Michael McVaugh, "The Development of Medieval Pharmaceutical Theory," in *Arnaldi de Villanova Opera medica omnia II: Aphorismi de gradibus*, ed. Michael R. McVaugh (Barcelona: Universidad de Barcelona, 1981), 1–136.
38 Cesalpino, *DMF*, fol. 272r: "In intermedia autem latitudine variam ubique proportionem esse caliditatis et frigiditatis, unde gradus praedicti oriuntur …. Appellant autem medici principium medium et finem cuiusque gradus."
39 Ibid., fols. 281v–282r.
40 Ibid., fols. 282r–283v.
41 Ibid., fols. 283r–284r.
42 Ibid., fol. 284v: "Alii porro sunt modi separationis per decoctionem, et distillationem, seu sublimationem, qui non sine manifesta alteratione per ignem perficiuntur."
43 Ibid., fols. 284v–285v.
44 Ibid., fols. 285v–286r.
45 Ibid., fol. 286r: "Quidam eo artificio ex radicibus ellebori nigri succum extrahunt, qui ciceris magnitudine haustus addito mastiche purgat sine noxa."
46 Ibid., fols. 286r–287v.
47 Ibid., fol. 286v: "Laticem suum celebrantes immunem ab omni putredine, qui elixir ab ipsis vocatur, et quinta essentia, ad omnes morbos etiam incurabiles, ut promittunt, sanandos. Sed videamus quid in distillatione et sublimatione medicamenta patiantur; hinc enim patere possit, quae utilitas ex hac arte in medicina praestetur."
48 On the development of alchemy in early modern Italy, see Antonio Clericuzio, "Chemical Medicine and Paracelsianism in Italy, 1550–1650," in *The Practice of Reform in Health, Medicine, and Science, 1500–2000*, ed. Margaret Pelling and Scott Mandelbrote (London: Routledge, 2005), 59–79.
49 Cesalpino, *DMF*, fol. 286v: "Solus igitur primus liquor retinet vini aliquas facultates, spirituosam scilicet substantiam odoratam a reliquo corpore separatam, quae multas utilitates affere potest. Nam citissime omnium pervadit ad intima corporis, substantia affinis naturae humanae spiritus reficiens et calefaciens, non tamen relinquens impressionem caliditatis ob maximam tenuitatem."
50 Ibid., fol. 287r: "Mesues docet ex oleo communi, quod ab ignitis laterculis, cum in eo extinguuntur, absorbetur, deinde confractis iisdem et in distillatorio conditis, acerrimam substantiam elicere aequipollentem naphtae. Sunt qui ex lapidibus bituminosis et ex electro sine ulla admixtione simile oleum eliciant."
51 Ibid., fols. 287v–288v.
52 Ibid., fol. 288r: "Species quaedam distillationis est, cum aqua non in aliud vas recipiens colligitur, sed iterum descendit, unde egressa est, ac veluti per circulum saepius ascendit ac descendit, in qua operatione solvuntur magis partes corporis in liquorem crassiorem veluti succum."

53 Ibid., fol. 288r: "Ex chalcantho privatim id genus olei quaeritur, causticum ad gangraenas sistendas; audent quidam etiam intus exhibere guttam unam aut duas cum iusculo ad putredines internas malignas in peste."
54 Ibid., fol. 288r: "Ex quibus colligere licet, si quis egeat omnibus facultatibus, quae in medicamento sunt, nequaquam ei opus esse distillatis uti, sed longe melior erit succus aut decoctio."
55 Ibid., fols. 288v–289r.
56 Ibid., fol. 288v: "Nam in fornacibus, quibus excoquitur aes aut argentum, corpuscula ascendunt non nigra ut resinis, sed luteo colore, aut candicante, aut vario. Haec superioribus fornacis lateribus cohaerentia concrescunt in cadmiam: similiter ex pyrite usto gignitur, ut testatur Dioscorides." Dioscorides, *Materia medica* 5.75.
57 Cesalpino, *DMF*, fol. 288v: "Ex cadmia vero sola aut cum aere sublimata fit pompolyx et spodium. … Quae omnia corpora terrea sunt, caliditatem quandam ex ustione retinentia, sed si abluantur, illam exuunt, et siccant sine morsu."
58 Ibid., fols. 289r–290r.
59 Ibid., fol. 289r: "Sublimatio igitur corporum separat partes exhalabiles, attenuat, et caliditatem auget. Quod si haec fiat per combustionem, immutat naturam corporum in terream substantiam cum quodam ignis vestigio."
60 Ibid., fol. 289r–289v: "Respondet Galenus in libro de Theriaca ad Pisonem in confectione salis theriaci multa ignis commercio reddi meliora, cum latens ipsorum natura in apertum editur. Nonnulla etiam ad quem volumus usum commoda reddi. Quod hinc patet. Nonnulla enim vires novas per ignem acquirunt. … Nonnulla per ignem mitiora sunt et sic usui magis commoda. … Acria omnia per ustionem acrimoniam deponere ac mitescere."; Pseudo-Galen, *De theriaca ad Pisonem* 18 (14:287–90K).

Bibliography

Primary Sources

Cesalpino, Andrea. *De medicamentorum facultatibus libri duo*. Venice: Giunta, 1593.
Cesalpino, Andrea. *Praxis universae Artis medicae*. Treviso: Deuchino 1606.
Cesalpino, Andrea. *Quaestionum medicarum libri II*. Venice: Giunta, 1593.
Dioscorides. *De materia medica libri quinque*, edited by Max Wellmann. 3 vols. Berlin: Weidmann, 1906–14.
Galen. *Opera omnia*, edited by Karl Gottlob Kühn. 20 vols. Leipzig: Karl Knobloch, 1821–33.
Pseudo-Mesue. *Opera omnia*. Venice: Valgrisi, 1562.

Secondary Sources

Clark, Mark E., and Kirk M. Summers. "Hippocratic Medicine and Aristotelian Science in the *Daemonum investigatio peripatetica* of Andrea Cesalpino." *Bulletin of the History of Medicine* 69, no. 4 (1995): 527–41.
Clericuzio, Antonio. "Chemical Medicine and Paracelsianism in Italy, 1550–1650." In *The Practice of Reform in Health, Medicine, and Science, 1500–2000*, edited by Margaret Pelling and Scott Mandelbrote, 59–79. London: Routledge, 2005.

Colombero, Carlo. "Andrea Cesalpino e la polemica anti-aristotelica e anti-spinoziana." *Rivista critica di storia della filosofia* 35, no. 4 (1980): 343–56.

Deer Richardson, Linda. "The Generation of Disease: Occult Causes and Diseases of the 'Total Substance'." In *The Medical Renaissance of the Sixteenth Century*, edited by Andrew Wear, Roger French, and Iain Lonie, 175–94. Cambridge: Cambridge University Press, 1985.

De Vos, Paula. *Compound Remedies: Galenic Pharmacy from the Ancient Mediterranean to New Spain*. Pittsburgh: University of Pittsburgh Press, 2021.

Gibbs, Frederick W. *Poison, Medicine, and Disease in Late Medieval and Early Modern Europe*. New York: Routledge, 2019.

Hasse, Dag Nikolaus. *Success and Suppression: Arabic Sciences and Philosophy in the Renaissance*. Cambridge, MA: Harvard University Press, 2016.

McVaugh, Michael. "The Development of Medieval Pharmaceutical Theory." In *Arnaldi de Villanova Opera medica omnia II: Aphorismi de gradibus*, edited by Michael R. McVaugh, 1–136. Barcelona: Universidad de Barcelona, 1981.

Ogilvie, Brian W. *The Science of Describing: Natural History in Renaissance Europe*. Chicago: University of Chicago Press, 2006.

Rankin, Alisha. *The Poison Trials: Wonder Drugs, Experiment, and the Battle for Authority in Renaissance Science*. Chicago: University of Chicago Press, 2021.

Strazzoni, Andrea. "Cesalpino, Andrea." In *Encyclopedia of Renaissance Philosophy*, edited by Marco Sgarbi, 1: 689–91. Cham: Springer, 2022.

13

Cesalpino's Theory of Disease: *De morbo gallico* in Context

Carmen Schmechel

Cesalpino dedicates a good part of the fourth book of his *Artis medicae pars prima* (1602) to the French disease, or "morbus gallicus."[1] His treatise comes after more than a century of confronting this disease in the European realm. After its appearance in 1495, a multitude of medical treatises had grappled with issues of the origin of the disease as well as with proposed treatments, ancient and newer (including chymical) ones. By the time Cesalpino enters the stage, the number of existing volumes, as Jon Arrizabalaga notes, "may have reached two hundred or more."[2] Among the most prominent writers one may count Niccolò Leoniceno (1428–1524), Girolamo Fracastoro (1479–1553), Giambattista Da Monte (1498–1551), Girolamo Cardano (1501–76), and Gabriele Falloppio (1523–62).

Cesalpino's own account eclectically but harmoniously reunites characteristics of the Galenic medical tradition with newer recommendations and remedies, including some that were seen as alchemical. Mostly, Cesalpino relies on ancient authorities: the Hippocratic corpus, Aristotle, and above all Galen. Occasionally he also veers into more modern territory including by supporting tenets that were popular with more chymically minded physicians. In his treatment of the topic of French disease, rather than defending one school of medical thought over another, as was typical of many of his predecessors, Cesalpino presents treatments and remedies side by side—be they Galenic, or from the Latin tradition, or the Arabic one—often with a sobering account of their side effects.

This chapter will highlight the intellectual lineage of some of his positions with regard to etiology, manner of contagion, and treatment including remedies.

1. Causes: Putrefaction, Heat, and Contagion

Cesalpino opens his treatise by saying that the cause of this disease is difficult to know, implying that a proper treatment of the disease presupposes a correct knowledge of its causes[3]—one of the main pillars on which university-educated physicians based their authority.[4] Cesalpino here adheres to a strand of "rational medicine," whose philosophical underpinnings he had laid out in the *Quaestiones medicae* almost a decade earlier.

Cesalpino notes that the disease is acquired either by a venereal or another kind of contact,[5] such as "sometimes through the breasts in the case of lactating infants, or through the whole body in the case of those who sleep in the same bed, sometimes merely through the bedsheets, such as happens in the case of itches."[6] His description is virtually identical to that of predecessors such as Sebastiano dell'Aquila (1440–1510), Gaspar Torrella (1452–1520), or Giambattista Da Monte.[7] With Girolamo Fracastoro's *De contagione* (1546),[8] Cesalpino's account shares the first two pathways: by direct contact and by fomites (contaminated linen cloth or bedsheets).[9] Regarding the third pathway proposed by Fracastoro—"at a distance"—while Cesalpino admits its possibility, he differs from Fracastoro substantially on the presupposition of physical, material seeds of disease as agents of contagion.[10] For Cesalpino, just as for Fracastoro's contemporary Da Monte, there is no need for such seeds in order to explain the transmission of disease. Putrefaction, along with the idea that this putrefaction can be "transmitted," is enough to explain contagion.

Let us now take a look at Cesalpino's description of putrefaction causing disease. He wrote:

> The contagium indicates putrefaction, that is, the external heat in putrefying matter, [which matter is] obstinate, so that it is not easy to remove. Therefore it excites a putrefaction similar to itself in another, not in the spiritous substance, because it does not travel far off, nor in the thin humors, because it is not communicated quickly ... but in the thick and especially the phlegmatic ones. The proof being the mucous substance emerging from the pustules, ulcers, boils. ... But seeing that it corrupts, it must be in excess: because it is due to excess that the corruption of primary qualities ensues.[11]

For Cesalpino, the close relationship between contagion and putrefaction is made possible by the external heat in the putrefying matter. The result of the process of contagion is negotiated—in an Aristotelian manner—between the strength and obstinacy of this putrid external heat, and the strength of the target body's own innate heat.

Because succumbing to contagion is a result of the external heat overcoming the innate heat, a brief review of Cesalpino's views on innate heat seems in order. These are revealed in the *Liber primus* of the *Ars medica* and seem based on Hippocratic and Aristotelian ideas current at the time. But they also resonate with a more recent reworking of these ancient ideas in a Renaissance Platonist vein, wherein the innate heat is not related to elemental fire but is an immortal spirit propagated from the heart and corresponding to the element of the stars. Cesalpino argues for the centrality of the heart as the repository of vital heat: "The heart ... just like the sun, disperses its vital heat, in the manner of light, throughout the whole body;"[12] the innate heat is "the instrument of the soul which is closest to it [to the soul]."[13] Cesalpino also quotes a well-known passage from the beginning of the Hippocratic treatise *On Fleshes*: "that which we call Heat, is immortal."[14] This passage had also been taken up by Cardano in *De subtilitate*, as well as by the renowned sixteenth-century physician Jean Fernel (1497–1558), whose Book 4 of *Physiologia* is entirely dedicated to the topic of innate heat; in both of their interpretations, this heat had a celestial source.[15]

The other strand of argumentation is based on a famous Aristotelian reference to the innate heat present in the semen as being analogous with the stars[16] (often coupled with a pronouncement from his *Physics* that "a man owes his birth to another man and to the sun.")[17] This source had been used by Fernel in *De abditis rerum causis*, to prove the celestial nature of innate heat[18]; Fernel explicitly contradicted an understanding of Aristotle's claim as an analogy[19] between the innate heat and the celestial one (which seems supported by Aristotle's own wording, ἀνάλογος), arguing that instead our innate heat is "celestial and manifestly divine."[20] Cesalpino's interpretation likewise implies the celestial and divine nature of innate heat, not by analogy but, as it seems, literally: "If indeed we are to consider innate heat, we perceive a most noble celestial portion in it."[21] By "portion" Cesalpino could mean that a part of the total quantity of innate heat would be "celestial."[22] This heat enacts not an elemental, but a celestial concoction which causes the growth of the sublunar body. It seems to me that this interpretation implies a Platonized Aristotle, a perspective which seems to have gained more favor with Cesalpino in his later years.[23] Moreover, this perspective seems to find further support when Cesalpino states that "there is something divine in diseases."[24] This is another (fortuitous or not) convergence with Fernel, who had repeatedly addressed "something divine in diseases" in his *De abditis rerum causis*, backing up the idea with a reference to the Hippocratic *On the Sacred Disease*[25] which Fernel reinterpreted to highlight the "divine." It is hence arguable that Cesalpino's ideas on vital heat resonate with a Platonized version of Hippocratic and Aristotelian views, a position not uncommon in his time.

2. The "tota substantia" Theory of Disease in Cesalpino's Predecessors

Possibly one of the ideas most rife with potential for disagreement among early modern physicians was the theory that some diseases could be understood as arising from the "whole substance," based on a reworking of Galen's theory of "change through the whole substance"[26] (καθ' ὅλην τὴν οὐσίαν, which in the Latin West became *tota substantia*). Galen had advanced a hypothesis for how a very small quantity of a poison may infect a much larger body; to account for the discrepancy, he argued that these are cases where the "whole substance" of the target body becomes vitiated. In the sixteenth century, in part, this theory promised remedies of a new type (antidotes) for a challenging disease; in part it resonated with the emerging concept of specific disease ontology. But the vicinity of this explanation with occult causes, possibly evoking alchemy, was not equally palatable for physicians of different philosophical convictions.

Cesalpino's own stance toward whole substance was multi-faceted. Some of Cesalpino's predecessors, and their own understanding of the *morbus gallicus* as a disease of whole substance, provide an effective foil against which Cesalpino's ideas may be understood. I argue that while writers such as Da Monte, Fernel, and Falloppio all adhere rather wholeheartedly to the idea of the French disease being a disease of whole substance, Cesalpino distances himself from them by proposing his own phenomenology of whole substance processes.

Da Monte, for instance, defines the French disease as a "bad distemper, hot and dry, in the liver, acquired by contagion,"[27] whose powerful drying effect is similar to that of preternatural heat.[28] He writes: "from those emanates a poison, in which a bad and venomous quality exists."[29] Thus it is a *venomous quality*, inherent in the poison that emanates from the infected person. Here, Da Monte proposed a place for an "occult" agency. When explaining how this disease adheres to the inner parts of the body and how it spreads within it, he claims that there is a double path: one related to manifest qualities, the other to an occult property (*a proprietate occulta*).[30]

The doctrine of "manifest qualities" was Aristotelian and had been the standard in traditional medical thought. But the *proprietas occulta* rested on an interpretation of on Galen,[31] to whose authority Da Monte referred, concluding that "when an affect is impressed equally within the whole body, then the natural principle is vitiated."[32] He explains the process thus:

> Hence it is no wonder that sometimes from one small pustule of scabies the whole body is infected. It should similarly not be surprising that from a small pustule or sore of this poisonous disease, the whole [body] becomes infected. Indeed if the liver is infected, which is the principal limb that serves everything else, when it has been infected, all else necessarily deteriorates. And thus declares Galen in book 6 of *De locis affectis*, that a little bit of the scorpion's poison, impressed upon any part, immediately reaches the heart or the brain, where he recounts of someone who was seen to have become cold from the scorpion's bite as if very cold water had been poured on his head. And it appears to be like a kind of spiritual power, just as with opium. Because a small quality [sic] of opium can make the whole mass of blood turn cold.[33]

Galen's theory, developed in regard to *pharmaka*, had become widely adopted in the Renaissance and after, for describing infectious disease. One strand of this adoption came from Avicenna, who in his *Canon of Medicine* had discussed "whole substance" as a mode of action of foods,[34] remaining largely true to Galen.[35] As mentioned earlier, the idea of whole substance, as it was transformed in the sixteenth century, went hand in hand with the view that certain diseases had causes that were "occult."[36] Perhaps the most prominent representative of this application of Galenic thought in the sixteenth century was Jean Fernel, who in his *De abditis rerum causis* dedicates a whole chapter to the diseases engendered by way of whole substance in the Galenic sense.[37] For Fernel, the idea of diseases of whole substance could better explain phenomena such as contagion, which were not always adequately served by the traditional humoral model. Fernel held that out of the diseases of whole substance, some were still caused by manifest qualities; others, however, by an occult cause.[38] As for the French disease, in *De luis venereae curatione perfectissima*, Fernel defines it as "an occult and contagious disease of the whole substance."[39] Its efficient cause, as he had expounded in an earlier short treatise, is a "poisoned and malign quality and a pernicious blemish" which "perverts the whole substance"[40] of the body.

Gabriele Falloppio's posthumously published *De morbo gallico liber absolutissimus* (1564) is another relevant case study which may be contrasted with Cesalpino's. A former teacher of Cesalpino, Falloppio likewise makes a strong case for the French disease being a disease of whole substance. He first distances himself from Da Monte, demonstrating that the French disease is not a "distemper" (*intemperies*) of any kind: be it hot and dry, or hot and humid, etc. It is, in his view, not even a disease "with matter" since there is no tumor or excess *in loco affecto*, such as in the liver.[41] In the end Falloppio concludes that the *morbus gallicus* cannot be understood within the framework of the four manifest qualities.[42] Instead, it is a new disease, unknown to the ancients but imported from the West Indies, transmitted by common contagion, and affecting mainly the liver through putrefaction.[43]

Having admitted the correlation of putrefaction with disease, Falloppio insists that not all warm and humid conditions result in putrefaction, since being warm and humid is one thing, and being putrid is another.[44] Bread also turns into blood, he argues, and yet they are different substances with diverse forms.[45] Hence, a hot and humid distemper is not *the disease* but only the *cause* of disease.[46] Relying largely on Galenic medical theory, Falloppio argues that the diseases originating in poisons—among which he counts the French disease—are infinite and that they are called diseases of the substance, since the whole substance is at work in them.[47] Falloppio's explanation of the development of disease rests on the idea of a correspondence or analogy between the poison and the spiritual substance of different body organs.[48] For the French disease, the analogy is between the poison and the "whole substance of the liver." Hence, the disease "is introduced in a hidden manner (*occulto modo*) and it infects the liver from its whole substance, whose measure we can neither know nor explain in words."[49] Because of this occult nature, the appropriate remedies will match the disease in that they, too, will act by manner of whole substance. Since "no medicine that is warming, or drying, cooling, or humidifying acts from its own substance,"[50] no medicine whose action relies on the modification of qualities will be effective. Hence "we need to discover a drug which heals from the whole substance"[51] by penetrating the body up unto the liver in a spiritual manner. Among the characteristics of such a drug he counts resistance to putrefaction and the capacity to impede ebullition or fervor; the latter requirement excludes certain foods such as fruits, since they are prone to triggering the morbid, fermentative ebullition of blood.[52] As an example of an efficient drug, Falloppio proposes precipitate of mercury, hailed as a "miracle of God" because the mercury is "resuscitated" from it.[53] Falloppio also speaks in favor of guaiacum as the antidote of choice, after performing other operations (evacuation, calibration of humors by means of nutrition, by drinking decoctions, and applying poultices). Along with other remedies commonly considered as alchemical, he also gives practical advice about how to observe the flux (*fluxio*) of humors and if needed, how to evacuate them using diverse *medicamenta evacuantia*.[54] Overall, Falloppio thus preserves many aspects of Galenic medical philosophy, while also adopting the stance that the *morbus gallicus* is an occult disease acting by whole substance. A few decades later, Cesalpino has to reckon with these writers' references to an occult cause, as well as with their adoption of Galen's *tota substantia*.

3. Cesalpino's Reworking of "tota substantia." His Own Incremental Model of Disease Spread

Cesalpino does not entirely reject the idea of action through the whole substance; rather, he reconceptualizes it so as to eliminate the occult agency. In the *Quaestionum medicarum libri II* (1593), Cesalpino had laid out how those drugs work which are said to act through whole substance.[55] Cesalpino differentiates between Galen's poisons and the disease venoms by stating that only the latter are contagious.[56] Moreover, the venoms originate in putrefaction, which in turn stems from a dysregulation in heat (hence, an *intemperies* in primary qualities).[57] While referring to the writers who claim action by *tota substantia*—such as Galen, Mesue, Avicenna, and others—Cesalpino seems skeptical of this mode of action insofar as it is said to act by some other, insensible power. In fact, he demystifies *tota substantia* explaining how these venoms and also some drugs act either through secondary qualities (ultimately derived from the primary ones), or directly by excesses of the primary qualities themselves. Heat plays a crucial role in enhancing propensities of matter such as attraction. Invoking occult virtues, Cesalpino argues, is merely taking refuge in ignorance, a way of avoiding explaining those modes of action in matter.[58] Instead, Cesalpino points out that the idea of occult qualities, claimed by some of his contemporaries to originate with Galen, is based on a misunderstanding of Galen's text, especially of the Fifth Book of *On Simple Drugs*, and that the correct understanding would still imply an action that is reducible to the effects and interactions of primary qualities.[59]

By tracing back the action and effect of drugs (such as poisons) to properties like weight, Cesalpino offers a more physical or quantitative theory of material action for *tota substantia*. Differentiating between various kinds of poisons, antidotes, and their respective modes of action, he does not deny that some of these do act in a way that may be called *tota substantia*, but he argues that what underlies the process are just physical phenomena that are harder to understand. The causes are material and sensible, though the manner of action be such that it may be called *tota substantia*. Importantly for medical practice, he argues that not just experience[60] needs to be used here in judgment, but reason and method[61] may be employed as well.

The inclination toward such a demystification of "whole substance" might point towards an influence from Averroes, whose philosophy of matter afforded a view focused on the active role of matter itself, as opposed to the presumed role of an occult agency external to matter.[62] According to Norma Emerton, for Averroes the substantial form is "determined by and emerges from a particular sort of matter."[63] In this perspective, which Emerton dubbed the "low view of the form," the formal power is inherent in matter, which pushes itself to rearrange its elements into a configuration of qualities allowing for new properties. Because Cesalpino relies precisely on such an exploration of primary qualities and their interaction in order to explain whole substance action, he seems to be taking a stance aligned with that of Averroes as regards the formal powers inherent in matter.

In the *De morbo gallico*, the tension between whole substance action and a kind of incremental action by primary qualities becomes the leading foil against which Cesalpino builds his theory of disease. Cesalpino accepts a manner of action which macroscopically would appear to involve whole substance, but to explain it, he proposes a different, incremental model of how disease spreads within the body at a more minute level. He specifies where the new putrefaction at the onset of disease is created: "Not in the spiritual substance, because it (the putrefaction) does not travel too long." Here the long travel refers to the spread of putrefaction within the human body, from the entry point (such as the genitals) to other organs such as the heart or the liver. Some of Cesalpino's predecessors, such as Falloppio, had argued that the disease spreads directly to the liver (which would qualify as a "long travel"). But Cesalpino differs. He argues that putrefaction travels short distances, affecting adjacent parts one by one, a position that had been advocated in part also by Da Monte who had argued that "the scabies first starts in one part, whence it permeates to the others one by one, until it makes the whole infected and in this manner reaches the liver, which, thus altered, produces such [altered] blood."[64] Cesalpino, however, downplays the traditionally central role of the liver, arguing that this disease spreads among adjacent internal body parts. He thus offers an alternative, incremental model of spread of disease within the body that does not map onto traditional descriptions of whole substance action. Instead of focusing on the liver's role in spreading the French disease, Cesalpino holds that the pustules in the genital area are caused by the putrefaction of seminal matter. This putrefaction is initially external in relation to the genitals; however, once contracted, the man's own semen becomes corrupted, at which point the corruption is internal.[65] This effect is exacerbated by the hot and humid nature of the genitals, which by itself entails a propensity toward putrefaction according to the Galenic model.[66] From the entry point, putrefaction spreads incrementally into the rest of the body, affecting adjacent parts (such as, firstly, the bladder), and triggering intermittent fevers (*hectica*).[67] Ultimately, putrefaction also corrupts the blood which becomes impure and full of mucous, according to Cesalpino's observations.[68] Within the body, putrefaction affects the internal organs including the brain, and disturbs their physiology by interfering with the natural processes of coction. Thus, the putrefaction undermines the organism's capacity to perform basic physiological functions (which rely on coction). It also imperils the capacity of the organism to heal, since humors fail to concoct prior to their evacuation.

To sum up, one of the most salient features of Cesalpino's medical philosophy is the question of how disease spreads within the body. There is a remarkable tension between two models which in principle would be competing, but which in Cesalpino's *Ars medica* tend to converge: the model of whole substance action, and the incremental model according to which adjacent parts of the body are infected one by one.

4. Remedies Old and New Cesalpino's Eclectic-Descriptive Approach of Old and New Remedies

Regarding cures for this disease, Cesalpino placed great emphasis on the eradication of the cause, namely, of the "venomous force" (*vis venefica*)[69] in nature. This being a difficult task, in the interim, individual bodies are to be protected from infection. An already infected person should first take care not to infect others; beyond that, various treatments may alleviate symptoms.[70]

Identifying appropriate treatments depended on whether one faced an "old" disease—for which already the ancients had recommended various remedies—or a new one that accordingly might respond to new drugs. Elsewhere, Cesalpino had noted the "many remedies brought from the New World, that is, the West Indies."[71] But Cesalpino's broader framework is Galenic, focusing on treating the individual condition of the patient within a multifactorial causation of disease. Since the disease attacks different body parts and differs in the young and in the old, and in the sanguine, choleric, or melancholic temperaments, treatments will also differ according to humoral balance and individual circumstances.[72]

For all the variation, however, one element is constant: the combatting of putrefaction. Therefore, common measures are, as for the plague, to "evacuate the excrements, and remove the remaining causes of putrefaction,"[73] a strategy known from Da Monte. There is, however, less agreement about how exactly to achieve this removal. Cesalpino argues for removing the conditions that are favorable to putrefaction in the first place, namely heat and humidity; the remedies will hence aim to cool and dry. Meanwhile Da Monte, who had held the French disease to be a "hot and dry" distemper, had, accordingly, been less of an advocate of dry remedies. (In this vein, wine, recommended by Cesalpino, was much less favored by Da Monte. Its "dry" character would not help a disease itself characterized by "dryness.") It was also essential, for both authors as well as for Falloppio, that the remedy have a nature that combats putrefaction. For example, for Cesalpino eggs and milk would not qualify, since they themselves are quick to putrefy.[74] Wine, however, had the beneficial quality of being fermentative and thus opposing putrefaction. Overall, there is some ambivalence regarding the fermentative nature of certain foods; it could either impede or promote corruption, an example of the latter being Falloppio's recommendation to avoid fruits due to ebullition.

Cesalpino recommends a wide array of remedies, freely combining those of the Ancients—such as wine—with more modern ones such as antidotes and mercury; the latter, however, are treated with much caution.

While Cesalpino gives some attention to antidotes (*alexipharmaca*), it is difficult if not impossible to tell whether he believed in their effectiveness. Certainly the side effects being considerable, Cesalpino, like Da Monte, recommends a certain order of steps in treatment, in which antidotes are only the last resort. One hint at what he might have held of the usefulness of some antidotes is given in the first Book of the *Ars medica*:

> Many, recoiling from arduous work, have tried to invent a briefer art of medicine. From the multitude of remedies, they have selected those that may be put to many uses, called *polychresta* by the Greeks, such as theriac and mithridatum, which are recommended not just against all poisons but against almost all diseases. Thus, indeed they do not require method, since they are considered to act by whole substance, which lacks method. In the same way, through the art of distillation, most potent liquors are extracted, which they call elixirs, and the fifth essence.[75]

Further Cesalpino writes of the "Fifth Essence" that it is said to possess an incorruptible celestial substance. But if this were true, Cesalpino argues, then the Fifth Essence should not only cure diseases, but also render man immortal, regardless of the deficiency in innate heat. This of course is impossible. This criticism appears to be directed at Empirics, who circumvent the traditional educational path as well as the intricacies of Galenic medical philosophy, which was focused on a long-term preventative regimen and was individually tailored to the patient's complexion. Neglecting all this, Empirics instead produce quick remedies for quick financial gain, making promises which they cannot keep.

While university-trained physicians often polemicized against Empirics, they also appropriated some of Empirics' remedies by "theorizing" them and finding a probable causal explanation, to confer legitimacy upon their use. For antidotes, the go-to philosophical framework was the whole substance theory, based on Galen—to which Cesalpino resorts in order to explain the "remedies which act by whole substance, called alexipharmaca."[76] Thus, he expounds on the mode of action of poisons: "The nature of the poison is to conquer everything else by means of its excess, and to convert [everything else] into itself."[77] Accordingly, antidotes, too, act upon the whole substance of the body. Notably, these references are not necessarily to be taken as an endorsement of the sort of occult *tota substantia* action that was advocated by Fernel. The term could have been used as a shortcut, while Cesalpino's understanding of it likely continues to imply the mode of action that had been laid it out in *Quaestiones medicae*. The poison may turn everything else into itself, but it remains relevant how exactly it achieves this.[78]

Mercury was another popular, but also controversial remedy against the French disease. As Arrizabalaga, Henderson, and French note, "mercury had been used in the treatment of skin disorders, including scabies and lice (pediculi), since the time of Avicenna and Rhazes."[79] As "Unguentum Saracenicum," it was widely used in Arabic medicine, making it one of the first options of treatment when the new skin disease made its appearance in Europe.[80] This background made mercury part of "rational medicine." It was also part of the alchemical medicine of Paracelsus. Leoniceno opposed mercury, arguing that the ancients either did not know it or abhorred it. Da Monte, a staunch supporter of Galenic medicine, is likewise dismissive of the newer physicians who follow the Arab alchemists in treating the French disease with mercury.[81] Galen, Da Monte argues, thinks nothing of mercury; and Da Monte shows how it can be deleterious, achieving often the opposite effect, since it alleviates the symptoms (superficial buboes) but not the cause of the disease (the distemper of the liver, *intemperies hepatis*). Mercury pills, he says, are an sensible poison (*venenum manifestum*).[82]

Cesalpino certainly departs from Da Monte's views significantly, as mercury seems more central with him. In fact, as Antonio Clericuzio has argued, Cesalpino belonged to an array of Roman physicians who adopted some Paracelsian remedies without explicit reference to Paracelsus and in spite of rejecting the more esoterical aspects of alchemical philosophy.[83]

For treating the French disease Cesalpino recommends mercury, such as in the form of cinnabar. Nevertheless, he also warns about the side effects. Differing from both Falloppio's enthusiasm and Da Monte's outright rejection, Cesalpino's hesitating endorsement might be part of a strategy to claim mercury compounds away from the medical practitioners outside the official schools. He wrote:

> The Empirics add cinnabar, which is most effective in dissolving thick and gummy humors, although it is dangerous when swallowed; it is safely applied to the private and external body parts. Yet, I have seen it dissolve suffocating tumors in the throat when taken orally.[84]

This passage shows Cesalpino's warning about the dangers of cinnabar, and his suggestions for safer use. Nevertheless, he also draws on his own experience, including cases when he found mercury effective. Elsewhere Cesalpino is more critical of the effects of mercury, describing its deleterious side effects in copious detail.[85]

Another remedy, wine, likewise does not enjoy the same degree of popularity with all authors. Da Monte, for instance, prefers to argue for abstinence from wine, favoring water-based decoctions. Falloppio recommends avoiding the specific wine that Galen calls *oligophoron*;[86] in general, he considers water preferable for drinking. By contrast, for Cesalpino wine acts as a therapeutic agent in multiple ways: as a simple excipient or as an active substance, applied externally to the skin or internally by drinking.

As an active substance, Cesalpino recommends "the drinking of wine against the established venoms."[87] He believes wine to have the power to modify the action of other substances, such as correcting the toxicity of the stomach[88] or the balance of the humors, or—through its qualities of being dry and cold—counteracting the effect of warm or humid victuals.[89]

External use of wine to cleanse the skin, as well as an antiseptic, is also documented by Cesalpino. This Galenic use is recontextualized for the new disease and the new remedies. If the ingestion of the potion from guaiacum wood failed to cause the heavy sweating that was expected, the legs and the back were wrapped in cloth that had been soaked in noble wine before adding fumigations of frankincense to aid breaking the sweat.[90] In another context, wine (or, alternatively, the patient's own urine) was used in frictions to alleviate the pain from the buboes and shield them from putrefaction as far as possible. Such solutions typically contained wine, vinegar, or brandy.

Wine was also a medium for preservation of the remedies, figuring in a list of excipients, along with honey or bear fat.[91] Cesalpino recommends various recipes which include a dry wine (*vinum austerum*) as a basis in which the actual remedy is to be added to make it more palatable, with the additional benefit of the dryness of the wine combatting humid putrefaction. In other cases wine was problematic. For instance, Cesalpino writes: "I do not praise the boiling of wine with wood, because its spirituous substance evaporates, and makes the potion unpleasant."[92]

Effects of drinking wine mixed with active substances could be, however, quite unexpected as well, as is evident in Cesalpino's story about the genealogy of the French disease. On the mountain of Vesuvius, Cesalpino relates, "there is plenty of that noble wine which is called Greek."[93] The story goes that while the French military camps were occupying the region, the Spanish had left a large quantity of wine unattended, which however had previously been intentionally contaminated with blood from "elephantiasis" patients in a nearby hospital. The French drank this wine, and shortly afterwards started to exhibit a milder form of elephantiasis.[94] Perhaps ironically, this is the confabulated story for which Cesalpino's otherwise rather dry treatise would become known.

In addition to treating the French disease, Cesalpino ascribes wine a palliative character, making the patient more cheerful and thus helping them to cope with the misery of disease. While this idea is rather universal, a reference is found in the Old Testament, in the Book of Proverbs 31:6, 7: "Let them drink and forget their poverty, and remember their misery no more."[95] Cesalpino in his turn recommends "Non ira, nec tristitia; sed hilaritas."[96] Experience might have taught Cesalpino that few methods to achieve *hilaritas* are as effective and reliable as wine.

5. Conclusion

Cesalpino's influence on later writings on the French disease is reflected in Jean Astruc's wide-ranging compilation first published in 1740.[97] Astruc notes Cesalpino's most relevant or most original tenets, including his mention of antidotes and the spurious genealogy of the disease involving infected wine. Other authors remember Cesalpino's treatise chiefly for this spurious genealogy,[98] contradicted for instance in Johannes Hartmann's medical thesis of 1611.[99] Another German author, Johannes Juncker, in 1624, mentions several of Cesalpino's remedies, including mercury.[100]

In sum, it may be said that Cesalpino's treatise is fully integrated into his own age. His predominant inclination toward the ancients is occasionally laced with alchemical overtones. While Cesalpino's understanding of the role of putrefaction in the French disease is fundamentally Galenic and largely in line with the ideas of his predecessors, his understanding of contagion also features some aspects and foci better explained on the background of a Renaissance framework that understood the *morbus gallicus* as a disease of whole substance. However, Cesalpino insists on his own interpretation of how "whole substance" should be understood, whereby he minimizes the role of occult powers, emphasizing instead a rational and methodic approach.

Notes

1   Today's consensus is that while this is likely to have been an ancestor of syphilis in the modern sense of the disease caused by *Treponema pallidum*, pronouncements about historical disease ontology cannot be made with certainty and hence hermeneutical caution is advisable. Venereal diseases like gonorrhea, syphilis, and others were not separated until their respective pathogens were identified in the late nineteenth century. Hence, early modern descriptions of *morbus gallicus* could have referred to any of them or to combinations of them. Additionally, historically minded physicians have observed that early modern syphilis might have been caused by a more virulent strain of *Treponema*, entailing more severe symptoms than today. In this chapter, I will refer to this affliction by its past name: "French disease." In this choice, I am following Arrizabalaga, Henderson, and French and other researchers who have argued that the contemporary understanding of disease should be taken into account, since the classification and naming of diseases are in part culturally determined.

2   Jon Arrizabalaga, "De morbo gallico cum aliis: Another Incunabular Edition of Gaspar Torrella's *Tractatus cum consiliis contra pudendagram seu morbum Gallicum*

(1497)," *La Bibliofilía* 89, no. 2 (1987): 145–57, at 145. For a more nuanced view of Arabic medicine in the West, see Dag Nikolaus Hasse, *Success and Suppression: Arabic Sciences and Philosophy in the Renaissance* (Cambridge, MA: Harvard University Press, 2016).

3   Andrea Cesalpino, *Artis medicae pars prima, De morbis universalis* (Rome: Zannetti, 1602), 543: "difficilis cognitu est." All translations are mine.
4   See Danielle Jacquart, "The Introduction of Arabic Medicine into the West. The Question of Etiology," in *Health, Disease and Healing in Medieval Culture*, ed. Sheila Campbell, Bert Hall, and David Klausner (New York: St. Martin's Press, 1992), 186–95, at 187.
5   Cesalpino, *Artis medicae pars prima*, 553.
6   Ibid., 539.
7   See Jon Arrizabalaga, John Henderson and Roger French, eds., *The Great Pox: The French Disease in Renaissance Europe* (New Haven: Yale University Press, 1997), 80; Giambattista Da Monte, *De morbo gallico tractatus* (Venice: Constantini, 1554), fol. 3r.
8   Girolamo Fracastoro, *De sympathia et antipathia rerum liber unus. De contagione et contagiosis morbis et curatione libri III* (Venice: Giunta, 1546), 29.
9   "Elephantiasis," he proposed (which was possibly leprosy) could be transmitted by fomites. Galen had treated of "elephantiasis," and many physicians inquired whether the "new disease" might not perhaps also be a variant of Galen's "elephantiasis;" clearly some of the symptoms and manifestations were similar.
10 Cesalpino also refers to contagion at a distance in *QM*, fol. 196v.
11 Cesalpino, *Artis medicae pars prima*, 544–5: "Primum igitur contagium putredinem arguit, calorem scilicet extraneum in materia putrescente, sed pertinaci ut non facile deleatur. Ideo similem sibi putredinem in alio excitat, non in spirituosa substantia, quia non in longinquum transit neque in tenuibus humoribus, quia non cito communicatur … sed in crassis praecipue pituitosis. Argumento est muccosa substantia emanans ex pustulis, ulceribus, tuberculis. … Quoniam vero corrumpit, in excessu esse necesse est, propter excessum enim primarum qualitatum corruptio fit." Thanks to Mark Thakkar for help with this passage.
12 Ibid., 6: "Cor praeterea in eo tamquam sol suum calorem vitalem veluti lumen in totum corpus diffundit."
13 Ibid., 80: "proximum animae instrumentum."
14 Ibid., 7: "id quod calidum vocamus, immortale esse."
15 Girolamo Cardano, *Opera omnia*, ed. Charles Spon, 10 vols. (Lyon: Huguetan and Ravaud, 1663), 6:764a. See also: Jonathan Regier, "A Hot Mess: Girolamo Cardano, the Inquisition, and the Soul," *HOPOS* 11, no. 2 (2021): 547–63, at 551; Hiro Hirai, *Medical Humanism and Natural Philosophy: Renaissance Debates on Matter, Life, and the Soul* (Leiden: Brill, 2011), 112–13 and 116; Jean Fernel, *The Physiologia of Jean Fernel (1567)*, trans. John M. Forrester (Philadelphia: American Philosophical Society, 2003), 256–301.
16 Aristotle, *Gen. an.* 2.3.736b34–37a1, trans. A. L. Peck (Cambridge, MA: Harvard University Press, 1943), 171: "the semen contains within itself that which causes it to be fertile—what is known as 'hot' substance, which is not fire nor any similar substance, but the pneuma which is enclosed within the semen or foam-like stuff, and the natural substance which is in the pneuma; and this substance is analogous [ἀνάλογος] to the element which belongs to the stars."
17 Aristotle, *Ph.* 2.2.194b13–14. Tr. W. Charlton.

18 Jean Fernel, *On the Hidden Causes of Things: Forms, Souls, and Occult Diseases in Renaissance Medicine*, ed. and trans. J. M. Forrester (Leiden: Brill, 2005), 482ff.
19 For this Fernel received criticism from those writers who held on to the "analogy" thesis in a more literal reading of Aristotle, such as Joachim Cureus; see D. P. Walker, "The Astral Body in Renaissance Medicine," *Journal of the Warburg and Courtauld Institutes* 21, nos. 1–2 (1958), 119–33, at 129.
20 Fernel, *De abditis rerum causis*, 487. For the Renaissance Platonist aspects of Fernel see Hiro Hirai, "Alter Galenus: Jean Fernel et son interprétation platonico-chrétienne de Galien," *Early Science and Medicine* 10, no. 1 (2005): 1–35.
21 Cesalpino, *Artis medicae pars prima*, 6: "Si vero calidum innatum consideremus, nobilissimam in eo portionem coelestem intuebimur."
22 There is also the possibility of text corruption and of "portio" appearing erroneously where "proportio" should have appeared. If that were the case, one could argue that Cesalpino invokes an analogical relationship, since "proportio" was the Latin word commonly used to translate the Greek *analogos*. While this would potentially weaken the Renaissance Platonic allegiance, for now this possibility is pure speculation.
23 The quoted passages are identical in the 1602 and 1606 editions.
24 Cesalpino, *Artis medicae pars prima*, 352.
25 See Fernel, *On the Hidden Causes of Things*, 117: "I used to weigh up these points silently, sometimes prompted at the time by the oracle of Hippocrates in which he affirms that there is a divine aspect present in diseases." Fernel referred to Hippocrates, *Morb. sacr.* 21 (6:6394L). Translation by W. H. S. Jones (Cambridge, MA: Harvard University Press, 1923), 183: "This disease styled sacred comes from the same causes as others, from the things that come to and go from the body, from cold, sun, and from the changing restlessness of winds. These things are divine. So that there is no need to put the disease in a special class and to consider it more divine than the others; they are all divine and all human." Forrester and Henry note that to see a divine aspect in diseases seems an over-interpretation of the Hippocratic text on the part of Fernel, see Fernel, *On the Hidden Causes of Things*, 117, n. 20.
26 Galen refers to this theory in several of his works, including *De locis affectis, De simplicium medicamentorum,* and the spurious *De theriaca ad Pisonem.* On Galen's theory of whole substance and its uses in early modern theory of disease, see Linda Deer Richardson, "The Generation of Disease: Occult Causes and Diseases of the 'Total Substance,'" in *The Medical Renaissance of the Sixteenth Century*, ed. Andrew Wear, Roger French, and Iain Lonie (Cambridge: Cambridge University Press, 1985), 175–94.
27 Da Monte, *De morbo gallico*, fol. 2r: "Dico quod est mala intemperies calida et sicca hepate per contagium impressa."
28 Ibid., fol. 2v.
29 Ibid., fol. 2r.: "ab illa emanat aliquod virus, in quo existit illa mala et venenosa qualitas."
30 Ibid., fol. 6v.: "Duplex est via, una per ea quae a qualitatibus manifestis operatur, alia quae a proprietate occulta."
31 For a nuanced account of Da Monte's adherence to, and modification of, Galenic causation of disease see Craig Martin, "Galenic Causation in the Theoretical and Practical Medicine of Giambattista Da Monte," in *Galen and the Early Moderns*, ed. Matteo Favaretti Camposampiero and Emanuela Scribano (Cham: Springer, 2022), 37–53.

32 Da Monte, *De morbo gallico*, fol. 3v: "Quando aliquis affectus aequaliter in toto corpore est impressus tunc principium naturale est vitiatum."
33 Ibid., fol. 4r: "Sic igitur non est mirum, quod ex una parva scabiei pustula totum corpus inficiatur quandoque. Pariter mirum non debet videri quod ex parva pustula vel ulcusculo istius morbi venenosi inficiatur totum. Si quidem inficiatur hepar, quod est principale membrum toti deserviens, quod cum fuerit ita infectum necessarium est omnia in deterius labi. Et ideo Galenus in sexto *De locis affectis* declarat quod parvum virus scorpionis in aliqua parte impressum pertingat illico usque ad cor vel cerebrum, ubi recitat de quodam, qui ex morsu scorpionis adeo infrigidari videbatur, ac si aqua frigidissima super caput eius inspersa esset. Et videtur quasi virtus quaedam spiritualis, sicuti etiam est de opio. Nam modica opii qualitas totam habet infrigidare massam sanguinis."
34 Avicenna, *Liber canonis* (Basel: Herwagen, 1556), 1.2.15, 68–9.
35 Martin writes that Avicenna's reworking entailed in part "eliminating the polemical context of Galen's writing," see Martin, *Galenic Causation*, 42.
36 On this topic see Peter N. Singer, "A Change in the Substance: Theory and Its Limits in Galen's Simples," *Archives Internationales d'Histoire des Sciences*, 70 (2020): 16–53; John Wilkins, "The Concept of Whole Substance in Galen's 'Simple Medicines,'" *Studia Ceranea*, 11 (2021): 479–91.
37 Fernel, *On the Hidden Causes of Things*, 533–48: "Diseases of the total substance, and how significant they are in the art."
38 Ibid., 537: "A disease of the total substance, whether a corruption in the simple sense or a putrefaction, sometimes arises from an obvious cause and sometimes from a hidden one."
39 Jean Fernel, *Universa medicina* (Geneva: Chouet, 1627), 419 (second pagination in second part of the book): "Lues Venerea totius substantiae morbus est occultus, contagiosus."
40 Fernel, *Universa medicina*, 604: "Neque earum temperamentum solum, verum etiam totam substantiam pervertit."
41 Gabriele Falloppio, *De morbo gallico liber absolutissimus* (Venice: Regazzola, 1574), 29–30.
42 Ibid., 36: "ideo concludo affectum hunc non esse intemperiem calidam et humidam, neque frigidam et siccam, neque calidam et siccam, quoniam hoc non possum iudicare ex aliquo."
43 Ibid., 19, 37.
44 Ibid., 33: "aliud est putridum esse, aliud esse calidum et humidum."
45 Ibid., 33–5.
46 This aspect harks back to a tradition, inaugurated by Leoniceno, of distinguishing between αἰτία (cause) and οὐσία (essence); on this see Martin, *Galenic Causation*, 43.
47 Falloppio, *De morbo gallico*, 39.
48 This idea had also been given support by Fracastoro, who had written: "Non omnia agunt in omnia, sed certa in certa solum, quae analoga dicuntur" (Fracastoro, *De contagione*, 1.8, 34).
49 Falloppio, *De morbo gallico*, 42: "morbus hic habet analogiam ad spiritum, et totam substantiam hepatis, ideo hic morbus *occulto modo* introducitur, et est ex tota substantia hepar inficiens, cuius mensuram scire, aut verbis explicare non possumus." [My emphasis.]
50 Ibid.: "nullum medicamentum calefaciens, aut siccans, refrigerans, aut humectans agit a propria substantia."

51 Ibid., 43: "si illud quod facit dolorem a tota substantia facit, debemus invenire medicamentum a tota substantia sanans … necessarium est igitur, ut spirituali modo penetrarit labes ad hepar."
52 Ibid., 58: "Fugite fructus … aptum ad ebullitionem, veluti mustum sanguinis."
53 Ibid., 57.
54 Ibid., 67.
55 Cesalpino, QM 1.12 and 1.13.
56 Ibid., fol. 196r.
57 Ibid.: "venenositas febris pestilentis ex maligna quadam humoru[m] putredine oritur, ideo omnis inter calidos affectus est, putredo enim a calore sit."
58 Ibid., fol. 198r.
59 See 11.763K, where Galen explains the relationship between whole substance and actions of the qualities.
60 The Galenic term for "experience" was πεῖρα. For an overview of Galen's pharmacological epistemology, see for instance Philip J. van der Eijk, "Galen's Use of the Concept of 'Qualified Experience' in His Dietetic and Pharmacological Works," in *Galen on Pharmacology: Philosophy, History, and Medicine*, ed. Armelle Debru (Leiden, 1997), 35–57.
61 As addressed in Galen's *De methodo medendi*, as the systematic μέθοδος.
62 For a discussion of Averroes' theory of matter see Norma E. Emerton, *The Scientific Reinterpretation of Form* (Ithaca, NY: Cornell University Press, 1984), 58, 80–2.
63 Emerton, *The Scientific Reinterpretation of Form*, 58.
64 Da Monte, *De morbo gallico*, fol. 3v.
65 Cesalpino, *Artis medicae pars prima*, 549.
66 This was a line of argumentation with a long history, being reinforced by predecessors such as Leoniceno, dall'Aquila, and Gaspar Torrella. See especially Niccolò Leoniceno, *Libellus de epidemia quam vulgo morbum gallicum vocant* (Venice: Manuzio, 1497).
67 Cesalpino, *Artis medicae pars prima*, 554.
68 Ibid.
69 Ibid., 557.
70 Ibid., 558.
71 Ibid., 16: "multa postea ex novo orbe India scilicet occidentali transportata sunt."
72 Ibid., 552, 558.
73 Ibid., 558.
74 Ibid., 586: "Minus ova, aut lac, quia facile corrumpuntur."
75 Ibid., 18–19: "Ideo multi laborem recusantes breviorem medicinam fabricare conati sunt. Ex remediorum multitudine ea seligentes, quae ad multos usus utilia sunt, polychresta a Grecis appellata, qualis est theriaca, & Mitridatum non solum ad omnia venena, sed et ad omnes pene morbos praedicata. Sic enim non egent methodo cum putentur a tota substantia agere, quae methodo caret. Eadem ratione per distillandi artem potentissimi liquores extrahuntur, quos elixires vocant, et quintam essentiam."
76 Ibid., 332: "Sed inter remedia, quae a tota substantia agunt Alexipharmaca dicta."
77 Ibid., 348.
78 In fact, earlier in "De venenis" he argues that what is understood by whole substance action is ambiguous (Ibid., 326: "Quid vero sit secundum totam substantiam agere, valde ambiguum est.").
79 Arrizabalaga, Henderson, and French, *The French Pox*, 139.
80 Johannes Fabricius, *Syphilis in Shakespeare's England* (London: Kingsley, 1994), 33.

81 See Da Monte, *De morbo gallico*, fols. 7r–v, 11r.
82 Ibid., fol. 13v.
83 Antonio Clericuzio, "Chemical Medicines in Rome: Pietro Castelli and the Vitriol Debate (1616–1626)," in *Conflicting Duties: Science, Medicine and Religion in Rome, 1550–1750*, ed. Maria Pia Donato and Jill Kraye (London: Warburg Institute, 2009), 281–302, at 288.
84 Cesalpino, *Artis medicae pars prima*, 570–71: "Empirici addunt cinabrium efficacissimum liquandis humoribus crassis et gummositatibus, sed haustum periculosum est, tuto ad pudendum adhibetur et ad partes externas. Vidi tamen per os haustum suffocantes tumores in faucibus dissolvisse."
85 See ibid., 572 for such a description.
86 Falloppio, *De morbo gallico*, 61.
87 Cesalpino, *Artis medicae pars prima*, 568.
88 Ibid., 566: "vino corrigente noxam ventriculi."
89 Ibid., 585–6.
90 Ibid., 569.
91 Ibid., 580–1.
92 Ibid., 567: "Non laudo vini ebullitionem cum ligno, quia spirituosa eius substantia evanescit, et ingratam potionem reddit."
93 Ibid., 548.
94 Ibid.
95 Proverbs 31:6. New International Version.
96 Cesalpino, *Artis medicae pars prima*, 587.
97 Jean Astruc, *De morbis venereis libri novem tomus II*, 2nd ed. (Paris: Cavelier, 1740), 855–8.
98 Ibid., 883.
99 Johannes Hartmann, *Dissertatio inauguralis de lue venerea, quam propugnavit Johannes Keilius*. In: Hartmann, Disputationes chymico-medicae (Marburg: Pauli Egenolphi, 1614).
100 Johann Juncker, *Compendiosa methodus therapeutica* (Leipzig: Steinmann, 1624). See Astruc, *De morbis venereis*, 910.

Bibliography

Primary Sources

Aristotle. *Generation of Animals*, translated by A. L. Peck. Cambridge, MA: Harvard University Press, 1943.
Astruc, Jean. *De morbis venereis libri novem tomus II*. Paris: Cavelier, 1740.
Avicenna. *Liber canonis*. Basel: Herwagen. 1556.
Cardano, Girolamo. *Opera omnia*, edited by Charles Spon. 10 vols. Lyon: Huguetan and Ravaud, 1663.
Cesalpino, Andrea. *Artis medicae pars prima, de morbis universalibus*. Rome: Zannetti, 1602.
Cesalpino, Andrea. *Quaestionum medicarum libri II*. Venice: Giunta, 1593.
Da Monte, Giambattista. *De morbo gallico tractatus*. Venice: Constantini 1554.
Falloppio, Gabriele. *De morbo gallico liber absolutissimus*. Venice: Regazzola, 1574.
Fernel, Jean. *On the Hidden Causes of Things*, edited and translated by John M. Forrester and John Henry. Leiden: Brill, 2005.

Fernel, Jean. *Universa medicina ... editio emendatissima*. Geneva: Chouet, 1627.
Fracastoro, Girolamo. *De sympathia et antipathia rerum Liber unus. De contagione et contagiosis morbis et curatione Libri III*. Venice: Giunta, 1546.
Galen. *Opera omnia*, edited by Karl Gottlob Kühn. 20 vols. Leipzig: Karl Knobloch, 1821–33.
Hartmann, Johannes. *Dissertatio inauguralis de lue venerea, quam propugnavit Johannes Keilius*. In: Hartmann, Disputationes chymico-medicae (Marburg: Pauli Egenolphi, 1614).
Hippocrates. *Prognostic. Regimen in Acute Diseases. The Sacred Disease. The Art. Breaths. Law. Decorum. Physician (Ch. 1). Dentition*, translated by W. H. S. Jones. Cambridge, MA: Harvard University Press, 1923.
Juncker, Johann. *Compendiosa methodus therapeutica*. Leipzig: Steinmann, 1624.
Leoniceno, Niccolò. *Libellus de epidemia quam vulgo morbum gallicum vocant*. Venice: Manuzio, 1497.

Secondary Sources

Arrizabalaga, Jon. "De morbo gallico cum aliis: Another incunabular edition of Gaspar Torrella's *Tractatus cum consiliis contra pudendagram seu morbum Gallicum* (1497)." *La Bibliofilía* 89, no. 2 (1987): 145–57.
Arrizabalaga, Jon, John Henderson, and Roger French, eds. *The Great Pox: The French Disease in Renaissance Europe*. New Haven: Yale University Press, 1997.
Clericuzio, Antonio. "Chemical Medicines in Rome: Pietro Castelli and the Vitriol Debate (1616–1626)." In *Conflicting Duties: Science, Medicine and Religion in Rome, 1550–1750*, edited by Maria Pia Donato and Jill Kraye, 281–302. London: Warburg Institute, 2009.
Deer Richardson, Linda. "The Generation of Disease: Occult Causes and Diseases of the 'Total Substance'." In *The Medical Renaissance of the Sixteenth Century*, edited by Andrew Wear, Roger French, and Iain Lonie, 175–94. Cambridge: Cambridge University Press, 1985.
Emerton, Norma E. *The Scientific Reinterpretation of Form*. Ithaca, NY: Cornell University Press, 1984.
Fabricius, Johannes. *Syphilis in Shakespeare's England*. London: Jessica Kingsley Publishers, 1994.
Hasse, Dag Nikolaus. *Success and Suppression: Arabic Sciences and Philosophy in the Renaissance*. Cambridge, MA: Harvard University Press, 2016.
Hirai, Hiro. "Alter Galenus: Jean Fernel et son interprétation platonico-chrétienne de Galien." *Early Science and Medicine* 10, no. 1 (2005): 1–35.
Hirai, Hiro. *Medical Humanism and Natural Philosophy: Renaissance Debates on Matter, Life and the Soul*. Leiden: Brill, 2011.
Jacquart, Danielle. "The Introduction of Arabic Medicine into the West. The Question of Etiology." In *Health, Disease and Healing in Medieval Culture*, edited by Sheila Campbell, Bert Hall, and David Klausner, 186–95. New York: St. Martin's Press, 1992.
Martin, Craig. "Galenic Causation in the Theoretical and Practical Medicine of Giambattista Da Monte." In *Galen and the Early Moderns*, edited by Matteo Favaretti Camposampiero and Emanuela Scribano, 37–53. Cham: Springer, 2022.
Regier, Jonathan. "A Hot Mess: Girolamo Cardano, the Inquisition, and the Soul." *HOPOS* 11, no. 2 (2021): 547–63.
Singer, Peter N. "A Change in the Substance: Theory and Its Limits in Galen's Simples." *Archives Internationales d'Histoire des Sciences* 70 (2020): 16–53.

van der Eijk, Philip J. "Galen's Use of the Concept of 'Qualified Experience' in His Dietetic and Pharmacological Works." In *Galen on Pharmacology: Philosophy, History, and Medicine*, edited by Armelle Debru, 35–57. Leiden: Brill, 1997.
Walker, D. P. "The Astral Body in Renaissance Medicine." *Journal of the Warburg and Courtauld Institutes* 21, nos. 1–2 (1958): 119–33.
Wilkins, John. "The Concept of Whole Substance in Galen's 'Simple Medicines.'" *Studia Ceranea* 11 (2021): 479–91.

Index

Accademia dei Lincei 4
Actuarius 203, 212
Africa 113
Agricola, Georg 171–6, 178, 180, 182
Albertus Magnus
   metals and 178–9, 181–2
   plants and 132
   stones and 171–2, 176, 181
Aldrobrandini, Ippolito see Clement VIII
Aldrovandi, Ulisse 3, 109
Alexipharmaca 44, 232–3
Alfred of Shareshel 132
Al-Kindi 215
Alpini, Prospero 113
Al-Razi 35, 38–9, 233
Altomare, Donato Antonio 39
Anaxagoras 56
Anguillara, Luigi 118, 160–1
Arabia Felix 113
Arber, Agnes 154
Arezzo 109
Aristotle
   Generation of Animals 39–40, 45
   History of Animals 20
   Metaphysics 21, 23–4, 42, 55–7, 90
   Meteorology 38, 132, 134, 172, 174, 178–81, 212
   Nicomachean Ethics 21
   On Divination during Sleep 34, 41–4, 61
   On the Heavens 58, 90, 93
   On the Parts of Animals 20, 40, 57
   On the Soul 57–9, 131–5, 138, 144–5
   Physics 55, 58, 91, 227
   Problemata 33, 42
Arnald of Villanova 215
Arrizabalaga, Jon 225, 233
Asia 113
Astruc, Jean 235
Averroes 2, 58, 215, 230
Avicenna

The Canon of 39, 174, 228
   celestial influences and 174
   diseases of the whole substance and 228, 230, 233
   hostility toward 35
   mineralogy and 171–2, 181
   practical medicine and 194

Bacon, Francis 19
Balduino, Girolamo 21–2
Barbaro, Ermolao 118, 160
Bauhin, Caspar 123, 160
Bayle, Pierre 1–3
bees 19, 26
Belon, Pierre 109
Benedetti, Alessandro 196
Benivieni, Antonio 34
Berengario da Carpi 194, 196–9
Bernard of Gordon 194
Biringuccio, Vannoccio 177–8
blood
   circulation of 1, 5, 40, 70, 193, 196–7
   diseases of 229, 231
   innate heat and 79–80, 180–1
   production of 201–2
   repletion of 202–3
   urine in 197–201
Bologna 109
Borro, Girolamo 4, 53
Boyle, Robert 173
Brahe, Tycho 88–91, 96–7
Brasavola, Antonio Musa 118, 160
Brunfels, Otto 154, 158, 162
Bruxius, Adamus 195
Bylebyl, Jerome 201–2

Calepino, Ambrogio 197
Calvi, Giovanni 25–6
Camerarius, Rudolf Jacob 141
Capivacci, Girolamo 22–3
Cardano, Girolamo

comets and 90
demons and 34
the divine and 37–9, 226–7
mineralogy 182
plants and 107–8
Cesalpino, Giovanni 3
Clark, Stuart 34
Clavius, Christoph 90
Clement VIII, Pope 1–2, 7, 171
Clericuzio, Antonio 233
Codronchi, Giovanni Battista 34
Colombero, Carlo 122
Colombo, Realdo 3, 5, 70, 196
comets 89–91, 96–7
Condorelli, Luigi 8
Costeo, Giovanni 123
Craig, John 88–9, 91
Craig, Thomas 88, 91
Cunningham, Andrew 70

Da Monte, Giambattista
  causes of syphilis and 225–9
  cures for syphilis and 231–4
  practical medicine 194
  soul and 39
d'Andrea d'Agnolino, Bernardino 3
dell'Aquila, Sebastiano 226
de Orta, Garcia 118, 161
Democritus 45, 56
Dioscorides
  as authority 109, 160, 162
  classification of plants and 19, 114–16, 119
  cures and 44, 113, 210, 215, 217
  dismissal of 19, 158
  minerals and 171–2, 178, 213
Donzellini, Girolamo 35, 38–40
Dorn, Gerard 178
dreams 34, 42–3
Du Chesne, Joseph 178
Durastante, Giano Matteo 36

Edinburgh
  James VI and 88–9
  teaching about Cesalpino and 92–8
  teaching of cosmology and 90–1
  university 2, 87–88
Edinburgh, Royal College of Physicians 89
Emerton, Norma 230

Empedocles 56, 136
Euclid 90–1

Faber, Johannes 4
Falcucci, Niccolò 194
Falloppio, Gabriele
  anatomy and 196
  causes of syphilis and 225, 227–9, 231
  cures for syphilis and 232–4
  teacher of Cesalpino as 3, 5
Ferdinand I, Grand Duke 7
Fernel, Jean 34, 40, 226–8, 233
Ferrari da Grado, Matteo 194, 197–8, 203–4
Ficino 55, 61
Fifth Lateran Council 2
Findlen, Paula 160
Fracastoro, Girolamo 225–6
Frankfurt an der Oder 88
Fuchs, Leonhart 119, 154, 158, 162–3, 209

Galen
  anatomy and 195–8, 200–3
  authority for practical medicine 35, 193–4, 204, 225, 229, 233
  criticism of 5, 33, 36, 45, 58–60
  De naturalibus facultatibus 197
  De usu partium 197
  interpreter of Hippocrates 37–9, 59
  Methodus medendi 194, 197, 213
  On Simple Drugs 210–12, 230
  On the Composition of Drugs According to Kind 213
  pharmacology 210–15, 217, 228, 233–4
  source for mineralogy 171–2
  theory of occult qualities 227, 230–2
Galenism 2, 5, 37–8, 209–11
Galilei, Galileo 2, 4, 25–6, 89
Garin, Eugenio 25
Gaza, Theodore 132
Gerard, John 160
Gessner, Conrad 122
Ghini, Luca 3, 109, 118, 160
Giacchini, Leonardo 35, 38–40
Giglioni, Guido 2
God
  as cause 5, 41, 71, 74–80
  dreams and 41, 43

Index

as prime mover 95
  providence 1, 37, 45
Guidi, Guido 3, 35, 38

Handsch, Georg 162
Harvey, William 1, 193, 196–7, 201, 204
Henderson, John 233
Heraclitus 40
Hermes Trismegistus 61
Hippocrates
  Airs, Waters, Places 38
  Aphorisms 37–8
  Aristotle and 33–6
  Decorum 38
  divine and the 37–9, 43–5, 59, 227
  Epidemics 37–8
  influence of 6, 35–9, 225–6
  On Ancient Medicine 39
  On Fleshes 38, 45, 227
  On the Diseases of Young Girls 45
  On the Nature of Woman 38, 45
  On the Sacred Disease 38–9, 45, 227
  Prognostic 37–40, 44, 59

Indies 3, 113, 118 (*see also* West Indies)
innate heat 5, 40, 70, 72–3, 77
Inquisition 2–4, 42, 45
intellect 1–2, 19–25, 41–2, 44

James VI, King of Scotland 88–9
Jansen, Kristian 15
Jollie, John 89
Juncker, Johannes 235

Kepler, Johannes 89–91, 96–7
Kincaid, Alexander 89
King, Adam 88–9, 91–7
King, Clement 91

Lais, Giuseppe 3
lenses 26
Leoni, Domenico 194
Leoniceno, Niccolò 40, 225, 233
Liddel, Duncan 88–9, 91
Linnaeus, Carolus 1, 123
L'Obel, Mathias De 109, 122–3
Lusitanus, Amatus 161

Maffei, Raffaello 107–8
magic 41–2, 44–5
Marbode 171, 176
Mathesius, Johann 173
Mattioli, Pietro Andrea
  authorities used 158–63
  materia medica 118, 154, 178, 209
Medici, Cosimo I de' 7, 109
Medici, court, family 53–5
Medici, Francesco I de' 7, 117, 157
Mercati, Michele 4–5, 7, 171
Mercuriale, Girolamo 3–4, 37–9, 194
microscope 25
mind
  human 42–5
  knowledge and 16, 20, 22, 24–5
  separability of 39–40, 45, 77
Mithraditic antidote 44
Monardes, Nicolás 118, 161
Mondino de' Liuzzi 198
Morton, Alan 122

Napier, John 91
Naples, university 39
Neri, Filippo 3, 5–6, 45
New World 231–2 (*see also* West Indies)
Nicolaus Damascenus
  author of *De plantis* 131
  influence of 139–40, 145
  plant function and 132–4
  plant reproduction and 134–8
  plants' souls and 142–4
Nifo, Agostino 21

Ogilvie, Brian 107, 123
Old Testament 235

Padua, university 33, 39
Paganelli, Cristoforo 153, 155–7, 159, 162
Pagel, Walter 197, 203
pantheism 5
Paracelsus 178, 182, 216, 233
Paris, university 88–91
Parker, Samuel 1, 15
Paul of Aegina 203–4
Pellicini, Antonio 155–6
Pena, Jean 89–91, 96–7
Pendasio, Federico 54
Piccolomini, Alessandro 22

Piccolomini, Francesco 54
Pietro d'Abano 40
Pisa
    botanical garden 3, 5, 108–9, 117, 163
    Sant'Anna Monastery 4
    university 2–4, 5, 25, 35, 53–5, 109, 154
plague 38
Plato 4–5, 22, 35, 37, 41–2
    Apology 60
    Cratilus 60–1
    Ion 61
    Phaedrus 61
    Statesman 60–1
    Symposium 60–1
    Teages 60
    Timaeus 57–8, 175–6
Platonism 2, 4, 53, 178
Platter, Felix 194, 197, 200, 202, 204
Pliny 44, 109, 136–7, 141, 171–2, 176
Pomponazzi, Pietro
    demons and 34, 36, 42, 44–5, 59–61
    epistemology 16–7
Porzio, Simone 3–5, 17, 40
Pseudo-Aristotle, author of *De plantis*, *see* Nicolaus Damascenus
Pseudo-Mesue, 35, 211, 214, 217, 230
Ptolemy 37, 90, 97
Pyrenees, the 176

Ramus, Petrus 90–1
Ray, John 1, 123
Reeds, Karen 123
respiration 5
Rome, university *La Sapienza* 2, 4, 55, 171
Rothmann, Christoph 96
Rucellai, Giovanni 26
Ruel, Jean 118, 141, 158, 160

Sacrobosco, Johannes de 90
Sands, Patrick 88–9, 91
Santing, Catrien G. 79
Sassetti, Filippo 113
Savonarola, Michele 194
Scaliger, Julius Caesar
    on plants 107–8, 119
    on prime mover 93–6
Seget, Thomas 91

Seitz, Jonathan 34
Seneca 176
Sennert, Daniel 174
Seton, Lord 89
Severinus, Petrus 178
Sibbald, George 89
Socrates 57, 60–1
Soul
    faculties of 132–5, 139, 145
    human 5–6, 42–5, 75–6, 144
    mortality of 59–60
    movement and 142–3
    nutritive 133, 180–2
    Plato's theory of 57–8
    sensitive 70–71, 138, 140, 143, 145
    temperament and 37, 39, 59
    vegetative 20, 71, 108, 116–17, 119–21, 123, 131, 180
Spinoza 1, 15
spirits 5, 40–1
syphilis 38

Taurellus, Nicolaus
    as critic of Cesalpino 1–2, 5, 15, 69–71, 73
    God and 75–9
Telesians 4–5, 54
Telesio, Bernardino 4
Thales 40, 71
theology 1–2, 4, 17, 33–4, 39, 60
Theophrastus
    as authority 109, 113–15, 145, 157–8, 160–1, 210
    generation of plants and 134–8
    knowledge of plants and 18–9
    methodology for classification of plants and 116–21
    plant sensation and 143–44
    rediscovery of 131–2
    Scaliger's commentary on 108
    spontaneous generation and 138–9
    stones and 171, 175
theriac 44, 213, 215
Tidike, Franz 123
Tonsis, Giovanni de' 36
Tornabuoni, Alfonso 7, 19, 109, 114–15, 117
Torrella, Gaspar 226
Tuscany 1, 26

Valori, Baccio 4, 53–6, 113
Van Helmont, Jan Baptist 173
Vasoli, Cesare 15
Vega, Cristóbal de 38
Vesalius, Andrea 3, 194–6, 198–200
Verino (II), see Vieri
Vieri, Francesco de' 4–5, 36, 53–4, 59, 61
Vimercato, Francesco 54
Vincent de Beauvais 132
Violi, Francesco 3

Vita, Belisario 113
Viviani, Ugo 2–3

West Indies 3, 114, 118, 229, 231–2
Wittich, Paul 88–9

Zabarella, Jacopo 16
Zalužanský, Adam 122–3
Zanetti, Luigi 195
Zerbi, Gabriele 196

www.ingramcontent.com/pod-product-compliance
Lightning Source LLC
Chambersburg PA
CBHW071821300426
44116CB00009B/1390